THAT OTHERS MAY LIVE

THAT OTHERS MAY LIVE

THE TRUE STORY OF THE PJs, THE REAL-LIFE HEROES OF *THE PERFECT STORM*

SMSGT JACK BREHM AND PETE NELSON

THREE RIVERS PRESS • NEW YORK

Published by Three Rivers Press,
New York, New York.
Member of the Crown Publishing Group.

Random House, Inc. New York, Toronto, London, Sydney, Auckland
www.randomhouse.com

THREE RIVERS PRESS is a registered trademark and the Three Rivers Press
colophon is a trademark of Random House, Inc.

Originally published in hardcover by Crown Publishers in 2000.

Printed in the United States of America

Design by Leonard Henderson

Library of Congress Cataloging-in-Publication Data
Brehm, Jack.
That others may live : the true story of the PJs, the real-life heroes of
The Perfect Storm / by Jack Brehm and Pete Nelson.
1. Brehm, Jack.   2. Parachute troops—United States—Biography.
3. United States. Air Force—Search and rescue operations.
4. Special forces (Military science)—United States.   I. Nelson, Peter, 1953–   II. Title.

UG626.2.B73 A3 2001
358.4'34'0973–dc21
00-048925

ISBN 0-609-80676-9

10 9 8 7 6 5 4 3 2 1

First Paperback Edition

DEDICATION

To my wife and best friend, Peggy, whom I love and adore. The greatest gifts God could have given me, my five children: Michele, Elizabeth, Bean (Laura-Jean), Matthew, and Jeffrey. You all supported me in a job I love, regardless of the heartache it could and so often does inflict. "In a box, hon'!"

To the crew of the Jolly 10, for the pain and suffering they and their families endured living up to the motto "That others may live."

To my fellow PJs and "every guy or girl next door" who puts on a set of greens one weekend a month to perform a duty that his or her neighbors could never understand.

And to my mentor, Mike McManus—no words are needed.

CONTENTS

PREFACE ix

ACKNOWLEDGMENTS BY JACK BREHM xiii

ACKNOWLEDGMENTS BY PETE NELSON xv

P A R T   O N E

CHAPTER 1: SHOOTING STARS 3

CHAPTER 2: DON'T SIT UNDER THE APPLE TREE 21

CHAPTER 3: BOZO WITHOUT A CLUE 32

CHAPTER 4: SUPERMAN SCHOOL 40

CHAPTER 5: BOZO RETURNS 51

CHAPTER 6: THE JOB 62

CHAPTER 7: CHERRY MISSIONS 78

CHAPTER 8: LIVING THE MOTTO 100

CHAPTER 9: BROTHERS 116

P A R T   T W O

CHAPTER 10: WITH ANYONE ELSE BUT ME 131

CHAPTER 11: THE BIRD THAT WAS NOT A BIRD 140

CHAPTER 12: THE NIGHT THE WIND BLEW 175

CHAPTER 13: KRYPTONITE 205

CHAPTER 14: DO YOU LIKE VAMPIRE MOVIES? 223

CHAPTER 15: THE HAND OF GOD IN THE HEART OF PITTSBURGH . . . 240

CHAPTER 16: ANYONE ELSE BUT ME 254

CHAPTER 17: '78-03 264

GLOSSARY 283

PREFACE

It's intrinsic to the nature of heroism that a hero is the last person who is ever going to call himself a hero, because the chief characteristic of true heroism is selflessness. That is perhaps what distinguishes true heroism from false heroism. False heroism might be the sports star who hits a lot of home runs in a season or scores a lot of points on a basketball court, all wonderful things to behold and cheer for, hugely entertaining, but nobody really puts anything on the line, or risks all that much, playing baseball or basketball. A sports idol is just that, an idol, not a hero. Any local fireman running into a burning house to save so much as a cat or a goldfish is more heroic, in the true sense of the word, than a sports idol. The famous only become role models because we know who they are and what they do. Fame and heroism are two different things.

This is a book about true heroism, deeds committed by a little-known group of men who think of themselves as anything but heroes, men who feel they are only doing their jobs, even when their jobs require them to do extraordinary things. They are called pararescue jumpers, or PJs, men who first came to the public's attention in Sebastian Junger's remarkable best-seller, *The Perfect Storm*. *That Others May Live* is a book about one man, SMSGT Jack Brehm, who serves in the Air Force's 102d Rescue Squadron, part of the 106th Air Rescue Wing, stationed at the Francis S. Gabreski Air National Guard Base in Westhampton Beach, Long Island. It's about Jack's life and times, his family, his adventures, the job he and his peers do, and why they do it. They are not men who, once in a lifetime, rise to the occasion in an emergency and jump into the ocean at great personal peril to save someone from drowning. They are men who train and prepare to do that, and more, on a daily basis.

The book covers a period from 1976 to the present. The reader will notice that in various places in the narrative, the tense shifts from past to present, or from present to past. This is intentional. Certain action scenes seemed best rendered in the present tense, for the purpose of effecting a sense of immediacy, while other scenes and expository information seemed better delivered in the past tense. Places where the tense is intentionally shifted have been marked by a series of eight asterisks.

There are places in the narrative where events have been rendered that took place twenty or more years ago. The reader might wonder about the conversations and events detailed herein, and think, "How could anybody remember what they said twenty years ago?" Indeed, most of us can't remember conversations we had a week ago, or what we had for lunch yesterday. The authors have tried to stay as true as possible to the veracity of events, remaining faithful in spirit, tone, feel, general structure and shape, chronology and import, but we acknowledge that in instances where producing exact verbatim quotations of things spoken long ago was beyond the collective memories of the parties involved we've had to reconstruct scenes and dialogues as best we could, creating conversations that can only approximate what took place in, for example, a loud helicopter among people under tremendous stress in a raging North Atlantic gale or between rescuers suffering from high-altitude hypoxia on an Alaskan mountain peak. Yet it's an ancient truism that a dozen men participating in a single event might, twenty years later, tell a dozen different stories about that event, making any individual narrator's version an approximation, framed by his own particular experience. *That Others May Live* is the story of one PJ's life, referenced by his fallible memories and filtered through his own personal recollections. We did have the benefit of logs, notes, photographs, and journals kept by the author throughout his career to assist us in our renderings, but in the end we must apologize for any instance in which individuals referred to or appearing in the book might feel that the author's version of events varies from their version. This is just one man's story, no more and no less.

It's hard to gauge to what extent one PJ's story might represent the stories of all PJs. Pararescuemen are not only one of the most elite forces in the military, they are one of the more unique groups of people anywhere. They are also as different from one another as any collection of individuals is going to be. Some PJs listen to classical music, some listen to rock, some listen to rap, and some probably listen to voices from outer space. The stereotypical pararescueman gets a testosterone high from being physically fit, and an endorphin high from exercising, and then he gets an adrenaline high after parachuting out of an airplane to a victim in need of medical assistance, and then he gets a spiritual, godlike feeling of omnipotence from saving somebody's life, and then he goes to a bar after the mission and has a few shots of tequila to celebrate, at which point he can become an extremely interesting and relatively unpredictable individual. Every pararescueman will share something with this stereotype, but every pararescueman will deviate from it, too. All share a unique approach to life, a sense of service and commitment to country, and beyond that a true feeling of compassion for their fellow man, which would be rare in any society, at any point in history, but which seems particularly rare in late-twentieth-century America.

ACKNOWLEDGMENTS

I would like to thank my co-author, Pete Nelson, for his ability to turn my crazy life and stories into such an amazing tale. To my agent, Jennifer Gates, thank you for your persistence and overall interest in pararescue. Simply put, without you this story would never have come to life.

To Kristin Kiser, our editor at Crown, thank you for your words of encouragement and all the direction that was needed to make this story flow.

Thank you, Mom and Dad, for giving me a strong foundation on which I was able to build a long and happy life.

To the rest of my large, extended family, and my friends, without your love and support my family and I may not have endured the hard times, but because of you I am blessed with a wonderful life. It is always a pleasure to share my happy times with you all.

I would also like to thank the Rocky Point school district, for their constant support of my children in my many absences over the years.

To my mother- and father-in law, Jane and Warren Stemke, thank you for giving Peggy and me so much support and guidance at our new beginning.

Thank you to all my fellow PJs, who contributed their time, effort and personal stories to paint a better picture of what we do.

—SMSGT *Jack Brehm*

ACKNOWLEDGMENTS

There are many people I'd like to thank, beginning with the Brehm family, Jack, Peggy, Michele, Elizabeth, Laura-Jean, Matthew, and Jeffrey, who took me into their home and filled me with food, stories, and admiration. Thanks also to Carol Martinsen, Sally Brehm, and Lorraine Fitzpatrick, and to Ken Stanley. From the 106th, I'm grateful for the cooperation and assistance of LTCOL Anthony Cristiano, LTCOL David Hill, CMSGT Alan Manual, MAJ Jim Finkle, Marty Martin, and for the support of all of Jack's friends. From the New York National Guard, I'd like to thank LTCOL Paul Fanning. Thanks to Douglas Thar, USAF Public Communications Division, the Pentagon, and to Bill Vargas, from Pararescueman's Association. From the Coast Guard, I'd like to thank Hugh O'Doherty for the long conversations and for steering me in all the right directions. Thanks to all the PJs who wrote to me with their stories, including John Alexander, Dana Beach, Dave Berrio, Ken Cakebread, Jeff Christopher, Bud Cockerton, Ken Dolan, Monty Fleck, Dan Galde, James Derrick, David Hammer, Greg Hehir, Chris Howk, Craig Kennedy, Jim Lundberg, Dr. Ron Lundrigan, Anthony Negron, Roger Porter, Daniel Routier, Jim Ward, and Dave Young, and apologies to those whose stories I couldn't use, not because they weren't great stories but simply because of the need to limit the scope of what we were trying to cover and say and show.

From Kirtland AFB, I'm grateful for the help given by SGTs Stephens, Copper, McDonald and Lee. From Patrick AFB, thanks to COL Bruce Davis and SMSGT Jeff Curl. At Lackland AFB, I'm extremely grateful for the time given me by men who had a whole lot more on their minds than talking to a journalist, including "cones" Keith Faccilonga, William Moore, Armin Sahdri, Robert Schnell, and Matt White, guys whose commitment and courage thoroughly impressed me. From the Instructors' Cadre, I'm grateful to SMSGTs Tony Alexander, Rod Alne, John Erickson, Blake George, Ross Kilbride, Kevin Kirby, Mike Mahoney, Doug McClure, Craig Showers, Jerry Sowles, and David Swan—thank you all for chatting with me, and for not making me do any pushups. Thanks also to, in Public

Acknowledgments

Affairs, Irene Witt and to LT Denise Kerr, the best ballroom dancer in the Air Force.

In Alaska, thanks to Bob LaPointe, Carl Brooks, Skip Kula, James Talcott, Mike Wayt, and particularly thanks to Mike McManus, who gave me so much of his time and went out of his way to introduce me to all the people I needed to talk to. He's a truly impressive gentleman and as great a guy as Jack said he would be. Among the PJs, from the class of '78-03, thanks so much to Dave Higgins, Joe Higgins, Randy Mohr, Chuck Matelski, "Slip" O'Farrell, Bill Skolnik, and John Smith, for the stories they shared and, on behalf of all the people they helped who perhaps never thanked them properly, thanks for the careers they had. Any one of these men could have filled a book on his own. Thanks as well to Debbie Judy for telling me about "The Jude."

Farther afield, thanks to Dany Brooks from the U.S. Parachutists Association, and to Dr. Jeffrey T. Mitchell and Don Howell from the International Critical Incidence Stress Debriefing Foundation, for their cooperation and for the vital work they're doing. Thanks to Kim Hong-bin for his bravery and for his efforts conquering the difficulties of trans-oceanic bilingual e-mail, and to Jack Stephens and Matthew Childs for their help with mountaineering questions. Thanks to Jennifer Simpson for her detective work. Thanks in Greece to Tassia Kavvadias, to Park Myoung-Soo, Linda Kim, and to her mother Haeja in Massachusetts for helping with translations, and to Utit Choomuang in Korea for being my main man in Asia. Thanks and a bottomless supply of effusive letters of recommendation to my research assistants Nicky Lewinson and Danielle "She-Should-Have-Her-Own-Sit-Com" Fugazy. Thanks also to my family, whose support has always meant so much to me.

In the publishing world, I'd like to acknowledge Sebastian Junger, whose fine book *The Perfect Storm* first introduced the PJs to the world. At Crown, I'm thankful to the support of the staff, to Rachel Kahan for her read, to editorial director Steve Ross for his enthusiastic support, and especially to Kristin Kiser for having faith in me and for her deft and pain-less editing. Thanks to supplemental outside readers Alan Gates and Doug Whynott for catching my mistakes, misphrasings, and omissions from draft to draft. At Zachary-Shuster, thanks to Lane Zachary, Todd Shuster, Esmond Harmsworth and thanks, finally, to my reader, agent, and best friend Jennifer Gates, whose vision and inspiration first shaped this proj-ect and without whom none of me would have been possible.

—*Pete Nelson*

PART ONE

PART ONE

1

SHOOTING STARS

As a PJ said to me once, "If you can't get out of it, get into it."

IN A C-130 HERCULES, FLYING AT 26,000 FEET, SMSGT JACK BREHM and five other men are preparing to jump. It's night. Amateurs and recreational jumpers don't jump at night, nor do they jump from 26,000 feet, but Sergeant Brehm is not an amateur. He's a member of the U.S. Air Force's elite pararescue team, a PJ, they're called, short for "para-rescue jumper," tasked with rescuing pilots who get shot down behind enemy lines. PJ is the abbreviation used in flight logs when a para-rescueman is a member of a flight crew. The pilot is P, the co-pilot is CP, the flight engineer is FE, and so on. It's dangerous to jump at night, and to jump from this altitude, and it's always dangerous to jump behind enemy lines, particularly when the enemy knows they've shot down an American pilot and have dispatched troops to find him. It's considered something of a coup these days to display, in times of war, the picture of a captured pilot on television, but PJs know they're charged with a higher calling than to simply prevent an enemy in Baghdad or Belgrade from gaining the upper hand in a photo-op contest. PJs do what they do "That others may live." This is their motto, their "prime directive." There aren't a lot of people who live by mottoes anymore, but if you're going to live by one, it's hard to think of a better motto. PJs wear maroon berets, and on the metal flash is the image of an angel enfolding the world in its wings.

Before the jump, the men in the C-130 check each other's equipment to make sure everyone has what he needs, and that all is in working order. The only light inside the airplane is red, so that their eyes will be accustomed to the darkness when they jump. They are also equipped with night vision goggles, but they won't use their NVG gear until they're on the ground. The binocular vision of the goggles greatly reduces their peripheral range and impairs depth perception, and they'll need peripheral range and depth perception to make it to the ground safely.

"Two minutes to target," Brehm hears the pilot say over the radio inside his helmet. "Airspeed 125. Scattered cloud deck at 13,000 feet."

"Clouds," one man says. It's unpleasant to jump into a cloud bank, particularly at night.

"Oh well," a second says, "I needed a bath anyway."

"That was you?" a third says. "I thought something died in the oxygen console."

"Gentlemen," the team leader says. Joking soothes the nerves, but it's time to be serious.

The jumpmaster stands by the open door, a large ramp at the rear of the airplane, and holds up two fingers, meaning in two minutes Brehm will step off the end of the ramp and out into the night. The men signal the jumpmaster with a thumbs up to indicate they've heard and understood his message. All eyes are on the jumpmaster. If he doesn't abort the mission in the next two minutes by holding up a closed fist, then it's a go. Brehm, who will be the high man in the stack, is last in line. He is also the oldest man in the line. Someday he'll be too old to do this job. Lately, as he's begun to consider retirement, silly fears or notions have been popping up. Superstitions. "What ifs" that he doesn't particularly care to tell anyone about. The vague notion that he is pushing his luck, a notion that can only come to a man who knows that for the better part of his adult life he has been very lucky. He once predicted he wouldn't live to see thirty, and he was sort of joking when he said it, but not entirely. He is now forty-two years old. There are few men doing this job who are older.

The jumpmaster gives the ready signal by holding his right hand in the air, thumb pointing at the ceiling. Then he gives the jump signal by pointing out the door. On a static line jump, the jumpers would follow each other off the ramp one at a time at one-second intervals, but this is free fall. They jump en masse, stepping off backward to hit the wind square on with their chests.

The adrenaline rush is immediate. As he falls, Brehm feels the same butterflies in his stomach you feel when an elevator starts down, but to a much greater extent. It keeps on coming as he picks up speed, a body-shuddering sensation. At the same time, once he steps out of the airplane, everything becomes suddenly quiet and hushed, which induces a sense of peacefulness.

Then there are the stars in the sky. People who for the first time spend the night sleeping out in the open under clear skies on the Great Plains of the American West, such as the Badlands of South Dakota, for example, feel overwhelmed because they've never seen so many stars before. People who camp high in the Rockies see more stars than people down on the plains see—viewed from ten or twelve thousand feet, the Milky Way becomes a tangible thing, no longer a figure of speech but a great river of light, or some massive migration of fireflies, so distinct and so real that you can't believe the planet Earth is a part of it. *It's* way over there, millions of light years away, and *we're* here, so how could *we* be part of *it?* Brehm is falling from 26,000 feet, almost five miles up—from as high as commercial airliners fly. At 26,000 feet, you see so many stars that you feel like you're one of them, a shooting star, falling to earth. In such thin air, with less atmosphere above you to obscure the view, the stars are brighter and more sharply focused, and there are more of them, and the blackness in between them is blacker and more intense.

"Number one okay," the first man reports to the team leader.

"Two okay."

"Team leader okay."

"Four okay."

"Five okay."

"Six okay," Brehm says.

Jack Brehm reaches terminal velocity, 125 mph, in about ten seconds. He falls a thousand feet in those first ten seconds. He'll fall about a thousand feet every five seconds after that. Terminal velocity describes the point at which the man's wind resistance, the mass of air molecules his body mass displaces as he falls, is equal to the force of gravity that pulls him earthward. Despite the stories of Galileo dropping objects of unequal mass from the Tower of Pisa to prove they fall at the same rate, wind resistance can affect terminal velocity and make objects of unequal mass fall at different speeds. Galileo just couldn't find a high enough tower. An Olympic speed skater in a $500 Speedo bodysuit might fall at a rate of perhaps 135 miles an hour, whereas a lawyer in a three-piece suit would fall more slowly. On a parachute team, you want everybody to fall at the same speed, but short stocky guys will fall faster than tall thin guys, who can tend to float a bit, so often a short stocky guy will have extra fabric sewn into the armpits or the crotch of his jumpsuit to handicap his rate of descent.

At five foot ten and 168 pounds, Brehm is neither stocky nor tall. He'll be in free fall for over two minutes, but he won't really get a sense that he's nearing the earth until around 4,000 feet. Unlike driving down a freeway at 125 mph, there are no telephone poles whizzing past him to indicate his speed or progress. He has a simultaneous sense of motion and motionlessness because he can feel the wind pressing against his body, but he has no point of reference. He knows he's falling, but he can't prove it unless he looks at the altimeter on his left wrist. It takes no strength or concentration to free fall for two minutes. It's nothing like holding your arm out the window of a car moving at 125 mph. It's more like lying on a pillow of air, so restful you could almost fall asleep. At the same time, falling through the sky causes an adrenaline release, the body's natural reaction to impending danger, and any way you look at it, falling five miles to earth is fraught with peril, if only because there's no margin for error. The adrenaline creates a sense of euphoria that can turn some men into adrenaline junkies, installing a craving for risk that can last a lifetime. It doesn't matter how many times you jump—the rush comes every time. You never get used to it. It's also, according to some, the best cure there is for a hangover. Jack Brehm is growing less and less interested in risk, the closer he gets to retirement, but at the same time he certainly likes the rush. He knows he's going to miss it.

"Stay tight but keep your intervals and maintain awareness," the team leader radios, though it's not really necessary, because everyone knows their job.

Each man has a green, six-inch-long Cyalume chemlight attached to the back of his helmet. They need to see each other in the darkness. Each man knows how to fly through the air, turn right, left, slow down, or speed up to avoid getting too close to each other. Still, seeing a team member's chemlight can be difficult if the weather is bad or there are lights on the ground down below. Tonight, because they are falling into heavy cloud cover, no lights are visible below. The lack of ground light adds to the sense of moving but not moving.

To protect his eyes from the wind and cold, Brehm wears a pair of clear plastic eye protectors called boogie goggles. It's very cold at 26,000 feet. The temperature drops about three or four degrees for every thousand feet above ground you go. At night, in a cold winter month, over a place like Kosovo or northern Iraq, the air temperature at 26,000 feet might be as cold as −30°. The wind chill at −30°, moving at terminal velocity, is about −70°. Any exposed skin at that temperature will become frostbitten in seconds. Against the cold, Brehm wears an ECW, or Extreme Cold Weather clothing system, composed of a Gore-Tex jumpsuit, worn over a down-filled jacket and down-filled overalls (sometimes dubbed a "Mr. Puffy" suit), worn over a woodlands green camouflage uniform, and, under that, expedition-weight polypropylene long underwear. He has on insulated Gore-tex boots, polar fleece mittens, and Gore-tex mitten shells. He wears a balaclava inside his helmet and a neoprene face guard. If he were to jump out of an airplane in midsummer over the deserts of Kuwait or Saudi Arabia, he would still wear such cold weather gear.

In addition to being cold, the air is also too thin to breathe. Brehm wears an MBU-12/P pressure-demand oxygen mask, which has a soft, silicone rubber faceplate bonded to a hard plastic shell, which creates a leak-tight seal over his nose and mouth, with a built-in dynamic microphone that allows him to communicate with the other members of his team. The mask is connected to a 106-cubic-inch portable bailout oxygen system, twin bottles of compressed oxygen that Brehm carries in a pouch on his left side. The unit weighs ten and a half pounds and will give him enough air to breathe for thirty minutes. The oxygen will provide him with some minimal protection, if he ever finds himself jumping into a smoke-filled environment, but the main reason to breathe it is to prevent hypoxia. Because the C-130, flying at the same altitude as a commercial airliner, was nevertheless not pressurized (you obviously can't bail out of a pressurized airplane), Brehm has been pre-breathing pure oxygen from a console since an hour before takeoff. C-130 Hercules tankers are built to carry parachutists and cargo, to refuel helicopters in midair, and to fly for long hours in any kind of weather on search missions, but they are not built for comfort.

The team has formed a circle, about thirty feet across. Each jumper faces toward the center of the circle so that they can keep an eye on one another. They'll hold this formation until they reach 6,000 feet, at which point they'll break off, each jumper turning 180 degrees away from the center of the circle. At 5,000 feet, each jumper begins his pull sequence, first looking over his shoulder to make sure the air is clear above him, then waving his arms to warn anybody who might be near him, then looking for his D-ring. In his mind, Brehm rehearses the pull sequence, even though he's jumped over a thousand times. There's a minimum of radio communication between the members of the team during free fall. Brehm hears only the sound of his own breathing and the wind in his helmet.

Still above the cloud deck, Sergeant Brehm looks at his altimeter, attached to his left wrist with a Velcro strap. He's been falling for a full minute, and the top of the cloud bank he's falling into begins at 13,000 feet. This coincidence presents a particularly difficult mental challenge, because the altimeter on his wrist only goes up to 13,000 feet. That is to say, it begins at 13,000, counts down to zero, then starts over again at 13,000, like the orbiting second hand on a clock, but when you jump from 26,000 feet and the cloud deck is at 13,000 feet, both your eyes and your altimeter tell you you're going to hit zero and frap, or go splat on the ground. It can be completely unnerving, and there's a strong urge to pull— many men have done so by mistake—because even though you know you jumped from 26,000 feet, and you trust that your memory of jumping from 26,000 feet is accurate, there is still a voice that questions what you think you know, the same voice we hear when we shut off the stove and leave the house, and two minutes later can't be sure we turned off the stove before we left. You really don't want to space out and get it wrong.

Brehm's altimeter reads 3,000 feet, the needle in the red zone. It means he's at 16,000 feet.

Unless . . . no, I'm at sixteen thousand.

He looks down and sees the cloud deck, illuminated by starlight. He has done this many times before, but it's always eerie. Tonight he sees only an ocean of charcoal gray. Jumping at night, particularly when you're in a cloud, is psychologically demanding because you have no sense of where you came from and no sense of where you're going. Night is, however, the best time to jump if you don't want to be seen, and Brehm does not want to be seen, because this is a military mission.

Compared to other ways of making war, the use of the parachute in military operations is still relatively new. The first successful parachute jump took place in 1783, when Sebastien Lenorman, a French physicist, jumped from a tower. In the early twenties, U.S. General Billy Mitchell staged a display of airborne infantry power at Kelly Field in Texas, dropping six soldiers out of a Martin bomber and proving that they could land safely and deploy within minutes of hitting the ground. The U.S. military leaders watching the demonstration were insufficiently impressed and chose not to develop a paratroops program. The German observers present, however, were quite impressed. The Nazis used paratroops to spearhead their Blitzkrieg assaults during WWII. The Allies didn't really get with it until 1940 and had to play catch-up for most of the war. The U.S. soldiers who dropped behind enemy lines during WWII used round parachutes, which gave them about as much control over where they landed as dandelion seeds in a summer breeze. Men landed in trees, with no way to lower themselves to the ground without breaking a leg, or worse, or they landed in lakes, where they drowned, or they hung up on wires or church steeples, or they landed in the middle of enemy troops, where they were captured or shot. They landed so far apart from each other that collecting themselves into a viable fighting force was often difficult and sometimes impossible.

It's a much more precise state of affairs today. Jack Brehm is, in fact, one of the most precise jumpers in the world, a member of the Air Force STARS demonstration parachute team. Tonight, Brehm is flying a HALO mission, one of the more extreme ways to jump out of an airplane. HALO stands for High Altitude Low Opening. By flying over enemy territory at 26,000 feet, the C-130 Brehm jumped from can avoid being hit by triple A, ground-based antiaircraft armaments, and it can also keep out of range of some SAMs, or surface-to-air missiles, including shoulder-fired Stinger-type missiles, which have a ceiling of about 7,000 feet. More to the point, in a combat zone a plane flying that high might not be taken for a threat, or it might be mistaken for a commercial airliner. An airplane flying in low over a combat zone would be sure to draw a response. If a plane coming in low overflies a river valley behind enemy lines, for example, within hours that river valley could fill with troops looking for any potential threat along the plane's flight path. A HALO jump puts men on the ground in a relatively short period of time while giving the enemy the least warning. The alternative is the HAHO, or High Altitude High Opening jump, where the parachutist does a clear and pull, opening his main chute as soon as he leaves the plane. Pulling from such heights can give the jumper enough drift time that, depending on the prevailing winds, or how strong the jet stream is, he can land as far as fifty miles from where he originally exited the aircraft. A HAHO jump protects the aircraft because it doesn't have to fly over (or anywhere near) the drop zone. The enemy might calculate the aircraft's flight path, but when the potential drop zone is more than fifty miles wide, there's not much they can do. The drawback to a HAHO jump is that the air is so thin at 26,000 feet that when the chute deploys, it can explode open with enough of a jolt to knock the jumper unconscious or rip the chute to shreds. Furthermore, if the jumpmaster or the navigator miscalculates the prevailing winds, or if the winds change, the jumper can miss the drop zone by miles. Each method of jumping has its own kind of beauty, but to someone like Brehm, it's the difference between skiing down a long gentle slope or taking a double diamond run full of moguls at top speed.

A HALO jump is the ultimate thrill.

Jack's altimeter reads a thousand feet.

He braces himself, because although clouds look puffy and soft from below, hitting one from above at 125 mph hurts. It stings, because raindrops may be round on the bottom, but they feel pointy on the top. Clouds may also contain ice crystals. Turbulence inside a cloud can be strong. Clouds often contain significant internal pressure differentials that can make an altimeter reading inaccurate by as much as a thousand feet.

"In the clouds!" the team leader says, even though everybody hits the cloud deck at the same time.

Within a few seconds of entering the cloud, Brehm is damp to the core. His ECW suit is waterproof, but it's like being sprayed with a fire hose. Water under that kind of pressure is going to find a way in—the only thing he could do to stop it would be to wear a scuba diver's dry suit. You don't do any kind of maneuvering inside a cloud, because you might hit someone. You maintain your position and hold your bearing. Jack Brehm experiences a sense of isolation and suspension, a cold nothingness all around him. It's hard to get used to. No matter how many times you've done it, it's still anxiety producing. Brehm stares toward the earth, straining to see something, anything, in the darkness below him, anything to reconnect him to the world.

This could end any time now. Just about now would be fine. How thick is this goddamn cloud anyway? What if this is more than just a cloud? What if it's actually ground fog?

He checks his altimeter again. The dial glows red, but to be safe, he's taped a green chemlight to his wrist to help him read it.

"I'm out," someone says.

Then he's out too. He takes a deep breath. He sees, far off to the south, the lights of a small town. The people in the town are going about their business, watching television, drinking in bars, making love, unaware that unannounced visitors are falling out of the sky just a few miles away. He scans the countryside below, looking for the headlights of any moving vehicles, any sign that they may have somehow been detected.

The circle has lost a bit of its structure in the clouds, but now that everyone's out, they re-form. Falling in formation like this is fairly standard fare at air shows, where professional jump teams put on demonstrations or try to set records for group jumps. It's a bit tougher to do at night, wearing an oxygen mask, carrying a forty-five-pound rucksack, with an M-16 strapped to your side. In a HALO jump, it's not done for show. It's purely practical, in fact essential, to know where your teammates are because everybody needs to deploy their chutes at the right time, and, at the same time. Otherwise you risk having your chute become entangled with someone else's in midair, an event that is usually fatal for both parties.

At 6,000 feet, the team leader gives the command.

"Break off!"

Brehm wheels about and turns away. He checks over his shoulder, waves his arms and, at 5,000 feet, deploys by reaching with his right hand for a steel rectangular ring at his right shoulder. Grasping the ring, he throws his right arm out and forward, as if throwing a right jab at somebody in front of him. This is the moment when he'll find out if he's had a malfunction. If his main chute fails to open, it may be because the pilot chute that pulls the main chute has gotten lodged in the vacuum that forms above a jumper's back as he falls, in which case Brehm needs only to roll his body one way or the other to break the vacuum. If his main continues to fail, he must disengage it by pulling a cutaway handle with his right hand and then his reserve rip cord handle with his left hand, all the while arching his back.

This time, it's not necessary. He's got a good chute.

He's not out of danger. He has to be aware of any malfunctions by other team members because he doesn't want to get hit by somebody else's cutaway chute, nor does he want to fall onto the chute of someone already under canopy. He really doesn't want somebody to fall through his own chute, as happened to a PJ named Scott Gearen, who in 1987 jumped from a CH-46 helicopter from 13,000 feet and opened at 3,500 feet, only to have a man above him crash through his canopy, destroying all but two cells of his parachute. Gearen fell 3,000 feet and hit the ground at an estimated 100 mph. From the neck down, he was okay, taking the brunt of the fall with his head and not his body. If you were going to fall from 3,000 feet and had a choice, you'd probably want it the other way around. According to one account, "An X-ray of his head looked like an exploded view of the human skull. All the bones were there. They just weren't connected." Miraculously, Gearen survived, and he still jumps, but now before he pulls he looks over his shoulder. Twice.

PJs all know Scott Gearen's story.

Brehm looks around for other jumpers. He looks up to check his own canopy. It's dark and hard to see, but everything appears to be okay. His lines are clear. He turns on the flashing strobe light on the back of his helmet, which tells the men in the air with him where he is and what direction he is moving in. He looks down below for the target. He can't see it, but it's the navigator's job to see it, not his. He performs a controllability check to make sure his chute is operating properly, testing his toggles, red nylon loops at the ends of the lines that control and change the shape of his parachute.

"All jumpers report in," the team leader says.

"Nav okay," the navigator says.

"Number two okay."

The team leader is number three.

"Number four okay."

"Number five okay."

"Number six okay. All jumpers have good chutes."

Brehm's ram-air parachute system opens perfectly, as it will about two hundred times, on average, before a malfunction. That is to say, it doesn't matter how old the chute he's using is—if he were to jump two hundred times with a brand-new chute, each time he'd be likely to have a malfunction, anything from impaired steering or breaking to a partial or complete failure to deploy. Some malfunctions can be fixed while falling, but others must be cut away. The old round S-17 static-line, troop-style parachutes are simpler, and have a near zero malfunction rate, but they aren't anywhere near as maneuverable as the MT-1X ram-air chute, a square, double-layered, 375-square-foot chute with an open nose that inflates the chute like an airplane's wing, the curved upper surface providing lift. As the high man, Brehm brakes to allow the others to drop beneath him.

"Nav got a good bearing?" the team leaders asks.

"Turning left ninety degrees to a heading of two-seventy magnetic," the navigator replies.

"Okay, everyone," the team leader says. "Check your position in the stack and let's get some separation. Nav—spiral down and give us some room."

There are essentially two formations that an element can move in while under canopy, either a V-shaped wedge or in a trailing line or stack, with the navigator as low man at the number one position, the team leader somewhere in the middle of the stack, and the high man at the number six position. Each team member needs to keep his eye on the navigator and follow his turns while maintaining his place in the stack. They follow the navigator because ram-air chutes are so highly maneuverable that you can't always tell which way the wind is blowing, the way you might if you were drifting along like a dandelion seed. You want to land into the wind, so that your forward momentum and the ground winds cancel each other out. Unbraked, a ram-air chute flies forward at about thirty mph. You don't want to be flying at 30 mph with a 30-mph ground wind at your back, or you'll hit the ground at 60 mph. It's considerably simpler during a daylight jump, when the navigator can look for smoke or a flag blowing on the ground to see which way the wind is blowing. At night, the jumpmaster, prior to giving the signal to jump, might drop a streamer with chemlights attached to it, or, if he doesn't want the enemy to see chemlights falling out of the clouds, he can attach chemlights that glow in the infrared spectrum, invisible to the naked eye but clearly visible to anyone using night vision goggles.

"Everybody keep your eyes open and look for airplanes," the team leader says. "And bad guys on the ground. Nav—you got any ground references yet?"

"Roger," the navigator replies. "Railroad tracks at twelve o'clock running east west. When we cross them, we got another five klicks to go."

"Number four," number six says. "Where the hell are you going? Bring it back to your left about forty-five degrees."

Brehm watches the ground below him. He sees no muzzle flashes, no tracer bullets, no campfires, no vehicle headlights, nothing to be concerned about, or rather, nothing to be concerned about beyond all the things he always has to be concerned about—trees, telephone wires, rocks, ditches, fences, water, anything he could fly into and hurt himself. The navigator is equipped with an array of electronic gear, including his compass, his radio, and a Global Positioning Satellite locater that's precise to within a few feet, equipment PJs can use to hone in on a downed pilot's locater beacon. Still, all the electronic gear in the world isn't going to help the jumper who misjudges the wind direction and hits a boulder hard enough to crack his helmet open.

"Okay," the navigator calls out. "Nav's got the DZ, two klicks at twelve o'clock. Looking good. Got the target in sight as well. Looks like the ground wind is out of the west. I'm starting to set up on a left base."

"All right," the team leader says. "Set up for landing. Everyone call out any hazards you see. You know how I hate power lines."

They are at 1,500 feet now. Brehm could remove his oxygen, but it's recommended that HALO jumpers breathe pure oxygen until they're on the ground, because breathing pure oxygen helps with night vision. Perhaps the most critical part of the flight is from five hundred feet down, a time at which the men in the element move closer together as they approach the drop zone. This is when an inexperienced jumper can screw up and jeopardize everybody else. An inexperienced jumper might stall his chute, panic, come out of it too fast by letting up on his toggles too abruptly, lurch forward and make contact with the man in front of him, or tangle chutes. Free falling from one hundred feet is just as likely to kill you as falling from 26,000 feet. A jumper might fail to judge where the ground is, flare his chute too soon and collapse it twenty or thirty feet above the ground. If he flares it too late, he could hit the ground too fast. Ideally, the parachutist will approach the ground in a half-braked position, moving with the wind, pass the target at about 1,000 feet, make a flat 90-degree turn into the base leg at eight hundred feet, turn 90 degrees back into the wind at five hundred feet, lower whatever equipment he may be carrying with him at two hundred feet on a twenty-foot strap so that he's not bearing the extra weight when he lands, and hit full brakes about ten feet above the ground, stopping all forward momentum. In a perfect world, your chute will fall gently to the ground, not catch in the wind and drag you along with it. In a perfect world, there are no swirling crosswinds, no obstacles or trees or wires to become entangled in, no turbulence to rock you from side to side, no boulders or rocks to try to land on, and the drop zone is a flat grassy football field. Finally, in a perfect world, there are also no enemy soldiers shooting at you.

"Turning final at eight hundred feet," the navigator reports.

"Number two, watch Nav's canopy on landing," the team leader says. "I'm following you."

SGT Jack Brehm carries a weapon, an M-16A1 rifle. It weighs 7.6 pounds and is worn on a sling over his left shoulder, with the muzzle pointing down. To rig it for jumping, he has duct-tape padding over the muzzle and sights to avoid entanglement with his parachute lines. This also prevents dirt from clogging his weapon if he falls on it while landing. If he had to, Brehm could fire his weapon as he lands, but that's not the idea tonight. That's never the idea. The image of men firing their weapons as they drop to the ground is strictly for the movies. If such a thing were to happen in real life, it would signify a dramatic strategic failure. In fact, if Brehm were ever to fire his weapon in earnest, it would be considered a sign of failure, which is not something you can say about most soldiers. The object of tonight's HALO mission is to get in and get out without being detected or captured. It's a covert SAR or Search and Rescue, as opposed to an overt SAR, which is how the Marines or the Army might attempt to rescue their people, sending in missile- or bomb-bearing jets in advance to clear the area, followed by multiple heavily armed helicopters with mini-guns blazing, followed by a team of men dispersed on the ground to set up a perimeter and blow the bejeezus out of everything that moves, after which the downed pilot can be plucked from the smoldering wreckage. The famous rescue of pilot Scott O'Grady from Bosnia was effected by the Marines something in this manner. PJs train for covert SARs, low-flying clandestine helicopter raids that put one or two guys on the ground to hoist the survivor out of danger under cover of darkness, or HALO or HAHO jumps, methods that risk as few people as possible to get the job done. There's no real rivalry between the services, except that when a rescue comes, everybody wants it. Whether a mission calls for an overt or a covert SAR depends on the situation on the ground.

Brehm, fully trained in tactical operations, is prepared and ready to fire on the enemy if he has to, but the idea is not to be discovered. Sometimes he wishes he had a silencer on his rifle, because then he could use it to shoot rabbits or squirrels for food, if he were ever in survival mode and so far into enemy territory that it would take him days to get out. The problem with a silencer is that if you have one on your weapon, you can be treated as an assassin if you're captured, and assassins are generally not treated well. No one, it goes without saying, wants to be captured or killed, but there is something even less appealing to consider. Every serviceman's worst nightmare is to be captured and then paraded around, either dead or alive, on the streets of someplace like Belgrade or Baghdad. Every soldier remembers the image on Somali television of pilot CAPT Michael Durant being dragged through the streets of Mogadishu, in October of 1993. That image alone helped change the outcome of events because it undermined American public support for what we were trying to do in Somalia. On a personal level, to a soldier, the more elite your unit is, the more you fear being captured and paraded, because it will bring dishonor to your unit, and Jack Brehm is a member of a very elite unit.

"Very elite" is, of course, redundant, but there are a number of military groups that claim, legitimately, to be elite, groups like the Green Berets or the Navy SEALs, and everyone likes to think of themselves as special and unique. The Air Force's pararescue team is unique in many ways. For one thing, it's one of the smallest special operations teams in the military. There are over 600,000 men and women in the U.S. Air Force, and only about three hundred PJs. They're also elite in that they have a single mission and only one basic reason to exist. Since World War I, it has become increasingly true that the key to winning a war has been to control the air above the battlefield, and to do that, you need airplanes with pilots in them, who will occasionally get shot down, despite all the best defense systems and precautions. Experience has shown us that most of the time, dominating the air will not, in and of itself, win a war, but the importance of airpower, particularly in light of recent conflicts like Desert Storm or Operation Allied Force, remains indisputable. For all the technology being developed to guide bombs and cruise missiles and reconnaissance drones, we will probably always need pilots, and pilots and air crews work better when they know someone is going to come get them if they get shot down. The more capable the rescuers, the more confident the pilots.

There are no more capable rescuers than the PJs. No one else knows how to fall five miles from the sky to rescue somebody. No one else trains to make rescues in such a wide variety of circumstances and conditions on a mountaintop, in the middle of the Sahara, or 1,000 miles out from shore in hurricane-tossed seas.

At five hundred feet, Brehm turns into the wind and descends at half-toggle. He watches below him, keeping his eye on his team members' chemlights. The high man's landing is somewhat tricky, with five other team members on the ground before him to avoid, but it's also easier, in that he can watch them land first and learn from their mistakes.

"Nav's in," the navigator calls out.

"Two's in."

"TL in."

"Four's in—shit, that hurts. Goddammit. I flared early again. I'm okay."

It looks fairly clear below, some kind of open field. Brehm tries to read any shifts in the wind, flies right to avoid one of his team members, turns directly into the wind again and lowers his Alice pack at two hundred feet.

"Five's in."

Brehm stalls his chute when he's about five feet off the ground. He lands on both feet, knees bent, but it jars him just a bit because he thought the ground was a few feet closer. He doesn't fall, which is a point of pride with him. He qualified for the Air Force STARS by landing ten consecutive jumps within a three-meter circle and standing up each time, sticking his landings like an Olympic gymnast. He has a number of dreams, but one of them is to land on the pitcher's mound in Yankee Stadium before a World Series game. Right on the rubber.

"Six in," he reports. "Still alive."

He reaches for his cutaway handle to free his chute as soon as he sets down, so that his parachute won't drag him along the ground if it's windy. The temperature is in the seventies. Jack Brehm gathers his chute together and hauls in his gear bag.

"Everybody bring it in and we'll meet on the north side of the target in five," the team leader says. "Good job, boys. Let's clear the DZ."

Brehm sheds his Mr. Puffy suit and unstraps his M-16. He takes off his helmet and his balaclava. He has short red hair, as much mustache as the Air Force allows, and freckles beneath the camouflage paint he wears on his face. There's enough ambient light that he doesn't need his night vision goggles. He collects his gear and rendezvouses with the other members of his team. The team leader is nearly Brehm's age. The rest are all younger, all men in their twenties. It's unusual for someone to remain a PJ for as long as Brehm has, for a variety of reasons. If you ever get knocked unconscious, you're out, because there's always a chance you'll have subsequent blackouts. If your eyes go bad enough, you're out. If you fail to maintain a peak level of fitness and can't pass the annual qualifying physical, you're out. In any rescue, the idea is to land as close as you can to the downed pilot, but sometimes you have to land a considerable distance away and cross miles of often difficult terrain, carrying heavy gear. When you find the pilot, you might have to carry him to where a helicopter can fly in and pick everybody up. In a purely physical sense, pararescue is a young man's game. In an emotional sense, it is, too. Jack Brehm has been doing this for twenty-two years, nearly four times as long as the average PJ's career.

At the rendezvous point, an argument is in progress.

"You're the navigator," number two says. "You're supposed to know these things."

"Don't blame me," the navigator says. "It's not like they gave me a GPS bearing for it."

"Well, I'm not following you then," number five says.

"I'm with him," number four says.

"Doesn't anybody have a cell phone?"

"It's right on the beach."

"No it's not."

"Let's ask the veteran," number two says as Brehm approaches. "Hey, Jack—this guy says Tracers is on 98A after Panama City Beach. I say it's before you get to Panama City Beach."

"Coming from where?"

"From Eglin? Or from Fort Walton Beach?"

"Well, if you take the fork after the bridge, it's before, but then you gotta go another ten miles. The fastest way to get there is to take 98 past Panama City and then circle back on 98A, which becomes Fort Beach Road. Then it's just after the beach. Why?"

"We're debriefing there in an hour," the team leader says. "I suggested the PJ section, but I was outvoted."

"Tonight's amateur night and they get college girls in there trying to make money for spring break," number four explains. Young PJs love strip joints. Old PJs don't mind them, either.

"I'll meet you there," Brehm says. "I need to stop at the motel first and make a phone call."

The training mission is over. They are on the property of Eglin Air Force Base, just outside of Fort Walton Beach, Florida. Dropping men from 26,000 feet is a complicated procedure, requiring all commercial air traffic in the area to be canceled or rerouted, something the Air Force only schedules a couple of times a year. Other teams of men will be falling throughout the evening. Such training missions are exhilarating, but at the same time, preparing for war is a grim business. There is trouble all over the world, in Iraq, in Kosovo, in Bosnia, Croatia, Chechnya, East Timor, the Congo—anywhere that American aircraft fly to police the skies, PJs have to go and stand watch and be ready to launch at a moment's notice.

That others may live.

Brehm's motel is right on the water in Fort Walton Beach. He opens the sliding-glass doors and stands on his balcony watching the ocean. The Gulf of Mexico doesn't smell the same as the ocean in New England. He's tempted to go for a midnight swim, but then he remembers he's done enough for one night. He's not tired. He rarely is after a jump, particularly not after a HALO jump. There's too much adrenaline in his system. The high doesn't go away when the mission ends. In some sense, that's when it begins. It's why guys generally want to go out after a mission and drink beers until the feeling goes away, not that you want the feeling to go away.

It's why his team members are at Tracers, helping college girls raise the funds they need by tucking dollar bills into their garter belts. Anything to further the cause of education. He calls home to Long Island. His wife, Peggy, answers.

"Hey," he says.

"Hi, John," she says, sounding sleepy. "How are you? How'd it go?"

"Did I wake you?"

"I was just resting my eyes."

"What time is it there?" He looks at his watch. "Oh shit. I keep forgetting the Panhandle is in a different time zone here. I'm sorry."

She doesn't mind being woken up. He asks her how his children are. She tells him Bean—Laura-Jean—did pretty good on her progress report. Matthew forgot to feed the puppy again, but Peg reminded him. Molly, the puppy, seems to have learned to pee only on the newspapers, so they're ready for the next step in her training. Jeff is good. The twins are good. Elizabeth, a freshman at Boston University, got A's on two papers she wrote, but that's no surprise because she's always loved writing and is thinking about becoming a writer. Michele and her boyfriend Greg went to the movies—they should be home soon.

Jack tells her there's a debriefing he has to go to at Tracers. She knows Tracers is a strip joint, but it doesn't bother her, because she also knows that there's nothing her husband values any higher than his family and nothing he would ever do to jeopardize that. He tells her he loves her and that he'll be home in three days. He thinks of how many times he's said that before and wonders how many times he'll say it again.

She thinks of how many times he's said that before and wonders how many times he'll say it again.

"Did you see the news?" she asks him.

"No, I didn't," he says. "What's happening?"

She tells him things are going wrong in Iraq. Saddam Hussein is refusing to allow U.N. weapons inspectors to inspect what they want to inspect. There's talk of a renewed bombing campaign. There's also talk of a possible war in Yugoslavia, someplace called Kosovo.

"Well," Brehm says, "with any luck, that'll have nothing to do with me." To be honest, though, part of him wants to go to combat—training to do something your whole life and then never doing it would leave you with a kind of empty feeling. He just jumped out of an airplane from 26,000 feet. There was a reason for that.

She reminds him that he's already scheduled to go to Turkey.

"Peg," he says, "I know. Okay? We can talk about it when I get back."

He hangs up the phone. He's got to start thinking about what he's going to do when he retires. Whenever that's going to be. It would be nice to have one last mission, one major rescue, so that afterward he could say he'd done it all.

It would be nice to go out on a high note.

2

DON'T SIT UNDER THE APPLE TREE

Whenever I go to a foreign country, I try to learn some-
thing about the culture before I go. Usually I read about that
country's religion. Before I went to Thailand, I read the
teachings of Buddha. Before I went to Saudi Arabia, I read
up on Islam. All the great religions have the same bottom line.
Christians put it this way: "Love thy neighbor as thyself." It
makes it hard to understand why there's so much fighting
over religion in the world. Pray to Buddha, or Allah, or God,
or Jesus—it doesn't matter how you address the envelope. It
all goes in the same box.

B ILL LOOKS GOOD," PEGGY SAYS. SHE THROWS HER SWEATER ON
the bed. "Do you think?"

"He looks real good," Jack says.

"How much weight do you think he lost?"

"Since when?"

"Since you saw him last?"

"I don't know. A lot."

"You said he used to look like Orson Welles."

"He was a big boy."

"I'm glad he looks good."

"He's doing great."

"I'm exhausted. You feel like waiting up for Bean? She told me today she thinks she's old enough to have her curfew extended."

"What'd you tell her?"

"I don't know. She probably is. I told her we could talk about it when you get back."

Peggy doesn't want to say the words "when you get back." Peggy doesn't want to talk about his leaving, but it's like trying to avoid the big blue elephant sitting on your couch. Jack's bags sit at the foot of the bed, unclosed, all but packed. Tomorrow he'll add his toiletries, his shaving cream, toothbrush, razor. Tomorrow night, when she brushes her teeth, Peggy will see the empty hole where his toothbrush ordinarily rests, and it's going to make her want to cry. Tonight is their last night together, and she doesn't want to cry on their last night.

"Did you call Elizabeth?"

"I talked to her yesterday," Jack says. "I'll call her again tomorrow."

"She's not used to being all alone when you go," Peggy says. "Bean was crying. She said it's because her friend didn't call her."

They both know Laura-Jean's weepiness has more to do with the sadness and the strain in the air than anything her friends have said or done to her.

"How's Matty?" Jack asks.

"Hard to read, as usual. Pretending he's cool with everything. He says his lacrosse coach isn't giving him much playing time."

"He will, once he gets to know him."

"He thinks he's too small."

"Tell him size has nothing to do with it."

"Not Matty—the coach thinks he's too small."

"Why? How big is the coach?"

"Not the coach—the coach thinks . . ." Peggy says, before she catches herself and realizes she's being teased. If she weren't so tense, she wouldn't be taken in so easily. She puts her arms around her husband and kisses him. His job is to make her laugh when she gets like this, and he's always been able to. Sometimes she seems like the most serious person in the family. The kids joke all the time, and they like to say to their father, "Why don't you go jump out of an airplane?" Peggy has a sense of humor, but her brow is often furrowed as she tries to think ahead and anticipate any problems, because it's her job, as she sees it, to keep everything in order and moving forward. She has fine eyebrows, beautiful brown eyes, high Slavic cheekbones, a narrow face, soft straight brown hair parted in the middle, cut shorter than she wore it when she was younger, off the neck now. Jack thinks she's beautiful when her brow is knit, and beautiful when she's smiling, but he prefers the latter. She wears the pants in the family, and he wears the parachute, and neither of them would have it any other way, but he knows he makes her worry. He relies on her faith and on her judgment. He could carry a full-grown man on his shoulders for miles, but he knows she's the strong one.

"What did you tell Elizabeth?" Peggy asks.

"I just told her that as far as I know, the mission's still in Turkey. I'm sorry I barked in the restaurant." It's a noise he makes when he's excited. He can't help it.

"I can't take you anywhere."

"Was it really loud?"

"Bill probably didn't think it was, but the couple across the room might have."

"I want to go watch the news for a second."

"Jack . . ."

"Don't worry—the kids are asleep." Peggy isn't afraid that the television will wake the children. She's afraid of what they'll hear, coming from the television, if they should awaken. She's in something of a bind because she knows that the more information she has, the better her decisions are going to be, and that the same thing is true for her kids, but she also knows that for the next three weeks, if not longer, everything on the nightly news regarding the war in Yugoslavia or events in Iraq is going to directly and personally affect every member of her family, each in a different way, none of them positive, and she wants to protect them from that.

"If Bean comes home," Peggy suggests, "switch it to the *Tonight Show.*"

Jack Brehm watches CNN in his living room. It's the third day of the bombing campaign in Yugoslavia—Operation Allied Force, they're calling it. The war seems to have considerable clarity of purpose—to stop, hamper, delay, or deter the Serbian government, led by Slobodan Milosevic, from executing a "cleansing" campaign against the ethnic Albanian/Moslem residents of Kosovo, a southern province of what was once Yugoslavia, between Macedonia and Montenegro in the Balkans. Everybody knows they've done it before, and everybody knows they're doing it again, attested to by footage of endless streams of refugees walking, riding mules, or driving rusted Belarus tractors out of their own country, fleeing Serbian troops who are burning villages, raping women, and executing or taking prisoner men between the ages of fifteen and fifty. The world sat back and watched it happen before, in Croatia and Bosnia, and in Rwanda, and there seems to be a consensus that we can't sit back and let it happen again. Jack agrees. Even Arab countries, with a few notable exceptions, like Iraq, seem to be backing the United States as it leads the NATO alliance in defending the Kosovars. Clarity of purpose, however, does not mean that an operation has structure or definition. Three days in and already the pundits are talking about exit strategies, as if you could know exactly how a war is going to go before you fight it. Brehm's years in the military have taught him to tune out the pundits. He pays attention instead to the physical details. NATO has about 430 aircraft in theater, the CNN announcer says. There are 200 U.S. planes in the air: F-15s, F-16s, F-117 Stealth fighters, British Harriers and Tornadoes, French Mirages, U.S. A-10 Thunderbolts or "Warthogs," AWAC command and control planes, KC-135 and KC-10 tankers, C-130 transports, radar jamming EA-6B Prowlers, B-1 bombers, B-52s and B-2 Stealth bombers, which, with a range of 11,500 miles, have flown all the way from Missouri to Serbia to drop new JDAMs (Joint Direct Attack Munitions) or GPS-guided bombs. There are also Tomahawk cruise missiles and unmanned Predator surveillance drones taking photographs or employing a new JSTARS technology (Joint Surveillance Target Attack Radar System) that sweeps the landscape with radar, looking for movements by tanks or armored personnel carriers. Brehm concerns himself only with the manned aircraft and the weapons the Serbs have to shoot them down, 20mm and 30mm antiaircraft guns, and sixty surface-to-air missile batteries, about two-thirds of those girding Belgrade, mostly Soviet-built Vietnam-era SA-2s and SA-3s, but also several mobile SA-6 batteries and who knows how many SA-7 shoulder-fired missiles.

The experts keep repeating that the Serbs have far more advanced anti-aircraft systems than the Iraqis had during Desert Storm, better radar for targeting, and more combat experience. They also have a number of fly-able but outdated MiG-21s and perhaps fifteen or twenty state-of-the-art MiG-29s, though on the first day of the war, NATO planes shot down three of the MiG-29s. Last night, they shot down two more MiG-29s attempting to fly into Bosnia. American pilots were reporting little resistance from the ground, wondering why the Serbs weren't launching their SAMs. Then reports of light resistance were proven premature when, only hours before Brehm involuntarily barked in the restaurant, the Serbs managed to shoot down an F-117 Stealth fighter about twenty miles outside of Belgrade. This is the event that holds Brehm's attention, because it's precisely the situation he's trained for over the last twenty years. The experts on CNN are calling the downing a lucky shot by the Serbs, a "golden BB." Jack barked in the restaurant when the TV said the pilot had been rescued.

"Do they know where he is?" Peggy asks Jack, appearing at his side.

"In a hospital in Italy, I guess," Jack says, turning the TV off, because he knows it's going to upset his wife. He puts his arm around her and says, "Let's go to bed."

In the bathroom, though, he's still trying to picture it. He has a fair guess what happened. His guess isn't based on anything the TV reporters have said. The Pentagon has admitted only that PJs were involved and won't say more than that for fear of compromising future operations. Brehm knows how PJs train and how AFSOC (Air Force Special Operations Command) plans such missions. It was either a pair of HH-53s loaded with assorted AFSOC personnel or HH-60s with two PJs, a gunner, and a flight crew—probably the latter, given the short notice and the time that would have been required to plan a joint mission. The HH-60s would have been armed with M-240 machine guns and 7.62mm mini-guns, which are electrically fired six-barreled Gatling guns, capable of putting out 6,000 rounds a minute, and possibly a 50-caliber door gun. Bad guys will sometimes move about, or even fire back, when they hear an M-240 or a 50-caliber machine gun shooting at them, but nobody dares lift his head when a mini-gun lets loose.

The F-117 Nighthawk pilot would have experienced a violent ejection, exiting his aircraft under a force of perhaps four or five Gs. He would have been somewhat disoriented at first. He would have been scared, knowing that whoever shot him down was probably sending troops to look for him. Once on the ground, the pilot would have applied the SERE (Survival, Evasion, Resistance, and Escape) training he was given. He would have found a place to hide. Holed up, he would wonder if the system was working. Are they coming? Tonight? Tomorrow? In civilian rescue work, rescuers can locate victims by honing in on an EPIRB, an Emergency Position Indicating Radio Beacon. There are commercially available emergency signal beacons that transmit GPS (Global Positioning System) data. Businesspeople in restaurants all around the world are already speaking to each other on cell phones with satellite uplinks. Much of the modern communications technology we take for granted was originally developed for military purposes. The system works fairly well for civilian rescues, but in combat, you always have to worry that the wrong people are monitoring your communications.

NATO forces in Operation Allied Force are flying out of Italian bases at Aviano, Cervia, Vincenza, and Brindisi. According to the maps on CNN, the closest friendly country to the site of the crash would have been Hungary, which only recently joined NATO. Wherever they launched from, the helicopters, according to the news, reached the F-117 pilot six hours after he was shot down. The helicopters would have been vulnerable to ground fire. Speed would have been paramount with enemy troops in the area. Once the pilot was located and identified, a PJ would have hoisted down on a cable to pick him up, riding a device called a forest penetrator, a small heavy buoy-shaped steel cylinder with paddles at the bottom that fold down in a Y to form seats. The forest penetrator was designed by the Kaman Helicopter Company in the early sixties to drop through the jungle canopies of Vietnam. To extract a survivor with a penetrator, the PJ places his legs over the injured pilot's as they face each other straddling the cylinder, in effect sitting on the pilot's lap. If the pilot's injuries are too severe, the helicopter will lower a Stokes litter, a caged aluminum basket that can carry someone even if he's unconscious. The helicopters would then have flown out of country, possibly using a different route from the route they flew in on, where ground forces might have been alerted by their ingress. Jack can visualize the whole thing. For all he knows, this is something he might be doing in a matter of weeks or even days.

"Bean told me she wants a piercing for her birthday," Peggy says.

"Oh yeah?" Jack says. He comes back into the moment. Tomorrow night, he'll be five thousand miles away. No sense being a million miles away now, on his last night home. He shuts the faucet off and dries his face. "What'd you say?"

"I told her I'd talk to you about it."

"Offhand, I think I'm against it," Jack says. "Did she say where?"

"I think her tongue."

"Well, that's better than some places, I suppose." He thinks, it's hard to have daughters. Hard to have sons, too, but for different reasons. The twins, Elizabeth and Michele, are drop-dead gorgeous—he remembers taking them to the mall when they were Bean's age and how the boys all looked at them, and how they looked back at all the boys. They were still babies, it seemed, when they first asked to get their ears pierced. At least that was just ears. Then Michele had her tongue pierced. Elizabeth had her belly-button done. What are you going to do?

The next day, Sunday, it's Laura-Jean's birthday, so they all go out to eat breakfast at the Rocky Point Diner. It's the same diner Jack and Peggy went to in high school, before they even knew each other. Say what you want about Long Island, Jack tells people, but it has great diners. When they get home, the answering machine is full of messages from friends, wishing Jack farewell and good luck. Peggy's sister Carol comes over to say good-bye. They don't have to leave for the airport until two or two-thirty, so Jack helps Jeffrey color Easter eggs, and then he plays him in a game of chess. Jack wins, but Jeffrey's game is much improved. Afterward, they wrestle a bit, until Jeffrey starts to cry.

"I'm sorry, buddy," Jack says, holding his son. "Was I being too rough?"

"No," Jeffrey says, sniffing. "I hurt my ribs last night."

"How did you hurt your ribs?"

"I don't know," he says. "I just did."

"I think he just needed an excuse to cry," Peggy tells Jack later, when she gets him aside. "Remember—all reactions today are not real. They're just cover-ups."

Jeff is mad that, again, his father won't be home for his birthday, April first. Bean is mad he has to leave before her birthday dinner tonight. Jack can see that Michele is worried about her mother, in the way Michele puts her arm around Peg or touches her shoulder. Matty is being quiet. Everyone is on edge because of him. As the time to leave arrives, everybody starts to scatter, "The Big Run Away," Peggy calls it, a phenomenon that happens each time he goes away, everybody saying good-bye as quickly as possible and then splitting off, because it's too hard to draw it out. Each kid hugs and kisses Dad and then walks away. It breaks Peggy's heart, each time. Each behavior tacitly acknowledges the fact that Jack's job is inherently risky. Every day he goes to work there's a chance that something might happen, which is something you could say about a fireman or a policeman, but what Jack does is often more extreme than that, and his family knows it. Having him go away on a mission only concentrates the feeling. Sometimes he wonders what they'd think if they really knew the risks he takes, because he knows he's far more aware than they are of what can go wrong when you try to refuel a helicopter in midair or parachute down to a ship adrift in twenty- or thirty-foot seas. His experience and training have taught him to accept those risks, but his family hasn't had the benefit of such experience or training—they've had to learn it the hard way.

He tries to see each of his kids one last time before he goes. Matt is reading. Laura-Jean is going through her closet. Michele and her boyfriend Greg take Jeffrey out into the backyard to distract him. There are ambiguities in life, and then there are those things you know with such an absolute certainty that they anchor you and keep a solid base under your feet, and one of those things, for Jack, is that he loves his children. Sometimes he thinks he loves his children more than other men love their own. That can't be true, but sometimes he feels that way. He hates going away. He's also excited to go away. He also knows that there is no better feeling than saving someone else's life. It's the other thing he does that gives his life purpose. Sometimes the two things conflict. So be it. He throws his things in Peggy's minivan. They pick up Jack's fellow PJ and friend Jimmy Dougherty at his house and begin the hour-long drive to JFK, where Jack and Jimmy will fly commercial to Istanbul.

They arrive at the airport around 4:00. There are televisions everywhere, and it seems like they're all tuned to CNN. Five hundred sorties were flown yesterday, a reporter says, involving two hundred planes attacking ninety targets. There's more footage of the wreckage of the Stealth fighter and Serbian teenagers dancing on the wings, kids Matty's age, sporting signs saying, "We're sorry—we didn't know it was invisible." The pundits say the loss of the $43 million plane is a propaganda coup for the Serbs. Of course, it would have been worse if they could display pictures of the captured pilot. Peggy and Jack both know he's flying to Turkey, where American pilots continue to enforce the northern no-fly zone as part of Operation Northern Watch. Back in December, in response to Saddam Hussein's decision to keep U.N. weapons inspectors from doing the job they were sent to do, allied forces launched an attack on Baghdad that included airplanes and cruise missiles, an escalation in the conflict that might have made bigger headlines if the world weren't so preoccupied with President Clinton's impeachment troubles. With the new war in Yugoslavia, reports of bombing raids in Iraq, which have continued sporadically since December, barely make it into the papers. Both Peggy and Jack know that it's still dangerous to fly over Iraq, and that there's still a chance of U.S. pilots getting shot down in hostile territory. They also know, without having to talk about it, that five hundred sorties over Kosovo in a day are five hundred reasons why Jack might be transferred from Operation Northern Watch to Operation Allied Force.

"Sometimes I think it was easier when the kids were little," Peggy says. She holds Jack's hand. She doesn't want to let go of it.

"How so?" Jack asks.

"I don't know. It was all physical. It was just getting them fed and put to bed at night, and then up and out to catch the school bus in the morning. I thought once they got older, it would be easier, but it's harder. It's all mental now."

"I suppose," Jack says. He wishes there was something else to say. He wants to promise her that he's going to be okay, that he'll be careful. It's nothing he hasn't said a hundred times before. He wishes there was a new way to put it. He wants to repeat what they talked about the night before, how lucky they are, how glad they should be, and how they should appreciate all the great things they have, but he's wary of saying anything that might remotely sound like fated last words. "You've got Michele and Elizabeth to help you—don't be afraid to delegate."

"I know," Peg says. *Why is it worse this time? Or does it always feel like it's worse than before?* She wants to tell him no one has ever loved anyone the way she loves him, that he's her whole life, and that without him she merely functions. It's nothing he doesn't know already. "You'll be in my prayers, you know."

"Yeah, well don't be afraid to delegate in that direction, either," Jack jokes. "We're really lucky, you know."

"It's more than just luck," Peggy says. "Don't you think?"

"What do you mean?"

"I mean, you don't marry somebody you've only known for two months and have it last twenty-one years by accident. God meant for us to be together, you know."

"I couldn't agree more," Jack says. She squeezes his hand and looks at the clock on the wall.

"This really bites."

"I couldn't agree more," Jack says. "I love you big. I'll be very careful, and I'll come home safe. What more can I say?"

"I love you too," she says.

"You want me to walk you back to the car?"

"No," she says. That would make saying good-bye harder. At some point she has to turn and go, and it might as well be now. She hugs him, kisses him, kisses him again, gives him a final hug, turns and walks away. She has to force herself to walk. She resists the urge to look back. Her insides literally ache.

In the car, driving back, she watches the time pass on the digital dashboard clock. Now he's boarding. Now they're taxiing. Now they're in the air. She can't keep the tears back, but why should she? She'll have plenty of time to hold them back in the next three weeks, unless the situation changes, and he's gone for longer than three weeks. . . . She can't bear to follow that line of thought.

"I don't want to do this anymore!" she screams in the car. "I'm too old for this! I don't want to do this anymore! I just don't! I want him home with me."

At Bean's birthday party that night, Peggy tries to be cheerful, and to sing "Happy Birthday" at the top of her voice and make sure that the kids know that everything is going to be okay, that this is just another mission, nothing out of the ordinary. She must be losing her touch, though. Three times during the meal Jeffrey reaches over and pats her arm and says, "Smile, Mom." She thinks about this getting ready for bed that night, that he's just a little boy, a week shy of twelve. That's too young to be worried about your mom, patting her arm and telling her to smile. He shouldn't have so much weight on his shoulders. For as long as she's been a mother, she's tried to protect her children, never by lying to them about the risks their father takes, every time he goes away and each day he goes to work, but by instilling faith in them, and optimism.

She cries again in the shower. It's a safe place to let go. The kids can't hear you, and the tears don't show. After she showers, she puts on one of Jack's shirts, one from the laundry—one that still smells like him—and goes to bed. She sleeps on her side of the bed. Moving over to his side would be bad luck. In her prayers she repeats the phrase that's been running through her head for the last three days, the way a song gets stuck sometimes. She says, *"Please God—watch over him and keep him safe."*

Jack is on an airplane somewhere over the Atlantic. He's thinking the things men think when they are headed into combat zones. He's thinking about his mentor, a guy named Mike McManus, a grizzly old veteran PJ who taught him everything he knows. Mike served in Vietnam but didn't like to talk about it, telling Jack less about combat than he might have preferred, but Jack learned not to press him on the subject. Jack once bought a veteran PJ a beer in a bar and said, well into the conversation, "Didn't you win a Silver Star in Vietnam?" only to see the veteran, a friend for years, bristle and say, "Is that why you bought me this beer?" Jack said no, forget about it, sorry, forget I asked, and he never did get the story. The veterans, he learned, would rather tell drinking stories than war stories. Still, within the pararescue subculture, many of the legendary PJs distinguished themselves in combat, guys like Bill Pitsenbarger, an Airman First Class who received the Air Force Cross posthumously, the first enlisted man to get one, for heroism in Vietnam, or Duane Hackney, one of the most decorated enlisted men in the history of the Air Force, a Vietnam-era PJ who once handed his parachute to one of his rescuees in a burning helicopter, grabbed another parachute and managed to pull the rip cord just as his helicopter exploded, blowing him out the gunner's door. Ted Hawkins. Chuck Morrow. Surfer Johnson. Randy McComb, who went down into the jungle in Vietnam from an HH-53 to pick up a wounded pilot, hoisting him out under heavy ground fire. When the pilot looked up at the vegetation overhead and said, "Shit, I had a hard enough time going through those trees on the way down," McComb loaned him his helmet and visor. They were halfway up the hoist when the helicopter pilot decided he was taking too many bullets and flew out, dragging McComb and the survivor through the trees as they evacuated. McComb hung on to the pilot but lost his eyesight in the escape and had to be hospitalized. He eventually regained his vision. Years later, back home and driving down a country road with his wife, lightning struck a tree, which fell on McComb's car and killed him. His wife escaped without a scratch. *There's a lesson in there somewhere,* Jack thinks.

Jack has heard the names and the stories that go with them. He knows, though he hasn't said this to Peggy, that if he could make one rescue in combat, he could retire a happy man. If he told her that, she'd say, "I thought you were already a happy man," and then he'd say, "I am," and have to explain, even though she already knows a combat rescue is a PJ's raison d'être. It's not that Jack has any particular desire to take part in an armed conflict, and there's no warrior's blood percolating in his veins, but he does have a sincere desire to serve his country, and the action in Kosovo (if that's where he ends up) is something he believes is right. He simply wants to do what he's trained to do for most of his adult life. It's not like poker, but if it were, making a rescue in a combat situation would be playing for higher stakes than he'd ever played for in his life. It's difficult to stop thinking about that. This could be his last chance.

Then he sees the telephone, lodged in the back of the seat in front of him. He wants to call his wife. He wants to be home, lying by her side. He pictures himself as a very old man, lying at her side. He wants that, more than anything, though the future is not in his control. He picks up the phone, then puts it back. There's nothing he can say that she doesn't already know. That's the nice thing about being married to your best friend. There's nothing you can say that she doesn't already know.

3

BOZO WITHOUT A CLUE

When I was a kid, maybe from the time I was ten or eleven, it was rare that a day went by when I didn't go to the beach. Winter spring summer or fall, I didn't care. The house where I grew up was only a block and a half from the Sound. On a clear day, you could stand on the cliffs and look across the Sound about twenty miles or so and see New Haven, Connecticut. In the winter, I'd just walk on the beach with my dog, Irish, who was actually a German shepherd, but we named her Irish anyway. As soon as it got warm enough to swim, in the spring, I'd be in the water, either alone or with my friends, Timmy Lent or Tommy Kitz or maybe the Rayner brothers. It may not have been terribly bright, but we used to dare each other to see how far out we could swim. One time we were probably a couple miles from shore and a guy came along and ordered us to get in his boat. He said, "Do you idiots have any idea how far out you are?" At the time, "far out" was an expression that meant you were hip or groovy, so we laughed, but he said we could get cramps, and that he was going to call the Coast Guard, so we got in his boat. All the way in to shore, he kept scolding us and asking us if our parents had any idea how far out we had been swimming, and as a matter of fact, if they'd known they would have killed us. In retrospect, the guy was probably right. We didn't know anything about the currents, or what was going on out there. I think I was a strong enough swimmer that I would have made it back, but there was no guarantee of that.

I've never been afraid of the ocean. There were times when maybe I should have been, but I think it's because I've always had a healthy respect for it. I know the ocean. I almost feel as at home in the water as I do on land.

IN 1976, NORTH AND SOUTH VIETNAM WERE REUNITED, AND SAIGON was renamed Ho Chi Minh City. Nevertheless, the United States was having a good self-esteem year, having extracted itself from Southeast Asia and said good-bye to Richard Nixon. There were the Carter-Ford debates, and there were Mondale-Dole debates too, but for the most part the country was busy recognizing its two hundredth birthday, with bicentennial festivities and tall ships from thirty-one countries sailing off the coasts to assist in the celebration. There were wars in Angola and Lebanon, and ongoing troubles in South Africa and Northern Ireland, but for the first time in a long time U.S. soldiers were completing their tours of duty and coming home safe and sound, to walk on beaches with their girlfriends, or eat at McDonald's, or go to the theaters and watch movies like *All the President's Men,* or *Taxi Driver,* or *Rocky.* Disco ruled the club scene, and the radio played tunes like "I Write the Songs" by Barry Manilow, or "Afternoon Delight" by the Starland Vocal Band, or "The Wreck of the Edmund FitzGerald" by Gordon Lightfoot. *A Chorus Line* ruled Broadway. *Charlie's Angels, Rhoda,* and *The Six Million Dollar Man* were on television. The newspapers told us Howard Hughes had died and was purported to have left his money to the Mormon Church, as well as to a Utah gas station attendant named Melvin Dummar. In the sports sections of the daily papers, we read about the Montreal Canadiens winning the Stanley Cup, the Steelers winning the Super Bowl, the Celtics winning the NBA championship, the Cincinnati Reds winning the World Series, and athletes like Franz Klammer and Nadia Comaneci prevailing in the Olympics. Hank Aaron retired with 755 career home runs that year. Gases from aerosol spray cans were causing damage to the earth's ozone layer, according to a National Academy of Science report, and an unknown disease at a Philadelphia American Legion convention killed twenty-nine people and left 151 others stricken. In Uganda, Israeli commandos staged a daring rescue at Entebbe Airport, where seven pro-Palestinian hijackers were holding hostages. Thirty-one people died in the raid, but 103 hostages were saved.

In 1976, on August sixth, John Bernard Brehm, called Jack by his family and friends, turned twenty. He was living at home with his parents, in the town of Shoreham, Long Island, while working a summer job mowing lawns. He'd gone to Suffolk County Community College for two years, and he had an associate's degree in marine biology, but that wasn't taking him anywhere he wanted to go. The house was a comfortable cedar shake–sided four-bedroom ranch on a wooded lot, on a narrow curving road lined with oak trees and pine. He saw *All the President's Men* and *Taxi Driver* and *Rocky* in the theaters that year and liked *Rocky* best. His favorite song on the radio was Paul Simon, singing "Fifty Ways to Leave Your Lover," unless it was Chicago, singing "If You Leave Me Now," even though no one had left him, and considering that he didn't have a girlfriend, no one was likely to leave him soon. He spent time puttering around in his boat, a twelve-foot aluminum Starcraft dinghy with a five-horsepower Evinrude motor on it, fishing for bluefish or stripers in the Sound, sometimes with his dad, or with friends, sometimes alone. Sometimes he'd cut the motor off and just drift.

It was not the only way he was adrift that summer.

In high school, he was mostly interested in girls, though not anyone in particular. He took Barbara Cummings to the prom, where he wore a brown tuxedo with brown velvet trim. He figured he looked pretty swank. He was also interested in cars, one in particular, a gold 1970 Ford Mustang that he bought from his sister Sally for $600. He liked to drive it fast, and knew he could have been more careful, but he wasn't worried about it. His favorite classes in high school were shop and science, and he ran on the track and cross-country teams, but none of this gave him any idea of what he wanted to do or how to make his way in the world. His father, Bernie, had worked as an electrician for thirty years and achieved the rank of Master Chief (E-9) in the Seabees Naval Reserves. Jack's mother, Rosemary, worked as a secretary at Suffolk Community College. Jack's sister Sally, three and a half years his senior, had moved out, but Susan, three and a half years his junior, was still at home, a junior in high school. By 1976, Jack Brehm was beginning to learn what we all learn, once it becomes irrefutably obvious that childhood is over—how uncomfortable you can feel in a comfortable place, like the house you grew up in, when everything starts to inform you you've overstayed your welcome and it's time to go. Mowing lawns was not, he had to admit, a career track.

As a kid, Jack liked riding his bicycle around Suffolk County, sometimes to the Grumman Aerospace facility in nearby Calverton, where he watched the first test flights of their F-14 Tomcat fighters. He liked spending time at the beach, or in the woods, playing war games with his friends, which could become fairly elaborate given that there were so many military veterans in the area with souvenirs their kids could put into play. The girls acted as nurses and carried the wounded off on genuine WWII vintage canvas litters. The boys wore real WWII steel pot helmets. Jack had a toy rifle that was battery-operated and made a *bam-bam-bam-bam-bam* noise when he pulled the trigger. The gun made him the envy of his peers, which included the Gallagher brothers, four of them in all. In war games, the Gallagher brothers often divided up on different sides. Two would be Americans, two would be Germans, and then they would go at each other like cats and dogs, fighting that went beyond play, and usually didn't end until someone was bleeding or crying or both. If Jack learned anything about fighting as a kid, he learned it from the Gallagher brothers.

At twenty, Jack could look out his bedroom window at the woods where they'd played at war and think, "This is crazy—I'm not supposed to be here anymore."

By 1976, Bernie Brehm was as interested in knowing what his son was going to do with himself as his son was. Bernard Brehm was a man of few words, from a time when men weren't expected to talk about their feelings. He'd served in the U.S. Navy in Africa and in the Pacific during World War Two, helping to clear out Japanese tunnels, and knew that the military was a place a young man adrift in the world could turn to for guidance, or at least employment. Despite the fact that his dad was a man of few words, by the autumn of 1976 Jack Brehm was fairly certain that his father was thinking it was time for Jack to get a life. He indicated as much, one morning at breakfast.

"Thought you might be interested in this," Bernie Brehm said, handing Jack an advertisement he'd clipped from Long Island's *Newsday*. It was simply a picture of a man in a helmet and jumpsuit, free falling, the words JUMP TO SAVE LIVES, and a phone number.

"Where is this?" Jack asked.

"I don't know," Bernie said. "Why don't you call the number and find out?"

Jack did. A SGT Jim Langhorn answered the phone. Jack told him he'd seen the ad in the paper. Langhorn invited Jack to drive down to what was then Suffolk County Airport, now Francis S. Gabreski Airport, in Westhampton Beach, just about where the toney part of eastern Long Island begins. Langhorn said he could see him at 1:00. Jack didn't expect anything to happen that quickly, but he checked his calendar and realized that that afternoon, and every afternoon for the rest of his life, was free.

"When you get to the gate," Langhorn said, "ask for the 106th Air Rescue Wing and they'll give you directions."

It was only a twenty-mile drive from Jack's parents' house to the southern shore of Long Island, but Jack had never been there before. Suffolk County Airport serviced the private planes of the wealthy New Yorkers who flew out to the Hamptons for the weekend. The man at the gate directed Jack to a collection of low buildings off to one side of the airfield, including an office building and, across the parking lot, the operations building. Jack parked his Mustang, got out and looked around. He saw ninety flat windswept acres, dry brown grass, and a field of grayish white concrete with lines painted on it, and on the horizon distant water towers and radio towers and low forests of scrub oak with leaves beginning to rust with the approach of autumn. There was a series of eight helicopter pods on the tarmac, odd-looking, ochre-colored barnlike buildings, more like tenement row houses than aviation facilities. He saw two larger hangars, in front of which were parked four Hercules C-130 turboprops, surrounded by service vehicles and movable risers. They were fat, stubby, low-to-the-ground, pugnacious-looking airplanes, painted park-bench green with a matte finish, two large four-bladed propeller engines on either wing and a large dolphinlike hump just above and behind where the pilots sat. They were nothing that made his mouth water, the way the F-14 Tomcat fighter jets he'd watched as a boy made his mouth water, but they were kind of cool-looking airplanes all the same, burly and intimidating.

He asked someone in the parking lot where the administration building was, and then he asked someone in the administration building where Sergeant Langhorn's office was, and only when he saw Sergeant Langhorn's uniform did it dawn on him. He was about to join the Air Force. It made him pause for a moment, but then he looked at the ad again, and the man in free fall, and figured it was something he could do. He told Langhorn, the 106th's recruiter, that he wanted to learn to skydive. Sergeant Langhorn tried to keep a straight face and said, "So you want to be a PJ, do you?"

"I sure do. What's a PJ?" Brehm asked.

"Pararescue," the recruiter said. "That's where you'll learn how to skydive. Scuba dive. Work as a medic. Can you swim?"

"I can swim like a fish. Sir," Brehm added.

"You don't have to call me sir," Langhorn said. "Did they tell you it's possibly the toughest job in the military?"

Jack had to think a moment.

"Well, that's what I want to be," he said. "I saw the ad in the paper." *What the heck? How hard could it be?*

He was clueless.

"Let me see if Sergeant McManus is around," Langhorn said, picking up the phone. "Master Sergeant McManus is in charge of the PJ section here."

Langhorn spoke for a moment, then hung up the phone and told Jack to follow him to the ops building. McManus was in his early thirties, small compared to some of the other guys Jack had seen walking around the base, maybe five-seven, and he bore a vague resemblance to Johnny Weissmuller, the Olympic swimmer and Tarzan portrayer. Brehm didn't know that McManus made Tarzan look like a wuss, but in his green flight suit and polished black boots, he was impressive enough. McManus was less impressed.

The kid looked like a matchstick. Literally, like a match on fire. Jack was a skinny little guy, but the thing that really stood out the most about him, the thing that people noticed first, was his hair. Brehm had a gigantic red afro. McManus had never seen anything like it, except perhaps on Bozo the Clown. He'd seen hippies come in before to enlist, but nobody like this. Yet it was McManus's job to read a man's character, and he liked what he saw in young Jack Brehm. He seemed to have a good attitude and great enthusiasm, right from the start. A fairly small man himself, McManus knew that size wasn't really as important as heart and guts. He never knew when he sent recruits through the Pipeline if they were going to make it, but he thought Jack had as good a chance as anybody. He'd sent guys who looked strong and athletic, and they'd wash out in two weeks. And the hair wouldn't be a problem—military barbers knew what to do with excess hair.

"How much do you weigh?" McManus asked Brehm.

"One-forty," Brehm said. McManus suspected it was more like one-thirty.

"Can you swim?"

"I can swim like fish," Brehm repeated. "I run, too."

"Well," McManus said, looking at Langhorn, "no harm taking the test, I suppose. Good luck, son."

Jack began the preliminary tests on December 20. He had to pass an IQ test as well as meet the physical performance standards, which required him to swim 1,600 yards doing the breast stroke, the side stroke, and the Australian crawl (no problem there), run an eight-and-a-half-minute mile, do six chin-ups, twenty-two push-ups, and twenty sit-ups. By the time he finished, he was exhausted, but happy.

They have to send me to PJ school now. The worst is behind me.

He was clueless.

On February 18, 1977, Jack Brehm joined the Air National Guard and was told he wouldn't be sent to Lackland AFB in San Antonio, Texas, for basic training until March. His friends threw him numerous going-away parties in the interim, where the music blasted, "Keep on a rockin' me baby . . ." and "Take it to the limit . . ." and "Love hurts . . ." and "Show me the way. . . ." At his going-away parties, much alcohol was consumed by all, particularly at a local bar in Rocky Point called the Dry Dock, on Route 25A, a beer joint with live bands on the weekends and disco on the juke-box. Jack wondered if he shouldn't be taking it easy on the beer, maybe focus on getting in shape for what lay ahead, but figured he'd deal with it when the time came, and besides, he wasn't buying—everybody else was. One night at the Dry Dock, a friend from high school named Cathy Cain asked Jack if he knew how to install the speakers she'd just bought for her car. The electrician's son told her no problem, that he'd be happy to help.

The following afternoon, Jack was at Cathy's house, working on her car. Cathy Cain lived with her grandmother, Grandma Jessie Brooks. Her cousin, Margaret Ann Stemke, was visiting. Cathy had invited Margaret Ann—Peggy—to several of Jack's going-away parties, but Peggy hadn't gone to any of them.

"That's him?" Peggy asked. She looked out the window toward the driveway, where she saw a pair of white high-top tennis shoes and a pair of feet sticking out from under the driver's-side door of a white and blue Maverick. "That's the guy who's going away?"

"Yeah," Cathy said. "You wanna meet him?"

There's something mysterious about a man who's had multiple going-away parties thrown for him. Whatever that something was, it wasn't enough to whet Peggy's curiosity.

"I don't think so."

"Oh, come on," Cathy said. "He's a really nice guy."

But Peggy had been seeing a boy named Tim, who had plans, real plans, to become a state trooper, or maybe a park ranger. If things worked out with Tim . . .

"I don't know. . . ."

"Just go out there and say hello," Cathy said. "He's a really nice guy."

In photographs taken at the time, Peggy Stemke looks a little bit like Madonna did before she became *Madonna*, a pre–prima donna Madonna, you could say, with shoulder-length brown hair parted in the middle. She was short, and pretty, not in a big-haired hoop-earringed Long Island sort of way, nineteen years old, working at the power company during the day and drinking in bars at night. She wasn't entirely sure what she was doing with her life, either, but she was pretty sure she'd be doing it in Long Island, unless she could think of something better. She dreamt of seeing the world, and to that end, she was going to travel agent school in New York City, two nights a week.

"So he's a nice guy—so what?"

"Suit yourself. It wouldn't kill you to say hello."

Why not?

She went out the front door and stood by the car, waiting for the head to emerge from beneath the dashboard.

In photographs taken at the time, you can look at Jack Brehm, with his freckles and his easy smile and his gigantic red afro, and think, "This guy has a sweet face." Or you can look at him and think what Peggy thought, the first time she laid eyes on him: *This guy doesn't have a clue. . . .*

She got in her car and drove away without saying a word.

4

SUPERMAN SCHOOL

The first thing I remember was walking in to report to the sergeant in charge, and as I'm standing there, this guy comes in, dripping with sweat, because he's just finished a run, and he's carrying this rock about the size of a football, and he says to the sergeant, "Permission to water my rock, Sergeant?" The sergeant gives him permission, so the guy takes the rock to the water fountain and pours water over it, and then he leaves, without ever taking a sip, and it was like a hundred degrees out that day. I thought, man, what kind of insanity am I letting myself in for?

JACK BREHM, WIDE-EYED AND EAGER, GANGLY AND SPRY, HIS LONG curly red afro intact, arrived at Lackland AFB outside of San Antonio, Texas, in March of 1977. It was the first time, not counting a few trips to Yankee Stadium with his dad and a vacation in Pennsylvania when he was ten, that he'd been off Long Island. He'd never been west of the Mississippi. It was the first time he'd had his head shaved. After six weeks of basic training, he reported to Lackland's Operation Location J, where he would find out whether or not he had what it takes to become a PJ.

There are several names for what Jack was about to go through. One is "Indoc," short for Indoctrination School. In 1977, it was referred to simply as OL-J, short for Operation Location J. Neither term describes it as well as the nickname "Superman School." The idea is to weed out all the candidates who are not supermen, though no one is a superman when he arrives. Some think they are, body builders or star high school athletes who come in, confident that they're big and tough and strong, and that hey can take anything the Air Force can dish out. Most learn they can't. Overconfidence can be self-defeating, because the idea is to identify candidates who can exceed their expectations of themselves. People who come in overconfident often disappoint themselves when the going gets tough, or doubt themselves, and disappointment and doubt can cascade to failure, though nobody flunks out—they simply make it tougher and tougher until you quit. Until you SIE, short for Self-Initiated Elimination. It is, by most measurements, the toughest school in the military, harder than what Navy SEALs or Marines or Army Special Ops candidates go through. At other schools, candidates might say to themselves, "They can beat me, but they can't kill me." At Superman School, the candidates say, "Well, they can kill me, but they can't eat me."

There were about ninety candidates reporting with Brehm, some guys right out of high school, others veterans cross-training from other branches of the service, and all of them volunteers, each with his own reason why he wanted to be a PJ. All of them were motivated by the desire to do good, to serve their country, to challenge themselves, and mainly to save lives. During the Vietnam era, some men who were drafted opted to become PJs because they preferred saving lives to taking lives. The recruiting pitch attracts candidates by promising them they'll jump out of airplanes, but it's far more of an education than a joyride. Becoming a PJ requires a variety of skills, which means candidates have to go to a number of different schools, including scuba school, jump school, free fall school, survival school, paramedic school, helicopter dunker training. They call this succession of schools the Pipeline. Men can apply for admittance to all these schools from other branches of the service, and wait their turn and hope they qualify. Indoc is supposed to prepare candidates physically and mentally for all the other schools. Sending someone through the Pipeline who couldn't handle the physical and mental rigors would waste everybody's time, not to mention the government's money. About 90 percent of all the candidates who make it through Superman School are tough enough to graduate the Pipeline. Ninety percent is also approximately the percentage of the candidates who SIE from Superman School. It's happened that in some classes, only one or two guys finish—there's no quota set by the Air Force. The Navy SEALs program, known for its toughness, graduates about 60 percent, partly because they prescreen their candidates, whereas pararescue takes on all comers. On the other hand, the horror stories and the reputation that precedes Superman School is itself a kind of prescreening mechanism. It's impossible to say how many Navy SEAL candidates would make it through Superman School, but it's a fair bet it wouldn't be 60 percent.

"ALL THE WAY DOWN, AIRMAN BREHM—THAT'S NOT HOW YOU DO A SIT-UP IN THIS PROGRAM! FINGERS INTERLACED BEHIND YOUR HEAD, DIRTBAG! DO YOU WANT TO TRAIN WITH US, OR WOULD YOU RATHER GO HOME?"

"HOO-YAH, SERGEANT . . ."

Brehm met the other candidates, but held off making friends right away, aware that nine out of ten of the guys he met wouldn't be around at the end. Candidates talked about the odds, usually where their instructors couldn't hear them.

"I heard some classes, nobody graduates."

"I heard some guys check into psych hospitals afterward."

"Not me man. I'm making it."

"That's what everybody says."

Most were young, but others were as old as thirty. Most were average size, under six feet. Brehm's roommate was a guy from Long Island named Bill Skolnik, another of Mike McManus's "guard babies." A guard baby is a man sent to Lackland and sponsored by a specific National Guard unit, which then has claims on his services, should he manage to graduate. Skolnik was a Vietnam-era Marine who'd left the service, bummed around, bartended in Tucson for a while, rode his motorcycle for a summer, and realized somewhere along the line that being in the military beat drifting around and sleeping in bushes. When Jack first walked into his room, Skolnik was standing in front of the mirror with his shirt off, exposing a massive upper body, and he was humming the Marine Corps hymn, "From the Halls of Montezuma," while making his pecs dance in the mirror. Jack thought, "This is one built Marine." He felt like 135 pounds of nothing. He wondered how he would ever compete.

"ARE YOU TIRED, BREHM? You look a bit tired, and that's really too bad, because I told you we were doing CHIN-UPS, NOT PULL-UPS— YOU DO KNOW THE DIFFERENCE, DON'T YOU, AIRMAN BREHM? CHIN-UPS IS PALMS FORWARD, PULL-UPS IS PALMS TOWARD YOU—IS THAT TOO COMPLICATED FOR YOU, BREHM?"

"Hoo-yah, Sergeant." Hoo-yah is a PJ expression that means, "Yes, I understand," or, "Yes, I agree," or simply, "Goddamn!"

"WHAT DID YOU SAY?"

"HOO-YAH, SERGEANT!"

Strong as Skolnik was, the instructors at OL-J made him look like a weenie. Most were combat-hardened Vietnam veterans, winding down into peacetime roles. To the young recruits, they seemed liked gods. They reminded Brehm of the characters in the *Sergeant Rock and His Howling Commandos* comic books he'd read as a kid, grossly exaggerated cartoon physiques come to life. They were MSGT Curt Phythian, SSGT Art Morrison, TSGT Steve Wofford, and SSGT Dan Byrd. They were unbelievable, the most awesome physical specimens he'd ever seen, monsters, but the way it worked was, however intimidated or awed Jack felt, he was also inspired, saying to himself, "Hey, maybe I can be like that."

The worst instructor, or the best, depending on your point of view, and whether or not he was in your face, was Sergeant Morrison, a black man dubbed "The Great Dark Shark." The Great Dark Shark was merciless, but not cruel, and had what one candidate recalls were "stone killer eyes." They were the kind of eyes that, when they glared at you from three or four inches away, made you forget to breathe. When the class ran in formation, they sang:

> Down at Lackland where the PJs run
> There is a sergeant named Morrison.
> He stands five-foot-eight with his hair packed down.
> His eyes are black and he sure can frown.
> If you're a wussy and never bark,
> May you know the wrath of the Great Dark Shark.

By the second week, half the candidates had quit. The plan is to start out brutal and then make it harder and harder each week, and the P.A.S.T. is prologue. P.A.S.T. stands for the Physical Abilities and Stamina Test you take to qualify for the privilege of being punished for another nine weeks, an initiation where, all in a three-hour period, you swim twenty-five meters underwater on one breath, swim 1,000 surface meters in twenty-six minutes, run a mile and a half in ten and a half minutes, do eight chin-ups in sixty seconds, and fifty sit-ups, fifty push-ups, and fifty flutter kicks (a flutter kick is a four-count scissors kick), each in under two minutes. The regimen increases in difficulty until by week eight you're doing seventy push-ups, seventy-five sit-ups, thirteen pull-ups, fourteen chin-ups, eighty-five flutter kicks, each in a two-minute period, as well as running six miles in under forty-five minutes, swimming 4,000 meters in eighty minutes, and swimming underwater for fifty meters on one breath. Those are the minimum evaluation requirements. You can earn extra points by exceeding the eval's minimums. Brehm did his best, though there was more to it than just training to make evals. He had to run everywhere he went between exercises. Candidates, broken into eight-man teams, had to run together, carrying a rope wherever they went, to emphasize teamwork. Brehm had to do pull-ups every time he entered the barracks and push-ups every time he exited. He had to do a hundred push-ups every time he screwed up and an instructor caught him, and worse, he had to do a hundred push-ups every time somebody else screwed up. Technically, Brehm wasn't required to perform another man's punishment, but from the start, PJs are taught to work as a team in everything they do. "No one can make it through this program alone," they are told at the beginning. If you don't do another man's punishment with him, you become identified as a non–team player, which makes you a dirtbag, and once the instructors start to think of you as a dirtbag—and they regularly get together to discuss who among the recruits is or isn't a dirtbag—you've basically had it. They'll do whatever they have to do to get you to SIE, and they usually succeed if they don't like you. Jack Brehm's attitude helped him, both his determination and his natural cheerfulness, which made it hard not to like him, such that if he came up a sit-up short or a couple seconds late, the instructors let it pass or gave him a second chance.

"WHO TAUGHT YOU PUSSIES HOW TO RUN? YOU'RE MAKING ME STAND ON THIS TRACK WASTING MY TIME. FIVE MILES! YOU'RE AT THIRTY-FIVE TWENTY, THIRTY-FIVE TWENTY-TWO, THIRTY-FIVE TWENTY-FOUR—YOU LOOK LIKE A BUNCH OF WOMEN RUNNING AROUND OUT THERE ON MY BEAUTIFUL OVAL TARTAN TRACK—PICK IT UP! MAYBE WE SHOULD GET YOU ALL TUTUS TO WEAR NEXT TIME—WHAT DO YOU THINK OF THAT, BREHM? YOU WANNA WEAR A TUTU WHEN YOU RUN?"

"NEGATIVE, SERGEANT."

"THEN PICK IT UP."

"HOO-YAH, SERGEANT."

"WHO'S THAT PUKING ON MY GRASS? DID I GIVE YOU PERMISSION TO PUKE ON MY GRASS, AIRMAN?"

The first major obstacle was "motivation week," otherwise known as Hell Week, the third week of Indoc. Hell Week meant inspections in the middle of the night, sleep deprivation, extra push-ups, extra sit-ups, the first ruck march, hiking with a thirty-five-pound pack, and more calisthenics in a basement room called the Dungeon, a place where Torquemada could have picked up a few pointers on how to torture the human body. The Dungeon was a long, narrow, and dank basement room, lit by a few bare lightbulbs, with a hard concrete floor that recruits scrubbed clean, again and again. There was a mural painted on one of the walls, a cartoon depicting recruits being kicked in the ass by barrel-chested sergeants. Brehm did his exercises on the floor. Sometimes he was allowed to spread a towel beneath him to serve as a cushion, but sometimes not. Sometimes he was allowed to do push-ups outside in a mud puddle, or march in the rain carrying a heavy pack, or run in the Texas sun until he felt like crying, or falling down, or both. Sometimes he was allowed to help carry, along with his team, a 450-pound sixteen-foot length of railroad steel on his daily run—again, to improve his sense of teamwork. Sometimes he ran the obstacle course unencumbered, but sometimes he'd run it carrying another man on his back. Candidates SIE'd in droves during motivation week, guys who lost sight of their long-term goals and focused only on their short-term agonies. Every night at chow, instructors would walk around the tables and lay Self-Initiated Elimination request forms and pens in front of recruits looking particularly weary, saying, "All you gotta do is sign here, and in two hours, you'll be eating steak, or watching some pretty girl wiggle her tits in your face at one of our famous San Antonio strip joints—anybody want to sign?"

Brehm's problem was pull-ups. He was a good swimmer and a good runner, but he lacked upper-body strength. At night, after chow, Brehm would go down into the dungeon and practice his pull-ups, with Skolnik helping him, holding him at the waist and lifting him. Skolnik pushed him, shouting at him, "Come on—you can do this!" as they trained, or simply "Hoo-yah, Brehm" during evals. Candidates helped each other, and took it hard when somebody quit—everybody tried to get everybody else through the ordeal. On the running track, Brehm pushed a guy named John Smith, who was somewhat stockier, bald, older, the only married guy in the bunch, a Vietnam veteran who during the war spent time as a flight mechanic, and later shoveled brass shell casings out the back of an AC-130 "Spector" gunship. Smith in turn helped a guy named Slip O'Farrell, another candidate who was cross-training, a former instructor at the Air Force's survival school in Spokane. The Higgins brothers, D.T. and J.G., pushed each other. The sons of Irish parents, born in Dublin and brought to California as infants, both were of medium build, brown-haired, fair-skinned, and opposite as bookends. J.G. was the serious one, the older brother, always taking responsibility for his younger sibling, trying to keep him out of trouble, which he invariably got into. D.T. had no sense of responsibility whatsoever, perhaps because he didn't need one—his older brother had enough for both of them. D.T. was always late for everything, always screwing up and making everybody do extra push-ups because his shirt wasn't tucked in or his boots weren't shined and under his bed. If you told him to comb his hair, he might comb half of it. During the morning run, D.T. sometimes ran with one eye closed.

"D.T.—what the fuck are you doing running with one eye closed?" Brehm asked.

"I'm conserving energy," he'd reply. "I'm laxin'."

He said "laxin'" because he was too lazy to pronounce the entire word *relaxing*.

Brehm ached at night, but no worse than anybody else. Guys were so sore that they'd walk up and down stairs with their arms folded across their chests so their pectoral muscles wouldn't shake. Jack did calisthenics in his dreams. After practicing pull-ups, some nights his biceps were so taut that he couldn't straighten his arms, but everyone had the same complaints. They talked at night about the Dungeon, and about which instructors were really pricks and which ones were just pretending to be pricks, but they talked mainly about the pool. The pool. Nothing the instructors ever put the recruits through on land compared to what happened in the pool.

"IT'S HOW YOU THINK ABOUT IT THAT MAKES ALL THE DIFFERENCE. MAKE UP YOUR MIND RIGHT NOW THAT IT'S ANOTHER TRAINING DAY AND YOU'RE GOING TO TAKE IT IN THE BUTT. IT'S A MIND-SET, GENTLEMEN. YOUR BODY KNOWS HOW TO DO THIS. YOU GOTTA GO PICK SOMEBODY UP IN A HELICOPTER, PEOPLE ARE SHOOTING AT YOU, YOU GOING TO SIT DOWN AND REST? YOU GOING TO GO OUT ON SICK CALL? IT'S NOT AN OPTION. MAYBE YOU DIE—SO WHAT? AT LEAST YOU DIED DOING SOMETHING WORTHWHILE."

The pool is twenty-five meters long and eight lanes wide, housed under a translucent fiberglass roof which offers some shade, but not enough. On a hot day in August, with a big red Texas sun beating down the walls, the water in the pool can get so warm that it no longer offers relief from the furnace outside. The pool is where the Wizard lives. The "Wonderful Wizard of Wig," some call him. The Wizard is who you see just before you wig out, the eyes you look into just before you pass out underwater and lose consciousness, the guy you think about the night before your weekly water confidence evaluation, when you know you've been screwing it up in training.

Brehm saw guys who were killing it in everything else, strong young men who had no problem with the runs or the calisthenics, but when they got to the pool, they'd lose it. They might appear calm and cool, but then Jack would look down and see that their hands were shaking, or their knees wanted to buckle. The instructors played head games with them, but some guys didn't need it—some guys did it to themselves. Fear of drowning is nearly universal, as natural as breathing, and in fact it's closely related. It's practically a given in the job that, on a watery planet, the majority of a pararescueman's rescues will take place in water, so his mastery over his natural fear of drowning must be absolute. You can push yourself beyond your comfort levels on land to the point of utter exhaustion and still know you have the option of stopping, resting, and recovering. You don't have that option in the middle of the ocean. Particularly not when you're underwater and running out of air.

To get a sense of it, try sitting still and holding your breath for as long as you can. Then try holding it for the same amount of time while walking. Then try it while running. Then try it while running with twin seventy-five-cubic-foot scuba tanks on your back. Now do it after you're already exhausted from exercising all day. Now do it with a 250-pound monster Vietnam vet sergeant on your back, who thinks you're a dirtbag, so he's hammering you, pulling your mask off, pinching your snorkel shut, trying to smoke you—and remember that if you fail to hold your breath, open your mouth, and inhale, you'll fill your lungs with water, not air.

"DON'T EVEN THINK OF SAVING YOURSELF FOR TOMOR-ROW, BREHM. THIS IS THE FIGHT YOU'RE IN NOW. WHAT COMES LATER COMES LATER. YOU'VE ALL GOT A LOT OF WINS UNDER YOUR BELT. START THINKING ABOUT THAT. HOO-YAH—YOU'RE THE BIGGEST BUNCH OF STUDS I'VE EVER SEEN!"

Brehm swam twenty-five meters underwater on one breath in a Speedo with fins. No problem. Then without fins. Easy enough. Then wearing a BC or "buoyancy compensator," an uninflated life preserver. Then wearing a BC and his combat fatigues, each additional item adding weight and resistance, until the twenty-five-meter underwater swim on one breath that took five kicks in a Speedo took eighteen kicks in full gear. He learned to perform tasks underwater while holding his breath, to tie knots, to take his equipment off and put it back on again, always with an exact eye to detail, because there is no margin for error underwater. If he didn't set his mask on top of his fins on the bottom of the pool precisely so, they made him do it again, and again, until he got it right. If he didn't give his instructors the correct "I'm okay" signal each time he surfaced, his left fist clinched in the air above him, they made him do it over. He treaded water wearing a twelve-pound weight belt, while holding his head and both hands out of the pool. At one point, they even tied his hands behind his back and his ankles together and threw him in the pool, "drown-proofing," they called it. To most people, the idea of having your hands and feet tied and then getting thrown into water over your head is the stuff of nightmares. Houdini made a living playing on just such fears. PJs get to where they look forward to it, because they learn that the only real trick is the mental one, where you teach yourself not to panic and eventually come to understand that you can take a deep relaxed breath, sink gently to the bottom, stay there, push to the surface, take another breath, sink to the bottom, surface, breath, sink, and do this almost indefinitely. PJs actually like having their hands and feet tied and getting thrown into the pool, because it gives them a chance to rest, relax, think about girls, sing songs in their heads. They *enjoy* a situation that would panic anybody else.

"JOHNSON—WHY DON'T YOU GET OUT OF THE POOL AND START THINKING ABOUT ANOTHER JOB! CARPENTER—DO YOU REFUSE TO TRAIN? THEN GET IN THE POOL NOW! SUCK IT UP! TODAY, CARPENTER—YOU ARE BECOMING A LIABILITY TO YOUR TEAM, AND THAT IS DISGUSTING!"

The fifty-meter underwater swim is one of the most difficult tasks recruits must accomplish. Brehm had no trouble with it, but others weren't so lucky, and each time they lost their focus or forgot where they were and came up for air, there'd be an instructor screaming in their faces.

"EXPLAIN TO ME WHY EVERYBODY ELSE ON THIS TEAM CAN DO THIS AND YOU CAN'T, CARPENTER? GO BACK AND DO IT AGAIN. DON'T STAND THERE WAITING FOR ME TO SAY IT AGAIN. DO IT NOW!"

Some recruits simply exited the pool, went into the locker room, and faced themselves in the mirror, knowing that by doing so they were out of the program, and that they'd failed and let themselves down. Some went into the locker room and cried. Some threw up. Some, like Jack Brehm, thrived. The PJ record for swimming underwater on one breath is held by a recruit who swam 133 meters and held his breath for two minutes and twenty seconds. An accomplishment like that is as much mental as physical.

"IT'S GOING TO BE WORSE THAN THIS IN SCUBA SCHOOL, GENTLEMEN, SO YOU MIGHT AS WELL GET USED TO IT NOW. COUNT OFF BY TWOS AND PREPARE FOR CROSS-OVERS."

Everyone dreaded cross-overs. Cross-overs tended to force the last few guys to SIE. Cross-overs simply meant that recruits would divide into two teams, facing each other from opposite sides of the pool, and then, at an instructor's signal, each team would swim underwater to the other side, one team swimming low along the bottom of the pool, the other swimming high just beneath the surface. Once across, they would surface, rest for fifteen seconds, then switch positions and cross over again. This would happen perhaps ten times in a set. Recruits would be exhausted by the tenth time. The catch was that as they swam, instructors would pounce on them, push them down and hold them, rip their masks off, kick or punch them, and, in whatever way they chose, try to drown them. Frequently, recruits would "see the Wizard" and either panic and surface or stay down and pass out, at which point instructors would haul the half-drowned recruit out of the pool, resuscitate him and give him oxygen to breathe. Once he was recovered, the instructor would ask him if he wanted to try again.

"Hoo-yah, Sergeant."

"WERE YOU TRYING TO SAY SOMETHING TO ME, DIRTBAG?"

"HOO-YAH, SERGEANT. I'D LIKE TO TRY AGAIN, SERGEANT."

"THEN GET BACK IN THE POOL, AND IF YOU FUCK UP THIS TIME AND PASS OUT, WE'RE GOING TO LEAVE YOU DOWN THERE. . . ."

It was terribly difficult, and sometimes cruel and brutal, but there was never a moment when the difficulty or the brutality or even the cruelty seemed the least bit desultory or pointless—there was always a reason for it. Brehm understood that more and more as the class shrank. No Superman School instructor is ever going to be as cruel or as brutal as the ocean in the middle of a hurricane, or the weather on a mountaintop when it's thirty below and the wind is blowing 100 mph. To rescue someone who's big and strong, you need to be bigger and stronger than he is. To rescue someone who might be panicking in the water, you have to be the last guy to panic in the water. To be part of the solution to a dangerous situation, you can't allow yourself to weaken, or lose hope, or quit, because then you become part of the problem. To save someone who's in such bad shape that he's given up hope, you have to supply him with hope and inspire confidence until he can, if possible, assist in his own rescue. And more than anything else, the point of it all is that you can always do more when you're part of a team than you can on your own.

By the time Jack graduated from Superman School, he'd done twenty-five thousand push-ups, twenty-five thousand sit-ups, eight thousand chin-ups, run over three hundred miles, and swam over seventy-five, much of that underwater. Over eighty candidates who'd started the program washed out. Brehm's class consisted of Bill Skolnik, John "Smitty" Smith (also called "Patches" because of his alopecia, which rendered him virtually bald), Vernon "Slip" O'Farrell, J.G. and D.T. Higgins, Mike Wilkey, Chuck Matelski and Jack's two new best friends, a farm kid from upstate New York named Randy Mohr and a guy from Toledo named Mark Judy. The three of them became known as the Three Musketeers. John Smith, because of his prior service and seniority, became the team leader. O'Farrell, already a sergeant, was second in command.

Brehm owed Skolnik for getting him through, but he wasn't so sure of where Skolnik would end up because he was a bit of a hothead and seemed to enjoy pushing Smith's buttons every opportunity he got. Brehm wrote it off to Skolnik's being an ex-Marine, just an interservice rivalry thing.

As they were packing their bags to head off to jump school at Fort Benning, Georgia, their first stop on the Pipeline, Brehm finally asked Skolnik a question he'd been meaning to ask for some time. Now that the pressure was off, there was no harm.

"Hey, Bill—what was it you did in the Marines, exactly? You never told me."

Skolnik didn't answer at first. Then finally he said, "I worked in the post office."

Brehm laughed.

"You worked in the post office?"

"Yeah—I worked in the fucking post office—you wanna make something out of it, Red?" Skolnik said, stepping toward Brehm. Everyone knew Brehm didn't like to be called "Red."

"No, man—I was just curious. I'd just assumed you'd done something . . ."

"Something what?"

"I don't know. I just didn't think you'd worked in the post office."

"You go where they put you," Skolnik said. "Why do you think I want to be a PJ?"

5

BOZO RETURNS

They call it the Pipeline, meaning you go to a series of schools, and at the end of the series, you graduate and you're a PJ. The class that leaves Indoc doesn't necessarily stay together, because some guys get held back if they become injured or develop medical problems in scuba school or jump school. Other guys from the class ahead of you who were held back might be added to your class. The appeal of pararescue, part of the recruiting pitch they make, is that you get to do all the schools, right in a row. The schools are open to members of other branches of the armed services, but they'll have to go through application processes and seniority situations and waiting lists. They say it can take someone from the Navy about six years, and someone from the Army about eight, to learn what PJs learn in eighteen months in the Pipeline.

From Lackland, you go to Army Airborne School at Fort Benning, Georgia, for three weeks, and then to Combat Divers School in Key West, Florida, where you learn to scuba-dive. That's four weeks. You do one day of underwater egress training—ours was in Norfolk, Virginia, but now it's in Pensacola, where you practice exiting a sunken helicopter in a dunk tank, first with a mask on in daylight, then in the dark, then in the dark upside down, using a HEEDS bottle, a small oxygen tank called a Helicopter Emergency Egress Device. The dunker was invented about five years after we'd left the Pipeline, but it's now part of it.

You do two and a half weeks at Survival School at Fairchild AFB in Spokane, Washington, and five weeks of free fall at the Parachutists School in Fort Bragg, where you do about thirty jumps and you also float in a wind tunnel, where you can practice keeping stable in a free-fall position. Next you do twenty-two weeks at Medic School, also at Fort Bragg, and finally you

*put it all together in a twenty-week program at Kirtland AFB
outside of Albuquerque, New Mexico, where you learn more
medical stuff, mostly trauma. Then mountaineering, combat
tactics, helicopter insertion and extraction, aerial gunner and
ground weapons training. When you're done, they give you the
maroon beret that distinguishes PJs from other service groups
like, for instance, the Green Berets. When you're done, and you
put the maroon beret on for the first time, it's the best feeling in
the world.*

*It's all pretty interesting, but maybe the most interesting
part is Survival School. It's probably the toughest program,
after Indoc. Psychologically, it's right up there.*

B REHM ARRIVED AT FAIRCHILD IN LATE SEPTEMBER OF '77. THE AIR
Force developed its Survival School—the only arm of the military to
have one—to train pilots and flight crews to survive if they're ever shot
down behind enemy lines in part as a response to the situation of the pilots
who'd been shot down and held prisoner in North Vietnam. Pilots in
Survival School learn how to avoid capture and how, if captured, to avoid
becoming a propaganda tool or a casualty in a prisoner-of-war camp. The
PJs who go in after downed pilots in combat situations do so with the full
intention of getting out again, with the injured pilot, as soon as possible,
undetected, and in a perfect world that's how it would work. The fact is
that when PJs head into areas of conflict, they are going to the places
where the world is the least perfect. They need to learn the same skills the
pilots learn, and then some.

Survival School included some academic work, learning in a classroom
about how to test a plant to see if it was edible or poisonous, or how to signal an airplane from the ground. The most challenging part came in the last
week, when trainees went out in the field and practiced E and E, or escape
and evasion techniques. Trainees traveled by bus to the Colville National
Forest, about sixty miles north of Spokane in the Selkirk Mountains, at the
very northeast corner of Washington State. It has terrain hilly and wooded
enough to get lost or to hide in. With Brehm were Mark Judy, Mike Wilkey,
and Chuck Matelski, as well as a survival instructor to supervise and
observe. The idea was to learn how not to die if a rescue ever went wrong
or if they ever got trapped behind enemy lines. Trainees entered the woods

equipped with nothing but a flight suit, a parachute, and a pocketknife. One man was allowed to carry matches, but only to be used as a last resort. They were supposed to learn how to start a fire by rubbing sticks together or using a flint. The mission was to spend five days following a map and a compass to a designated location, traveling a distance of perhaps eight or ten miles, without getting caught. Teams of aggressors dressed as Russian soldiers searched for them, both on foot and from the air in HH-1 Huey helicopters, and if they were caught, at whatever stage of the escape and evasion they were in, they'd have to start the program over. Aggressors usually came looking at dusk, with occasional patrols during the day. By midnight or so, Brehm and the others knew the aggressors were pretty much cleared out. Brehm learned things like covering up anything he had on him that might reflect light and give him away—his belt buckle, for instance. He learned how to be quiet. It started out as kind of a game, but it got real very quickly. Particularly the hungrier he got.

The weather was cold for September. They used their parachutes for shelter. The chutes they were given came with white, green, tan, and blaze orange panels for a reason. They could use the white panel to conceal themselves in snow, the green panel in the tropics, the tan panel in the desert, and they could use the orange panel to signal an airplane overhead. Brehm and his team learned how to fashion a parachute harness and a shroud into a rudimentary backpack. The nylon material could be used to catch rainwater or collect morning dew for drinking water. At night, to conceal where they slept, they'd each dig a hole, which they'd cover with the appropriate-color parachute shroud, and cover that with branches or leaves, then crawl in, wrapping themselves in the remaining shrouds for warmth. They also learned how to use their parachute lines to fashion fishing lines and snares to catch animals to eat.

Eating occupied much of their time, or rather, searching for something to eat did. Jack made a mental promise to himself to eat anything there was to eat, and never flinch or falter, because he wanted to keep his strength up at all costs and learn as much as possible. They ate all the edible plants they could find, from roots to wild blueberries. They snared a squirrel, cooked it on a spit and ate it. They turned over a log and found a snake, cooked it and ate it. They found a deposit of turtle eggs and ate them. They found a termite mound. Brehm ate about fifty termites. They didn't taste like chicken—they didn't taste like anything, really. He wasn't too fond of spitting the wings out, because they caught in his teeth and stuck to his uniform. The worst thing he ate was a grasshopper. He never did find out what it tasted like, because he didn't have the courage to bite down. In fact, he thought he could swallow him whole, but it kicked all the way down. Brehm learned that to eat a live grasshopper, first you've got to take the hind legs off. There's not much meat on the legs, anyway—it's not like they're drumsticks on a Thanksgiving turkey.

Such training is intended to make the candidate appreciate the carnivore that he really is and to make him understand what he's capable of when he's really really hungry. He becomes part of the food chain at a primary level, no different from the bird that eats the worm to sustain itself; so if the candidate eats the bird, or if he eats the worm, it's the same thing—one life ends so that another can continue. Going two or three days with nothing substantial in one's belly can make a rational person start to feel capable of rash or desperate acts, as Wilkey found out when he caught a snapping turtle, a big one, maybe the size of a dinner plate. For a while, everyone stood around speculating as to just how much meat the thing might have inside that shell, and just how you were supposed to cook one—in the shell like a lobster or shucked? Finally the question was, how were they going to kill it? It was suggested that somebody pull the head out and somebody else cut it off, until Wilkey decided to do it the old-fashioned way—after all, what would you do if you didn't have a pocketknife? It is, however, a lot harder to bite the head off a snapping turtle than it looks. He bit down as hard as he could, sawing his teeth back and forth, but couldn't sever the spine, and ended up twisting the shell, rotating it clockwise a couple of revolutions while biting down with all his might until the head came loose. Brehm looked on in awe.

"That does it," someone said. "I'm definitely not letting you suck my dick tonight."

Escape and evasion training is also intended to make the pararescueman appreciate what a pilot shot down behind enemy lines might be going through. A PJ undergoing escape and evasion training comes to understand that if the rigors of survival school are hard on him, despite his tremendous physical conditioning, a pilot without that conditioning would have an even more difficult time of it. E and E is serious business, because the alternative to escaping or evading is getting captured and being brought to a prison or POW camp, where a U.S. Air Force pilot is likely to be interrogated and/or tortured. During the conflict in Vietnam in the sixties and seventies, PJs were credited with saving as many as two thousand U.S. servicemen from just such a fate.

By the end of the Pipeline, Jack knew how to parachute out of airplanes, and hoist down from helicopters, and shoot a machine gun, and scuba dive under water, and climb mountains. He'd learned how to diagnose and treat a wide variety of medical problems, how to live in the woods for days without food or water, and how to drink fairly large amounts of distilled spirits in off-base cantinas. He was looking forward to going home to Long Island for a little R&R and a chance to catch up with family and friends before starting the job. He felt strong and young and capable of handling anything life handed him.

The question remained, was he ready for true love?

When Peggy's cousin Cathy got engaged to Tom Bazata, her friends and family decided to throw her an engagement party at the Rocky Point firehouse, one of the few buildings in the area with a hall large enough to hold the clan. It was April 1978, and Peggy was there, along with about seventy other family members and friends. Peggy'd been taking the train into Manhattan two nights a week, a dreary two-hour ride each way, attending travel agent school. She liked looking at maps and brochures from far-off exotic places. Ireland looked good. Greece. Maine, even. Rocky Point was a place she knew by heart. Her father, Warren, was at the party, a switch-man at the phone company. Peggy's mother, Jane, was there too. Jane managed Cooper's Stationery in Port Jefferson, just west of Rocky Point. Peggy's older brother Warren Jr. and her sister Lorraine, a year her junior, were talking to Cathy's fiancé Tom by the food table. Peggy's kid sister Carol, fifteen, was being a bit of a pest, asking if Peggy could give her a ride to a friend's house, when Peggy noticed a new face in the crowd, or rather, a vaguely familiar face, one she couldn't place.

She noticed him, first of all, because he was wearing a cowboy hat, and in 1978 you didn't see a lot of cowboy hats in eastern Long Island. You still don't. The Bozo hair was gone. In fact, nearly all the hair was gone. The freckles were still there, but now they were obscured by a deep New Mexico tan. More to the point, something had changed in the eleven months since she'd last seen him. The body was transformed. The 135-pound weakling, formerly built like a matchstick, was now, well . . . ripped.

Cut.

Chiseled.

Buff.

It was instant lust. Jack, Peggy noticed, was wearing blue jeans and a T-shirt and cowboy boots. A tight T-shirt. Probably the same T-shirt he'd worn the last time she'd seen him, but now it was tight across his chest.

His friend, Randy Mohr, was wearing overalls and a derby. She didn't know what to make of the derby. She didn't really care, though—she was far more interested in Jack. Jack and Randy were feeling absolutely bullet-proof, young and free and in the best physical condition of their lives. They'd just finished the Pipeline, where they'd jumped and swam and dove and flown and crammed more information into their heads than they would ever have believed possible, plus they had something most guys in their early twenties don't have—a sense of purpose or mission. Randy was on vacation before taking up a posting in Florida. Because Jack had been sent through the Pipeline by the 106th, he owed the Westhampton base a minimum of two years of service, after which he'd be free to apply for positions in other PJ units. But all that would come later. For now they were feeling their oats. They'd never felt such oats.

The next night, Peggy was at the Dry Dock with her cousin Freddie, Cathy's brother, when she spotted Jack over by the jukebox. The room was dimly lit, with dark wooden tables on a dark wooden floor. The only light came from the beer signs in the window, the jukebox, and the light behind the bar. The cowboy hat was gone, but the friend in the derby was there.

"That's him!" she whispered.

"Who?" Freddie said.

"Jack Brehm. You know him, don't you? You went to high school with him. Call him over here."

"Why?"

"Because I'm going to get him to date me," she said.

"What?"

"I'm going to get him to be interested in me," she said. "Call him over here."

Freddie called Jack over. Jack and Peggy chatted for about five minutes, and then Jack went back to his friends.

"Well?" Freddie said teasingly. "Is he interested in you?"

"He's getting there," Peggy said.

A week later, at the Dry Dock again, this time with Cathy, Peggy was standing at the bar when Jack suddenly filled the space next to her.

"Hey," he said.

"Hey," she said, trying to act nonchalant. "What's new with you?"

"Oh, not much," he said. "Just hanging out."

"Who are you here with?"

"My pals, Tom and Tommy."

"You have two friends named Tom?"

"No," Jack said. "One is named Tom and the other is named Tommy."

They chatted animatedly, and Peggy was at her charming best. Making progress. The jukebox played "Boogie Oogie Oogie" and "Three Times a Lady" and "It's a Heartache." Jack listened to Peggy and smiled, but he seemed distracted. He glanced briefly toward the door. When he finally caught the bartender's eye, he ordered two beers. As the bartender brought them, a pretty, dark-haired Italian girl walked past and nodded to Jack to follow her. Nodded in a way that didn't give Jack much of a choice. *Really* nodded. Jack excused himself and said he'd be right back.

"Where's he going?" Cathy said. "Who the hell does she think she is?"

"I don't know," Peggy said.

He said he'd be right back. That means he's interested.

Stephanie was waiting by the jukebox. Jack had been dating Stephanie for a few weeks, but the relationship had gotten extremely heavy, way too fast, and tonight he wanted to go out with the boys. The problem was, it was a Saturday night. You don't want to leave an Italian girl from Long Island sitting home on a Saturday night, and if she catches you, you don't want her to see you talking to some other girl.

"I don't believe you," she said. "You have some nerve. I can't believe you didn't call me."

"I wanted to go out with the guys. . . ."

"The *guys?* That didn't look like the guys you were talking to at the bar. You call that a night out with the guys?"

"She's my friend's cousin. . . ."

"I don't care who she is—I saw the way you were talking to her."

"What way was that?"

"You know which way. Don't be cute with me."

"I don't even know her."

"Does she have a name?"

"Her name's Peggy. Look, Stephanie . . ."

"I thought you said you didn't know her?"

"Well, I know her name. . . ."

"If you want to talk to her, go talk to her. I don't give a shit who you talk to. You wanna talk? Talk! Talk until your lips fall off. I saw the way she was looking at you. If you think . . ."

"Stephanie . . ."

At the bar, the cousins conspired.

"What's he saying to her? Who is she?"

"I don't know. I've never seen her before."

"Did he come with her?"

"I didn't see them come in. They sort of look like they're together. I mean, it looks to me like they're having a fight."

"About what?"

"How the hell should I know?"

"Go over there and find out."

"Find out what?"

"Just find out what's going on."

"Oh, right—I'm supposed to walk over there and say, 'Excuse me, but we were wondering what you two were fighting about. . . .'"

Peggy waited at the bar, while some Bee Gees fanatic—there were many on Long Island in 1978—pumped a week's pay into the jukebox, punching up the numbers for "Stayin' Alive," "Night Fever," "How Deep Is Your Love." The bar was crowded. Loud. Smoky. Cathy was on reconnaissance. Jack was in more of an escape and evade mood.

"All I wanted to do tonight was relax," he told Stephanie, glancing toward Peggy to make sure she hadn't left yet. "It's a little hard to do that with you hanging around in the background."

"The *background?* I'm in the fucking background now?"

"Maybe that was the wrong word . . ."

"Maybe you should just stop talking altogether."

"If you want to stay here, I'll be happy to go somewhere else. . . ."

"Well I'm not happy to stay here, and in fact, I'm leaving—right now!"

Stephanie left the bar. Jack's heart was broken, but then he took a sip of beer, and it was all healed. He noticed Cathy Cain standing nearby. They chatted for a moment, and then she turned and went to the bar.

Where did Cathy go? What was taking her so long?

"He just broke up with his girlfriend," Cathy reported.

"He did?" Peggy said. "That was his girlfriend?"

Gee, that's too bad.

"He says his friends left and he doesn't have a ride home."

"We'll take him home! Tell him we'll take him home."

They drove him home. Getting out of the car, Jack leaned over and gave Cathy a polite kiss on the lips, just a peck, to say thanks for the ride. When it was Peggy's turn for a kiss good night, she made the most of it, because she knew it might be the only chance she'd have. Not that she wanted to appear easy or anything—she wasn't going to *French kiss* a boy the first time their lips ever touched, but she made sure the kiss was longer than he expected, softer than he expected.

Holy shit, Jack thought. His knees were literally weak. All the physical training in the world isn't going to help you when you're kissed like that. *Jesus—was that what I think it was?*

Jack got the message, and called the next day. Jack, Peggy, Cathy, and another friend went to Westhampton Beach that afternoon and parked on Dune Road. They walked the beach. The following weekend, again in a group of people, Jack and Peggy went to the Great Adventure amusement park in New Jersey. That night he slept over in the apartment Peggy was sharing with her sister Lorraine, but that was it—just sleep.

"I tortured him," Peggy recalls. "I wasn't going to get involved with him until I knew he was going to be serious."

They started seeing each other every day. One night, Peggy decided to stop torturing him. Jack took a two-month gig house-sitting for a fellow PJ named George Gonzales, a.k.a. Gonzo. Jack had temporarily moved back home with his parents and was looking for a place of his own, a place where he could have overnight company. Peggy saw him at Gonzo's house and stayed with him there. They had dinner parties, like grown-ups, and invited their friends over, just for drinks, or to watch a new show on television called *Dallas.* It was the end of the sexual revolution, the final days of casual sex, before anybody really knew that unprotected lovemaking could lead to herpes or AIDS or pregnancy. . . .

Well, they knew about the latter. Peggy and Jack knew, but they were young, hot to trot, and sometimes you just feel lucky. And sometimes you're not lucky, or at least you're not lucky in the way you think you want to be lucky.

Peggy came over to Jack's house one night in May. The front door was open, so she walked in and caught him coming out of the shower with just a towel around his waist. Another time, this might have led to something glorious and inspired, but tonight Peggy was crying. Jack asked her what was wrong.

"I don't know if you want to hear this."

"What?"

"I think I might be pregnant," she told him.

"Oh," he said. "Oh shit."

They sat on the edge of the bed, side by side. Jack put his arm around Peggy. She put her head on his shoulder. For two hours they cried, and held each other, and talked about what they were afraid of, both of them acknowledging that this wasn't exactly how they'd ever expected it to happen. Jack knew, without Peggy having to tell him, that one way or the other, she would have the baby, with him or without him. If that was the case, he knew it would be better with him than without him, and he knew that he wanted to do the right thing, and he knew that even though he hadn't known Peggy Stemke all that long, he loved what he knew about her so far. Seeing her deal with this only made him admire her more—her strength, her fairness, and her faith. It wasn't like they were the first couple this had ever happened to—they would figure out how to get through it.

"I'm getting a test tomorrow," Peggy told him. "I guess there's not much we can do until we know for sure."

The next day during her lunch hour Peggy and her friend Maureen drove to the Planned Parenthood Clinic in Patchogue, where her suspicions were confirmed. That afternoon, she and Jack talked about what they were going to do. It was early June, less than two months since they'd first spoken at the Dry Dock. Neither one of them felt they really knew each other all that well, but then, how well did you have to know someone? Lust, it seemed to both of them, wasn't enough to base a partnership on, but hadn't this become something more than that? The way she handled things impressed him. He'd been trained not to panic. Her courage was even more impressive. Jack felt nowhere near ready to become a father and didn't know anyone else his age who was one. That didn't matter. At Superman School he had learned to confront and accept risk. He had learned that he had the power to rise to any occasion that might present itself, but he had learned something more important than any of that. He had learned that there's one thing more important than courage or faith, training, intelligence, intuition, strength, or luck.

Teamwork.

But that had to do with things like hurricanes, earthquakes, typhoons, avalanches, airport raids, terrorist attacks, and all-out combat in a war zone. This was different. This was bigger than that. This was marriage. He needed to talk to somebody, preferably somebody older, with more experience in such matters. Talking to his father was out.

Brehm was wondering if there was anybody at the base he could talk to when he found Mike McManus alone in the locker room. He didn't really know Mike, his NCOIC, very well yet. He was the Non-Commissioned Officer in Charge at the base, responsible for the PJ section. Jack sensed a kind of affinity between them, but then it could be that Mike just liked everybody. Mike outranked Jack, but he never abused his rank. He seemed like a good guy, a fair man. Jack noticed something else slightly odd about McManus—he would hold the door open, not just for women but for everybody, always the last guy to enter a room. Jack decided to confide in him and told him what had happened, expecting some kind of macho advice like, "Screw her—you've got your own life to live—stand up for yourself, PJ!" Instead Mike, who was thirteen years older than Jack, with two kids of his own and a wife, Marie, a schoolteacher, told him he'd do great, that he had the right kind of stuff to be a father.

"I do?" It was exactly what Jack needed to hear.

"Sure."

"Oh."

"Another PJ marriage proposal," McManus said with a smile.

It was a friend at the Dry Dock who finally talked a bit of sense into Brehm, who was having cold feet and thinking of calling the whole thing off.

"Look, man," the friend said, "nobody knows if it's going to work out, down the road, but I know one thing. I know for a fact that you're not going to be able to live in Rocky Point with a kid ten miles down the road in Port Jeff. That's the only definite thing in this equation." Jack nodded. "Look at it this way—if it doesn't work out, it doesn't work out, but at least you gave it a shot. If you don't give it a shot, you'll never know, will you? And you'll never be able to live with that."

Brehm drove to Peggy's parents' house. They were out for the evening. They sat on the front steps.

"So what do you think?" Peggy asked.

"Well," Jack said, "I think we should get married."

"I don't want you to say that just because I'm pregnant."

"I would have said it anyway," Jack told her. "Just not as soon. I love you."

"You know," she said, "you haven't really officially asked me yet."

Brehm got down on one knee.

"Will you marry me?" he said.

"Yes," Peggy said.

It was a warm spring night, late May, no moon but a sky full of stars. They could smell the ocean. There were dishes in the sink containing the remnants of the pasta Peggy had made for dinner. They weren't scared, nor were they without fear. Everything lay ahead of them. Whatever love was, they were going to learn it.

6

THE JOB

Some of the finest men I've ever known served honorably and courageously in Vietnam. That's a given. That's what I know now.

What I knew then was somewhat different. What I knew then was mostly about my cousin Tommy. My sister Sally was closer to him than I was because they were closer in age. His dad walked out when Tommy was little, so my Aunt Gloria had to raise a girl and three boys by herself. My dad ended up being their male role model. I remember watching the draft lottery on television, and I think they'd only drawn something like six numbers before Tommy's birthday came up, and he was given the number four, which meant there was no question he'd be drafted. My Aunt Gloria was hysterical, but my dad, who was a Navy veteran, tried to reassure her that everything would be all right. Nobody could reassure Tommy. We went over there one day, because my mother had bought him a shaving kit, and he was furious, saying, "You guys are just sending me off to war—you don't even care!" I think I was maybe fourteen. My dad and he had some heated debates about the war. Tommy was a really smart kid, with good S.A.T. scores, and I remember he gave my sister a book he'd read called Johnny Got His Gun, *about this soldier who wakes up in a hospital and realizes he doesn't have any arms or legs, and he can't smell or taste or see or hear, and somehow he even realizes he doesn't have a face, and then he remembers that he was in a battle, and now he's in a hospital, but he doesn't know if it's an American hospital or an enemy hospital. After a full year of mental anguish, he finds a nurse who knows Morse code, so he taps out an SOS message in Morse code with his head, and a nurse responds by tapping in Morse code on his forehead, "What do you want?" at which point, his mind just explodes. Something like that. It was a pretty gruesome story, but when I read it, I realized what Tommy was afraid of.*

What we heard from him, once he went to Southeast Asia, was that he hated it from day one, and every letter he wrote said, "I've got to get out of here." He had nightmares. He stood guard and took some fire. There was no welcome-home party for him when he got back, that I can recall, though I remember there were yellow ribbons on my Aunt Gloria's house. When he came back, he was totally different. I had nothing in common with him. Gradually, the family realized he had a drug problem, though all I thought was that he was smoking a lot of pot. One day he and my sister were sitting in the car in the driveway when my Grandma Barbara walked out to the car and got in and announced that she wanted to smoke some marijuana and find out for herself what all the fuss was about. That's the kind of woman she was. So they smoked a joint, and afterward she said, "Well, I still don't see what the fuss is all about."

Tommy died of a heroin overdose. He was in his car. He was twenty-two.

IT WOULD HAVE BEEN A LOT TO HANDLE, JUST LEARNING THE JOB, without a wedding to plan on top of that.

A date was picked. The wedding was to be held on July 28, 1978. The ceremony would take place at Peggy's home church, St. Louis de Montefort, in the town of Sound Beach, with the reception at a restaurant called the Miller Place Inn. Peggy's parents helped make the arrangements. Jack's parents were less enthusiastic, for a couple of reasons. In part, they'd already been burned once when Jack's older sister Sally canceled her own wedding and left her parents with a hefty bill, only to sneak off a month later and marry a man named Vincent whom Bernie and Rosemary Brehm had never met. Now their son was marrying somebody they hadn't met, somebody they didn't know from Eve, a girl he hadn't even invited over for dinner yet to introduce to them in a proper way. Somebody who, as far as they were concerned, was robbing the cradle. She was younger than Jack, but no matter. They were aware of the pregnancy. Jack was as helpful as he could be with the planning and preparations, under the circumstances, given his limited knowledge of weddings and what went on at them. Peggy, coming from such a large family, was more than a little surprised to learn that the first wedding Jack would ever attend would be his own.

Jack felt enormous pressure because of his forthcoming nuptials, and because he also had a new job to learn.

The beginnings of pararescue can be traced back to an emergency that took place on August 2, 1943, when a C-46 developed engine trouble over the jungles of Burma, forcing all twenty-one of its passengers to bail out, including high-ranking Chinese officers, members of the U.S. Office of Strategic Intelligence and a young newsman named Eric Sevareid. A flight surgeon, LTCOL Don Flickenger, and two of his medical assistants, a SGT Harold Passey and a CPL William McKensie, volunteered to parachute into the jungle to rescue the survivors. Jumping was the only way to reach them. Flickenger had jumped from an airplane before. His assistants had not. They landed, treated the survivors, and thirty full days later walked out of the jungle and into civilization. In 1947, the same year that the Air Force became a separate branch of the military, a U.S. B-17 crashed into the jungles of Nicaragua and a doctor named CAPT Pope Holiday jumped in to rescue the pilot, LT Robert Rich. It became apparent to the Air Force that having a team of parachute-trained medical personnel standing ready to give a quick response to emergencies in inaccessible areas was a necessity, particularly when airpower was sure to play a larger and larger role in conflicts worldwide. Pararescuemen made rescues during the Korean War, using helicopters, of the sort seen on the old television program $M^*A^*S^*H$, and SA-16 seaplanes. During the cold war, PJs stood alert to rescue the pilot every time a U-2 spy plane flew, though in the case of the U-2 pilot Francis Gary Powers, shot down over the Soviet Union in 1960, rescue wasn't possible. As the conflict in Southeast Asia grew in the 1960s, so did the need for pararescuemen, which led to the creation of the Pipeline. PJs served nobly in Vietnam and also stood alert, during the 1960s and 1970s, to rescue astronauts for NASA's space program, which continued into the Space Shuttle era.

The purpose of pararescue training is still to rescue pilots who've been shot down behind enemy lines or to come to the aid of service personnel who find themselves in other such dire circumstances, anywhere on the globe. However, to maintain their combat readiness in peacetime, the PJs in addition to their training duties answer calls to rescue civilians, taking on, generally speaking, any task other rescue agencies can't handle, rescues too tough for ordinary measures. Coast Guard ships and aircraft, for example, effect rescues in U.S. territorial waters, within about two hundred miles of the coast, but beyond that, or to get to somebody quickly, you need men who can jump out of airplanes or helicopters that can refuel in midair, such that when the Coast Guard, which is in charge of all off-shore rescues, gets a job they can't respond to they call the Air Force. PJs also assist the Coast Guard when it asks for their help: for example, when John F. Kennedy Jr.'s private plane went down off Martha's Vineyard in July 1999 killing him, his wife, and his sister-in-law. The PJs will launch for famous people or civilians, for U.S. citizens, or for the lowest-ranked seaman on a foreign-registered ship. About 40 percent of pararescuemen are members of the active-duty Air Force, and the rest are members of Air Force Reserve or Air National Guard units. Reserve pararescue units include the 301st RQS (or Rescue Squadron) at Patrick AFB in Florida and the 304th RQS in Portland, Oregon. Guard units include the 129th RQS at Moffett Field in California and the 210th RQS in Anchorage. Jack's unit, the 102d RQS, subsumed by the 106th Air Rescue Wing, was established in 1975 and assigned to cover the northeastern United States and the North Atlantic, operating roughly from Greenland to the north and the Bahamas to the south and about 1,500 miles east to the halfway point between Long Island and Woodbridge AFB in England, where active-duty Air Force PJs were stationed to cover the other half of the Atlantic.

Jack had about 250 co-workers at the base, a number that swelled to over 1,000 on drill weekend, when the 106th's entire complement showed up once a month to train. Other personnel at the base included pilots, mechanics, communications people, recruiters, media relations personnel, motor pool, parachute shop, engine shop, hydraulic shop, electrical shop, security police, central base processing office, medical clinic, mail room, sheet metal shop, auxiliary ground equipment, and life support. Jack worked in the PJ section, on the ground floor of a two-story, World War II–vintage operations building with green shingles and a flat tar roof, hung ceilings, tile floors, fluorescent lights, and little for the eye to rest upon in comfort, save for the old black and white aviation photographs that lined the hallways. There were about eight PJs on the team. Each man had a large closet-sized locker for his personal and professional gear, changes of clothing, extra boots, hats, wet suits, flight suits, combat gear, scuba regulators, packs, camping gear, clean socks, clean underwear, a shaving kit, spare sunglasses, extra car keys, mementos from missions; the inside of every man's locker door was festooned with photographs of *Playboy* playmates, girlfriends, wives, nieces and nephews and children, or the letters their kids had written them while they were away on a TDY, a "temporary duty" tour. In the middle of the locker room were two enormous tables, perhaps six feet across and fifteen feet long, upon which the PJs could assemble their packs and kits and inspect their parachutes before launching on a mission. There was a medical clinic, where the various medications and narcotics they used to treat patients were kept under lock and key, a shower room, an operations dispatch center containing telephones and communication equipment, and a briefing room, something like a small movie theater, with a podium up front, a blackboard, and a retractable movie screen. The rest of the PJ section housed storage bins for all the equipment they might use in the course of a rescue, from parachutes and scuba tanks to climbing ropes and medical kits.

Jack quickly learned that although the ads made the job sound exciting, when nothing exciting is happening the life of a PJ is, relatively speaking, dull as dirt. You do PT, meaning you physically train by running, swimming, or lifting weights because the job requires you to maintain the same level of fitness achieved at Indoc, but beyond that you work in the supply room taking inventory, or you read medical bulletins to stay current as to new procedures or medications, or you read manuals to learn how to operate or repair new equipment or gear, or you read military regulations, or you pack medical kits, inspect alert gear, clean weapons, attend to administrative details, and stare at the telephone.

Altruism explains part of why PJs live for the mission, but the rest is that it breaks the monotony. Jack wanted a mission as soon as possible. Until you make your first save as a PJ, you're still considered a virgin. Until your "cherry mission," the first nontraining mission where you actually rescue or recover somebody, it's all just talk. He waited for something to happen, with the macabre mixed anticipation of the transplant surgeon on New Year's Eve who knows drunk-driving accidents are the best source of transplantable organs, waiting eagerly for the phone to ring, even though he knows it's going to be bad news.

Brehm also wanted a mission because he wanted to have something to say, instead of just sitting there like an idiot, the nights he found himself in the company of veteran PJs with real stories to tell. McManus seemed to have the best stories. From Pennsylvania mining country, he'd worked as a kid as a clown diver, entertaining tourists at fancy Florida hotels. McManus told him how, after Vietnam, he took a group of fourteen front-line PJs fresh out of Southeast Asia and tried to retrain them at Loring AFB, outside of Caribou, Maine, about 150 miles north of Bangor, far from any major population center where they might have done more serious damage. They'd come straight from a war and were all in need of psychological counseling, probably, decompression for sure. They were in jail every week, drinking copious amounts of alcohol and setting things on fire, or stealing fire trucks and Air Force property, getting in brawls at base football and basketball games. "Guys had a lot of energy," Mike said, typical of his tendency to understate. It wasn't until he got everybody into rock climbing that they started to calm down, he explained, adding, "They'd come back from that so tired that they couldn't cause much trouble anymore."

While Peggy worked or looked for apartments (it seemed like the good ones all said, "No kids"), Jack made himself useful at the base during the day and went out at night to an off-base PJ hangout called the Matchbox, a bar about a quarter of a mile from the main gate, so named perhaps because there wasn't a PJ's wife who hadn't thought of burning the place down. If you were a PJ, you stood about as good a chance getting hurt in a brawl at the Matchbox as you did jumping out of an airplane. A PJ, in a brawl, has a special sense of entitlement, in that, as a trained medic, he knows he probably isn't going to do anything to another guy's face that he won't be able to fix later. It wasn't always the most comforting thing to be sitting on a barstool next to Bill Skolnik, probably the best guy you'd want at your side if a fight were to break out, but sometimes it seemed that if he were sitting next to you the odds of a fight breaking out automatically went up. The management welcomed the PJs, despite their bellicose propensities, and often let a group of PJs with four dollars between them drink all night, because they kept the other riffraff in line, the bikers and transients, derelicts, troublemakers, and random skells who drank there because all the other bars in Westhampton Beach were too chic and upscale, catering to the Hamptons crowds, and wouldn't let the Matchbox's clientele in the door. It was easier for management to ask a PJ to throw somebody out the door than call the cops, when calling the cops too many times in a given month could get you closed down as a public nuisance. It was a symbiotic relationship. Sometimes the PJs would apply their escape and evasion training, when one guy would hide under the pool table until the barmaid locked up for the night, and then he'd come out of hiding and let the other guys back in, and they'd drink beer until the sun came up. Once, a member of the 106th arrived at the

Matchbox on his bowling night at 4 A.M., already drunk, only to find the place dark, so he threw his bowling ball through the window and let himself in, unaware that the place had installed silent alarms. He was calmly drinking a beer at the bar when the police arrived, but when management learned it was a guy from the base who'd broken in, they said they wouldn't press charges if he'd agree to fix the window. Another PJ named Dave Lambert was always the first guy to show up for work and the last guy to leave the Matchbox, night after night, and it remained a mystery how he did it, until finally Jack asked him where he lived.

"I'm living in the bushes in front of the Matchbox," Lambert said. It was a warm summer, after all, and a PJ's survival training teaches him how to live in the bushes.

The veterans introduced Jack to a PJ tradition at the Matchbox, the art of "fire-breathing," which involved drinking 151-proof rum—unless Al Snyder was around, and then you had to drink schnapps, because that, and Budweiser, was all he drank. Al was one of the older PJs in the squadron, about thirty-four. Between the demanding physical requirements and the huge amount of time it takes to stay current and qualified in all the various disciplines, the average length of time a PJ stays in the business is about six years. Jack listened to stories of how Mike McManus broke his butt—fractured his sacrum, to be technically correct—jumping out of a C-130 back in May of 1976, though he was jumping again by September, four months after the accident. Jack became aware, both from knowing the man and from hearing what people said about him, that he'd probably never meet anybody as tough as Mike McManus, who was five foot six and 160 pounds of cast iron and willpower. He was also a helluva nice guy, Jack realized, and had seemed to take a liking to his young red-headed recruit.

They stayed up late, shooting pool, taking turns buying rounds or pitchers of beer, telling stories, and Jack absorbed it all and felt enormously lucky to be a part of this group of men. He heard Al Snyder and Bill Hughes talk about one of their finest saves, hauling their friend Don's ass out of the path of a herd of charging bovines during the running of the bulls in the Azores. It wasn't easy to find schnapps in the Azores, but what there was of it, Don had had too much. They talked about a PJ named Bob Harrison, who was boxing in the local Golden Gloves tournament at 155 pounds and doing pretty well for himself. Harrison told of how he and Billy Hughes had gone out in an HH-3 "Jolly Green Giant" and hauled a young couple off a boat that had gotten frozen in the ice of Long Island's

Great South Bay in January of 1977, and how cold it was. Al Snyder had to buy Harrison another schnapps at the thought of it, declining one for himself on the grounds that his wife was about eleven or twelve months pregnant, so he wanted to stay sober in case she needed him to drive her to the hospital. The fact that she was so pregnant hadn't stopped him from coming to the Matchbox, but at least she knew where to find him. Men talked of how long they thought they might be PJs and what they might do when they quit, guys like Mike Durante, Dave Lambert, Carl Frolich, Scott Hursh, Rich Melito, and George Gonzalez. They talked about some of the new guys coming through the Pipeline, guys like John "Mickey" Spillane and Jimmy "Doc" Dougherty, and Dave Ruvola, men McManus had sent to Lackland, knowing he'd get anybody who didn't SIE back to serve with the 106th. They talked about the "Guard bums" on the base. Guardsmen were required to serve one weekend a month and two weeks during the year, thirty-eight days total. Guard bums were the guys constantly scrambling for work, trying to pick up as many man-days as they could, or signing up for as many schools as they could, sometimes, it seemed, to avoid ever having to get real lives.

One night at the Matchbox, they came up with a plan to raise money for the PJ "Fund of Funds" by staging intra-pararescue boxing matches in a ring outside the section after Saturday drill and selling beer at the matches. The idea was to use the money from the Fund of Funds to throw Christmas parties for the base or to buy flowers for anybody whose wife had a baby. The first match was between Scottie "Hurricane" Hursh and Timmy "Mauler" Malloy, and they started a rumor that Timmy had gotten caught doing Scottie's girlfriend, just to spark a little interest. Nobody pulled any punches—both men took a brutal beating, and a lot of beer was sold. Jack was scheduled to fight Dave Lambert the following Saturday until the NCO Club found out the PJs were selling beer without a liquor license and told the base commander, who pulled the plug on the scheme. The next scheme was even better—a "Name That Moon" contest, in which ten PJs formed a human pyramid and then dropped their gym shorts, and then a picture was taken. Pictures were taken of their faces as well. It cost a buck for the chance to match the correct face to the correct moon, and whoever got the most right won half the pot. The Fund of Funds netted over two hundred dollars.

In May, McManus called a briefing in the Ops building and told the squadron there were going to be two missions coming up the second week of June. Neither was anything to get excited about, but one was a bit more interesting than the other. The first mission needed men to fly an HH-3 Jolly up to Burlington, Vermont, in order to get water rescue training for the copilot. The other afforded some "lucky" PJ a chance to be part of history. The Air Force was attempting something that had never been done before, flying helicopters, in this case three HH-53s, across the Atlantic ocean, from Eglin AFB in Ft. Walton Beach, Florida, to Woodbridge, England. The flight would require repeated midair refuelings, and that was always a tricky proposition. Aboard one of the helicopters would be some general, McManus wasn't sure who. They were calling it Operation Volant Vault. The PJs would be "duck-butting" the mission in the C-130 the HH-53s would be taking fuel from, at least until they were halfway across the Atlantic, and then a C-130 from Woodbridge would meet them and escort the general the rest of the way. A duck-butt mission means you serve as an escort, on hand in case anything goes wrong and your services become needed. PJs duck-butt it every time *Air Force One* flies, for example, following behind, ready to go get the president if *Air Force One* were to crash and leave him stranded on a desert island. Because it involved midair refuelings, Volant Vault qualified as an "increased risk mission." It's considered an increased risk any time you have to parachute from a plane, or refuel in midair, or fly in really bad weather, or under combat conditions. Men were assigned to missions for a variety of reasons, from aptitude to availability, but most of the time it was a question of who needed what kind of training.

"I'll go to Vermont, what the hell," Dave Lambert offered. "I hear the maple syrup up there is fresh this time of year."

"Count me in," Scott Hursh said.

"Jack, why don't you and Harrison take the duck-butt?" McManus said. Volant Vault was, of the two, the least preferable mission, an escort service job where nothing was likely to happen, and giving it to Jack was a sign that he was a "newbee" and lacked seniority. Another newbee on the team was Bill Skolnik, who'd had to repeat a course in the Pipeline and finished behind Jack. Jack was glad to see his old friend, both because he was glad to see him and because it meant he wasn't the greenest rookie on the team anymore.

The C-130 tanker took off the afternoon of June 13. It was a Tuesday, a drizzly afternoon, gray and overcast, the same day the Jolly was due to fly back from Burlington, approximately 250 miles due north of Long Island.

McManus and Skolnik had been added to the flight to Vermont, but when Al Snyder asked to go, McManus figured Al needed the opportunity to lead a mission and pulled himself off. That bumped Skolnik as well, because Skolnik needed to qualify on an HH-3, and McManus was the only guy who could have certified him. Skolnik wasn't entirely happy about it, but there was nothing to be done. Peggy drove Jack to the base because she needed his car to run errands. She had a friend who was going into surgery that same night after a horse he had been riding fell and crushed him, and Peggy needed the car in case she had to go to the hospital. She parked next to Scott Hursh's yellow Volkswagen Beetle.

"Hurricane Hursh," Jack said as he got out of the car. He thumped the Beetle on the roof with his fist. "Middleweight champ of the 106th."

"Tell me you're not still thinking of boxing Dave," Peggy said.

"Can't—the commander pulled the plug," Jack said. He was disappointed, because he'd looked forward to having a boxing nickname. Jack "The Ripper" Brehm sounded about right. Oh well. "Why don't you come kiss me good-bye?"

She was happy to oblige. He told her that if everything went off according to schedule, he should be back at the base by 6 P.M. She said she'd meet him there then, or if she couldn't, she'd leave a message with somebody to tell him where she'd be. He thought it was funny, how he was learning new things about her all the time; tonight, for instance, realizing how much he could count on her to be there, to pick him up, or for anything else, really—realizing how reliable she was, and that was a good thing, but it was the kind of thing most people would know before they got engaged to someone, not something they'd discover later. Sometimes when he thought of how little they knew about each other, it scared him, but then he remembered that what little he did know, he liked.

Or loved.

The flight out on the C-130 was uneventful. Brehm and Bob Harrison were joined in the back of the plane by the loadmaster, in charge of the airplane's cargo. There were red nylon benches along the sides to sit on, and whoever wanted to could sit at one of the scanner windows on either side of the aircraft, in front of and below the wings, positions manned whenever a C-130 is used in a SAR, or Search and Rescue mission. There's a console at each window that allows the observer to flick a toggle switch to drop a flare, a smoke signal or a dye package to mark a location, whenever he thinks he might have seen something. The C-130 rendezvoused with the helicopters over the North Atlantic, south of Nova Scotia. There was nothing to see during Volant Vault, just rain and fog out the window, no sky to look at and sometimes no ocean. There wasn't much to do, either, other than check and recheck their gear. They had with them a pair of MA-1 kits, each consisting of a seven-man inflatable raft and its accompanying paraphernalia, as well as medical supplies. They had wet suits, masks, fins, snorkels, and twin fifty-pound scuba tanks. Were they to deploy, they'd be jumping into the ocean with about 160 pounds of gear on. They flew at between 2,000 and 10,000 feet, depending on where the weather was best, but low enough that they didn't need to use supplemental oxygen. The back of a C-130 provides a space about the size of a school bus, plenty of room to be alone with your thoughts. They listened over the intercoms in their helmets as the pilots communicated about weather information or made arrangements to refuel.

The HH-53s would need to refuel perhaps a dozen times between Westhampton and Woodbridge. Crew members on the helicopters were required to don bailout parachutes during air refueling due to the increased chance of a collision. Brehm didn't know it at the time, but his friends Randy Mohr and John Smith, stationed at Eglin, were on one of the helicopters, there to help if anything went wrong. Refueling would be the most dangerous part of the journey. To refuel a helicopter in midair, first the tanker flies out in front of the helicopter, both aircraft slowing their forward speed to about 115 knots. The C-130 unspools a ninety-foot long six-inch-wide reinforced black rubber fuel hose from a pod under either of its wings. At the end of the hose is a device called a drogue, a twenty-five-pound steel coniform "female" receptacle, which the helicopter pilot tries to hit with his probe, a telescoping twenty-foot-long pipe that extends from the lower right side of the chopper. He has to hit the drogue with at least 140 foot-pounds of pressure to connect. It takes 420 foot-pounds of pressure to disconnect. The coupling is self-sealing. The fuel is pumped across from the C-130's own tanks, measured in pounds. The tanker releases the fuel, a high-octane mixture called JP-4 that burns hotter and cleaner than gasoline, at a rate of one thousand pounds a minute. In a perfect air refueling, the chopper's tanks are topped off in one smooth shot, but occasionally contact is broken due to turbulence, so a second attempt must be made. Sometimes if the pilot thinks he's received enough fuel, he'll cut it short and tell the tanker pilot he wants to wait until they reach clearer air, or that he wants to climb or descend to different altitudes, where the flying might be smoother, to try again. The drogue is stabilized by a small basket-shaped parachute, which keeps it from flailing wildly about, but it can still be difficult to hit the drogue, particularly in bad weather with poor visibility. It's a dangerous procedure because the helicopter has to fly so close to the C-130 to make the connection. Once the probe hooks up with the drogue, the pilot can fly off a bit and put some distance between himself and the airplane, but during the actual connecting maneuvers, the rotors of the helicopter miss the C-130's tail stabilizers by as little as twenty feet. Anyone who's flown on commercial airliners knows that aircraft can lurch about in the air due to winds or turbulence, often by a distance greater than twenty feet. A sudden shift in wind direction or a catastrophic wind shear could cause the two aircraft to collide. Pilot error could cause the same thing. The drogue could make contact with a helicopter rotor and knock the chopper out of the sky so fast that nobody would have time to jump to safety.

The HH-53s flew on an east-northeast heading at about 130 knots. Two hours out, they hit "bingo fuel," meaning they were past the point where they could return to shore on their own. They had made three successful midair refuelings without incident when Jack heard the radio in his helmet come to life. He was expecting to hear from the crew flying out to rendezvous with them. His mind was on other things, like where he was going to live, and what kinds of apartments Peggy was finding. He was thinking about whether or not he'd be able to raise a kid on a PJ's salary, or if he'd have to get a second job. Guys raised kids on a PJ's pay, but nobody ever said it was easy. Lots of them took second jobs, as cops, EMTs, prison guards, firemen, bartenders, anything. He was wondering if his parents were going to come around and welcome Peggy into the family. Some of the time, he was not thinking about much at all, staring out the observation window at nothing.

It wasn't a greeting from the tanker from Woodbridge. Instead, it was a communication from the Rescue Control Center at Scott AFB in Illinois, about twenty-five miles east of St. Louis, where all pararescue rescue operations are coordinated. Scott had an urgent message to pass along to the general in the helicopter below. RCC couldn't relay the message directly to the general's helicopter, which lacked the proper high-frequency radio equipment to communicate with RCC directly. The C-130, on a mission, acts as the communication platform for all the other aircraft. Scott didn't know the C-130 accompanying Volant Vault was from the 106th.

"Please inform the general," RCC said, "that an HH-3 from the 106th has crashed outside of Plattsburgh Air Force Base in New York. All seven on board confirmed dead."

"Understood, Scott," the pilot said. He didn't ask for a reason or an explanation. There was a long period of silence. Jack looked at Bob Harrison and pointed to his headset to say, "Are you hearing what I'm hearing?" Harrison nodded. More silence, or rather, the drone of the C-130's four propeller engines and the wind.

"Jolly, this is King," Brehm's pilot said at last. His voice was calm, matter of fact. "Message for the general from RCC at Scott. Please inform that an HH-3 from the 106th Air Rescue Wing has crashed outside of Plattsburgh Air Force Base in New York. Seven confirmed dead."

"Roger, King," the helicopter pilot replied.

Then nothing.

Hearing the news a second time made it sink in. Nobody said anything. There was no message from the general to indicate he understood that the men in the tanker above him had just lost seven of their friends. The decision was made to carry on with Operation Volant Vault. The tanker from Woodbridge met them, and the plane from Westhampton Beach turned around. Jack Brehm had half the Atlantic Ocean to contemplate as they flew back to Long Island. Everyone listened to their radios, awaiting further news, perhaps word that there'd been some kind of mistake, or that a survivor had been found. Everyone lived with his own thoughts, wondering what happened, and whether or not the men in the Jolly had known what was happening to them at the time. *Would it be better to know you were going to crash, and make some kind of preparation with your Maker, if you believed in such a thing, or would it be better to be taken without warning?* Jack Brehm thought only that he'd made some assumptions that he shouldn't have made, and couldn't make again. He'd assumed he was going to see Al Snyder and Scottie Hursh and Dave Lambert again, and now he wasn't. He'd assumed, as young men often do, that he was going to live, if not forever, then for a very long time, and now that wasn't necessarily as sure a thing as he'd thought it was.

He wanted to cry. It would have been quite a natural reaction, he knew, to cry, but he didn't cry, maybe because tough guys aren't supposed to cry, or because nobody else was crying and he didn't want to be the only one, or because it hadn't really sunk in yet. Everything felt suspended, up in the air, literally and figuratively. The closer to Suffolk they got, the more nervous he became, because he knew that once they landed, it would all be confirmed. It sunk in, rather unexpectedly, when he looked out the airplane's right side paratroops door as they landed and saw Scottie Hursh's VW Beetle, and knew that Scottie was not going to get in his car and start the engine and rattle off into the night, the way he had a hundred times before. Somehow, seeing the car made it all concrete and real. Suddenly, everything was irrevocably different. The idea that he could easily have been on the helicopter with the men who died was inseparable from the loss he felt. He'd been lucky, and they hadn't, and it made no sense, and everything was different, and unpredictable, and all he wanted to do was cry. Everyone on the tanker with him was being completely stoical, unemotional, almost blasé about it. What was wrong with them?

When the plane stopped moving and the door opened, he saw McManus standing next to a pickup truck, ready to unload everybody's mission gear and take it back to the Ops building. Jack saw people going about their business, as if nothing had happened, not speaking, and knew only that he had to get away from them, and be alone.

He ran from the plane. It was raining. He ran down the flight line and stopped running when he reached the parking lot, where he sat down on a curb and covered his face with his hands. His sleeve was too wet to dry his eyes with it. Some time later, he wasn't sure how long, he felt someone sit down beside him.

It was Mike. For a moment, McManus didn't say anything. They sat side by side in the rain. McManus had served in Vietnam and knew something about losing friends.

"Hey, man," he said. "You gonna be okay?"

Jack didn't answer. Both men knew that at some level, there was nothing to say. That it would be something they would need to face each in his own way, at his own speed.

"It's part of the job, you know?" Mike said.

"I know," Jack said.

"Take your time," Mike said, "but when you're ready, come on into the section because I'm going to need your help."

In the section, most of the PJs on the team had gathered, the full-timers, McManus, Gonzo, Hughes, Harrison, and the part-timers who arrived after punching out on their full-time jobs—Rich Melito, Jay Jinks, Mike Durante. Somebody was passing beers around. McManus asked who would be available to pull honor guard duty to escort the caskets home.

He also lined up guys to take turns staying with Marlene Snyder and to fend off the press, in case they came around asking questions. His information on the crash itself was sketchy, but as best as he could piece it together, they'd been headed home, following a highway that ran along a valley between mountain ranges, and then they turned back, for whatever reason. Mike didn't know the reason. It was dark, visibility was poor due to fog and rain, and somehow they thought they were farther down the valley than they were. If they'd have been a hundred yards farther south, or a hundred yards farther north, or twenty feet higher in the air, they would have missed everything, but as it was they'd turned and clipped the top of a mountain.

Jack got a ride home from Bob Harrison, forgetting that Peggy was going to come get him. They drove south on Old Riverhead Road and turned right on Montauk Highway. They'd gone about a mile when they passed Peggy, coming the other way in Jack's gold 1970 Ford Mustang. Harrison honked the horn and flashed his lights, but Peggy didn't see them, so he turned around and set off after her, catching her as she turned into the base. Jack ran from the car and threw his arms around Peggy, tears welling up once again in his eyes. She started crying in response, for the wrong reason. She assumed his tears meant that he didn't want to marry her. He assumed that she must have heard about the crash on the news. She hadn't. It took a moment to straighten the matter out. He finally explained to her that three PJs and four crewmen had died in a crash in Vermont.

"This is unbelievable," Peggy said.

"I know."

"No," she elaborated. "I mean, yeah, that's unbelievable too. The reason I was late was that I was on the phone with the hospital." Her friend had died in surgery.

They held each other for a long time.

"Let's get out of here," Jack said.

They went home, dried off, made coffee. They decided they needed to go for a walk. They'd walked about five or six blocks when they saw a church, a small white chapel, set back from the road. They decided they might find some comfort there, a way to get out of the rain in both a literal and a spiritual sense. Peggy was the more religious of the two, but Jack was more than happy to accompany her up the steps. Sometimes you just need to close your eyes and ask the questions, whether or not you get the answers.

The church was locked.

They sat down on the steps and held each other. Everything seemed stacked against them. This was their life, and death was apparently going to be a part of it. It was as if God was sending them a message, and if he was, then the message went something like this: All you've got is each other.

The following week was filled with funerals. On Monday, June 19, Al Snyder was buried in Pine Lawn cemetery, at a ceremony where the surviving PJs surrounded his grave, and then each drank a shot of schnapps, throwing the shot glasses in after his coffin, on top of which was Al's maroon pararescue beret. That same night, his widow gave birth to a boy and named him Alan Craig. Jack and Peggy talked about it that night and tried to imagine what it would be like, to bury a husband and have his child all in the same day. They couldn't imagine. Jack wanted to promise Peggy she'd never have to find out, but if this was the job, how could he promise?

The day after Snyder's funeral, a week after the crash, it was Scottie's turn. Dave Lambert's funeral had already been held in upstate New York, near his parents' home. By now, there'd been enough memorials and funerals and words spoken. The loss was easier to bear, even joke about, and sometimes it seemed like laughter moved the grieving process along faster than tears. The plan was for Brehm and McManus and the others to do a water jump a half-mile off shore and release Scottie Hursh's ashes in the sky over Shinnecock Inlet. On the day of the ceremony, a helicopter was taxied out onto the apron in front of the Ops building. The PJs were suiting up in the locker room, preparing to leave, when the Ops commander, Major Frank, informed the group that the other thousand men of the 106th were standing outside in dress uniforms at full attention.

"Why?" McManus asked.

"They want to salute Scottie's remains as we take him to the plane," Major Frank said.

"Scottie's already on the helo," McManus said.

"I know," Frank said. "What do we do?"

"Well," McManus said, "I suppose we've got to give them something they can salute, don't we?"

Jay Jinks found a rock and put it in a helmet bag, which was carried with great solemnity to the aircraft, and the entire base saluted the rock. Half an hour later, as his family stood on the beach, his fellow PJs gave Scottie "Hurricane" Hursh's ashes back to the sky. All that was left behind was a silver coffee can with the words *Contents: one Scott B. Hursh* typed on a piece of paper Scotch-taped to the side.

7

CHERRY MISSIONS

There was a PJ stationed out in the Pacific Northwest who got handed the worst nickname. It wasn't his fault in any way, but for the first seven or eight missions he went on, either they got there too late or the injuries he treated were too severe and the victims died, so guys started calling him "The Bagger." All he did was put people in body bags. Of course, you learn that you can't save everybody, that you have to accept the fact that your training and your abilities have limitations, and that death is part of the job. Sometimes you develop a dark sense of humor as a coping mechanism, maybe the way doctors or morticians can have dark senses of humor. Still, you really ache to have a good first mission, partly because you've been preparing for it for so long that you blow it out of proportion. You want to get off on the right foot. At any rate, you don't want people calling you "The Bagger." In the rescue business, that's a nickname you hope doesn't stick.

SOMETIMES JACK HEARD ABOUT THE CHERRY MISSIONS OF HIS former classmates on the PJ grapevine. He stayed in touch with Mohr, Judy, and Smith, and they stayed connected to the other guys, more or less. Pararescue constitutes one of the smaller elite forces in the military, never more than about three hundred at any given time. As PJs from one unit join up with PJs from another unit on a training mission or temporary duty tour, eventually they either meet everybody else in pararescue or they've heard of them. There wasn't any sense of competition between Jack and his classmates to see who might "lose his cherry" first, but at the same time, Jack didn't want to be the last.

Slip O'Farrell's first official "save" was barely that. A fishing boat, the *Melba Gal*, had lost its bilge pump and was slowly sinking in the Gulf of Mexico, so O'Farrell's helicopter flew a pump out to them. He'd been posted to Tyndall AFB in Panama City, Florida, an Air Defense Weapons Center where he got assigned to work as a drone jockey, hooking and fishing unmanned Air Force target drones out of the sea, not exactly the kind of rescue work he had in mind, but the Air Force doesn't have that many strong swimmers, so PJs are occasionally used in nonrescue capacities. The helicopter crew would also clear the area before such practice sessions and fly "bikini watch" along the beach to make sure nobody swam out too close to the drone recovery area. The drones were small airplanelike craft with heat generators at the wingtips. Fighter pilots would practice locking on to the drones and firing unarmed heat-seeking missiles at them. The unarmed missiles didn't do enough damage to bring the drones down, so usually the drones would fly back to base when the practice session was over, deploy parachutes, and drop on shore. The exception was when a fighter-jock got lucky and managed to put a missile directly up a drone's tailpipe, which was, naturally, what they all tried to do. When they succeeded, recovery was a bit more difficult. One time a fighter-jock shot down a drone, about five miles out in the Gulf, in a steady rain with twenty-knot winds and seven-foot swells, conditions deemed too difficult for the drone recovery boat on the scene to deploy their swimmer. About six feet of the drone's nose stuck straight up out of the water—the other twenty-four feet were submerged. O'Farrell decided he'd give it a try. He swam to the sinking drone, then dove down about ten feet to find the drone's recovery loop, where O'Farrell attached a cable from the helicopter's cargo sling. He saved the Air Force the cost of the drone, about $250,000, only to be chewed out by the Ops officer when he returned to base for deploying without a second PJ onboard as a safety swimmer.

O'Farrell preferred the term "Sky God" to PJ. His hoo-yah attitude was second to none. He needed all the attitude he could muster for his first real save, which transpired after he'd been reassigned to Kadena AFB in Okinawa. Two crew members on the USS *Thomas Jefferson*, a Polaris-class submarine operating in the South China Sea, had been stricken with an unknown illness. Submarine captains don't like to stop, and they don't like to stay on the surface any longer than they have to, with Soviet spy satellites orbiting overhead, so O'Farrell was forced to hoist down to the conning tower while the ship was under way. The HH-53 pilot had to angle his craft 45 degrees forward into the wind to maintain his position, which blinded him to any hover reference. As a result, O'Farrell could only swing back and forth over the conning tower, while the flight engineer tried to place him gently down. After a few minutes of futility, O'Farrell took off the safety strap and leaned out from the penetrator, intending to drop to the conning tower, something like the way Tarzan used to jump from vines onto the backs of elephants. The difference was that Tarzan didn't have that far to go if he fell off the elephant. O'Farrell would have hit the hull of the ship. If he survived that, he still would have been washed off the deck, sucked through the ship's propeller, and ground into so much Purina shark chow. He made it, climbed into the hatch, and saluted the skipper, reporting in by saying, "Bond—James Bond." O'Farrell told the skipper it would be a lot easier to take his crewmen off the ship if they didn't have to play pendulum. The skipper reversed his engines and stopped the sub long enough to allow O'Farrell to hoist the men off safely.

Chuck Matelski's first assignment took him to Fairchild AFB in Spokane, primarily a base for B-52 long-range bombers, with a few P-38 trainers on hand. PJs at Fairchild flew in HH-1 Huey helicopters, a nonrefuelable two-bladed Vietnam-era airframe, which was considerably smaller than the HH-3 Jolly Green Giants or the HH-60s, but it was capable of carrying two to four litters, depending on how they were arranged. Several of Matelski's early missions involved med-evac'ing premature babies from towns like Boise or Missoula and taking them in portable neonatal units to Spokane, where the only hospital with a neonatal-care facility was located. His first rescue took him deep into the Rocky Mountains of Montana, the Bitterroot Range, where a party of elk hunters had gotten in trouble. It was May 1979. There was still a lot of snow in the higher elevations, but lower down the spring thaw had begun. The hunters had ridden in on horseback, along mountain pack trails far from the nearest road. There were six of them, five hunters in their forties and fifties and an outfitter leading them. They were below the snow line and had come to a clearing when one of them was thrown by his horse. One of the hunters managed to ride out and flag down a highway patrolman, who radioed for rescue, then stayed on the scene to direct the helicopter. Matelski looked down from the helicopter on the Clark Fork and the Kootenai Forest, an endless sea of pine and spruce, hemlock, arborvitae, Douglas fir, and larch. The Huey hovered over trees that were themselves over a hundred feet tall.

He took a long ride down the hoist, through the trees to the site of the accident, next to a riverbed. The victim was a man in his forties, dressed in basic hunting clothes, boots, jeans, and a plaid wool shirt. Matelski determined that the man had fractured his lower back. One of the other hunters was a doctor, who'd managed to stabilize the victim and give him aspirin. Matelski called for a Stokes litter. In the Huey, they hooked up an IV of saline solution, to help administer meds, mostly painkillers, because the hunter was in a huge amount of pain.

Jack practiced following a compass underwater. He shined his boots. He lifted weights in the weight room at the base. He waited for the phone to ring.

Joe "J.G." Higgins's cherry mission was as nerve-wracking as Slip O'Farrell's. Joe was posted to the 67th ARRS at RAF Woodbridge in England. ARRS stood for Aerospace Rescue and Recovery Service, the branch of the Air Force overseeing all PJ operations. Higgins's first mission was a water recovery, in a place called The Wash, a large notch in England's east coast where the Ouse and Welland Rivers empty into the North Sea. British and American pilots use The Wash for bombing practice and strafing runs. An American F-15 fighter had gone down not far from where a British Lightning jet had crashed a month earlier. The plane had simply flown too low, dipped a wing and hit a wave at about 600 miles an hour. There was no hope of survivors, but the Air Force still wanted to bring the bodies up if they could. Finding the plane wasn't going to be easy, not because the waters were deep, but they were extremely murky, with strong currents and heavy tides. A British salvage ship, loaded with sonar and recovery equipment, had been looking for the Lightning jet for weeks. All the PJs had to assist them in their search were wet suits, scuba tanks, and their eyes.

They'd been out about a week diving search patterns from a small boat without much luck, in part because they only had half an hour of slack water between tides. The tide was coming in, so Higgins suggested they drift with the current and tow him along, riding the anchor, a small Danforth anchor with a hinged blade on it. He was clipping along at five or six knots, at a depth of perhaps fifty feet, when he saw something out of the corner of his eye. There was no way to signal the men up top, and the only way he could think of to stop the boat was to jam the anchor in the sand, which jerked the boat to a dead stop and knocked the men on the boat off their feet.

Higgins had to make a quick adjustment as well. To ride the heavy anchor, he'd partially inflated his buoyancy compensator, an adjustable life preserver, something like the opposite of a weight belt. Once he let go of the anchor, his BC immediately started taking him up to the surface. He grabbed the anchor rope and hung on to it, upside down, while he bled the air out of his life preserver. If he'd risen uncontrollably to the surface, he would have gotten the bends, possibly to a fatal extent.

They marked the spot with a buoy and went back the next day to recover the pilots. Pieces of the airplane were scattered across the ocean floor, but a large section of the fuselage was intact, a long dark shape in the cloudy water. The danger lay in the fact that the pilots, who sit in tandem side by side in an F-15, hadn't ejected. The escape pod is something like a space capsule, about the size of a Volkswagen. In an ejection, the pod virtually explodes out of the airplane. A guillotine-like device severs the cables and wiring at the back of the pod, a detonating chord cuts the sheet metal, and then twin rockets, with engines more powerful than those on the jet itself, fire to free the capsule, which is equipped with a parachute and flotation bags. An un-ejected escape pod in a crashed plane underwater is a rather hazardous place to be because there's a chance the pod could blow at any minute. You don't want to be working in the pod and have it fire on you. Worse still, you don't want to be halfway in or halfway out of the pod when it fires.

The window was shattered and the pilot was missing, his body ripped from his seat at impact. The copilot was still in his seat, untouched, as if calmly waiting to be recovered. Higgins had with him cotter pins, which he intended to insert into the escape pod's ejection handles to render them safe. Unfortunately, the ejection handles were too damaged for Higgins to insert the pins. He was scared, but his training in the pool at Lackland had taught him how to recognize fear and what to do about it. He calmed himself down, calculated the risks and assessed the situation. He worked carefully—very carefully—with his partner to extract the copilot. When they got the body out, they bagged it and floated it to the surface. Pieces of the pilot later washed ashore.

Jack bided his time. He watched the Reagan-Carter debates on television, and news of the ongoing hostage crisis in Iran. He practiced low and slowing out of an HH-3 helicopter, jumping into the ocean from ten feet above the surface at ten knots. He also learned that Peggy was having twins. She'd been watching her diet carefully, but felt she was gaining too much weight for it to be a single birth. When Jack put a stethoscope to her belly, he swore he heard two separate heartbeats. Her original obstetrician suggested she was simply overeating, so she found an obstetrician who had a sonogram machine, which told her what they'd suspected, that she'd been eating for three, not two. Jack was impressed with his first real medical diagnosis. He brought two stethoscopes home from work one night and they both listened. They listened the next night too, and the next, and the next. Sometimes he'd fall asleep listening, and wake up with his ears aching from the pressure of the stethoscope.

At work, he listened for the phone to ring. Sometimes when it rang, it was Mark Judy or Smitty telling him they'd heard about someone else from their class.

"You hear about D.T.? Oh man, this one's a beaut. . . ."

Joe Higgins's brother Dave "D.T." Higgins had a mission that was typical D.T. and soon after became the stuff of legend and myth, much of it erroneous, but then, legend and myth have never cared much for the facts. It did indeed involve a tropical island, half-naked island girls and copious amounts of alcohol and island spirits, but it wasn't quite the idyll in paradise PJ folklore has made it out to be.

The call came at 8:30 in the morning. D.T. was stationed at Kadena AFB in Okinawa. There'd been a going-away party the night before for the NCOIC, and the section had boozed it up pretty good. D.T. was in the alert room at the PJ section, reviewing the previous evening's lessons while prioritizing his daily tasks, trying to decide whether to sleep, watch television, or play cards, when the Klaxon sounded, signaling a mission. An airman, part of a six-man weather research team out of Tinker AFB in Oklahoma City, had taken ill, afflicted with a 106° temperature and red spots all over him, while stationed on an island about six hundred miles south of Guam, a place called Woleai Atoll, actually a six-island group in the Carolines, U.S. Trust Territories. It was a jump mission, involving an eight-hour flight on a C-130. PJs love the jump missions the most—some guys go years without getting one. Higgins expected they'd fly there and be waved off and told to go home—that sort of thing seemed to happen all the time. His partner was PJ SSGT Jim Derrick, who was two weeks away from PCS-ing (Permanent Change of Station) back to the States. If they jumped, Higgins and Derrick anticipated a brief mission, twenty-four hours at the most. They arrived around 5 P.M.

From the C-130, the main island looked the size of a postage stamp, perhaps five hundred acres total. Without a good wind line, a jumper could blow right over it. One option was to jump into the water and swim ashore, but the surf looked rough. They noticed a small cultivated field in the middle of the island and decided to try for it, jumping round chutes with a limited steering capability. Higgins missed it.

D.T. hit a coconut palm so hard he broke the faceplate on his helmet. He also broke the tree, which was growing out of a WWII bomb crater, which was full of water, which he splashed into, only to find himself surrounded by twenty "Sumo wrestlers in diapers." The D.T. legend would have it that they were a primitive people, untouched by civilization, though in fact many of them had gone to American universities as part of a program training them to return home to Woleai to run their government, once sovereignty was granted. Derrick landed in a cultivated taro root field which, he soon learned, had been fertilized with human feces, and smelled accordingly. He was immediately surrounded by topless island women, who led him to his partner.

The patient, an Airman First Class named Carmichael, had acute tonsillitis, an inflamed infection that a German nurse who was island-hopping the South Pacific with her husband, their boat moored in the lagoon, had tried to treat by giving Carmichael a shot of penicillin. Unfortunately, he was allergic to penicillin, and in fact to most antibiotics. Higgins and Derrick rehydrated the patient with an IV drip and radioed the Rescue Coordination Center in Guam, where the flight surgeon on call recommended medications that Higgins and Derrick didn't have in their medical kits. Higgins and Derrick applied icepacks to the patient and waited. A Navy P-3 Orion flew out the next day and dropped canisters containing a synthetic penicillin called Keflex and a drug called Solu-Medrol, which Higgins and Derrick added to the drip. The drop was around ten at night. The German nurse's husband had never seen an air drop, and came to the field in the middle of the island to watch. D.T. later learned that the nurse took the opportunity to have an affair on her yacht with one of the weather guys from Tinker. At any rate, the new medications did the trick. Carmichael's temperature was soon down to 102°.

The second trick was getting off the island. The Rescue Coordination Center in Guam arranged for a civilian single-engine Cessna 172 seaplane to fly over from the island of Truk. When he got there, the pilot told Higgins and Derrick it would be such a long flight to Guam that he only had enough fuel to take out two passengers. The patient obviously had to be one of them. Derrick had a wife and family in Okinawa, packing to leave, so Higgins volunteered to stay behind.

He waited to be picked up. He drank beer with the weather guys from

Tinker, whose generator had gone down halfway through their six-month mission, leaving them with nothing to do but get hammered every day and annoy the indigenous population. All the Tinker guys had for food was beer, cases of olives, and do-it-yourself pizza kits, so D.T. made friends with the natives and shared meals with them, mostly rice, dried fish, and fruits. Stories of Higgins lying on the beach sipping piña coladas with beautiful island girls rubbing suntan lotion on him are grossly exaggerated.

The locals, perhaps four hundred natives on the island, were indeed friendly, offering him a fermented coconut milk drink called *tuva,* but it was vile and tasted like rotten eggs. The Woleaian women were friendly as well, even flirtatious, but they came from a part of Micronesia where the definition of beauty is rather different from what it is in the United States, and looked, to Higgins something like big fat ugly Eskimo guys. Higgins claims he wanted nothing to do with them.

Jim Derrick recalls that the women weren't all fat or ugly, and that one, an attractive twenty-five-year-old American Peace Corps volunteer, one of the women who'd greeted him topless when he landed, had joined them (topped) around a bonfire at the weather station, the night before he flew out on the Cessna. She might have been from Boston, or Chicago, or possibly from Seattle—some details simply get lost with the passage of time.

As Higgins tells it, he was stranded. Virtually shipwrecked. A supply ship from Truk was supposed to come get him in three days, but the ship developed problems on route and got pulled into dry dock. After eight days (no point in calling in *right* away), Higgins radioed back to Kadena. The base told him not to worry, they hadn't forgotten about him. He finally hitched a ride on a 140-foot tour boat that was taking Japanese WWII veterans back to the islands they'd occupied to conduct burial ceremonies for the soldiers who'd been left behind. The tour boat took Higgins as far as the island of Yap. Yap had a small commercial airport. Higgins was supposed to catch a flight to Guam, but the Air Force sent his tickets to Truk instead. Eleven days from the time he'd launched from Kadena, D.T. caught a flight to Guam, where he was told he'd have a flight to Okinawa the next day. That flight was canceled. Higgins was told, "Maybe tomorrow." Higgins also didn't have any money on him. For some reason, he did have his checkbook, but he didn't have any ID, no dog tags, nothing, so nobody would take his checks. He also didn't have a change of clothes, which wouldn't have been an issue except that during his stay on Woleai it was hot, so he'd cut the sleeves off his shirt and the legs off his BDU (battle dress uniform) pants, which made him look something like the proverbial guy stranded on a desert island. His beard had grown. His hair was a mess. He was deeply tanned from maintaining a beach watch while he waited to be picked up. Because of how he looked, he couldn't get served in the mess hall. He managed to cash a check for twenty dollars with a colonel who trusted him, money he used to stock up on supplies at the airport snack shop.

Meanwhile D.T.'s teammates at Kadena worried. Information on him was sketchy, particularly after he left Woleai. When he finally landed back at Kadena, a full two weeks after he'd launched on what was supposed to be a twenty-four hour mission, fifty members of the team greeted him at the airfield. Higgins appreciated the welcome-home party, and accounted for his delay, explaining that the natives had seen him falling from the sky, thought that he was a god, and carried him on their shoulders to their village, where they coronated him. His teammates responded by sticking Higgins in a body bag, filling it with ice, and hanging him upside down in a Stokes litter.

Different versions of the story circulated on the PJ grapevine. It figured that if something exotic was going to happen to one of Jack's classmates, it was going to happen to D.T. He heard a rumor that D.T. got busted back to tech sergeant for not getting home sooner, but knew that if it were true, D.T. was the sort of guy who always bounced back. He heard a considerably less amusing story when Randy Mohr called him and told him about his cherry mission.

Randy Mohr, Mark Judy, and John Smith in fact all shared the same cherry mission. Shortly before Thanksgiving 1979, several helicopter and C-130 crews launched from Eglin and headed south across the Gulf of Mexico to Puerto Rico, then flew across the Caribbean to Georgetown, Guyana. The global political situation was a mess. Violence and discord had broken out in Nicaragua, Afghanistan, Yemen, and Iran. Terrorists ruled the headlines. No one knew what to expect in Guyana. Judy manned a C-130 tanker. Smith and Mohr were posted on separate HH-53s. As brand-new PJs, they weren't included or consulted in the planning sessions and didn't know much about their mission other than that an American congressman from California, Rep. Leo J. Ryan, had been killed at a small airport in the jungle, where he'd flown to investigate a religious colony, and that there were apparently "a lot of bodies" at a jungle compound. It was believed that there could still be armed hostiles in the area. On the chance that there were, Smith and Mohr were armed with GAU-5s, a brush gun something like a truncated M-16.

They were housed in an abandoned building at the Georgetown airport. On their first flight to the compound, a three-and-a-half-hour journey, they thought how beautiful Guyana seemed, the jungle canopy below gorgeous to behold, a rolling ocean of foliage. Smith had seen jungles in Southeast Asia, but it was new to Mohr. Smith's helicopter was in a holding pattern at 1,500 feet, about a mile downwind from the compound, when he smelled it. Mohr could smell it from five miles away. Smith thought the smell was something like a compost pile in a garden, only much stronger. Mohr, who grew up in agriculture, compared it to a "really nasty pig farm."

When they landed, they found 917 bodies on the ground, all former members of a religious cult known as the People's Temple, led by a charismatic paranoid psychopath minister named Jim Jones. From their helicopters, looking down, it appeared that a massive quilt had been laid on the jungle floor, bright colors of red, yellow, blue, and green. The rotor wash only kicked up the smell as they landed. Most of the bodies were gathered around a blue-roofed open pavilion. They'd been there for about four days, lying in the equatorial sun, so they were all burned and bloated. In many cases, the soft tissues had swollen so that tongues protruded from mouths, and on many corpses the eyeballs had popped out of their sockets. There weren't as many flies or maggots on the bodies as Smith or Mohr expected. There were Air Force combat controllers on the ground, directing helicopters and setting up landing zones, and there was an army grave registration team at work, identifying and bagging the bodies of the people who'd participated in one of the largest, and perhaps most baffling, mass suicides in history, after Jim Jones decided that the end was near and forced his followers to drink a cyanide-laced punch.

The smell of decaying bodies was overpowering. Some men vomited. Others were issued surgical paper masks, which they could pinch across their noses and treat with liquid peppermint drops to block the smell, but the stench was everywhere, the way a skunk can spray a dog in the backyard and perfume the whole house for days. It came through the masks. It came through the body bags. It was in the mud. Mohr and Smith did without masks, summoning all the hoo-yah they had in them to deal with the sickening conditions. PJs are tasked primarily to rescue survivors, but recovering human remains is also part of their mission, and these were American citizens whose bodies needed to be treated with respect and dignity. It was hard to do that, sometimes, particularly after the second day, when Smith and Mohr discovered the nursery. Smith had kids the same age as some of the children of Jonestown, innocent children who'd had cyanide squirted down their throats from syringes by grown-ups they loved and trusted. What trust more sacred was there to violate? It made him sick, seeing the children.

Mohr had a harder time with it. He'd pick up a small body bag that weighed only fifteen or twenty pounds, and it would make him so angry that he had to kick one of the big bags, knowing he would lay down his life before he'd hurt one of his own kids.

At first they brought the bodies out nine and twelve per flight, but with over nine hundred bodies to recover, that was going to take forever. They were under orders not to stack the bodies on top of each other in the helos, which would have been disrespectful, but they did learn to pack them in sideways, sardine style, until they could bring out up to fifty at a time. At the airport in Georgetown, away from the eyes and television cameras of the media, the helicopters were unloaded and the bodies were placed in metal caskets to be flown back to the States. The PJs were left to consider what it all meant, and they were left with the smell. When it was over, they burned their clothes and buried their gear, and washed and fumigated their helicopters. They showered and scrubbed themselves as best they could, but the stink clung to them. Afterward, they were given three days of R & R on the beaches and in the bars of Puerto Rico, and that helped. Lying on the beach and absorbing the rays of the sun helped them feel clean again. Glasses of vodka and pink grapefruit juice helped them forget about it, but not entirely. Mohr thought of a letter he'd found, written by a woman as she was dying from the cyanide-laced punch. The letter was addressed To Whom It May Concern: *Please understand that we had a good life here. We had everything we needed. We had a hospital, and a bakery, and a pineapple farm, and a hog farm. Please don't think we were all a bunch of lunatics, just because Jim Jones flipped out at the end. The idea he had was a good idea. . . .*

Call him a dumb old farm kid, but Mohr remained unconvinced.

Jack was happy for Randy, and Mark, and Smitty, but he wasn't envious. His own cherry mission had come a month earlier, and afterward he understood something he hadn't understood before.

Jack's call comes on September 27, 1978. There's a problem on a 627-foot Greek freighter, *Thermopylai*. The Greek captain of the *Thermopylai* has sent out a distress signal. His wife and two daughters are sick. They're having trouble breathing. He doesn't know why. The ship is 600 miles off shore. Rescue Control Center at Scott classifies it an increased risk mission, in that it will be a night pickup requiring multiple air refuelings. Jack has a party to go to later, some friends from high school, but isn't sorry in the least that he might miss it. He leaves the base at 7:30 P.M., on a windy warm night at the tail end of summer. The weather out over the North Atlantic is, they are told, moderate to rough. Brehm wonders why the captain's wife and daughters have taken ill, when apparently no other members of the crew have.

Even with earplugs and a helmet, the noise inside an Air Force HH-3 Jolly Green Giant helicopter is deafening. One of Jack's helicopter flight engineer pals called his aircraft "ten thousand rivets flying in loose formation." It's as if you're caught in a hailstorm, the sky kicking out hailstones the size of baseballs, so to protect yourself you put a garbage can over your head. Some have described it as like being inside a paint mixer. Even with foam earplugs and protective helmets, the sound thumps through the skull and massages the soft tissues. After a while you feel it more than you hear it. It's even louder with the gunner's window open. It's not a particularly pleasant experience, and after an hour or two, you get what they call a helo-headache. It's especially unpleasant in bad weather. The ceiling for an HH-3 is around 12,000 feet. Above 12,000 feet, the air thins, flight becomes "mushy," and the craft doesn't respond well to control inputs. It makes it difficult to fly above bad weather. Often when a PJ flies out on a rescue mission, the weather is bad. Sometimes, it's weather that nobody else would dream of flying in. Weather no one else is capable of flying in.

The pilots are in radio contact, arranging for refueling. The tanker flies under the helicopter, just off to the right. Every so often, moderate to severe turbulence jars the helicopter and the men inside it, sort of the way you might feel if you're driving in a panel truck on the freeway in a hurricane, except that it's more three-dimensional. In the air, you go up and down, not just side to side. Brehm wears a gunner's belt, an eight-foot strap that goes around his waist with a tether secured to the floor of the chopper, in case he should accidentally go out a door or window. Jack's pilot is LTCOL Nick Dawson. Dawson has been with the 106th since before it converted to a rescue unit, formerly an F-102 pilot and the squadron commander. It's his cherry mission too, the first time he's flown a helicopter on a rescue. The copilot is Marty Martin, a quiet, religious man and a former Vietnam helicopter pilot, brought in to the 106th to help retrain their fighter pilots. The flight engineer is Dale Stitz, the NCOIC of the other flight engineers and a helicopter technician. Jay Jinks is the other PJ. Jinks and Brehm wear black neoprene wet suits. Jinks is seated on a red nylon seat just behind Jack, hanging I.V. bags from the ceiling of the helicopter.

"Gonzo show you his pictures from Mt. McKinley yet?" Jinks asks Jack.

"Seen 'em," Jack says. "Pretty amazing."

"You gonna go to McKinley?"

"Some day," Brehm replies.

"Prepare for AR," Nick Dawson tells his crew over the intercom. As he dons his bailout chute, Brehm listens to the conversation between pilots on the intercom, hoping not to hear anything unusual, like "Rats" or "Oops," or something stronger. Other than donning the bailout chute, there's nothing Brehm can personally do to prepare for AR, except try to become Zen about it. Looking down, he can't see the ocean below.

"Jolly one-one," the chopper pilot says, "how's it looking?"

"Cleared into observation position," the tanker pilot replies.

Turbulence suddenly jolts the HH-3. Jack looks at the face of Jay Jinks. Jay doesn't look worried. Jay Jinks is six-two and 225 pounds of solid muscle. His nickname at the base is "The Spoiler," supposedly because he's so big that after he's been with a woman, she's spoiled for any "ordinary" man. The refueling should take no more than a minute or two, but in the turbulence, Dawson seems to be having trouble hitting the drogue. Even without turbulence, to make a midair refueling, the C-130 has to fly about as slow as it can, while the helicopter flies as fast as it can. Flying as slow as it can renders the tanker unstable. Brehm listens as Dawson tries again and again. Pilots and crews and PJs all grow accustomed to hitting "bingo fuel," the "point of no return" that might make an untrained individual nervous, but even trained individuals don't like going very far beyond it. Each unsuccessful effort to hit the drogue seems to up the ante. Dawson tries again. No. Again. No.

"I can't do it," Dawson finally says to his copilot. "Why don't you give it a try?"

"Negative," Martin says. "You can do it."

"I'm trying."

"I can't see anything cross cockpit," Martin says. "You have to do this."

Jack looks out the window again, trying to see if he can tell what the problem is. He assumed it was simply the turbulence, but now he thinks it could be something else. Then he notices that he can barely see the tanker. This is not a good sign. A powerful searchlight from the helicopter, mounted on the nose of the HH-3, ordinarily lights up the tanker during refueling, which helps the helicopter pilot maintain his intervals. All Jack can see are the tanker's position lights. He learns that's all Dawson can see too; the bulb in the helicopter's search light has burned out. It burned out as soon as Dawson flicked the switch. Dawson can't see the drogue, except as it is silhouetted by the light on the C-130's horizontal stabilizer, which shines toward the tanker's left wing. He's literally taking stabs in the dark.

Finally Jack hears Dawson again.

"Contact made," Dawson says. Jack sighs with relief. He knows he's not the only one on the helo to do so. "That was interesting." A few minutes later, Dawson comes on the radio again. "On-load complete, 1200 pounds. Thank you much, Kingbird, and don't go anywhere."

Jack realizes they have at least one more midair refueling before they can get home.

He checks the MK-13 flare he keeps in the pocket of his wet suit. He checks his life support vest pocket for his strobe lights and his pen gun flare. If he somehow ever gets lost at sea, he knows his teammates from the 106th will look for him at night, and if they do, he will signal them. He has improvised his own personal survival kit, consisting of extra water, flares, chemlights, spare strobes, and extra batteries. The blackness of the ocean at night can be to your advantage, though success still depends on the weather. Spotting a strobe in heavy twenty- or thirty-foot seas would be a bit like finding a penlight in a cornfield. Jack doesn't think he'll die at sea. Something just tells him that.

"Why do you think it's the wife and the daughters?" Brehm asks. "Because they're smaller than everybody else?"

"Dunno," Jinks shrugs. "We'll find out when we get there."

Brehm mulls it over. Why would the females on a ship be taken ill and not the males? Why would the smallest people on a ship succumb and not the larger ones? Maybe it was just seasickness. Maybe everybody else on board was used to heavy seas but the wife and kids weren't.

The helicopter jolts suddenly to port. They are in the middle of a storm, not severe enough to qualify as a true Nor'easter, but enough to make things interesting.

Brehm smiles at Jinks.

"Wouldn't be any fun if it was easy," Jinks says.

"Got it," the news comes over Brehm's headset. "Port side, boys."

Below, Brehm sees the lights from the *Thermopylai*. The procedures for boarding ships in foul weather depends on the ship. If a vessel is small, or if the deck is cluttered with rigging or antennae or swinging block and tackle assemblies, the protocol is to come in low and slow, jump from the door of the helicopter into the water and swim across. If the ship is large and the deck is clear, they can put a man down using the forest penetrator. It's important that no one on the ship touch the penetrator cable before it's grounded, because helicopters generate a huge amount of static electricity, enough to knock someone on their ass and injure them. The deck of the *Thermopylai* is clear, so Dawson decides they can use the hoist. The ship is heaving wildly in heavy seas. A man going down on the penetrator as the ship comes up to meet him could take a heavy blow stepping off. Conversely, if he steps off as the ship falls, he could drop ten or fifteen feet before landing.

The pilot makes radio contact with the freighter and is told that the crew is standing ready. The procedure during a rescue is for the ship to turn until it's heading about 30 degrees to the right of the wind direction, such that if the wind is coming from due north, the twelve o'clock position on a clock, the ship will point to the one o'clock position, which allows the helicopter to hover into the wind and still see the ship. Were the ship to point directly into the wind instead of cocked to the side, the helicopter pilot would lose it beneath his own aircraft. A carbon-arc beacon from the roof of the freighter's bridge sweeps the sea, as does a smaller light from the foremast.

Just don't embarrass yourself. This is what I've trained for. This is what I do.

Jinks will go down first. The HH-3 will have to refuel again for the return flight, but while in hover, they want to stay as light as possible. They'll gas up again after the pickup is made.

Jay Jinks mounts the penetrator, steps out the door, and disappears from sight. He has with him a medical kit in an "Alice pack" on his back. As soon as he hits the deck, he will go below to triage the patients. Brehm stands back from the door. He checks his medical kit one more time as Dale Stitz, operating the winch, lowers Jinks at a rate of about three or four feet per second.

When it's his turn, Brehm taps the tattoo on his butt for luck. The tattoo is of the unofficial PJ logo, a pair of Jolly Green Giant footprints, derived from the nickname for the helicopter. Each graduating class from Lackland leaves an identifying graffiti, a pair of green footprints, painted somewhere on the base, on the water tower, even on the bottom of the pool. In addition, all PJs have green footprints tattooed on their asses, a tradition started by a couple of PJs in a tattoo parlor in Thailand after a night of heavy drinking during the war in Vietnam.

Brehm gives Stitz the thumbs up sign. Brehm straddles the penetrator and steps out into the night. Conditions are stormier than expected. It's raining. He is wearing his scuba fins, mask, and snorkel, in case he ends up in the drink, but the 80 mph rotor wash from the helicopter catches his fins and makes him spin wildly on the cable, while below the lights of the pitching ship go round and round in a blur. The sea is moving, and the ship is moving with it. The helicopter is drifting, moving both with the wind and against it, and Jack is dangling from a cable in the middle of all of it, spinning. Without a single stationary point of reference, he is quickly disoriented. He spots two crew members on the deck. Then he doesn't see them. He thinks he's approaching the *Thermopylai*, then it seems farther away. Then close. Then he can't see it at all. He's immersed in total darkness. He can't see the cable three inches in front of his face. He looks down but can't find the lights of the ship below him. No lights anywhere. How could that be explained? The ship suddenly sank? Unlikely. He went blind? Hardly. Something is obscuring his vision. He's in total blackness. And it's hot.

Don't embarrass yourself.

He feels the seat of the penetrator suddenly yanked up into his spine, and then he's a hundred feet above the ship and moving up, not down. Stitz has hoisted him up at high speed and told Dawson to "pull collective," or lift the helicopter straight up, because they have inadvertently lowered Jack into the ship's smokestack. Heat from the ship's stacks has created unstable air above midships, making it hard for Dawson to hold steady. Brehm hangs in the air for what seems like a long time, from a height that, if he were to fall into the ocean, would probably kill him. There's the ship. He's lowered again. When he finally reaches the deck, the ship is rolling so wildly that he can't stand up. He's also a bit dizzy. He asks the crew if anybody saw what happened on the first attempt. They don't speak English. He looks at himself and realizes that he has somehow become covered in soot. He dusts himself off.

Brehm is led down two decks to the captain's quarters. The captain of the ship is a Greek who speaks only broken English. His wife is about thirty years old and speaks no English. Jinks is trying to interview the captain. How long have they been sick? Not long, the response, maybe a day. What were the first signs? He doesn't know. Have they been given anything? Aspirin. Jinks tells Brehm the situation. The two-year-old is dead. The four-year-old is extremely ill. The wife is sick as well, seated in a chair, wrapped in a blanket. The captain is next to her, holding her hand. They all look like they've been crying, their eyes red and watering. The four-year-old has a bad cough, the mother a sore throat. They feel out of breath. Jack asks the captain what the ship is carrying, and he replies that it's carrying grain. The ship smells faintly wheaty, Brehm thinks, maybe like fresh-cut grass.

"What do we do about the little one?" he asks. It's against ARRS regulations to transport "deceased."

"We can't leave her here," Jinks says. "I mean, we could but . . ." The look in the mother's eyes tells them they can't. Jinks gets on the radio with Dawson and explains the situation. Dawson contacts the C-130, which contacts Scott RCC. Finally word comes back—Dawson gives Jinks and Brehm permission to bring the two-year-old up with them.

"We're still going to need a children's hospital," Jinks says. "What's closest? Boston?"

"Probably."

Brehm explains to the captain they need to get his wife and daughter to a hospital as soon as possible. The captain is ailing but tells Brehm he will stay with the ship. They help his wife and daughter to the deck. If anything, the seas are worse, thirty-foot swells that lift and roll the freighter. It's raining harder as well, coming down in curtains. The problem is that the four-year-old is too small either to ride the penetrator or fit into a Stokes litter. Jinks goes up the penetrator first with the two-year-old in his Alice pack, then returns with the pack empty. The four-year-old is too big to fit in the pack, so he cuts two holes in the bottom of it for her legs and fits her in, papoose-style. Brehm hoists up with the mother, and Jinks follows with the child moments later.

"Call RCC and tell them we have two females, one approximately thirty years old, one four, illness unknown at this time," Dawson says to the pilot of the C-130.

In the helicopter, the dead child is placed on an OD, an olive drab two-pole canvas litter, and covered with an olive drab wool military issue blanket. The mother, with blankets wrapped around her as well, sits opposite her dead child, holding her four-year-old daughter. Brehm wonders what he'd think or feel in her place. How awful this must be for her. He gives her a headset to protect her ears from the noise, disconnected from the intercom. She cannot take her eyes off her dead child. For the return flight, Jinks sits on the missions pyrotechnics box, by the left gunner's window. Brehm looks out the right gunner's window as the lights of the *Thermopylai* fade in the distance.

"Jolly one-one," Nick Dawson says with Boston still hours away. The weather is worsening, the flight back rougher than the flight out. That's not a good thing, particularly for a frightened woman who's probably never flown in a helicopter before. "Pre-contact position."

"Clear for contact," the tanker pilot replies.

Brehm begins to don his bailout chute when Jinks shoots him a glance, nodding toward the mother, then shaking his head slightly from side to side. Wearing the bailout chute is only a precaution, but she doesn't know that, and there's no way to explain it to her. There's no reason to make this any harder for her than it already is.

The second refueling is as hairy as the first. It feels as though it takes Dawson forever to make contact. Jack tries not to look worried lest he scare the mother. Jinks is expressionless. Finally Dawson announces that he's made contact. Everybody breathes a sigh of relief, and Jinks rolls his eyes at Brehm as if to say, "That was a little too close." The tanker passes the HH-3 enough gas to get to shore. The Greek woman knows nothing of what has happened. Brehm watches her. She is lost in her private anguish, her arm around her four-year-old, her eyes on the shape beneath the blanket on the litter across from her. *How do you go on, after losing a child? That's the worst thing that could happen to anyone.*

Brehm and Jinks check the mother's and daughter's vital signs every half hour, monitoring their temperature, pulse, blood pressure. Marty Martin asks if anybody would mind if he says a prayer, just to keep everybody focused. Nobody minds. Dawson has a son the age of the little girl. Marty Martin's wife is pregnant. Jay Jinks has small children of his own, and Jack's wife is pregnant with twins. They are thinking about their own children, and they are thinking about the little girl they are carrying. They all want her to live. They know they will be utterly heartbroken if she doesn't.

The tanker gases them up one more time as they cross the shore of southern Long Island, giving them enough fuel to fly to Boston, then returns to base. RCC has directed the helicopter to fly to Boston, since Boston's Children's Hospital is the closest children's facility. As they approach the city, Brehm sees the lights of Fenway Park, where the Red Sox are playing the Tigers. They land at Logan Airport, where an ambulance meets them. Brehm and Jinks ride in the ambulance to the hospital where a team of nurses and internists meets them with gurneys ready. The helicopter refuels on the ground while they wait. Brehm and Jinks take a cab back to the airport.

The flight home takes them over Providence, Fall River, Warwick, New London. A direct line from New London to Westhampton Beach would take them over the ocean, but instead they turn west above New London. It's always safer to fly over land. They'll cross the Sound farther down. For a while, Jack watches the cars streaming up and down the coast on Interstate 95. He's thinking about the woman and her daughter. He considers calling the hospital once he gets back to Long Island to find out for certain what the diagnosis is. *What would I do if I lost a child? How could I go on?* He remembers the mother's face when he pulled the blanket over the two-year-old. He watched the worst thing that could ever happen to somebody. Yet rather than feel low or depressed, he knows that part of him feels exhilarated. The mother and the child are probably going to live. Without him, they might not have the chance. He's been personally responsible for altering somebody else's destiny. When the little girl grows up, she might marry and have kids of her own. Brehm doesn't feel ennobled by this, like he's some kind of hero, or did anything particularly brave or difficult, other than getting lowered into a smokestack, and that's more stupid than brave. He doesn't deserve any great credit, and isn't going to ask for any, and he doesn't feel special, or in need of patting himself on the back, but at the same time he feels great. High. *Maybe it's an adrenaline rush. Maybe I'll feel this way after every rescue. In which case, this is a great job.*

At the base, he expects some kind of welcome, somebody to say "well done." If anybody got a welcome, it must have been the C-130 crew, who returned hours ago and have already gone home. The only person waiting for the HH-3 is a single mechanic.

"How's my bird?" he says. "If you wrecked it, I'll kill you."

That's it? That's the greeting he gets?

No one else is around. It's about 12:30. He tries to imagine the kind of shit his PJ friends are going to give him for going down the smokestack. Little early to play Santa Claus, don't you think, Brehm? At least you're well sooted for the job. What were you trying to do—give yourself a protective charcoal filter coating? That some new camouflaging technique you invented?

He showers, and realizes he still has time to make the party his friends were throwing, and he feels like he could use a beer or three, so he drives to Rocky Point. He's pumped, dying to find someone to tell his story to, now that he's lost his cherry. At the party, a handful of people remain. He sees his pal Ted Sawicki and tries to tell him about the mission, but Ted would rather talk to the girl he's with. The music is too loud, the Beatles' "She's So Heavy" is cranked to eleven, and everybody is drunk or stoned. One guy is trying to relive a scene from the new movie *Animal House* where John Belushi crushes a beer can on his forehead. It's not that Brehm wants to brag, but something happened to him today that's a lot more important than John Belushi's movie antics.

"You'll never guess what I did tonight," he tells a girl he barely knows, seated on the couch.

"You know what Jerry did?" she says. "He ate the whole pizza we ordered and didn't share it with anybody."

"*We* didn't order the pizza—*I* ordered the pizza—if you want a pizza, order your own fucking pizza. There's nothing stopping you."

"All I wanted was a slice," the girl says, laughing. "You wouldn't be so defensive if you didn't know you were guilty."

"I'm not being defensive."

"Don't try to deny it."

"I'm not denying it."

"Oh—now you deny you're denying it?"

"That's not what I said."

Brehm thinks, *Oh forget it.*

He goes home. Peggy is asleep, so he doesn't wake her. He can't sleep. He doesn't feel like watching television. He opens a beer, then finds some paper and makes notes to himself. He writes:

> *At the party, I finally gave up and sat in a corner. I looked around the room and realized that there was no one in that room who could even remotely relate to what I had seen and done that evening. I had flown 650 miles out to sea and back in a helicopter, joined up with an airplane for fuel, been lowered into a ship's smokestack, saw the anguish of two parents who had just lost the most precious thing in their lives, and could not even stay together to comfort each other. I'd flown home in weather that almost caused us to run out of fuel 200–300 miles out to sea. What could I say to any of them to make them understand? That's when I decided to never even try. I would keep those stories to myself and share them only with the other guys who do what we do. Even then, it's best if it only comes up over a beer, with all the emphasis on the funny parts. Otherwise it's just another war story.*

*   *   *   *   *   *   *   *

The following morning, the phone woke him up. It was Mike McManus, telling him he needed to take the clothes he'd worn the night before and seal them in a Ziploc bag. There was a chance they'd been contaminated. "Probably no big deal," Mike said, "but we should be careful."

"Do they know what it was yet?" Brehm asked.

"Well," McManus said matter-of-factly, "they're still waiting the results of the autopsy, but I guess a Coast Guard cutter took twelve more people off the ship. They're talking about a possible plague, but they're . . ."

"Did you say *plague?*" Jack asked. "As in, *bubonic* plague?"

"Well that's what they were saying at eleven this morning. Something infectious, anyway," McManus said.

"But it's not?"

"Well, I don't know if they're done with their tests yet, but now I'm hearing they think it might be something called phosphegene."

"Which is what?"

"I think it's a gas the Germans used during World War One," Mike said.

"Oh," Brehm said. "Well, that's a relief."

"How do you feel?" Mike asked.

"I feel great," Jack said.

"Good," Mike said. "Just give me a call if you notice anything. These guys were exposed for weeks and you were only onboard for an hour, so I wouldn't worry about anything."

When the *Thermopylai* arrived in New York harbor two days later, it was boarded by health inspectors who found traces of a phosgene-based pesticide that had been used to spray the hold of the ship prior to its being loaded with grain. Some of the gas had leaked into the ship's living quarters, creating a long-term low-level exposure. Jack looked up phosgene in a medical book. The book said that phosgene-based pesticides and fungicides were commonly used in agriculture. Phosgene, synthesized in 1812 by a chemist named John Davy, was also used by the Germans at Verdun in 1917, fired over the trenches in liquid-filled artillery shells. It smells like new-mown hay. It can take up to seventy-two hours for the symptoms to appear, though usually they're evident within twenty-four. It kills after it's inhaled by combining with water in the tissues of the respiratory tract to form carbon monoxide and hydrochloric acid. The acid dissolves the alveolar-capillary membranes in the lungs, the permeable blood-air barrier where the red blood cells pick up oxygen. Death occurs as the lungs bleed out, choking the victim.

"I'm never going to live to thirty, am I?" Brehm asked Mike at the section, when he heard the news, but Mike didn't have an answer.

8

LIVING THE MOTTO

Jack was always very protective of me and of Susan—I'm his older sister by three years, but I always called him my big brother. When I called off my engagement, a week before the wedding, my father supported me all the way and said, "If you have any doubts, don't do it," but my mother was furious. Jack sat her down and had a long talk with her. I don't know what he said, but evidently it worked because eventually she came around. He was always very strong. He helped me through my divorce in all kinds of ways.

—SALLY BREHM

THINGS COME TOGETHER. THINGS COME APART. FRIENDS MARRY, and friends divorce. Friends pass away. Sometimes when more things seem to be coming apart than coming together, you can feel like you're losing ground, unless you're raising a family, watching your children grow, and then you're less likely to feel like you're just spinning your wheels. Any man or woman who's ever worked long hours at a lousy job just to put food on the table and keep enough Cheerios on hand for the little ones to throw around the kitchen knows what it means, in one sense, to do whatever has to be done, "That others may live."

Jack jumped into fatherhood the hard way and hit the ground running. Jack and Peggy Brehm learned to be parents at the same time that they learned to be married. Jack learned as well what most people learn when they start to try to raise a child—what kind of sacrifices his own parents must have made, raising him. He took naturally to fathering, but with twins he didn't really have a choice. One got baby A and the other got baby B. Peggy had done some baby-sitting before having kids of her own, but Jack had absolutely no previous experience. The first wedding he ever went to was his own, and the first baby he ever held in his arms was his own.

Michele was the pleasant baby, always smiling. Elizabeth was "The Grinch," prone to tantrums, hairless and pouting, fond of giving her fraternal twin sister tongue lashings in baby gibberish. At night, Jack and Peggy would put the babies in bassinets on either side of the bed, and whoever got the Grinch tended to do a lot more baby walking in the wee hours. Baby Bassinet Bingo, they called it. Peggy had the luxury of an extended family to call upon for baby-sitting and for advice. Her mother gave her perhaps the best advice of all. "One day a week," she told Peggy, "you and John have to go out," Peggy recalls. "Even if you don't have any money. Just go window shopping. Go for a walk on the beach."

Jack's extended family grew to include the men he worked with. McManus was a fair man who gave you all the respect in the world if you did your job, and as Jack got better and better at doing his job, Mike took Jack under his wing and mentored him in the ways of the world, both on and off the base. Mike had two girls, Kelly and Kimberly, six and four at the time, but among the younger PJs, Jack was the only man with kids, which made his house the hangout of choice. Guys would come over, play with the twins, and drink beer. Jack's best friend, Jimmy Dougherty, took them to the beach to fly kites. Jack's other best friend, John "Mickey" Spillane, helped Jack build "the world's largest retaining wall" in his backyard. Sometimes, Dougherty would unintentionally scare the girls when he'd drop by with bruises on his face, usually from getting in a fight, like the night at the Matchbox when some guy punched him for no reason while he was talking on the phone. Dougherty simply had, Jack ultimately concluded, a face people liked to hit, kind of a baby face with a crooked smile, sort of a what-me-worry? expression that got him into fights he never started. The night Mickey Spillane lost two front teeth when one of the participants' girlfriends jumped him from behind and knocked his face into a table, Peggy asked them not to come around so much when they'd been fighting, for the kids' sake.

Jack brawled. Jack drank beer. Jack made bets with the other PJs in the section, usually five-dollar food bets involving whether or not somebody could eat a large quantity of food in a short period of time. No puking allowed. Another bet went to whether or not Jack could lift the entire weight rack in the base gym. He couldn't. Another involved the shark darts PJs wear when diving in shark-infested waters. Strapped to their legs like a dagger, a shark dart was nothing more than a CO_2 cartridge with a large-bore needle attached, used to jab any menacing shark and instantly inject it with enough air to embolize and kill it. The bet was whether or not a shark dart could blow up a cantaloupe. It could. The follow-up bet went double or nothing on watermelons.

Watermelons blow up good.

Jack played with his babies. Jack heated baby bottles at oh-dark-thirty in the morning. He walked his babies back to sleep and changed diapers. He went off on training missions. On one training mission at Lake Placid in upstate New York in the month of January, the Dumb Ass Bare Assed Club was established, a PJ tradition involving getting drunk and taking your clothes off and doing something stupid. As Mike McManus told Jack, "You get enough PJs together and give 'em alcohol, and sooner or later somebody's going to show you his ass." At Lake Placid, the Dumb Ass Bare Assed Club decided they would take all their clothes off, run out back through about twelve inches of snow, and lie down in the ice-cold waters of the Chubb River. It only counted if they got completely submerged in the stream. It wasn't so bad, though some of the PJs felt compelled to give it a yank or two before they went back inside, just so the waitresses would know they were guys.

McManus, even though he was the leader, was as likely to get the team into trouble as anybody. He was one of the most accomplished men in the history of pararescue, and at the same time just one of the boys. Jack had to admire him for that. Mike's problem was that he'd always been a man of his word, and he occasionally waxed loquacious after a night of fire-breathing. One night in a bar in Lake Placid he made a drunken promise to let the owners of the bar jump out of his helicopter. There were two owners, both with long hair and beards, resembling bikers, or perhaps the front men in the band ZZ Topp—at first glance, they weren't going to be mistaken for PJs. Mike never expected them to show up the next day at the airfield. He hadn't expected them to remember the offer he'd made the night before—after all, he barely did—but there they were the next morning to remind him, good to go. A promise is a promise. He put them in flight suits, and managed to tuck their hair up inside their helmets, but there was no way to hide the beards, and they weren't going to shave. Letting a civilian jump from a military aircraft, let alone a civilian who has never parachuted before, is a potentially career-ending violation of clearly stated Air Force regulations. McManus wasn't worried for himself so much, but he wasn't sure how he was going to convince the rest of the crew to go along with him. The person ultimately in charge of anything that happens on an airplane is the pilot.

"These guys are PJs?" the pilot asked him, incredulous.

"Uh, yeah," McManus said. "Special Ops. They're on leave."

"Special Ops?"

Brehm had to struggle to keep a straight face.

"Yeah," McManus said. "They're Jedi Knights from the 24th." There is no 24th, and there hadn't been any Jedi Knights in the U.S. Air Force since a long time ago in a galaxy far, far away. Afterward the pilot confided to Brehm, "I might have bought the 'PJs on leave' story if I hadn't seen the way their eyes popped out of their heads when the FE opened the door."

Jack was as wild as any of them, always ready for mischief, always with a gleam in his eye when pranks were afoot. On another training mission in Yaphank, Long Island, they were working with a squad of SAR Techs from Trenton, Ontario—SAR Techs being the Canadian equivalent of the Air Force's pararescue, minus the combat training. Brehm and his fellow PJs showed their friendly rivals from north of the border how to lower a volunteer Canadian in a Stokes litter off a building, belaying him with ropes halfway down a local fire station's burn tower. Brehm and his fellow PJs then demonstrated for their SAR Tech guests how to put out the flames if, in an emergency, the volunteer Canadian from north of the border in the Stokes litter halfway down the burn tower were to somehow catch on fire, and the only water you had to put him out was the beer you drank for lunch. Part of being an effective rescueman, it goes without saying, requires being prepared for any situation. The friendly Canadians later responded by demonstrating how, in an emergency, say perhaps an escape and evasion situation, you can use an American PJ named George "Gonzo" Gonzales's stocking cap for a latrine, though to avoid detection by the enemy afterward, you need to bury the stocking cap deep in the American PJ's rucksack, such that it can take days to figure out where the smell is coming from. For good measure, the Canadians tipped an outhouse over, door side down, while Gonzo was inside of it. They also threw an orange MK-13 signal flare in, figuring they'd smoke Gonzo out through the bottom of the crapper, but instead the flare exploded the methane gas that had accumulated at the bottom of the hole. Gonzo wasn't hurt, but he wasn't happy, either.

Jack worked out every day, trained in the gym, swam at the YMCA pool, and ran on the streets of Rocky Point. He worked on his house, reinforcing the nest in which he intended to raise his brood. He re-sided the house, finished the basement, replaced the windows, built a deck, installed glass doors, replaced the oil burner, insulated the attic, redid the kitchen cabinets, and built a second bathroom. He learned the routine, both at home and at work. He learned certain PJ traditions, which included welcoming new PJs to the team by taking them to the Matchbox and drinking shots of tequila. Most newcomers tried to keep up with the veterans, to prove to them that they were "one of the guys," and sometimes they even tried to show they could outdrink the veterans, but it never worked, mainly because the senior PJs always plotted in advance with the waitress to, at a prearranged signal, bring them shots of tap water instead of tequila. She would of course continue to bring the newcomer shots of tequila. A new PJ named John Canfield, who'd never been outdrunk by anyone in his life, got so hammered at his initiation that when they all got back to the section to sleep it off, he went into the bathroom, ripped a toilet out of the floor, and smashed it against the wall, shouting "Death to Commies" before passing out.

Men bond in such foolishness. Men do crazy things out of a fondness for each other, and in doing so create a story to tell, because telling a crazy story later is easier than coming right out and saying they love each other. Men bond in physical activity, whether it's on a sports team or a work crew, which may indicate that men do indeed come right out and say it—men just use body language instead of a spoken tongue. Men who run together, or who drink together, will say things to each other that can't be said under normal, sober circumstances, confessional and personal things that only come out when their guards are down. From day one at Lackland, running from task to task carrying a length of rope, or a 450-pound length of railroad steel, pararescuemen are taught that teamwork is everything, the most important thing you can ever know, friendship a valuable thing for purely tactical reasons. Sharing adventures is bonding. Jumping from airplanes is bonding because afterward everybody on the team is cruising on adrenaline. Saving a life may be the ultimate adrenaline rush. It has a spiritual component, too, which in part explains why doctors sometimes develop God complexes—altering somebody else's destiny is indeed playing God, in the best sense. It gives you a high that lasts a long time. Combine the godlike sense of purpose you get from saving a life with the sheer endocrine mega-buzz of risking your own life jumping out of airplanes or swimming in raging seas to save that life, and you might begin to get a sense of how PJs feel when they've completed a mission.

It makes for absolutely incredible friendships.

It's unconditionally hell on marriages.

Jack and Peggy saw young couples come in to join the 106th and get pregnant right away. The PJ would pull a temporary duty tour and be gone for months at a time, and come home, and go off again, and they'd be all right for the first year, and the second year there'd be tension, and pretty soon they'd be in big trouble. A PJ who ran the PJ team out of Moody AFB in Georgia once joked with Jack they didn't need a flight surgeon—they needed a team divorce attorney. McManus would find PJs whose marriages were in trouble coming to him and begging him to get them a TDY somewhere, anywhere, because they had to get away from their wives. McManus usually took the blame for it, telling the wives, "That's life in the Air Force. . . ."

Life in the Air Force means a lot of things. It frequently means being broke. Part of the IQ test for becoming a PJ involves weeding out anybody who goes into it for the money. A new PJ, in 1999, at the starting E-3 pay scale, earns $1,179 a month, base pay. With twenty years' experience, a PJ's pay at E-3 increases to $1,274.70 a month, base pay, meaning he takes home $95.70 more each year, or $7.97 each month, to spend on Mercedes-Benzes and European vacations. A midlevel E-6 PJ with twelve years' experience earns $2,010 a month, base pay, or about what a high school graduate temping in an office can earn if she's really good at alphabetizing. The top pay for an enlisted man, for example a chief master sergeant at the E-9 level with twenty years' experience, is still only $3,375.90 a month, base pay, or roughly where a brand-new Ivy League college graduate with a business major starts, working at a New York stock brokerage or investment banking firm. Sometimes a PJ on a temporary duty tour, sent somewhere where there's no nearby Air Force base or government mess available, can also pull down a meal allowance of $11.21 a day. A PJ's pay increases with time in service, but also goes up as he acquires rank. Rank comes from progressing with your on-the-job training, as well as from the completion of CDC, or Career Development Courses, which can be taken via correspondence. Courses can also be completed by attending formal schools. Base pay can be supplemented with incentive pay, flight pay, dive pay, hazardous duty pay, or by going TDY. It also helps that while in places like Turkey, Kuwait, or Saudi Arabia, a PJ's income is tax-free. A young PJ might volunteer for a two-month tour to Thailand or a three-month tour to Iceland, while the wife stays home with the kids, alone, making mortgage payments and car payments and probably working a job herself, calling the plumber when the pipes break or the septic system backs up, punctuated by occasional long-distance phone calls in which she learns her husband is going on a dangerous mission. PJ wives learn quickly to harden themselves. They grow stronger and stronger, or else they break. A PJ wife has to readjust each time her husband comes home. He doesn't know what's been going on, because he's been away. He doesn't know what the new school schedule is, or when the kids have to be put to bed. She learns to be really independent from him when he's away, because she has to take care of everything herself. Sometimes when he comes home, she resents him just for shaking up the system, even though she knows his intentions are good. Even couples who aren't separated by work can still become estranged when they learn it's easier to behave like a single person than like someone in a couple. Instead of compromising and coming together, people learn to take care of themselves. Instead of, "We'll do this," it's, "I'll do this and you do that and see you later." PJs and their wives sometimes have to adjust to a seemingly endless cycle of feeling single, then married, then single, then married, then single, then married.

Part of the problem is that the PJs have never been fully manned. Each year, the 106th might send ten candidates down to Lackland and feel lucky if they get one man back who makes it all the way through. The shorter the manpower available, the more guys feel pressured to do double duty. The only solution would be to lower their standards at Indoc and not wash out so many people, but they won't do that.

As a family increases in size, it becomes a double bind. The more kids a PJ has, the more money he needs, so the more he has to work, but the more kids there are, the more they need a father at home. Some men on active duty can be gone as many as 240 days out of the year. The older the kids get, the more they need parenting, because they can't be set in a playpen and given a toy and forgotten about anymore—they start needing rides to sport practices, or doctor's appointments. A PJ wife can start to resent living like a single parent, when she knows that in reality she's not one. She's supposed to have help.

The men have to constantly readjust too. PJs with good marriages, relationships on solid ground, look forward to coming home. PJs with rocky marriages don't, and often feel as if they're leaving a situation—climbing a mountain in Alaska or scuba diving in the Florida Keys, where the problems they face are concrete and tangible and they know how to solve them—only to return to a situation where the problems are less graspable and the solutions are all unclear. The espirit de corps in a bar can be a more comfortable thing than facing a rocky marriage at home. A PJ might come home after a two-week deployment and the first thing he really wants to do is go have beers with his buddies and debrief the mission and swap stories. He doesn't exactly feel closer to the men he serves with than he does to his wife, but he does feel close to them. He sees less of them than he does of his wife, so he doesn't want to pass up the opportunity to spend time with his buddies. It's also harder to take a buddy for granted, because there's always the chance you'll be sent off in different directions and not see each other again for months, years, or ever. PJs who fly on tough missions together become friends for life. Sometimes a PJ might even feel he owes somebody his life—you're not going to have a beer with a guy you owe your life to? Many is the PJ who's rolled home at two in the morning, totally slammed, to a wife who says, "When did you get in?" and the PJ replies, "Noon."

It can make the wife feel rather unimportant and neglected.

Peggy learned to cut Jack a lot of slack, and he learned he didn't need a lot of slack. She knew that men on missions work really hard, and want to play just as hard when it's all over. She knew that when Jack had time to himself on a TDY, after working a sixteen-hour shift he'd get used to doing exactly what he felt like doing. He ate when he wanted, he slept when he wanted, and then he'd get a pass and go wherever he wanted to go, and nobody could tell him not to, because he'd earned it and he deserved it. PJs are their own bosses when they're on TDYs or missions. There are no officers in the pararescue corps, only enlisted men, who get used to taking care of themselves and thinking for themselves. For his part, Jack understood and appreciated what Peggy went through when he was gone, and he accepted a simple fact. When he was gone, he was his own boss. When he was home, Peggy was the boss. He learned to leave his job at the office. He saw the families of other PJs suffer, when work and marriage failed to mix, and knew if he wanted to hang on to what he had, he had to work at it.

Sometimes, however, it's a good thing when work and marriage don't mix. At Eglin, Randy Mohr got engaged to a fellow PJ's sister, a woman named Linda, from Cleveland, Ohio. She was five years his senior, and he'd been living with her for three months, but it was a volatile relationship, full of disagreements, disputes, and loud arguments. One of the disputes had been over the size of the wedding—Randy wanted a small wedding, a small reception, and maybe a big party. Linda wanted to invite the Pope. Plus guest. Mohr's father had rented a tux, and his mother had bought a dress. Linda's parents had rented a hall, hired a band and a caterer, all while Randy tried to warn everyone that there was always a chance he'd be called away on a mission. His unit was told they were on standby to fly to Costa Rica a week before the wedding. Mohr went ahead with his bachelor's party, got drunk, and ended up hurting his leg, falling after trying to shinny up the mast of a sailboat. He hurt himself badly enough to be put on DNIF status, qualified only for Duty Not to Include Flying. When the mission became a go the next day, Mohr begged the flight surgeon to put him back on flight status. "It sounds like you don't really want to be married," the flight surgeon said. That was true, but that was only part of it. The other part was that Mohr couldn't live with the idea of his teammates facing dangers without him. The mission was to take part in a peace-keeping force, tasked to stand alert on the border of Nicaragua and be prepared to go in and rescue any Americans who might be taken hostage or need evacuation as the Sandinistas overthrew the Somoza government in Managua. The mission was tedious. Mohr spent nearly three weeks cooped up on the USS *Saipan*, trying not to go insane from the boredom, but it was better than getting married to the wrong person. He called Linda a week before flying to Central America and told her the bad news, saying simply, "Linda, you won't like this, but I'm going out of country." Secrecy forbade him from telling her where he was going, which he knew was going to piss her off, and in fact he sort of counted on it. When the commander of the mission, a full bird colonel, told Mohr he was willing to fly him home for the wedding, Mohr replied, "You can't give me a direct order to get married, sir." Mohr felt the mission was an act of divine intervention.

Some PJs simply marry for the wrong reasons, as did Jack Brehm's friend Bob LaPointe, a veteran PJ McManus first met in Vietnam. LaPointe was an ex-seminarian who was drafted in 1969, subsequently enlisting in the Air Force to become a PJ because he decided he'd rather save people than kill them. He was single, a tech sergeant working in Alaska, when he learned that married PJs not only earned almost twice as much money as their single counterparts but were also allowed to live off base. He was sick of the dorm he had to live in, and tired of being broke. He decided then and there to get married, even though there was a slight hitch in his plans to get hitched, in that he wasn't dating anybody and didn't know any women. It was after Happy Hour one night at the NCO club at Elmendorf AFB, where he'd gotten particularly happy, that he decided to go out and find himself a bride, eventually cornering a woman at an Anchorage dive called the Pine Club. He bought her a beer and said, "I hope you believe in love at first sight, because it's staring you right in the face—you wanna get married?" When she told him she had a son, his first thought was, "Great—that's more money for me." After being married for six months, he slowly realized that all his extra money was going to support his new family, and that "Kids eat—not only do they eat, but after a few hours, they want to eat *again.*" Food cost money. His marriage lasted two years, largely because his wife knew she had a good thing going, relatively speaking, and refused to grant him a divorce, until finally he volunteered to "go remote," which in the Air Force means taking an assignment where you're not allowed to bring your family. In LaPointe's case, his remote assignment was to the demilitarized zone between North and South Korea. It's not the most comfortable place in the world, but it was better than where he was living. He told his wife he wasn't going to send her any money, either, at which point she agreed that getting divorced was probably a better course of action. LaPointe gave her everything he had and went to Korea, wiser but not necessarily sadder.

Jack Brehm called home whenever he got the chance, and wrote letters. He begged off when things got out of hand when he was away on missions. PJs with good marriages behave themselves when they're pulling a TDY in Thailand or the Philippines. PJs with less to lose sometimes misbehave. There are places in this world, places that are not top secret but are nevertheless known primarily to military personnel, in the Philippines or Thailand, where an airman can eat three meals a day and still have enough left over from his $11.21 per diem to buy a lap dance in a strip joint or brothel. He can afford more than that if he skips dessert. Brehm knew that if he did anything to jeopardize his marriage, Peggy would kick his tattoo all the way from Montauk to Staten Island. Peggy knew that Jack wouldn't let things get out of hand, in part because it simply wasn't in his nature, and in part because she knew he valued his children and would never do anything to harm them.

Friends got divorced. Marriages turned sour. Jay Jinks got divorced. It was Jinks's wife, Anita, who'd counseled Peggy at her first PJ funeral, after the crash in Vermont, telling her she could cry all she wanted to, as long as she learned when it was time to let go and when it was time to keep it in. You let go in private and stayed strong in public, Anita advised. After the divorce, Peggy wondered if Anita was keeping it in or letting it out. There was another PJ who was married but who had, it was common knowledge, a bad habit of "falling in love" when he was away on TDYs. No one expected his marriage to last. Mike McManus's wife, Marie, a school-teacher, seemed to be drinking too much, probably to relieve the stress when Mike was away, but they were fighting all the time—their marriage was on the rocks, too.

Jack flew missions. Sometimes there'd be several in a month, and then months would go by without a call. On one mission, on a warm day in August, Brehm and a new PJ named Larry Arnott were called out to pick up a fisherman on a seventy-foot fishing trawler about eighty miles south-east of Montauk, Long Island. Arnott was new to the job but relatively old for a PJ, already thirty when he went through the Pipeline, with prior ser-vice in the army, where he'd been an officer. The initial report said the fisherman had incurred "severe head injuries from being hit in the face with a block and tackle." Based on the initial report, the NCOIC decided they should bring the flight surgeon, a part-time guardsman who just hap-pened to be in that day. Brehm "low and slowed" to the trawler, jumping out from ten feet above the water at ten miles an hour, and swam to the boat, where he reached the victim and realized he couldn't tell the front of the guy's head from the back. The sailor, lying on the deck in a pool of blood, had been hit in the face with the block and tackle, but he saw it coming and ducked back, such that he was struck at a moment when his head was already up against a steel bulkhead. The blow crushed it from both directions. He was gurgling in his own blood, unable to speak, but he was conscious, and understood Brehm when he explained that it was going to be too loud on the helicopter for them to communicate. Brehm told him if he started to have trouble breathing, because his neck and face were still swelling, he was to give Jack a signal by holding up two crossed fingers. "At that point," Jack said, "I'm going to have to cut an airway into your throat—do you understand?"

The victim gave him a thumbs up.

Onboard the helicopter, Brehm and Arnott started an IV and suctioned the patient's airway. For some reason, the flight surgeon didn't seem inter-ested in attending to the victim. Five minutes later, the patient began to fran-tically give the crossed fingers sign. Brehm asked the flight surgeon if he wanted to perform the cricothyrotomy to help the guy breath. The flight sur-geon declined, shook his head no, and leaned back in his seat. Jack was holding a scalpel and scissors when the patient waved him off, telling him the suction was working again. They made it to the hospital without further trouble.

After turning the patient over to the hospital's emergency room personnel, Jack asked the flight surgeon why he'd refrained from treating the patient. "I'm just not used to seeing patients in that condition," he replied. Jack later learned that in civilian life the guy was a gynecologist.

Jack decided not to ask for the flight surgeon a few weeks later, when the base got a call around five in the afternoon to recover a seaman from a 250-foot U.S. registered freighter sailing three hundred miles southeast of Moriches Inlet, on Long Island's south shore. The report was that the seaman had been bleeding from a head wound for over twelve hours and no one on board the ship could stop the bleeding. The exact nature of the injury was unspecified. Due to the distance from shore, the decision was made to send a C-130 and two HH-3 helicopters. They launched at 6 P.M., expecting that it would be dusk by the time they made the hoist, and dark during the air refueling on the way home.

"You gonna wait up for me?" Jack asked Peggy, phoning home before leaving on the mission.

"Do you know what time you'll get in?" she asked.

"Not precisely," Jack said. "Probably not before eleven or twelve."

"Possibly later?"

"You never know."

"Have you been a good boy all week?"

"I certainly have."

"And you've worked very hard?"

"Yep."

"Well then, why don't you go to the Matchbox with the guys afterward," Peggy said, "because I'm thinking I'm going to go to bed early tonight. I didn't get much sleep last night."

"I adore you."

"Of course you do. I'll see you later."

*   *   *   *   *   *   *   *

The trip out is uneventful. Brehm hoists to the deck of the freighter, where he's met by a crewman who leads him belowdecks to the ship's "clinic," little more than an office with a first-aid kit in it. Seated in a chair is a nineteen-year-old seaman, holding a cotton ball in his hand. He looks younger than nineteen, with dirty blond hair cut short and wire-rimmed glasses, and he's wearing a Yankees cap. The cotton ball in his hand is tinged pink with blood, but not soaked with blood. The right side of the boy's jaw appears to be slightly swollen.

"You thee?" he says, showing Jack the cotton ball, then shoving it into his mouth. "Ith thill bleebing."

"What's bleeding?"

"My toof," he says, removing the cotton ball. "My tooth. They pulled it yetherday morning."

He opens his mouth, and Jack looks in. He sees a red hole, oozing blood where the guy's wisdom tooth once was. He can't believe it.

"That's it?" he says. The boy shoves the cotton ball back in.

"Ith been bleebing for twelve hourths."

Jack looks at the first mate, who is standing at his shoulder. Scott AFB is responsible for fielding the calls and ascertaining just how serious an emergency might be, but you can't really tell over a ship-to-shore radio when somebody is exaggerating or putting a spin on something. If they say it's a head wound and it's been bleeding for twelve hours, you have to pretty much believe that's what it is and respond accordingly. Jack Brehm is ordinarily a cheerful, good-natured guy, but he does have a temper.

"Do you realize what you're saying?" he says to the crew. "We've got five guys in one helicopter, and five guys in the other helicopter, and eight guys circling overhead in a tanker, and we all just flew three hundred miles over open ocean and risked our lives because you've got bleeding gums? This is ridiculous."

None of the crew members knows what to say. The kid with the tooth extraction switches to a fresh cotton ball. He throws the old one toward the wastebasket but misses. He tries not to make eye contact with his rescuers. Jack realizes going back with somebody is still better than going back with nobody. It's probably not the kid's fault. He returns to the patient. "What's your name, kid?"

"Joe," the kid says.

"Well, Joe," Brehm says, "you got your stuff packed?" The kid points to a powder blue Samsonite suitcase. Who boards a Merchant Marine ship carrying a powder blue Samsonite suitcase? "You might as well grab it and let's go."

Night has fallen, and the seas have gotten rougher. The winds have picked up as well. The pilot of the lead HH-3 has difficulty maintaining a hover reference in the darkness. A hover reference is any visual object that remains motionless, such that the helicopter pilot can keep a stable hover and not drift around in the sky. In the open ocean, a good hover reference is hard to come by. In the open ocean in stormy weather, it's nearly impossible. It takes forever to get off the ship. Toothache Joe wants to take his suitcase. Ordinarily a critical patient would be taken to the trauma center at the University Hospital at Stony Brook, Long Island, on the north shore about ten miles west of Rocky Point, but since the guy looks like he's probably going to make it—in fact, he looks pretty excited at getting his first helicopter ride—the pilot decides to drop him off at Southampton Hospital, which is on their way back to base. There's a strong sentiment that they've already wasted enough time and av-gas on the guy.

"Precontact position for refueling," the pilot says.

"Roger that, Jolly One," the tanker pilot replies.

Brehm's lead helicopter hits the drogue on the second attempt and takes on enough fuel to get home. For some reason, the trail helicopter has trouble. Brehm listens on the radio as the pilot of the trail chopper makes multiple attempts. His copilot reports how many minutes of fuel they have left. A message comes in from the pilot of the C-130.

"Jolly Two, you might want to start reviewing ditching procedures. We're gonna do this, but you might want to get the book out, just in case."

"Not to worry, Jolly Two," the pilot of Jolly One adds, "we gotcha if you do."

"Roger that," the pilot of the trail helicopter says, "but it's not going to be a problem. I'm going to stick this sucker."

Brehm looks at the kid. His tooth must be killing him. The noise from the helicopter can't be helping any. Brehm looks around for an extra helmet but can't find one. He gives the kid two orange foam rubber earplugs and gestures that he should shove them in his ears.

"THIS YOUR FIRST HELICOPTER RIDE?" Brehm shouts above the engine noise.

"WHAT?" the kid asks.

"I SAID, IS THIS YOUR FIRST HELICOPTER RIDE?"

"YETH."

"IT SUCKS, DOESN'T IT?"

"WHAT?"

"NEVER MIND."

The attempt at conversation takes his mind off the trail helicopter's problems. Then he hears that Jolly Two has made contact, taking on enough fuel to return to base. He breathes a sigh of relief. He's glad they didn't lose a helicopter over a toothache. A good ten minutes passes before the next problem arises. The trail chopper has an electrical fire in the cabin, reporting smoke and fumes. Brehm tries to look out the gunner's window but can't see a thing. They're flying at about 125 knots. He wonders how far away shore is.

"Jolly Two—how's that fire going?" the pilot of the C-130 asks a few minutes later.

"I think we got it," the pilot reports. "We isolated the circuit and pulled the breakers and it seems to have stopped."

"Does it *seem to*, or has it stopped?"

"It's stopped," the helicopter pilot says. "We're clear of smoke."

"Do you have a viable aircraft?" the C-130 pilot asks.

"Affirmative," the helicopter pilot says. "I'm thinking though that maybe once we hit the beach at Montauk Point, we set it down there and let maintenance drive out and have a look. Why fly another sixty miles if we don't have to?"

"Roger that," the C-130 pilot says.

The two helicopters fly in tight formation to Montauk, where Jolly Two lands on the beach. The C-130 radios ahead to have the crew of Jolly Two picked up. The pilot also radios to the police in Southampton, asking where they can land Jolly One, since Southampton Hospital doesn't have a helipad. The police say there's a baseball field at Long Island University in Southampton, maybe a mile from the hospital. An ambulance will meet them there.

The C-130 returns to base. Jolly One finds the field, which has been illuminated by the headlights of police and fire department vehicles. Brehm thinks, *Geez, this is a lot of guys to disturb for a toothache*. Jolly One executes high and low recon passes, circling the field, looking for obstacles. They see none. As they make their landing approach, two vehicles suddenly bolt out of the way, lights flashing. They land. Jack tells the crew of the HH-3 to wait for him, because he'll get a ride back to the helo as soon as he drops the kid off, then accompanies the patient in the ambulance. At the Southampton Hospital emergency room, the doctor on call examines the kid. It doesn't take long.

"So what do you want me to do with him?" he asks Brehm.

"I don't know," Brehm says. "He says the bleeding won't stop."

"Well, it doesn't require stitching," the doctor says. "Give him a gauze pad to bite on."

"What do you want us to do with him?"

"I don't care what you do with him," the doctor says. "Send him home." The doctor leaves.

"Where do you live?" Brehm asks Joe.

"New Jersey," Joe says.

One of the volunteer firemen gives them a ride back to the ball field. The Jolly One crew was probably thinking their nightmare mission was over. Seeing the kid again infuriates the pilot. By now Brehm feels sorrier for the kid than he does for himself.

"What the fuck are we supposed to do with him now?" the pilot screams. "Fly him back to fucking New Jersey?"

"I'm thinking we should take him to the Matchbox and buy him a beer," Jack says.

"He's your problem now, PJ," the pilot growls, spinning up the engines. "And by the way, Jack—interested in knowing why those fire trucks took off when we landed? Look out the window—we almost hit those power lines that we *never saw!*"

It's a slow night at the Matchbox. The kid tells Jack that unfortunately he doesn't have any money. Jack tells him not to worry about it. He wonders where Joe is going to sleep tonight. There's probably a vacancy in the bushes out front. Doc and Mickey are at a table by the pinball machines. Jack and the kid join them, just as COL Bernie Giere, the base commander, walks in. He spots Jack and approaches.

"Just stopping by to see how the mission went," Bernie says. "Any problems?"

"Nothing serious," Brehm says.

"How's the survivor?"

"Why don't you ask him, Colonel?" Brehm says. "That's him in the baseball cap with the suitcase."

"What's he doing here?" Giere asks.

"He's being treated," Brehm replies.

By the end of the evening, the kid has to admit his toothache feels much better. Brehm drops him off at the Westhampton train station, not far from the Matchbox, at 2 A.M. Jack isn't sure when the last train in to New York City is, but the kid says it doesn't matter. "There's always another train," the kid says. Jack tells him he can't argue with that.

9

BROTHERS

Never give up a friend. They're too valuable. We make the biggest difference in this world when we deal with people one on one.

PEGGY LEARNED TO COPE. SHE HAD A DAUGHTER, LAURA-JEAN, ON March 28, 1982. On October 7, 1983, her son Matthew was born. Even the littlest ones seemed to know it when their father was missing for any length of time. At the age of three, Michele would pop in a cassette of Pure Prairie League and sing "Amy" into the tape player and cry in front of the speakers, saying, "I want my daddy home." The kids sensed it when their mother was upset when their father was gone and would often do silly things to make Mommy laugh, or propose trips to Grandma and Grandpa's house to take Mommy's mind off whatever was upsetting her. They didn't realize that she simply missed her husband. She and the other PJ wives would look after one another, and invite each other's kids on outings, to walks on the beach, game farms, bird sanctuaries. Peggy and Barbara Dougherty and later Laura Spillane taught themselves how to do things around the house, paint or put up paneling, and they worked together on each other's projects.

Jack didn't care about the house. "In a box," he told his wife, "I'd live with you in a cardboard box." Sometimes the money got so tight that living in a cardboard box didn't seem like such a distant prospect. When Jack came home from a particularly long TDY the family would take a trip to Toys "R" Us, where they'd fill a shopping cart with gifts. Michele got a hula hoop after one TDY and became an expert hula-hooper. Peggy held the purse strings and learned to budget. She scrimped and saved, and robbed Peter to pay Paul. She fielded the calls from the collection agencies when they came. She did child care, taking in other people's children, though she had her own babies to raise. She clipped coupons, and made enough macaroni and cheese over the years to fill a swimming pool. During the holidays, she worked at a department store in Rocky Point, both for the extra money and for the discount. Their furniture was used, and their kids' clothes were often hand-me-downs, with the occasional brand name Reebok or Nike sneakers, purchased when one of the kids absolutely had to look really cool at school, though they'd get the twenty-dollar Nikes, not the forty-dollar Nikes. Somehow, the money would always come. Somehow, they always made it. One Christmas, an anonymous stranger left five hundred dollars in the mailbox, signed "Santa Claus." "Santa" turned out to be Peggy's cousins, George Reid and Tommy Donovan, but all the same it proved there is a Santa Claus.

Laura-Jean was an exquisitely patient child, quiet and calm. Matthew was sweet, and somewhat pampered as the first boy in the family. Jack was often gone for the little accidents, and the bigger ones requiring stitches, as when one of the twins pulled a hutch down on herself, or inhaled a bead from a broken hair clip. He made sure that he brought his kids presents from wherever he was sent, Saudi Arabia, or Turkey, or even Iceland, where there's not a lot to buy to bring home. His children gave him a lot more, in the letters they sent.

Peggy developed a love-hate relationship with the telephone. She did her best not to worry when Jack was gone and the phone rang late at night. Sometimes it would be a hang-up call, probably just a wrong number, but even so, her imagination often got the better of her. Sometimes she'd think a hang-up was actually the base, calling to make sure she was home, because they were about to send over a chaplain to tell her that something bad had happened to her husband. If a car pulled up outside late at night, it was even worse.

Four months after rescuing the fisherman with the smashed face, Jack and Larry Arnott were sent to Nevada to take part in Operation Red Flag, a war game exercise in the Nevada outback. Brehm and Arnott were to perform a CARP jump, an acronym for Controlled Aerial Release Point, something like the opposite of a HAHO jump. In a CARP jump, you come in low and fast, and bail out from about eight hundred feet. Eight hundred feet would be too low to jump from a helicopter, but from a C-130, the airplane's forward momentum gives the jumper enough wind speed to open his chute. Jumpers wear reserve chutes, but if you can't deploy your reserve above five hundred feet, the point is moot. The idea of a CARP jump is to spend the minimal time possible in the air. Brehm, Larry Arnott, and Mike Durante, all from Long Island, and a PJ from Florida were tasked to reach a drop zone that the jumpmaster had to recognize solely from aerial photographs given him the day before. Ordinarily there would be a target, an inverted V, with the stem leg pointing into the wind to indicate its direction, but tonight there were to be no visual aids, no targets to head for, only a brief "Clear to jump" from a concealed ground party. The jumpers would be allowed only one pass at the target. Upon landing, Brehm and Arnott and the others were supposed to move about ten kilometers across the terrain, recover a survivor, transport the victim a few kilometers from the recovery site, and be picked up by a helicopter. The difficult part would be the landing. You hit the ground really hard performing a CARP jump, because you're still carrying with you some of the airplane's momentum. You use S-17 parachutes, which open quickly and descend just as fast. You're on the ground about twenty seconds after you leave the airplane, and you don't have time to check the ground winds or be choosy about your personal landing zone. You land where you land. The only other time Jack had done a CARP jump, he broke his arm.

The jumpmaster held his right arm straight out from his shoulder, palm open, fingers extended, thumb up, the hand signal indicating their final approach to the DZ. Everyone was in full combat gear. Jack could feel his heart pumping, and said to Larry Arnott, "If I die on this jump, I die happy." Arnott had no response. Moving to the door, Jack noticed that the right side of Larry Arnott's rucksack had come loose, falling to the left. Arnott hesitated a moment, but there was no time to fix the rucksack, and they weren't going to get a second chance at the DZ, since the idea was to emulate a combat mission, where it would be too dangerous for an airplane to circle back if something goes wrong the first time. The jumpmaster gave the signal to go. Arnott jumped. Brehm followed a second later. A static line opened their chutes. Brehm fell in a spiral, forced to pull his risers apart to stabilize himself. Jumping in full combat gear, carrying a rucksack, a medical kit, and a weapon makes you aerodynamically unstable and can cause the jumper to spin on exit, which can twist his lines and prevent the canopy from fully inflating, giving him a rapid rate of descent. A moment later, Brehm was down, landing on the slope of a hill and sliding all the way to the bottom on his belly, a distance of perhaps a hundred feet. He was scraped and scratched but all right, thinking, *Thank God for tree suits*. He'd landed in a valley, a wash strewn with boulders the size of washing machines and minivans. Wind speeds on the ground had to be twenty-five or thirty knots. It was a violent landing, but there was nothing broken or bent. He collected his parachute, stashed his gear and went to look for the others, moving stealthily because according to the rules of the exercise the "enemy" could be anywhere. He found the PJ from Florida and the two of them eventually holed up in a scrub brush and waited. Forty-five minutes passed, with no sign of the others. They were supposed to rendezvous at the north end of the DZ.

Then Brehm heard screaming, and someone shooting blank rounds from an M-16, three shots in a row, an SOS signal. He hesitated, thinking it could be a trap. Ten minutes later, when he again heard shots, he decided it wasn't a trap and came out of hiding. Walking up the valley, they met Mike Durante, who told them Larry Arnott was dead. A few yards away, Arnott's body lay crumpled on the ground. His head had hit a rock about the size of a large footstool upon landing, so hard that the rock penetrated Arnott's helmet. His chute appeared to be okay, with no evidence of a malfunction. Death had been instantaneous.

They'd mistakenly jumped five miles short of the drop zone, and from a height of only five hundred feet. Brehm thought, *Two seconds.* If he'd jumped two seconds sooner, when Larry had jumped, it would have been him hitting the rock. He'd never come so close to death.

His main thought afterward was this: There's no point fearing things that are out of your control, so you might as well do what pleases you. He could have been in Larry's position on the CARP jump, but he wasn't. For Peggy, the accident only confirmed what she already knew, that any time Jack went away, even if it was for a simple training exercise, halfway across the globe, or around the corner on Long Island, there was a chance that he might not come home. They talked about it on the phone that night. Larry was a man who didn't seem to need to put down roots, casual in most respects, a guy who, for example, lost a lot of money one day by blowing off calling his stockbroker, for no better reason than that the surf was up and he and Jack had a chance to go ride some waves. He was an accomplished glider pilot and had taken Jack flying one day. Jack figured Larry wasn't going to be a PJ for long, destined for a commission as an Air Force pilot. The very morning of the day he died, Arnott had stood next to Jack at the airfield, staring up as a fighter plane passed overhead, screaming across the blue Nevada sky, and said, "What am I doing here when I should be up there?"

When they cleaned out Larry Arnott's locker, they found a button, pinned to one of his caps, that read: *REPORTS OF MY DEATH ARE GREATLY EXAGGERATED.* It went up on the memorial wall, at the far end of the 106th's locker room, next to a photograph of Arnott, next to pictures of Scott Hursh, Al Snyder, Dave Lambert, and the other PJs who'd died in the line of duty. Seeing Larry's picture on the wall only made Jack realize what a loner Larry was. Nobody even knew Larry had a girlfriend until the funeral.

It also made Jack glad all over again that he wasn't a loner, that he had a family to come home to. It made him want to rededicate himself to his kids, even though he'd never lost the sense of dedication. He became a believer in "quality time" as long as it coincided with quantity time, so he spent all the time he could playing with his kids, giving them the same level of commitment he gave the Air Force. When he was on a mission, the Air Force owned him, but when he was off duty, he became the property of his family.

Not long after Larry Arnott died, the golden boy, Mark Judy, married a woman named Debbie Hansen. Jack was happy for his old friend, because he had an idea of what marriage held in store for him. The wedding was April 24, 1982. Mark's bride had been working at the base at Patrick, where she was crossing the street when he approached and asked her if she needed help, crossing the street. She smiled at the dorky line and said, "What are you—a Boy Scout?"

His wedding marked the end of an era, because Mark Judy was a true ladies' man, more by default than by choice, a smoothie and a charmer in the best sense of the word. He made the people he met feel special. He shook their hands, looked them in the eye, and was never judgmental. Jack considered Mark one of those guys it was impossible not to immediately like, maybe the most charismatic person he'd ever met. He expressed it in his body language, which was casual, relaxed, confident, positive, cheerful, serene. His friends knew him to be extremely intelligent, intensely focused, and fiercely loyal. He was almost always smiling. With his dark hair and his trimmed mustache, he looked a bit like the Olympic gold-medalist swimmer Mark Spitz. He was a little guy, smaller in stature than most of the other PJs but no less tough, five foot nine, maybe 135 pounds. "I've got a body like a Jaguar," he liked to tell people. He had a tattoo of a crab, not a jaguar, on his left wrist. He came from Toledo, Ohio, and joined the PJs mostly because he had to get out of Toledo and couldn't think of how else to do it. Because of his size, he was the guy the Great Dark Shark tried the hardest to wash out of Indoc, telling him he had no chance, that he was too weak and too scrawny to be a pararescueman, but Judy kept screaming back, "NOT ME,

SERGEANT MORRISON—I'LL NEVER QUIT. HOO-YAH!" Judy's fear of drowning at the bottom of the pool was overridden by a fear of going back to Toledo, which he described as being a town "like nowhere at all." Not even the Wizard of Wig could make him go home again.

In bars, the guy could pick up women without even looking at them. To Jack Brehm, it was uncanny. He and Randy Mohr couldn't figure it out. Judy would just walk past a group of girls, and they'd come to him. It wasn't like he was so incredibly good-looking, like Tom Selleck or something. Women loved him. As the Three Musketeers, they'd go out together, three single young men in the prime of their lives, and Mark would attract a group of girls, and Jack and Randy would end up talking to the leftovers, which was okay, because Judy was only attracted to tall skinny blondes. He'd met Hansen when she was working at the base at Patrick, and she clearly had something special and unique about her, something that told Mark he wanted to spend the rest of his life with her, but she also had something in common with some of Mark's past loves. At his bachelor party, Jack told him, 'Mark, you realize Debbie looks exactly like that girl from Toledo you were dating.' "

"Maybe a little," Judy said.

"Mark," Brehm said, "she could be her twin. She's identical."

Judy served at Patrick AFB with John Smith, and together they performed a number of rescues. They rescued a team of firefighters who were fighting a range fire at the Kennedy Space Center when the winds shifted, trapping and burning them. Judy picked up lost divers and plucked sailors from sinking boats. He helped search the rubble when a five-story condominium in Cocoa Beach collapsed while under construction, falling like a stack of pancakes and trapping workers inside. Judy rescued shark attack victims from the water, which meant swimming in the same water where the blood-crazed sharks were circling. They med-evac'ed another shark bite victim from Del Ray Beach, south of Daytona, when the sheriff called and said the area was too remote to reach by truck. Judy and Smith responded to a call from an oceangoing tug hauling a barge where a sailor had gotten himself entangled in the cable mechanism and was hurt badly—the weather was so fierce that when Judy went down on the hoist, he swung wildly back and forth in the wind, yelling "HOO-YAH!" the whole time and having the time of his life.

Judy's main task at Patrick, as part of the 39th Aerospace Rescue and Recovery Service, was to stand alert for space shuttle launches. PJs had been involved in the space program since the fifties, where they were tasked to support a joint CIA-Air Force project called Corona, officially part of a space exploration program called Discoverer, but in fact a program that sent camera-bearing spy satellites over the Soviet Union and China. The satellites ejected capsules containing film cassettes that dropped into the open ocean; PJs parachuted in wearing scuba gear and recovered them. During the period of manned space exploration, PJs were tasked to support launches and to recover astronaut landings. The Navy covered the primary landing zones. PJs flew in the event that a space capsule splashed down too far from the primary landing zone for the Navy's carrier-based helicopters to reach it. In May of 1962, when Scott Carpenter's *Aurora 7* Mercury spacecraft splashed down, after three orbits, 250 miles from the nearest recovery vessel, two pararescuemen deployed from an SC-54 and jumped in to attach a flotation collar to Carpenter's capsule. In March of 1966, when *Gemini 8*, carrying astronauts Neil Armstrong and David Scott, aborted after six orbits and splashed down five hundred miles east of Okinawa, a three-man team of PJs jumped from an HC-54 to secure the capsule with a flotation collar until a Navy ship could arrive. During the *Aurora 7* splashdown, network television commentators referred to the PJs as "Navy frogmen." From that mission on, the words *USAF RESCUE* were emblazoned clearly on PJ equipment, everything from helicopters to wet suits.

To support the shuttle program, PJs trained to parachute down to astronauts who, following the space shuttle *Challenger* disaster, had been equipped with bailout capabilities in the event of emergency, a Mode VIII contingency in rescue parlance, involving a man on the ground or in the water needing immediate assistance. PJs trained to reach space shuttles that were forced to make emergency landings on distant airfields. The PJs at Patrick trained on a mockup of the shuttle, working Mode VII contingency rescues, a worst-case scenario in which a crashed shuttle falls to earth or into the ocean. The PJs worked in acid-proof, vulcanized rubber dry suits designed to protect them from the hazardous hypergolic fuels that could leak from a damaged orbiter and potentially explode, and learned how to power down a partially submerged shuttle, open the emergency hatch, and extract the occupants. Mark Judy was the instructor for Mode VII scenarios, probably the most complicated and dangerous of all contingencies.

On April 7, 1984, two weeks before his second wedding anniversary, Mark Judy was working a missile test launch from a Trident nuclear submarine, flying in an HH-3 to "clear the box," which meant moving all boats and aircraft out of the missile range before a shoot, approximately a twenty-square-mile area. He'd flown a shuttle launch earlier in the day. It was unusual to stand alert twice in a 24-hour period. There was a Russian "fishing trawler" on the scene, most likely loaded with surveillance equipment, but there were a couple of Army Blackhawk helicopters keeping an eye on it. It was a moonless night, around 2 A.M., and the weather was bad. The seas were rough, rolling waves fifteen or twenty feet high. The submarine ran just below the surface, a mast raised to mark its position, which pilots of patrol aircraft inside the box could use to orient themselves to make sure they'd be out of the way when the missile was fired. A submarine tender sailed nearby, carrying about two hundred civilian observers, even though the launch was supposed to be secret. Had they been looking, they would have seen the pilot of the helicopter Mark Judy was flying in experience a moment of spatial disorientation and begin drifting backward with his tail down. Before the pilot noticed the problem, the helicopter lost altitude, and then the tail hit a wave and snapped off, dropping the helicopter into the ocean.

Brehm got the message when he walked into the PJ section the next morning. He'd been away on a TDY, practicing free-fall techniques at March AFB in California. Mike McManus called him into his office and told him he had some bad news. He went over what had happened the night before, in as much detail as he could provide. The helicopter had floated upside down for almost three hours. The sub tender even managed to get a nylon line around it before it sank. The gist of it was, Mark was missing. It didn't look good.

Brehm couldn't believe it. "What's the status?" he asked. "Have they recovered anybody?"

"There were eight in the crew and they've got three, I believe. I think they got the pilot and the copilot and another guy."

"But nothing on Mark?"

Mike shook his head.

"I know he was your friend," Mike said, "so I thought maybe you'd want to fly down there to assist in the search."

"That's all right with you?" Jack asked.

"I've already made the call," Mike said.

Jack left for Florida the next morning. There was nothing he could have done about Larry Arnott, but in Mark's case, it seemed as though there was still a chance of finding him, and besides, this was his best friend, one of the best guys he ever knew. He wanted to believe that somehow that was going to mean something, as if friendship conferred some variety of magical properties, such that a best friend could find a guy where other people couldn't. Maybe it was denial, but Jack told himself that he was going to be the one who picked him up. He just had a feeling. He could picture it. He practiced what he was going to say, convinced that he'd find his fellow Musketeer, and they'd laugh when they met up again, and it would go down as just another funny chapter in their lives.

Jack searched for three days. When he wasn't searching, he tried to keep Debbie Judy informed. She'd received a call the morning of the accident, telling her the helicopter had crashed twenty minutes after the missile launch, but a reporter on television said the accident had occurred twenty minutes *before* the launch. If that were true, it meant they'd ignored the accident and launched anyway, and then delayed making any rescue efforts until it was too late. With a ship on the scene, and Army Blackhawks already in the air, it seemed to her as if more could have been done. Jack did his best to call her whenever he heard anything.

He also called home every night and told Peggy what he'd been up to. She tried to reassure him that everything was going to be okay, but she also knew that part of what she had to do was help him accept the reality of it, once it appeared that Mark was truly gone. Jack told Peggy that the pilot, two copilots, and two range officers aboard the helicopter survived the crash. One of the survivors remembered seeing Mark Judy moving toward the rear of the helicopter immediately after the crash, which meant he'd probably survived the impact. Judy had been wearing a helmet, and he also had on LPUs, or Life Preserver Units, which are worn under the arms attached to a vestlike harness that buckles in front, and must be manually inflated with CO_2 cartridges. By the third night, all that they'd found of Judy was his helmet, unscratched and undamaged, and his LPUs, inflated and floating outside the aircraft.

"What does it mean?" Peggy asked. "Did they fall off?"

"Maybe," Jack said. "I guess. I mean, they could have fallen off, I suppose, but they're saying it's more likely he took them off. They don't inflate on their own."

"Meaning?"

"Meaning if he was conscious enough to inflate them, he was probably conscious enough to remove them."

"Why would he have taken them off?"

"Well, if the helo didn't sink right away, he might have figured there could have been somebody still inside it and swam back in. I don't know why else he'd take his LPUs off."

"Oh God. He went back in?"

"Maybe."

"Oh my God. I thought you said the helicopter stayed afloat?"

"It did, but the seas were extremely rough. He could have hit his head, or . . . Anyway, if he did go back in, he probably went down with the helicopter."

They didn't have to say that going back into a sinking helicopter to save somebody was exactly the sort of thing Mark Judy would have done.

"Are you all right?"

"Not yet," Jack said. Definitely not yet. "I will be."

"Do you know when you're coming home? Is it too soon to say?"

"Soon," Jack said. "Things are pretty much wrapping up down here. Did anybody call about Scott Simpson's bachelor party?"

"I wrote down a message for you."

He didn't much feel like going to a bachelor party, but life goes on.

He called Debbie Judy one last time. She sounded bad. She'd had a dream that Mark was on a desert island. She'd even entertained the notion that the Russians had captured him for some reason and were holding him prisoner. Her friends were telling her Mark wasn't dead. Jack knew he needed to put her uncertainties to rest.

"Debbie," he said, trying to keep his voice level and even, "Mark isn't out there. We've covered almost thirty thousand square miles. We're picking up stuff the size of paper cups, but we still haven't found anybody. I think if there was someone there, we would have found him."

He heard a sense of peace in her voice when she spoke next.

"I don't think anybody but you could have told me that," she said. She told Jack that Mark had told her once he loved Jack like a brother.

"I felt the same way about him," Jack said.

From his room in Florida, he looked out at the ocean and the night sky. He knew it was foolish to think he could change things that were beyond his control. On a rescue you do your best, and you hate losing anybody, but if a patient doesn't make it, you can also say to yourself, "Tonight was the night when the guy's number came up—everybody has to die sometime." Why was it so much harder to say that when it was a close friend whose number came up?

He had a lot of time to think that night. He thought about brothers. He'd grown up with sisters and never really had a brother. He loved his sisters, but sometimes he wished, growing up, that he'd had a brother. Buddies like Randy Mohr and Mark Judy were as close as he'd ever come. He liked having "brothers," even if there were quotation marks around the word. He thought about Matthew, growing up in a house with three girls. It would be nice if Matthew had a brother.

He also wondered how fair it was to the kids to raise a family with a job where there was always a chance of leaving them fatherless. Of course, firemen did it, and policemen did it, but he knew PJs who said they were going to wait to get out before starting families. He'd thought of it before, even though he'd never really had a choice in the matter. Mark's death made him think of it again. He swore he'd never leave his family fatherless, but the bottom line was, it was beyond his control. What he did was intrinsically valuable, he knew, and he never questioned that it was, but at what price if it hurt his family?

If it ever gets bad for them, I'll get out. I won't be selfish. I'll do something else. If I get too old to do the job, or if it ever gets too hard for my family, I'll get out.

He thought of Randy Mohr. Randy had known when to get out, or rather he'd been told, pretty convincingly, when it was time to get out.

After his first two years were up at Eglin, Mohr decided to reenlist. Mark Judy had already signed on for six more years, at the rather exciting prospect of being transferred to Patrick to form a team to work the space shuttle launches. That sounded good to Mohr, as did the $23,000 reenlistment bonus the Air Force was offering PJs who re-upped. It was a good deal for everyone, considering that it cost the Air Force about a quarter of a million dollars to train a single PJ, so they preferred to pay a bonus to encourage veterans to re-up rather than start from scratch with recruits. Mohr went to the administration building at Eglin, which was directly across the street from the PJ section, and signed his name to all the necessary reenlistment papers. He was thinking of how many antique cars he could buy with $23,000, how he could maybe even make a down payment on a house, and how Cocoa Beach, between Patrick and Canaveral, was reported to have the best surfing in Florida. He was going to be a PJ for life, he'd decided, when he turned down a hallway to leave the building. At the end of the hallway was a glass door. Beyond the glass door, he could see the building where the PJ section was housed. He got halfway down the hall when he was suddenly bathed in a wash of golden light.

Randy Mohr was raised Catholic. He didn't think of himself as super-stitious, but he was religious. He stared at the golden light. He squinted and turned his head to make sure it wasn't just the sun shining on the glass door in some odd way. It wasn't. He looked around to see if there might be anybody else there to witness this thing with him. There wasn't. The light was intensely bright, but not hot, and it was inside the hallway, defi-nitely in the building, not on the other side of the glass door. It was so bright that he couldn't see past it. He couldn't see the PJ section across the street. It was an opaque, golden light, not white, like sunlight. He crouched down and turned his head, trying to see under it. He stood up again. He didn't hear any voices. The light didn't seem to have any mean-ing to him, until he turned his head, and then he saw a sign. Literally. He saw a sign on the wall, about a foot in front of his face, at eye level, and the sign said *Outbound Assignments,* marking the office at Eglin where you go when you decide not to reenlist.

He looked at the light again, and it was gone. Through the glass door, he again saw the PJ section across the street.

The light had come between him and the section. It had stopped him, blocked his way. He saw the *Outbound Assignments* sign, and then the light was gone. The meaning of that seemed pretty clear. He went into the Outbound Assignments office, told them he'd changed his mind, quit the PJs, and never told anybody why, except for Mark Judy and Jack.

When Jack called Randy Mohr in Olean, New York, to tell him the news, Randy didn't believe him at first, and thought he was playing a joke.

"Randy," Jack said. "Mark is dead."

"Yeah, right, asshole," Mohr said, and hung up the phone. Jack thought, *Oh my God—he really doesn't believe me.* He waited half an hour for Mohr to realize he wouldn't make a joke like that, then called him back. Randy asked Jack to tell him what happened, so Jack told him, in as much detail as he could provide. He told him the search was being called off.

"How's Debbie?" Randy asked.

"She's holding it together," Jack said. "She's hurting though."

They talked about "The Jude." Randy told him how, before Judy got married, he and the Jude would go to bars and try to meet women. "Except given that he was handsome and charismatic and I was an obnoxious bas-tard," Mohr said, "so I always got 'The Friend.' One night I said, 'Hey Mark—how come when we go out, you always get the beautiful one, and the one I get is always ugly and weird?' Jude said, 'Hey Randy—did it ever occur to you that the girls we meet are probably saying the same thing?' "

Jack laughed. Mohr said if he hadn't seen the Outbound Assignments sign, he probably would have reenlisted, and if he had, he probably would have been on the helicopter with Judy.

"It just fucking isn't fair," Mohr said.

"What isn't?"

"It doesn't make sense. I mean, why take him and not me?" Mohr asked. "Why would God spare an obnoxious ugly bastard like me? Forget about me—what about my boss? My boss is a fucking dirtbag idiot. He's a scum-sucking slug who doesn't deserve to draw breath. Why take a man like Mark Judy, the best guy you could ever hope to know, and leave behind a fucking dirtbag scum-sucking slug who doesn't deserve to draw breath?"

"You got me," Jack said. Thoughts of his family returned.

If it ever gets bad for them, I'll get out. I'll do something else. I'll know when it's time. Somehow, I'll know when it's time.

PART TWO

10

WITH ANYONE ELSE BUT ME

My dad is just the worst driver. He hates to drive. Usually my mom does all the driving, but sometimes she's not there and my dad has to drive. When we were little and my dad was driving in busy traffic, like maybe we were crossing the Tappan Zee Bridge at rush hour, we'd just put blankets over our heads and close our eyes and pray and wait for it to be over. I remember one time after I got my driver's license, I was following him somewhere, and we were approaching a railroad crossing, and when he went across the tracks, not once did his brake lights light up. He just rambled right across the tracks, and pieces of the car were falling off and bouncing down the road, and he just kept on going, without ever slowing down.

He's also terrible with money. He has no concept. If he has any money on him and you ask him for it, he'll give it to you.

—Michele Brehm

THE WAR IN YUGOSLAVIA CONTINUES TO ESCALATE, AS EVIDENCE OF massacres and atrocities accumulates. President Clinton warns of the possibility of the war spreading, "a war with no natural national boundaries." The estimated total number of displaced refugees seems to double daily, 100,000, then 200,000, then perhaps as many as half a million. A Pentagon spokesman announces that the United States will be sending more planes, five more B-1 bombers and five more Prowlers. An aircraft carrier, the USS *Roosevelt,* is sailing for the Adriatic, and that throws another seventy-five planes into the mix. A week later, the Pentagon says they're sending twenty Apache helicopters and thirteen new Stealth fighters and that airpower resources are being shifted from northern Iraq to Yugoslavia. Peggy knows that the more airplanes and pilots NATO sends, the greater the chance that Jack will be moved from Turkey. Worse, for Peggy, are the photographs of three American soldiers, Staff Sergeants Andrew A. Ramirez, Christopher

J. Stone, and Specialist Steven M. Gonzales, captured by Serb troops while on patrol in what they thought was Macedonia. Peggy can't look at their faces without seeing Jack's.

Jack arrives in Istanbul, at 1130 hours, Monday, March 29, and five hours later reaches Incirlik AFB, where PJs from the 129th Rescue Squadron out of Moffett AFB in California are having a going-away party for themselves and a welcome party for the 106th. Jack has a couple beers with the guys before jet-lag overtakes him. "What's been happening?" he asks. "Not much," he's told. He hits the sack around 10:00 P.M. local time. Early the next morning, there's a briefing on the situations in Kosovo and Iraq. In short, they're told, it's heating up in Kosovo and cooling down in "the box," the no-fly zone of northern Iraq. It seems possible that PJs from the 106th may be moved 1,300 miles northwest to the Yugoslav theater. Nobody would mind too much, because they all want to get in the game. They know it's not a game, but that's what it feels like—as if they're sitting on the sidelines, out of the action, when they're ready and willing to play.

On Jack's third day in country, he reports at 0900 hours for a briefing at the HAS (Hardened Aircraft Shelter) and is issued a new PRC-117D radio, with satellite uplinks. As the team leader on his Jolly, he'll be the one who carries the radio and talks to the "war lord" if or when the call comes that the box is hot. He has all day to learn how to use his radio. On his fourth day, he's briefed on routes in and out of Iraq, ground threats, evasion areas. The base commander has invited them all to a barbecue that evening. He spends the afternoon loading his survival vest with MK-13 flares and pen guns, programs his GPS, then works out. On his fifth day, he reads reports, plays with his new radio, and then at 1600 hours they're told that ten French mountain climbers have gotten in trouble in the mountains forty miles north of Incirlik. Two HH-60s launch, but twenty miles out, in the foothills, they hit weather they can't fly in and turn back. Nobody calls the next morning, which probably means the Turks got them. Jack plays with his radio.

A week in country, he breaks his new radio.

His frustration grows. They're waiting to move up to the FOL, the Forward Operating Location, where they'll sit alert for Northern Watch, the mission to keep Iraqi planes out of the northern no-fly zone. Nothing goes right. On the day they're supposed to fly a simple training mission, the Turks withhold approval to take off, reasons unknown, so instead Jack drives around, trying to get his radio fixed. The next day, the weather is bad. Jack watches the movie *Saving Private Ryan*. Someone jokes that they should be watching *Groundhog Day* instead, a film where a man is trapped in an inexplicable time warp, forced to repeat the same day over and over again. The next day, Brehm's team tries to move forward, but this time two cloud decks, one at 3,000 feet and another at 7,000, trap the helicopters in a cloud sandwich and force them to return to base after being airborne for only an hour. The day after that, the weather stops them thirty minutes out. Then it's the weekend, and the PJs are told they won't try again until Monday. On Monday, they load the helicopters and are good to go when the Turks again deny them permission to fly, without giving an explanation.

Groundhog Day.

Finally, on Tuesday, April 13, the weather is good, and the Turks give permission to fly. Three HH-60s taxi out of the HAS. Yet on the ramp Jack's helicopter develops problems with the horizontal stabilizer, part of the tail. It won't move to the full down position. They radio the other two helos to go on ahead. Fifteen minutes later, the horizontal stabilizer is fixed. They run down the checklist to prepare for takeoff one more time, but this time the copilot notices problems with the hydraulic system. Brehm slips out the HH-60's right side door to check and sees hydraulic fluid streaming off the engine cowling. They shut down the aircraft and find hydraulic fluid pouring off both sides. A mechanic determines the problem is with the SAS, or Stability Augmentation Stabilizer. If the rear stabilizer hadn't given them problems initially, they would have been in the air when the SAS malfunctioned, and then they would have crashed. Now two-thirds of his team has advanced to the FOL, but Jack's left behind. At least Jimmy Dougherty is with him.

"This is worse than *Groundhog Day*," Brehm says to his friend. "At least *Groundhog Day* was funny."

They stand down. The next day they load up, only to be told their diplomatic clearance has expired. The day after that they have clearance, but the tower won't let them fly, because they need a hard copy of the clearance orders.

And so on.

Back home, Peggy buys a spool of yellow ribbon and ties a piece around a slat in the picket fence in the front of the house. She'll do this for each day Jack's gone. She's switched over into survival mode, which means sleeplessness, loneliness, and an exhausting attempt to keep everybody else busy and happy. Over the years she's heard people call her "Super Mom," the "Mother of All Mothers," and "Saint Peggy," and she's never taken it seriously, but she's always done anything she could for her kids. When Michele, a finicky eater ever since she was little, went to college in Albany and found that she couldn't eat the food they were serving in the cafeteria, Peggy overnighted meals to her daughter in Ziploc bags, even though she and Jack were paying the full cafeteria fee, because she knew that if she didn't, Michele simply wouldn't eat.

This time, to take the kids' minds off Dad being gone, she's planned a vacation. The kids are loading up the car, getting ready to drive down to Myrtle Beach, South Carolina. Peggy picked a resort more or less at random from a brochure, thinking, "Well, we have to go somewhere. . . ." Heading south with her will be Michele, Michele's boyfriend Greg, Laura-Jean, Matt, and Jeffrey. Her sister Lorraine, her two kids, Michael and Kristen, and her husband, Jim, who is recovering from cancer, will follow in a second car. For the last several months, Peggy and Jack have been helping drive Jim to the Sloan-Kettering hospital in Manhattan, first for CAT scans and then surgery. The strain has been tremendous. Everyone needs a vacation, but Peggy thinks she's crazy, planning something so ambitious. Shortly before departure, the phone rings. She expects Lorraine to call, but instead it's Jack.

Her heart pounds.

"Hey," he says. "I had a minute, but I can't talk long. . . ."

He sounds great. He says his flight was long and obnoxious. He asks her if she's ready for the trip. She says Greg is helping load the roof rack. Jim is feeling strong, still looking forward to the drive.

"I got a note from Jeffrey's teacher, thanking me," she says. "I called him and told him Jeffrey might be moody. Bean's upset—another of her friends at school attempted suicide. That's two in two weeks."

"That's horrible," Jack says. "She's okay with it?"

"Seems like she is. She's been worrying about her S.A.T. scores, and Uncle Jim, and now you, so, you know, it's hard. She has a lot to deal with, but like she always does, she's trying to handle it on her own."

Jack knows Bean got her independent side from Peg. It's hard to talk, because there's a delay on the phone, which means they have to talk over each other's echoes. Jack tells her everything is pretty quiet. They both know he can't tell her what he's doing when he goes away. He's not allowed to say anything on the telephone that could provide information to the enemy. He can't say where he is, or what he's doing, or what his plans are. Occasionally the Air Force will monitor outgoing calls to make sure security isn't being violated. Violators can be subject to disciplinary actions ranging from court-martial to having an Article Fifteen letter placed in your file noting that you've discussed classified material, which can keep you from being promoted. Peg realizes how late it must be in Turkey, with its eight-hour time difference. Jack tells her he has to hang up now. There's never enough time. Never. She tells him she loves him. He tells her he loves her.

Three hours later, Peg and the kids are headed down the road. Super Mom has a pair of walkie-talkies to use to stay in touch with Lorraine and Jim. They drive until one in the morning, and by the time they stop it's hard to find a vacancy, so all nine of them share one room. It takes two hours to get everybody processed through the bathroom in the morning, but it's Jeffrey's birthday, so to celebrate they go out for a birthday breakfast. At breakfast, Jeffrey and Matt get in an argument, so Peggy banishes Matt to the car until he calms down. This is Matty's pattern, how he reacts when Jack leaves, acting out because he knows he can push his luck with Dad gone. Peggy's patience level today is low.

The next day it rains. They make the motel in Myrtle Beach by 10:30, and Peggy's heart sinks. The "resort," which looked pretty good in the brochure, is a dump. It's half under construction. Even when it's finished, it's still going to be a dump. There's no water in the pool, no ice in the ice machine (which nevertheless manages to make loud noises) but plenty of bugs in the rooms. There are no other vacancies in town, thanks to hordes of college students on spring break, so she decides they'll make the best of it. They find a T.G.I. Friday's for dinner. When Michele tells the waitresses it's Jeffrey's birthday, they make him stand on a chair while they sing "Happy Birthday" to him. He turns beet red, particularly when everyone else in the restaurant cheers, but he's grinning from ear to ear.

It's news to no one that vacations are relaxing for everyone but the mother. All the same, Peggy feels like she's trapped in a Norman Rockwell painting, up to her elbows in dirty laundry and unwashed dishes, while the kids frolic on the beach. She tries to be up and cheerful for her kids. On Saturday, they all drive go-carts at a nearby amusement facility with miniature golf and video games, but even seeing everybody else having fun makes Peggy sad, because she wishes Jack were there. Sometimes it's actually worse to enjoy yourself alone than it is to feel miserable alone. Joy is something you want to share, too.

While everyone else is playing video games she takes the time to pull herself together, but then, back at the motel, all hell breaks loose. When she asks Matt to pick up his dirty clothes, he argues with her, in a way he wouldn't if Jack were there. She tells him to watch his mouth and not get fresh. Greg, half joking, pins Matt to the bed and tells him to apologize to his mother, but Jeff sees Matt pinned to the bed and takes the opportunity to smack him on the butt, which outrages Matt, who then swears he's going to kill Jeff. Bean tells Matt to grow up, which only makes him madder. Peggy tells Bean to butt out. Bean shoots her mother a dirty look. When Michele joins in, it's the last straw.

"That's it!" Peggy says. "I have lost my ability to listen to this garbage. You can all have dinner by yourselves. You have pushed me past my limit."

She grabs her book and her glasses and leaves, walking a mile and a half up Ocean Boulevard to a Kentucky Fried Chicken, where she dines alone, thinking she has another week of "vacation" to go.

On Easter Sunday, they open Easter baskets Peggy's sister Carol sent. The days pass. They win prizes at an amusement park. They eat at a Dairy Queen. Peggy does laundry. She referees disputes and settles arguments. She watches her kids for signs of serious stress. She thinks, *I never asked to be the single mother of five.* She does more laundry. She worries about her brother-in-law, who some days seems fine, but other days seems tired. It's to be expected, she knows. They're worried, of course, about a relapse of his cancer. On the last day, she lets the boys get temporary tattoos. Jolly Green Giant footprints on their butts are out. She agrees that for their last meal, they can all eat at the Hard Rock Cafe.

Finally, on Wednesday, they pack up and hit the road by 11:30 A.M. The plan is to drive six or seven hours and then stop and see how they're doing. Outside of Richmond, Virginia, Peggy finds a great oldies station, and she and Bean sing along. When she hears Kim Carnes singing "It's a Heartache," she remembers that it was on the jukebox at the Dry Dock the first night she met Jack—the first night she kissed him. These are good memories. She misses him, but she's happy to be headed home. Maybe getting back into a routine will help.

They stop at McDonald's at 4:30, and she begins to worry again, about Jim, about Jack, about everything. They stop for gas at 7:30, and discuss how far they want to drive. She's still worrying. Lorraine feels good. Peggy feels good. They estimate they can be home by 2:00 A.M. if they push it. Peg takes a Vivarin to stay awake. At 10:30, they all stop for gas and coffee at the Dunkin' Donuts next to the gas station. While they're stopped, Matt says he can't stand the smell of bananas emanating from a cooler in the back of the minivan and sprays the car with his cologne, forgetting that his mother is allergic to perfume. Peggy tries not to get too upset, but the smell is awful. They drive with the windows open for as long as they can, but it's too cold to leave them open long. Turning on the heater makes the smell worse.

Outside of Wilmington, Delaware, she starts to feel bad. She feels a cramp in her left shoulder, and she worries about it, because she had a bad cholesterol report at her last physical. An ache in the shoulder can sometimes be an early-warning sign of heart attack. She feels clammy and breaks out in a cold sweat. Her heart pounds. Perfume gives her migraines, but this doesn't feel like a migraine. This is in her chest. She calls Lorraine on the walkie-talkie and says she's getting off at the next exit. They find a motel. She barely makes it through check-in, heads for the room, and locks the bathroom door behind her.

Something is wrong. She has to hold it together. She splashes her face with cold water, trying to slow the pounding in her chest. Maybe all she needs is a good cry—maybe she's been keeping too much inside. She buries her face in a towel, so the kids can't hear, and then cries for Jack. It doesn't help. Afterward she feels worse. She wants to call her sister Carol, but by now it's 1:00 A.M. She knows she's only making it worse by panicking. She tries to lie in bed, but she can't calm down. She starts to feel dizzy and recognizes she's hyperventilating. She gets out of bed and lies on the bathroom floor. It's hard and cold, and offers some relief. She tries to go back to bed, but her thoughts race. At 3:30 A.M., she can't take it anymore. Something is definitely wrong, and she thinks, "John will kill me if I don't get help." She wakes Bean and asks her to go down the hall and get Lorraine, who drives her to a local hospital, where Peggy is quickly hooked up to an EKG machine and a heart monitor. Her heart rate is 128 beats a minute.

"I took a Vivarin around seven or seven-thirty," she tells the ER doctor, "but I've taken those before. I just haven't been sleeping much lately. I think that's it. I had coffee at ten-thirty or so at Dunkin' Donuts, but . . ."

"Tell me," the doctor asks, "have you been under any unusual stress lately?"

Then whatever it is that's been holding her together gives. She falls apart. She tries to explain, between sobs. She tells him about her husband,

and the war, and Jim's cancer. When she's finished, the doctor says only, "No wonder." He tells her her feelings are real. He prescribes Elavil, a mild tranquilizer, to take the edge off. She finally returns to the motel at about a quarter to five. She's tired, and she worries that she won't be rested enough to drive when she gets up. Finally she sleeps.

When she gets home the next day, around four, there's a message on the machine from Jack, saying he's going to call at five. She doesn't want to worry Jack by telling him what happened, but she knows she has to. She's been doing this for twenty-one years. Why is this TDY worse than any of the others? When he calls, he tells her he can only talk for fifteen minutes. They have a good telephone connection, no echoes.

"So how are you?" he asks.

"I've been better," she begins. She gives him a summary of what happened. She tries not to leave anything out, but she has only fifteen minutes, and she doesn't want to do all the talking—she wants to hear his voice. He listens, and feels bad, wishing he'd been there at her side, though if he'd stayed home she probably wouldn't have had the palpitations in the first place. He thinks of all the times she stood at his side in hospitals. He tries to think of something he can say to calm her. He can't tell her about Groundhog Day, or how he's frustrated at not being in the game—that he's not even close to the game. He can't really tell her anything, except to say, "Don't worry about me."

"I know those words aren't enough, Peg, but *don't worry* about me."

"Please come home," she says, crying again. She realizes begging him to do something that's impossible for him to do will make him hurt a bit, and that's wrong, but it only seems fair, considering how she's hurting. She wants him to hurt, too. "I'm sorry for . . ."

Then the line goes dead. They're cut off. She curses. It's happened before, but it's so unfair. The only person in the world she needs to talk to, and they only have fifteen minutes to begin with, and then they don't even get that. It's unfair. It bites. She wants the phone to ring again, and then it does.

"They tell me we have one more minute," Jack says. "But I couldn't let it go without telling you I love you."

"I love you, too," she says, calming down. "I'm sorry."

"Don't worry about it," he says. "Just take care of yourself, Peg, and don't worry about me. Now listen. I have to fly somewhere, and then I'll be back." He thinks he may have said too much.

"Fly where?"

"I can't tell you that," he says, "but then I'll be back. . . ." He can't tell her that things aren't going well, because then she'll worry, and he won't be able to explain exactly how it is that things aren't going well. "I might be back later than expected . . . but then I'll be home. Soon. Okay?"

"Okay."

"I'll try to call again in a week, but I can't promise."

"I know."

"I love you, Peg."

"I love you, John."

The thing is, the not knowing drives her crazy, and the knowing drives her crazy. The news, the war, but mostly the not knowing. Surface mail takes too long and ranges from sporadic to worse, e-mail never gets through, and the phone doesn't do it, even when she connects. *Fifteen minutes? Are they serious?* When it doesn't ring, she wants it to ring, unless it's bad news, and then she doesn't want it to ring. When the light on the answering machine blinks, sometimes she's reluctant to hit playback, but still, not knowing is worse.

That night, she prays again. Same old same old—nothing new about the prayer. *Just keep him safe. That's all I care about. I don't care about me. Just keep him safe. Make him be okay.* It's the same prayer she offered when he flew to Turkey. The same prayer she offered when the Turks denied Jack's team permission to fly, and again when the weather turned them around the first day, and again when the weather turned them back the second day, and again when operations postponed the mission for the weekend. She said it the night the malfunctioning horizontal stabilizer grounded Jack's helicopter, and again when the control tower told Jack's team their diplomatic clearance had expired, and again the next day, when the Turks stopped Jack's team from flying because they needed a hard copy of the orders.

A cynic, or maybe a believer, might say Peggy Brehm's prayers are wasting U.S. taxpayers' dollars, but Peggy wouldn't mind it if it were true.

11

THE BIRD THAT WAS NOT A BIRD

You have to learn mountaineering skills because there's always a chance that a pilot is going to be shot down in a mountainous area where it would be difficult to reach him, even under friendly conditions. We're flying over mountains in Iraq, and in Kosovo, and places where it's easy to hide an antiaircraft battery. Sometimes you're not as worried about the guy getting shot or captured by the enemy as you are that he could succumb to the elements. And if you're racing against time with an enemy patrol trying to reach and capture your guy, whoever has the better mountaineering skills wins.

I climbed Mont Blanc in France back in September of 1982 with a PJ named Rod Alne. We got thrown out of a couple bars one time in the village of Chamonix, a restaurant, because we were told they had menus in English, but when we asked for them, they wouldn't give them to us, which made us think they didn't want our patronage. We also collect souvenirs wherever we go, because our unit had a trophy room, so if you go on a ship, maybe you grab a life ring or a coffee mug with the ship's name on it. In France, my buddy Scott Simpson and I used our mountaineering skills to climb up this hotel's balcony and steal a French flag. A couple days later, the flag had been replaced, so a friend of Rod's, a PJ named Bill Jones, thought he'd climb up and steal that one, except that whoever had put the flag out had figured out how we'd done it the first time, so they greased the railing. When Jones jumped for the railing, he fell two stories to the ground. He was okay, but he was in shock, saying, "I can't believe it—they greased the rail."

Rod got pissed at me when we were climbing an ice face. I was up probably forty or fifty feet, and when I got to the top, I laid my ice ax down instead of sticking it firmly into the ice and double-checking to make sure it was secure. When I bumped it, it went flying down the ice face and landed right at Rod's feet. It didn't hit him, but it could have, and these things weigh maybe four pounds—it could have killed him.

Mountains are dangerous places. You go there because there's no place else you can go where you'll be that tested, and the more you're tested, the more you learn. Sometimes you learn it the hard way, but you learn it.

ON APRIL 1, 1987, APRIL FOOL'S DAY, PEGGY GAVE BIRTH TO HER last child, a boy, Jeffrey. Jeffrey was a sweet, smiling baby. Perhaps because he was still feeling good about his new son, a month later, Jack ran a personal best time of two hours and fifty-one minutes in the Long Island Marathon. Having once predicted he wouldn't live past thirty, every year beyond that milepost seemed like a gift. Almost without noticing the time passing, as if it had sneaked up on him somehow, Jack realized he was now a veteran PJ. He felt comfortable in his job, confident, without anything like the sense of fatigue or burn-out that other PJs retiring early seemed to feel.

One day, a few weeks before Christmas in 1988, McManus asked Jack if he wanted to get a beer at the Matchbox after work, because he had something he wanted to talk to him about, an "opportunity" Mike said. By now Mike was divorced, remarried to a woman named Debra Carnes. Jack had spent many nights at the Matchbox with Mike, talking about women and marriage. He'd seen Mike at his lowest, and was glad to see him so happy again. It was snowing when Jack left the Ops building, three inches already on the ground, but he knew that in eastern Long Island, it was just as likely to rain the day after a snow as stay cold—they would still need luck if they were to have a white Christmas. Mike was already in a booth, nursing a beer, when Jack joined him.

"So what's the opportunity?" Jack asked. "For you or for me?"

"Well," Mike said, "both, if it works out. I've been more or less offered a chance to go up to Alaska and set up a PJ team there. When Debby and I flew up there last month, we really liked the place, so I met with Colonel Taylor, the wing commander there, and we pretty much hit it off. He didn't say so in so many words, but the job is mine if I want it." Jack knew that Mike had never really taken to Long Island, an acquired taste even for people who were born there. He congratulated Mike and told him it sounded like an exciting prospect.

"It depends on what kind of funding I get," McManus said, "but it sounds like we could really do something pretty neat up there." With all the oil money coming in to the Alaskan state coffers, Mike said he had high hopes that he'd be adequately financed, able to order everything he needed to supply his team, instead of taking hand-me-down equipment and used helicopters from the regular Air Force, the way a lot of guard units had to. He had dreams of putting in a professional-quality weight room, maybe even a pool for guys to train in. The governor seemed determined to install a first-class rescue system. Jack was amazed. Mike was nearly forty-five years old, an age when most PJs had retired, and here he was beginning a whole new phase of his career.

"You're going to love it," Jack said. "From what I've heard, Alaska is going to be just your kind of place."

"It could be your kind of place, too," Mike said. "I'm going to need some good experienced PJs up there, so I'd prefer to take the guys I really like with me."

"Who else are you thinking of inviting?" Jack asked.

"Steve Lupenski is one," Mike said. "Some others. I'm not really spreading it around just yet. I figured you'd have to talk it over with Peggy and the kids, but I just wanted to give you the heads up on this as soon as I could. But the other thing would be that once I'm gone, they're going to need a new NCOIC at the base, and you'd be the guy I'd recommend. You'd be pretty much the only guy on my list, as a matter of fact. I know some people are probably going to feel passed over if they hire you for NCOIC, but I'd rather have the best man get the job, not somebody who's simply been here the longest."

"Hmm," Jack said. *Wow* was what he wanted to say.

"I mean," Mike added, "I can't guarantee you anything, and we still have to post the job, so you'd have to go through the application procedures and be interviewed and all that, but there's no rule that says I can't recommend somebody. So think about it and tell me what you want me to do."

As Jack drove home, he had much to think about. He tried to keep the two ideas separate. He was momentarily excited about the idea of going to Alaska, starting fresh in a new place. He pictured the mountains, the forests, the sea, the glaciers, the whole glorious magnificence of the Alaskan experience, but at the same time he couldn't picture relocating. He would talk it over with Peggy that night, but as he drove home he felt as if he already knew what she'd say, and that he was going to agree with her. Her extended family was like nothing he'd ever experienced before, and it was a big factor in why their marriage was as happy as it was. Instant baby-sitters. Instant grown-up company. Instant playmates for the kids. Instant emergency end-of-the-month loans. Car pools to pick the kids up from soccer or cheerleading practice. Readily available emotional support, and plenty of parental eyes, everybody keeping tabs on everybody else's children, much to the chagrin of the children, who felt as though they couldn't get away with anything. It seemed as though if Jack and Peggy moved then her sister Carol would have to move, too, and her sister Lorraine, and her parents, and Jack's sister—as it was, everybody lived within a few blocks of one another. Putting all the kids into new schools seemed harsh. Moving to Alaska might be good for his career, but it would be bad for his family, and his family came first.

On the other hand, becoming NCOIC would also be good for his career, and he wouldn't have to move to do it. He realized that, at first anyway, he'd be learning on the job, and that he was relatively young to be an NCOIC, which meant that there would be guys with more seniority who'd need to be greased or assuaged, but if Mike believed in him (and he knew Peggy believed in him), then he'd be a fool not to believe in himself. He couldn't have asked for a better teacher or role model.

"I think we're going to have to pass on the thing in Alaska," he told Mike the next day, "but I'm definitely interested in the job here."

"Let me talk to Stratameier and Giere," McManus said, referring to the squadron commander and the base commander. "You know you still have to go through the standard selection process," McManus added.

"I understand that," Jack said.

"I'll get back to you."

Jack was excited by his prospects. All the same, Mike's change of station came as a mixed blessing. Jack felt that half the things he knew he'd learned from Mike. Mike had been there when the helicopter had crashed in Plattsburgh. He'd been there when Jack found out Peggy was pregnant. He'd been there when Mark Judy died. He'd been there when Larry Arnott died. And for all the harsh and hard moments, there'd been hundreds of lighter joyous moments, jumps out of airplanes, training runs side by side, Dumb Ass Bare Assed escapades and beers shared in bars all over the globe. Sure they'd see each other again, and stay in touch, but life without seeing Mike on a regular basis was hard to contemplate.

On January 24, 1989, Jack and McManus flew their last mission together. A trawler had overturned in icy cold waters, five miles out from the base on a south-southeast heading. The Coast Guard was on the scene, but they needed medical assistance. Jack joked that given how cold it was, it was sort of a preview for what Mike could expect on his new job. Thermometers at the base registered a mere 24° Fahrenheit. Brehm and McManus low-and-slowed in, entered the water wearing wet suits and swam to a 44-foot Coast Guard ship that had pulled a sailor off a capsized 87-foot fishing boat. The other crewmen had been rescued, but the sailor on the Coast Guard ship was suffering from severe hypothermia and needed to be med-evac'ed to a hospital immediately. Jack and Mike hoisted the victim up, treated him for hypothermia on the helicopter and administered CPR all the way to Stony Brook Hospital, even though the victim had no vital signs and was quite likely dead. The general rule in rescue is, you don't pronounce a cold body dead because cold bodies can sometimes be resuscitated even after being submerged for long periods of time. If the guy warms up and he's still dead, *then* he's dead, which was exactly what the doctors at Stony Brook pronounced him, forty minutes after the HH-3 landed.

There was a farewell party for Mike McManus at the NCO club on the base before he left for Alaska. It was a gloomy winter day, but the wives helped decorate the place to bring in some cheer, Peggy and Barbara Dougherty and John Spillane's fiancée, Laura, stringing up white Christmas lights and *FAREWELL* and *GOOD LUCK,* and *BON VOYAGE* banners. Jack called Major Jeff Frank, who'd been the original squadron commander for the 106th back in 1975, when McManus first came onboard to build the team, and got him to fly up from South Carolina as a surprise. Jack gathered together a number of retired guys who'd been there in '75— Bernie Waters, Dickie Forrestal from the motor pool, Mike's pal despite all the vehicles Mike and his PJs kept wrecking. The PJs wanted to buy Mike a hunting rifle, figuring that's what men going to Alaska need, but they didn't know what kind to buy, so they gave him a cashier's check for $400 and told him to buy a rifle with it, if the idea of hunting appealed to him. There were real gifts, and there were gag gifts. For example, when it was time to clean up after a mission, Mike would always walk from his locker to the showers and back wearing a towel with a slit cut in the middle of it, thrown over his head, something like a terry cloth poncho. He also hated it when he'd leave his shampoo in the showers, so instead, before showering, he'd simply glop a big blue dollop of Head & Shoulders on his pate at his locker and walk around like that, sometimes talking to people or taking phone calls. One gag gift was a new bath towel, with a slit neatly

Twenty-four hours before departing for basic training in February 1977.

No more long hair: Jack's basic training photo.

Jack and Peggy begin their new life together, July 28, 1978.

"Air Force beats Army," July 1977. The class of '78-03 victorious in the Great Chattahoochee Raft Race. *Bottom, from left:* Jack Brehm, John Geerlings, J. G. Higgins. *Top, from left:* Slip O'Farrell, D. T. Higgins, Bob Wagner, John Smith, Mark Judy, Bill Skolnik. (*U.S. Army Photo*)

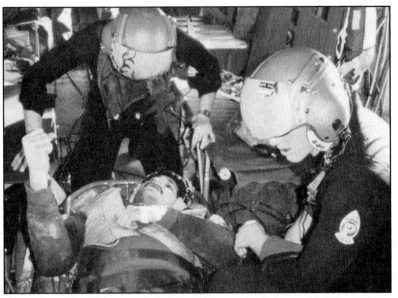

Saving lives is all in a day's work for the PJs. PJ Robert Olson, *left,* and Jack, *right,* monitor Ronald Cunningham's condition, July 14, 1981.

The Jolly 85 that crashed on June 13, 1978, killing all on board, including three PJs from the 106th: Al Snyder, David Lambert, and Scott Hursh. *(106th Combat Visual Information Section)*

Jack gives a tour of an H-60 to Alan Craig Snyder, son of Al Snyder, who died one week before Alan was born. *(106th Combat Visual Information Section)*

Tell me this doesn't look like fun. Hoo-yah!

Jack finally gets to summit Mt. McKinley, June 1991. With Skip Kula, *left*.
(*Jack Chapin*)

Jack and his father, Bernard Brehm.   Jack and his mother, Rosemary Brehm.

Chief Edward O. King's retirement party at West Point in 1997. From left: Jimmy and Barbara Dougherty, John and Laura Spillane, and the Brehms.

COL David Hill, Jr., 106th Wing Commander, and Peggy and Jack at the Senior NCO Academy Graduation in 1994. *(LTC Anthony Cristiano)*

Groundhog Day in Turkey, May 1999. *From left:* Jack, Jonathan Davis, Jimmy Dougherty. *(Rob Marks)*

Peggy's support staff while Jack was in Turkey (celebrating Jack's return). *Top, from left:* Peggy, Jim, Peggy's sister Lorraine, Jack. *Bottom, from left:* Greg, Michele, Peggy's sister Carol, Bean, Jaimie, Elizabeth, Mark.

Above: Jack gets support from mentor Mike McManus as he races his first Ironman-distance triathlon. (*Laura-Jean Brehm*)

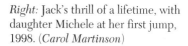

Right: Jack's thrill of a lifetime, with daughter Michele at her first jump, 1998. (*Carol Martinson*)

Jack's proudest achievement—the Brehm family. *Top, from left:* Peggy, Matthew. *Middle, from left:* Laura-Jean, Elizabeth, Jeffrey. *Bottom, from left:* Michele, Jack. (*Carol Martinson*)

cut, sewn, and hemmed in the middle, a refinement on the simple tailoring Mike had done on his own towel with his survival knife. When the party moved to the Matchbox after the NCO club closed around two in the morning, Mike showed up wearing nothing but his new towel, buck naked underneath it. A PJ named John Canfield immediately tackled him and wrestled him to the floor, McManus's ass and balls flying all over the place. It was a miracle no one put an eye out.

On the day he left town, beginning the long road trip north to Anchorage, Mike and Debby stopped by Jack and Peggy's house in Rocky Point intending to say a quick good-bye and get on the freeway, but they ended up staying until midnight, drinking beers and talking about old times. Mike brought Jack a parting gift, a pair of brand-new Cochran jump boots, shiny black dress boots for those occasions when a full dress uniform was called for. Jack had always been too cheap or too broke to pony up the forty bucks for dress boots, polishing up his standard Air Force issue jungle boots instead, and Mike had always teased him about it. McManus finally got on the road in the wee hours of the morning, determined not to spend another night on Long Island, only to be harassed on the Long Island Expressway by an insane motorist in what appeared to be a black Monte Carlo. There's nothing particularly uncommon about encountering insane motorists on the Long Island Expressway, but at two in the morning, when it's just you and the lunatic tailgating you at 100 mph and flashing his high beams, when all you're trying to do is leave in peace, it's particularly irritating. McManus wasn't worried for his safety, because he had his weapons in the car with him, and was in fact loading his sidearm, concerned more that the noise from the weapon was going to wake up his wife than about shooting the moron in the Monte Carlo. He finally lost the guy at the Throg's Neck Bridge, and he was happy to see him veer off, but he couldn't help but think it a fitting farewell, and good riddance.

The spring and summer were relatively uneventful. Jack ran the section, thankful that there were no major challenges, just a daily routine of paperwork and training. He knew that Mike had left behind some fairly large shoes to fill, but whenever Jack found himself in doubt about a decision, asking himself "What would Mike do?" usually led him to an answer, and if it didn't, he could always pick up the telephone and go directly to the source. In April, John Spillane married his girlfriend of five years, a woman named Laura Hohman. In May, Jack ran the Long Island Marathon for the eleventh consecutive year. In August, he swam, biked, and ran a half–Iron

Man race, called a Tin Man, in Lake Placid. Search and rescue missions were few, and routine—patients who needed to be med-evac'ed, sailors who were a few days late for dinner and needed to be found. Things stayed quiet until 1990, when Iraqi troops invaded and occupied Kuwait.

A prolonged and complex multinational military buildup followed, preparations for what became Operation Desert Storm, the Gulf War. Active duty Air Force PJs, under the control of AFSOC (Air Force Special Operations Command), were tasked to support tactical combat teams, which meant joining up with combat controllers to establish landing zones, or with the 82d Airborne to seize Kuwaiti or Iraqi airfields. PJs under AFSOC were to parachute in and then perform the functions of old-fashioned field medics, treating anybody who might be hurt in the jump. The Guard and Reserve pararescue units, under the ACC, or Air Combat Command, would ordinarily have been tasked with the traditional assignment of going after downed pilots, but it was decided at the higher levels that the HH-3 and HH-60 Pavehawk helicopters the Guard and Reserve units were flying, aircraft that were rated for low- to medium-risk combat situations, were not going to be safe to fly in the high-risk environment over Iraq. The 106th specifically was deemed non-combat ready, as a unit, because their pilots and mechanics were undergoing conversion training, the squadron recently having switched from HH-3 to HH-60G air frames, and until their training was completed, they weren't going anywhere. There was still a chance, however, that PJs from the 106th might be sent to supplement or replace the active duty PJs in theater.

Guys asked Jack what he thought the chances were that they'd be sent. Prewar propaganda aside, it looked as if it was going to be huge. The newspapers were full of stories about Iraq's state-of-the-art Russian-made air defense systems, their stockpiles of nerve gases and biological weapons of mass destruction, and particularly Saddam Hussein's "crack Republican Guard." Saddam did his part to frighten everybody by speaking of how it was going to be the "Mother of All Battles." The Iraqi army proved, in retrospect, fairly ineffective, managing to stage a partially successful raid on the animals in the Kuwait City Zoo and set a couple hundred oil wells on fire before grabbing the first jeep, bus, bicycle, or skateboard available back to Baghdad, once Desert Storm commenced. Before it started, however, the average American was deeply concerned, if not outright terrified, with what might happen if nerve gases were used, or if Saddam managed to hit Jerusalem with one of his SCUD missiles and do enough damage to draw a nuclear response from Israel. In the early stages of the conflict, PJs from the 106th deployed to Patrick AFB to help fly coverage for an accelerated program of space shuttle launches carrying classified military payloads, meaning, everyone knew, spy satellites to be placed in orbit over the Middle East.

At the Brehm household, it was the first time the kids were old enough to worry about what was going on in the world. The twins were eleven, Laura-Jean was eight, Matt was seven, and Jeffrey had turned three on April first. Elizabeth had developed into the sensitive one, the romantic, easily moved to tears by a story with a sad ending, or better yet by a romantic story with a happy ending. She loved to write—stories, poems, journals, anything as long as she could let the words flow out of her and put them down on the page. She was nonconfrontational, but her emotions were largely evident and accessible, unlike Michele, who played her cards closer to the vest. Michele was confident, willful, more willing to explore and try new things, more self-reliant, more fun-loving, and a better athlete than her twin sister. Elizabeth envied the way Michele didn't care what other people thought, and how she seemed to have a clear sense of reality, of who she was and what she wanted. Both girls were old enough to understand that their father might have to go to the Middle East. Peggy tried to turn the television off whenever she saw the kids watching the news about Desert Storm, but she couldn't keep it off all the time. The White House needed the American public to back the war, and to a certain extent used scare tactics to get the support it needed, emphasizing Saddam Hussein's history of brutality and his prior use of nerve gas on his own people.

If the propaganda campaign worked on grown-ups, it frightened the daylights out of young children. Elizabeth cried. Michele used the tension as an excuse not to do her homework, saying, "I was too upset last night to study." Laura-Jean was the gregarious one, thoughtful of others, sensible and silly at the same time, able to charm her father with little effort, but as the war developed she grew clingy, reluctant to leave her father's side. Even Jeffrey, who was only three, seemed to know that something bad was about to happen somewhere, and that his dad could be involved in it somehow. He was a sensitive child, extremely patient, and a bit of a mama's boy, but neither he nor Peggy seemed to mind. Jeffrey seemed oddly tuned in for someone so young, always staring at the news on CNN whenever he got the chance. Matthew seemed to be handling it well, but Peggy knew that was an act. Matty was the kind of kid who seemed quiet and shy at first, observant and smart but slightly detached or remote, until you got to know him, and then you realized he had the driest sense of humor in the family, a subtle wry wit he used to tease his siblings, usually without seeming mean. He was small for his age group but good at sports like hockey, soccer, or lacrosse, and highly competitive, like his dad, whom he idolized. Admitting Dad was at risk meant admitting Dad was something less than invincible, which wasn't Matthew's position on the matter. Peggy tried to keep her cool but lost it one morning when she was trying to get Matthew out the door and onto the school bus. The phone rang. It was a teacher from the school at Rocky Point.

"How are you doing?" the teacher asked.

"I'm fine. What do you mean?"

"Well, it's just that I heard the 106th was being deployed today."

Peggy's knees weakened. It was all she could do to get Matthew on the bus. As soon as she could, she called Jack at the base, who reassured her that they were not being activated, but rather they had simply been placed on alert.

During the "Mother of All Battles," Jeffrey became obsessed with the pictures on TV, favoring CNN over Barney or cartoons. Pictures of buildings blowing up, or buildings about to blow up, taken from cameras in the nose cones of flying bombs and missiles—what could better capture the imagination of a three-year-old boy? Peggy would say to Jeffrey, "You can't watch this—turn it off," and confiscate the remote control, but sooner or later it would be on again. When Michele won $365 on an Instant Lotto ticket that Peggy cashed for her, she said she wanted to take the whole family to the Great Escape Amusement Park in Lake George. Jack, on alert, couldn't go, but Peggy and the kids went. They went on rides, and played arcade games, ones not involving guns, and stayed in a motel, and ate out in restaurants three meals a day, and forgot about the war that was going to happen, any day.

Desert Storm began in January and lasted until April 6, 1991. The main air campaign was waged in the first month. The 106th waited to be called up, and the PJs were polled for volunteers to deploy in the Gulf on two separate occasions. Jack volunteered both times but was never called. He volunteered without Peggy's knowledge, because he didn't want to worry her prematurely, and because he knew she'd understand if he ever did get called. It wasn't just a sense of duty that made him want to go—it was more a sense of purpose, the thing that gave his life meaning and shape.

Peggy knew that. She also knew Jack was probably volunteering to go without telling her. She was elated when the war ended as quickly as it did.

As the war wound down, Jack got a call from Mike McManus in Alaska, who said that once the squadron was off alert, he had a training mission Jack might be interested in, a team that was going up Mount McKinley in Denali National Park. After all the tension of waiting out Operation Desert Storm, and the disappointment of not going, climbing McKinley seemed, to Jack, like just the ticket.

There was one thing he had to take care of first. Two days before he was due to fly to Kulis Air National Guard Base in Anchorage, Jack's next door neighbor, Carl Waage, called. Carl was a few years older than Jack and lived with his wife, Maryanne, his son Kris, and his daughter Carla. Carl drove delivery trucks for *Newsday*. He and Jack would drink beers in his kitchen and talk about the Mets, and their kids, and the jobs they'd had. Carl had worked as a flagpole painter, not as dangerous as the things Jack did, he said, but scary at times. More dangerous, perhaps, was the job he'd had scraping and repainting the insides of underground storage tanks, which, the doctors thought, was possibly where he'd inhaled the chemicals that had given him a rare degenerative lung disease. Carl was awaiting a double lung transplant, and now that spring had arrived, and the motorcycles or, as doctors call them, "donor-cycles" were coming out of the garages, it looked as if Carl's time on the waiting list was coming to an end. That was, in fact, why he'd called—would Jack mind driving him to the hospital to pick up a fresh pair of lungs?

Jack felt honored, but wondered why Carl hadn't asked his wife. Probably because he didn't want to worry her. Better to call her from the hospital. The lungs were waiting. Jack drove Carl to the hospital. Carl was calm, confident, thrilled that his hospital room had a great view, eager to get it over with, and anxious to hear about Jack's trip to McKinley when he got back.

"Take a lot of pictures," he said. "When you get back, we'll sit on the porch and drink a beer and you can show me your pictures. I'll see you soon."

* * * * * * * *

On the sixteenth of May, three days into his climb of Mount McKinley, his group climbing the West Buttress route, Brehm writes in his diary that he has a slight headache and that he slept only three hours the night before. The entry for Friday, May 17, records the first inkling of trouble: *Arrived*

9,800 feet at 1200 hrs. The whole area from 8,000 feet to 10,000 feet is in a total white-out all day with a light snow falling. Temp. approx. 20 degrees F, winds 10 kts [knots]. The troops are happy we have yet to get stuck in any one place. I'm doing great physically, no blisters, and I feel strong, and you know me, I couldn't be happier. Found out yesterday that a group of Koreans are frozen out at 17,000 feet. One dead, one with frostbite, whole arm, three hypothermic, and one missing.

But you can't necessarily trust the information you get on a mountain—news items relayed via word of mouth—as climbers pass each other on the way up or down. It's like a big game of telephone, a situation where facts might get distorted, even at sea level—add impaired thinking at altitude to the mix and you can have an obscuring of facts of major proportion. Brehm takes the news of the Koreans with a grain of salt, because it might not be true. His diary entry for May 18 notes, *"There's no place in the world I'd rather be."*

On May 20, they make Windy Corner at 13,500 feet and reach a bowl at 14,000 feet, around 4:30 P.M., a place called Fourteen Camp, which affords them a breathtaking view of Denali National Park and the Alaskan Range. The trip from 11,000 to 14,000 is a bitch, maybe the toughest part of the route. The skies are clear and the sun is intense all day, almost too hot. Brehm's pulse an hour after arriving is sixty beats a minute. On Brehm's rope team are PJ "Skip" Kula and a Navy SEAL named Jack Chapin. PJs Mike Wayt and Steve Lupenski are on team two. PJ Carl Brooks, a British Special Ops guy named Mike Blinkhorn, and a civilian, Brian Abrams, make up team three, while PJs Steve Daigle and Garth Lenz make up team four. Three other guys have gone up the West Rib route, but that's a more technical and thus more dangerous climb, leading through a place called the Valley of Death, where chunks of ice the size of railroad cars can come crashing down, so you have to cross it early in the morning before the sun heats the ice above you. The West Buttress group is for men with less mountaineering experience. Rudolf Kula is a PJ from Cleveland who graduated the Pipeline a few classes behind Jack's, and because he's the PJ with the most experience on McKinley, he's in charge. Lupenski was one of the PJs from the 106th who relocated to Anchorage with McManus to help start up the Alaskan wing. PJ Wayt, a twenty-eight-year-old Japanese-American Air Force brat, is climbing McKinley for the first time, as is Lupenski. It will be Brehm's first climb above 15,000 feet, assuming all goes well. Chapin and Brooks are developing blisters and may not go any farther. The total number of people staying at Fourteen Camp this day is probably about thirty, including three park rangers who've been stationed there for twenty-four days and are due to be replaced and rotated down the mountain. Fourteen Camp, sometimes called Doc Hackett's Camp, after Bill Hackett, one of the first men to climb the West Buttress route back in 1951, is one of two staging areas on McKinley. The other is at 17,000 feet. They are places where you recover and reorganize your thoughts and await news of good or bad weather either above or below you.

All seems well. A diary entry for May 21 records that with an oxygen saturation level of 86 percent, Brehm's pulse, at 8:30 P.M., is sixty-four beats per minute. The entry ends, *Some Girl Scouts knocked on our tent selling cookies tonight.*

Girl Scouts? The next day Brehm reads the entry and can't remember what he was thinking or why he wrote it down. He might have been dreaming. It's possibly a sign that he needs to rest.

The plan is to spend some time shuttling gear up the mountain and caching it, but mostly the idea is to rest for the next leg of the climb. At 14,000 feet, it takes about three days to acclimate to the altitude. Acclimating to altitude requires a variety of biological adjustments, but the main way the body compensates for the lack of oxygen is by manufacturing additional red blood cells, which carry oxygen from the lungs to the rest of the body. If we could remove the soul from the body and take away the thing that makes us human, we could then think of ourselves as simply an ongoing, enormously complex chemical reaction, a kind of controlled fire, or an assembly of a trillion small fires going on in each individual cell. Without oxygen, fires go out. Chemical reactions slow down. When you're climbing, the thinning air acts like a damper. You can eat three or four times the amount of calories that you might eat at sea level, but without oxygen the fuel inside you only partially burns. The technical term for the general malaise you feel at high elevations is hypobaric hypoxia. It frequently leads to mountain sickness, which generally occurs at 8,000 feet or higher. Affected individuals develop symptoms within four to six hours, reach maximal severity in twenty-four to forty-eight hours. Basic mountain sickness often abates three or four days after exposure. The most common symptom of hypobaric hypoxia is a skull-busting headache, but other symptoms include vomiting, dizziness, labored breathing, and ataxia, or a lack of muscle coordination. Confusion can occur because even the ideas in our heads, including the memories we carry around with us and the dreams we have at night, are themselves chemical reactions that require oxygen. At high altitudes where the oxygen is thin, thoughts and dreams and memories begin to turn fuzzy and lose structure, as if oxygen were the glue holding them together. The psychological symptoms of mountain sickness are things like despondency, irritability, or impaired memory. Thinking becomes work. Sometimes hard work, and it doesn't matter how smart you are to begin with—you get dumber. At 14,000 feet, no matter how fit you are, you get a little bit weaker with each passing day. You sleep at night, but without oxygen sleep does not bring the kind of rest you need and you can wake up feeling more tired than you were when you went to bed. At some point, it requires as much emotional strength to keep going as it does physical strength.

On May 22, the three new park rangers arrive, among them a man named Roger Robinson, who the Alaskan PJs have worked with before. The rangers being replaced head down the mountain to Talkeetna, skiing down part of the way and no doubt feeling better and stronger with each meter they descend. Shortly after their departure, a group coming down the mountain reports bad news. The rumor of fatalities among a team of Korean climbers is false; however, a Korean named Kim Hong Bin is in serious trouble, a second Korean less so. In addition to the Koreans, there are two other parties at 17,000 feet, about twelve people altogether. Kim Hong Bin is an expert skier and one of Korea's leading mountain climbers, a man who made it to 23,600 feet on Mount Everest in 1989 and 23,900 feet on Pakistan's 26,260 foot Mount Nangaparbat in 1990, though no one at Fourteen Camp has any way of knowing this. If they had, they might suspect it could have been a fear of failing to summit three times in a row that got Kim Hong Bin in trouble. From Kim Hong Bin's perspective, how could he turn back, knowing that on his two previous ascents he'd climbed higher than the summit of the mountain he was now climbing?

The staging area at 17,000 feet is a relatively flat narrow plain at the crest of the West Buttress's headwall, an area on the mountain where the angle of ascent increases to 55 or 60 degrees. At the bottom of the headwall is a *bergschrund,* an area of crevasses where the glacier flowing down the mountain breaks off. The vertical slope is mostly ice and bullet-proof snow, sculpted at various locations into *sastrugi* ice, where the ferocious winds create waves and sawtooths and stalactites. From 17,000 feet, it's another 3,320 vertical feet to the summit, a hike of perhaps five horizontal miles. A moderately steep ascending traverse, beginning at 17,200 feet and dubbed the

Autobahn because a German party got in trouble there once, takes you to Denali Pass at about 19,000 feet. You climb a short headwall to a flat area called the Football Field, and then it's a half a mile of plodding up the peak ridge to the summit. Along the way, you may encounter couloirs, knife-edged ridges, frost-fractured schist columns, and snow or ice cornices—no one in their right mind would call it an easy walk, but the degree of incline isn't as steep as the headwall between 14,000 and 17,000 feet. Climbers regularly go from Seventeen Camp to the summit and back in a day. Brehm's party has already cached supplies at 16,030 feet (between 14,000 and 16,030, it's much too steep to cache anything) with the thought of moving the whole show up the following day.

"Is there a problem?" Brehm asks Kula, who explains the situation with the Koreans.

"Koreans?" someone says. "Well, that figures."

"Why?" Jack says. "What's wrong with Koreans?"

It's explained to him that there's nothing wrong with Koreans, except that they seem to come to Alaska with a sense that if they don't make it all the way to the summit, they will then have to return to Korea disgraced and dishonored. Everybody climbs mountains to push themselves and test themselves, but if you push too hard sometimes you flunk the test. A week before, someone at Fourteen Camp says, a group of Koreans at 18,000 feet pulled out when they all got sick.

"The other problem is," a park ranger standing nearby says, "we just got here, and we're not really acclimated, so we don't have anybody who can go get him. We were actually wondering how you guys felt about that."

There is a French helicopter called a Lama, little more than an aluminum frame and a transmission connecting the motor to the rotors, with a place for the pilot to sit, which is light enough to fly to the summit, but the weather has to be perfect, and today it's too windy. Major storm systems crossing the area can be forecast out of Fairbanks, but the mountain generates its own weather as air masses rise up its slopes and cool to form clouds and wind. According to meteorological records, Mount Washington in New Hampshire, only 6,288 feet high, is supposed to have the worst weather in the world, according to measurements taken at the weather station on the summit, with steady 100 mph winds in the wintertime and a world record wind speed of 231 mph measured on April 12, 1934, but that may only be because there are no meteorological records for Mount McKinley, the tallest peak this close to the Arctic Circle. There's no weather station atop McKinley. Brehm and Kula and the others discuss their options. Possibly somebody already camped at 17,000 feet could bring the stricken climber down, but unless that person has training in rescue techniques, the odds are poor that either the rescuers or the victim will make it, particularly if the weather changes.

"Where is he?" Brehm asks the ranger. The ranger points to a place high atop the headwall.

"Right about there, I'm guessing," the ranger says. "At the top of the fixed line."

"What'd they say the symptoms were?"

"They found him unconscious at eighteen and carried him down to seventeen, I think," the ranger says. "That's all I know. I guess they got him in a tent and a sleeping bag."

"Who brought him down?"

"I don't know."

It sounds to Brehm, though he'll reserve his diagnosis until he sees the patient, like high altitude cerebral edema, or HACE, a swelling of the tissue lining the brain at high altitudes that begins as the worst headache you've ever had in your life and ends in unconsciousness and, if left untreated, death. It happens like this. The body responds to hypoxia, or oxygen starvation, by increasing the blood pressure, which accelerates the release of leukotrienes, which increases arteriolar permeability, allowing the passage of fluids into extravascular locations. In other words, your blood pressure rises so high your blood vessels spring leaks. Strenuous exercise only makes it worse, and climbing is strenuous exercise. A guy goes into his tent to rest and doesn't come out, and at first you think maybe he's just sleeping, so you leave him be, but then you can't wake him, and you pry back his eyelids and see two fixed dilated pupils.

Li'l Orphan Annie eyes, PJs call them.

A similar thing can happen to your lungs when the lack of atmospheric pressure induces a pulmonary edema, a swelling of the lung tissues that expresses itself as short or labored breathing, full of crackles and rales, an abnormally fast heartbeat, possibly blue skin, and a general weakness, lethargy, or disorientation. Climbers, to test for the signs of possible pulmonary edema, frequently cough and spit and check their saliva for signs of blood. Pink spit is not good. Body fluids change color at altitude. If your pee turns bright orange, it means you're dehydrated, a condition that can really sneak up on you, because you forget how dry the air around you is.

Mountaintops are like arctic deserts, with near zero percent humidity, air that sucks the moisture out of you, drying out your lungs, particularly breathing as deep and as fast as you do, even when the wind isn't blowing, and when it is . . .

You don't want to think about when the wind blows, and the wind inevitably blows.

There's really only one way to treat altitude sickness. Get the victim lower. It's sort of like the guy who goes into the doctor and says, "My arm hurts when I do this," and the doctor says, "Well then, don't do that."

"We can go," Skip Kula tells the rangers. It makes perfect sense. They are acclimated, prepared, and they have experience in such matters. It isn't why they're on the mountain, but it would make the climb a bit more interesting, Brehm thinks, though it could mean forgetting any summit attempt for the entire party. They've come prepared for a training mission, not a rescue, and don't have all the equipment they need, but rescue equipment is already in place, stored in a chest at 17,000 feet for just such an emergency. The PJs have a single Saber walkie-talkie with them, a National Guard issue sixteen-channel programmable FM radio. The rangers have handheld walkie-talkies and will be able to maintain radio contact with Brehm's group for as long as the batteries last. Batteries don't last very long in extreme cold. Jack Brehm, Wayt, Lupenski, Lenz, Daigle, Kula, Brooks, Abrams, Blinkhorn, and Chapin get in their tents and try to sleep. They awake at 5:30 A.M., the morning of the twenty-third, and leave Fourteen Camp at 7:00 A.M. hoping to reach the Korean by late afternoon. Wayt and Lupenski leave a half an hour before the others, because they've been leading the way and killing it the whole trip, young and in shape and feeling good. Some guys just take to altitude better than others. And then there are the freaks of nature, the guys who in the parlance are simply "genetic," climbers like Reinhold Messner or the late Alex Lowe, guys who could climb to the summit and back in a day. Wayt and Lupenski aren't genetic. They're just young and in shape and feeling good.

Before leaving that morning, Jack Brehm takes his Gore-Tex and pile hat off and applies a heavy coating of sunblock to his already reddened face and neck, SPF 50. With his fair skin, he has reason to worry about sunburn. Inexperienced climbers wear hats and goggles, but they don't realize how fierce the sun can be at that elevation, and don't take into account the fact that it's going to reflect off the surface of the snow and bounce back at you from all angles, and this with considerably less oxygen between you and the sun to block or filter the ultraviolet rays. People get sunburned inside their nostrils, or on their gums if they're walking along with their mouths open, sucking air. Skip Kula once got sunburned on the roof of his mouth. It's particularly important that Brehm, Wayt, Daigle, and Lupenski keep their hats on because before the climb they all shaved their heads at a party at Mike McManus's house, leaving only Jolly Green Giant footprints above the hairline.

They set off toward the headwall. People in Anchorage are still asleep in their warm beds, or eating cornflakes, watching the *Today* show.

Brehm and Kula reach the unconscious body of Kim Hong Bin around 6:30 P.M. after an exhausting eleven-hour climb that took two hours longer than anticipated, with only a few five-minute breaks. Wayt and Lupenski are waiting at the top, eating, rehydrating, and just resting. Lenz, Abrams, Chapin, and Daigle follow at their own pace and will be there soon. Brooks and Blinkhorn took themselves off the rescue and stayed at Fourteen Camp because they were having physical problems. Brehm finds the tent. Kim is tucked inside a sleeping bag. He has one other Korean with him, a man who speaks a very broken form of English. A quick examination of the Korean confirms Brehm's original diagnosis. Hypothermia and cerebral edema. His pupils are dilated and sluggish and he is unresponsive to stimuli. His pulse is extremely slow, as is his breathing, and his core temperature, taken with a rectal thermometer, is down to about 88 degrees. Whoever placed him in his sleeping bag inexplicably left his arms outside the bag. They are now frozen solid. Kula suspects that the Korean's hands, seriously discolored, have somehow been frozen, thawed, and refrozen, which means he's probably going to lose his hands.

"Do you know what happened?" Kula asks the Korean waiting with Kim Hong Bin.

"No," the second Korean replies.

"Who was climbing with him? Was he with you?"

"No."

"He wasn't with you?"

"Alone. Climbing alone."

"Solo."

"Yes. With a partner."

"He was climbing solo with a partner?"

"Yes. But his partner got sick. He went back."

"And you found him?"

"Excuse me?"

"You found him?"

"No. We give him oxygen."

"That's good."

"I'll ask around," Brehm says, hoping he can find someone who knows more about what happened.

No one at Seventeen Camp has come out of their tents to greet the rescuers, so Brehm goes knocking. Tents become insular fortresses on mountaintops, and people rarely visit each other or interact. The tents at 17,000 are even more insular because you have to dig a deep trench to pitch them in, or else they'll blow away. Standing on the Autobahn, looking down, you could have a hard time seeing the camp, even on a clear sunny day, because the tents are so dug in. Brehm has some luck. A Frenchman from one of the other parties says he believes Kim had been placed in his tent by another group two days earlier. He thinks a couple of expedition guides found the guy up by Denali Pass, dazed and vomiting, with a weak pulse and aching lungs, too sick to move. The Frenchman and members of his group took turns checking on Kim, at least until the other Koreans arrived, but there'd been no change. The fact that Kim's arms were outside his bag when the PJs found him indicates to Brehm that no one looked too closely at the injured climber's condition, but it's been Brehm's experience that people often prefer to close their eyes and hope for the best instead of opening them and learning the worst. A second group of Koreans say they couldn't help their countryman because they have a sick climber of their own to attend to, a man suffering from headaches and periodic unconsciousness—the early stages of cerebral edema. The man is barely conscious, but Brehm manages to administer doses of Decadron, a synthetic adrenocortical steroid, to reduce the swelling, and Diamox, a carbonic anhydrase inhibitor that promotes diuresis and controls fluid secretions.

Four hours later, the man is in better shape.

Unfortunately, Decadron and Diamox are tablets and must be given orally every four hours. They work prophylactically as well, but they won't help somebody who's already unconscious. Even if the other climbers at Seventeen Camp had been able to diagnose what was wrong with Kim Hong Bin, there is little they could have done, and perhaps they knew that the only real treatment is to descend. They could have used their body heat to warm up the Korean, but it's an exchange, and what heat he gains you lose. The rule in such situations seems to be this: You have an obligation to help somebody else who's in trouble if you can, but you're not obliged to put yourself in jeopardy, and it's your call as to exactly what that means. Mountaineers have, of course, second-guessed themselves, and each other, for centuries over such things, asking when it's the right thing to do to help and when it's the wrong thing to do, reliving what they could or should have done after a tragedy. Brehm hasn't come to judge anybody. He also hasn't come to second-guess himself.

"This Frenchman over there thinks the guy's been here for a couple days," Brehm says. As he speaks, it begins to occur to him that he's very tired and still has a long night ahead of him.

"That's what the translator tells me," Kula says.

"He said before the guy passed out, he said his lungs ached, so we might have pulmonary edema on top of whatever else."

"This guy's in rough shape. We need to talk about whether or not we can do this."

"Whether?"

"Not whether—how. Let's see what we've got to work with."

The rescue cache is a six- by four- by two-foot wooden container, painted red with a white cross marked on the top of it. A twelve-foot pole with a red flag on the end of it marks the location, in case the box was to be covered over by blowing snow. Brehm and Kula open the box, which is crammed with 600-foot lengths of perlon climbing rope, each with a tensile strength of 1,800 pounds, as well as carabiners, pickets, and snow anchors, called snow flukes. They find a couple of K bottles of oxygen, a spare tent, spare sleeping bags, and a first-aid kit. The rangers had assured them that there would be enough rope to reach Fourteen Camp. A Cascade litter, essentially a seven-foot-long molded plastic bucket, is roped to the back of the box. Brehm unfastens the litter while Skip sorts through the ropes. Garth Lenz and Steve Daigle and the others arrive.

"What's the situation?" Lenz asks.

"The situation sucks," Kula replies. He radios to the park rangers what they've found.

The ground they stand on is bare, windswept pink granite and hard-packed snow, a treeless expanse about the size of a couple of football fields. Looking down, you can see Fourteen Camp, then endless mountain ranges as far as the eye carries. The view from here is legendary. A wounded climber under his own power might be able to descend the same way he'd come up, but an unconscious man has to go down the hard way, lowered on ropes following a couloir or crease in the headwall, which is partly visible from Fourteen Camp. Jack Brehm begins tying lengths of rope together, using a series of double fisherman's knots, but to do so, he's forced to remove his heavy down-filled mittens, leaving only a thin pair of navy blue polypropylene liners between his bare skin and the wind. His fingers are quickly numb, which slows the knot-tying process. His thought processes slow down as well, something he's aware of but can do nothing about, other than to work carefully and double-check each knot he ties to make sure it will hold. Hypoxia robs a man of his ability to reason, like a computer that's not getting enough juice to drive its programs, and that includes spatial reasoning, such that a knot might look fine from one angle and wrong from another. Brehm works carefully, knowing that a flawed brain is, at some level, incapable of accurately measuring or assessing itself. He's tied knots like this a thousand times and has faith that his hands will remember what to do. He hopes muscle memory is more reliable than mental memory—that's what Mike McManus always taught, the reason he wanted his PJs to jump a hundred parachute jumps, just to establish muscle memory—"Fifty jumps is when you're dangerous, because that's when you start to think you know what you're doing. . . ." Jack wonders what Mike's up to, and whether or not anyone has informed him that a rescue is in progress. *Maybe he's watching television right now, or sipping a hot cup of* . . . Then Jack realizes that his focus is drifting, and he tries to concentrate anew on the tasks at hand.

They establish an equalizing triangular anchor system, using snow flukes, an ice ax, and a rock. Each anchor will bear a third of the load, or about two hundred pounds. In theory, any one anchor should be strong enough to hold, were the other two to give way. From above, two men will hold the rope at all times, lowering it hand over hand, braking with a four-carabiner rig. Two men will go down with the litter and guide it over any potential snags, as well as traversing it around obstacles or crevasses, which will be taxing where gravity prefers to pull things down in a straight line. There will be no way for the men going down with the litter to communicate with the men up top, though conceivably the rangers at Fourteen Camp might be able to spot the litter with their binoculars and radio up progress reports. Going down the headwall with the litter is going to be the hard part. Whoever's in the best shape should go. Skip Kula polls his team members. There's no call in this kind of situation for false bravado— claiming to feel better than you actually do is only going to get everybody

else in bigger trouble. Jack Brehm and Skip Kula have been working fever-
ishly since their arrival and need to recover. Lupenski and Wayt have been
working with them, but they got there first and have had some time to
recover. Abrams, the Brit, and Chapin, the Navy SEAL, shake their heads.

"I'm pretty good," Lenz says.

"I could be better," Daigle says.

"I'm fine," Wayt says.

"Same here," Lupenski answers.

"So we can do this?" Kula asks. "Everybody feels good about it?"

Everyone nods.

Steve Lupenski and Mike Wayt will go down with the litter. They are
strong as bulls, and as fed, rested, and acclimated as anyone within a thousand miles could be. They've also been displaying sound judgment and are
perhaps the most mentally ready members of the group. At this time of
year, light will not be a problem, available twenty-two out of twenty-four
hours a day. Even at the darkest part of the night, the light will still be
greater than a full moon at sea level. Getting him a thousand feet lower
might help the Korean, so it's decided to begin lowering Kim Hong Bin
immediately. Delay could mean death. Left untreated, high-altitude cerebral edema can often proceed with great rapidity, from stupor to coma to
death from massive cerebral hemorrhaging. Hypothermia is an equal danger. Eighty-eight degrees is an extremely low core temperature. Death
from hypothermia works like this: First your peripheral blood vessels con-
strict to prevent the blood from reaching the cooler extremities.
Adrenaline is released. Heart rates and respiratory rates increase. Blood
pressure goes up. The body generates heat from shivering, which can continue until the core temperature drops to about 86 degrees. The shivering
ceases when glucose or glycogen, or the insulin needed for glucose trans-
fer, is no longer available, and there's no fuel left to burn. After the shivering stops, cooling is rapid. Respiration, pulse, and blood pressure
decrease, the blood pH decreases, and electrolyte imbalances occur. The
heart, which is racing, slows down and becomes highly irregular, sputter-
ing and backfiring like some ancient two-stroke lawn mower engine running on fumes. Electrocardiographic changes occur, with, according to the
textbook, "prolonged PR, QRS and QT intervals, obscure or absent P
waves, ST-segment and T-wave abnormalities and J or Osborn waves
present at the junction of the QRS complex and ST segments." In other
words, a last few sparks of the fire that used to be you fly up into the sky,

and then the fire goes out. Cardiac and respiratory arrest occurs at around a core temperature of 68 degrees.

If Kim lost consciousness before reaching the shivering stage, it's possibly a good thing because it might mean his body still has some fuel left. However, moving someone that cold can bring on a heart attack. The sleeping bag and blankets they wrap him in before securing him to the Cascade litter insulate him, but sleeping bags only contain and slow the release of your own body heat. They give heat back to you, but they don't generate it. The way you stay warm in an arctic environment is to work up a sweat, get your body temperature up to 101 or 102 degrees, and then trap that heat in the air around you.

"Hang on a second," Wayt says. "Have we got anything to cover the guy's face?"

"Don't block his airway," Kula says. "Just cinch the bag up good."

The temperature is about zero, not terribly cold. Thirty below zero would be about normal for this elevation at this time of year. Jack Brehm and the others are, however, becoming increasingly concerned with the wind, which has been blowing at 15 to 25 knots during the day but which has now increased to 40 to 60 knots, somewhere on the Beaufort scale between a Force 9 gale and Force 11 violent storm. Any winter activities enthusiast knows that the wind layer of your clothing is as important as the insulting layer, perhaps more important. The First Law of Thermodynamics states that energy cannot be created or destroyed. The Second Law of Thermodynamics states that heat will flow from hot to cold objects. Blowing on a cup of hot coffee cools the coffee by increasing the number of cooler air molecules that come in contact with the warmer coffee molecules. The same thing happens when wind blows across the human body. The irony is that up so high, where there's so little oxygen, so much of it can come at you all at once in the form of wind. A 50-knot wind at sea level feels quite different from a 50-knot wind at 17,000 feet—up that high, it feels dangerous, as if your clothes and your skin don't so much stop the wind as filter it as it blows through you and sucks the heat from your core. Even with 99 percent of your body covered, you know a wind like that stands a good chance of killing you. All you can really do is get out of it.

Brehm feels himself weakening as he fights the desire to become lazy and bug out and let somebody else take over, but for his entire career he's never wanted to be the guy who flagged, the guy who dragged the others down by losing enthusiasm. He has a headache. Thinking is becoming difficult. They've done a major climb in eleven hours and haven't had time to stop and rest once they reached their goal. He's anxious. He wishes the wind wasn't picking up. Feeling the wind gusting, Wayt and Lupenski, wearing only wind shells, polar fleece and polypropylene long underwear, decide to don their down insulating layers, just in case. They expect to zip the guy down in an hour or so and probably won't need the extra layer, but you never know. If you have too much insulation on, and you work up a sweat, you can overheat, even in conditions like this. The down makes them bulkier, but that might make them more comfortable and help pad them, if they ever need to sit on or lean against the irregular ice surfaces of the couloir.

"We're set," Wayt says.

"Steve?" Kula asks.

"Let's do it," Lupenski says, looking in the direction of the wind, which seems to be coming down on them from the top of the mountain.

"Don't eat all the cheeseburgers in Talkeetna—save some for us," Brehm says.

"I want to go, too," the Korean translator says, stepping forward. A new development. Kula assesses the change in plans. It's unlikely that Kim Hong Bin is going to wake up and need translating, but the guy, whatever his name is, seems to be in pretty good shape, and it's really up to him.

"You okay?" Kula says. "Are you rested?"

The translator nods.

"When's the last time you ate?"

"Just eat," the translator says. "Much food."

Kula agrees that he can go, as long as he doesn't get in the way or interfere. The translator nods his head to say he understands. Then he tries to pay Mike Wayt a compliment, and probably means to say something like, "You are very brave," or perhaps, "You are very selfless," but what actually comes out of his mouth is, "You are very handsome."

Wayt doesn't know what to say.

They begin lowering the Korean around eight in the evening, letting out a few feet of rope at regular intervals. Mike Wayt works on the Korean's right side, anchored to the lowering rope, just above where it's tied to the litter, with Lupenski on the Korean's left, tethered to the bottom of the litter. The translator follows on his own. Kim Hong Bin weighs about maybe 140 pounds. After the first 150 feet of rope, the three men are out of sight. For the first thirty minutes, Brehm and Daigle at the belaying station can feel the tug of the weight as it descends, but after a certain point the friction of the rope against the rock face and the play in the perlon fibers makes it harder and harder to tell what's going on, the way fishing with a lot of line makes it harder to tell when you've got a bite. You could lose all or part of your load at the other end and not know it unless you start retrieving line. Muscling the litter back up if something were to go wrong down below isn't really an option.

They drop the litter down about five hundred feet, and then the storm hits. It is perhaps nine o'clock. The wind picks up to 60 or 70 knots, with intermittent white-outs. It's ferociously cold. Anyone who hasn't already donned his down insulating layer does so now. Kula tells the others to set up tents as soon as possible. Chapin and Abrams have been digging in, but they are the least familiar with mountaineering, so Kula reminds them to use common sense and to stake everything down so that it doesn't blow away. He tells Daigle that they're going to need to eat. Daigle says he'll see what they've got. Brehm and Lenz pay out line. In wind this fierce, the temptation is overwhelming just to curl up in a ball and protect yourself. Brehm thinks, *If it's this bad for us, it's got to be worse for the guys down below.*

It is. Wayt and Lupenski have by now pretty much given up on zipping the guy down in an hour. It is grunt work, pure and simple, moving the litter, nudging it this way and that, lifting it over obstacles or stopping it from skidding down too fast, looking below them to check where they place their crampons, occasionally stepping on and harpooning their own pant legs, ripping the fabric, down feathers flying. They use the rope as an anchor, but they don't want to let it bear the entire weight of the patient. When the storm hits them, their situation goes from bad to worse. Hard granular snow is pelting down on them from above, to where they can't look up without getting hit in the face hard with a shovelful of pebbles. As long as the line is being payed out from above, they have no choice but to keep moving. Sometimes the white-out conditions cease, and they can see the camp down below, and the lights and shapes of somebody coming up to meet them below the *bergschrund,* but they still have a long way to go. They are tired. They are not comfortable. They have no choice. They keep going.

"The guy's slipping," Lupenski says.

"I've got him," Wayt says. The translator looks on.

"No—he's slipping inside the litter."

Kim Hong Bin has slumped down inside his plastic sled, turned a bit to the side, and his face is clogging with snow. He needs to be repositioned and adjusted, but it's difficult to work with him while the litter itself is moving. On a true rescue mission, they would have a radio with them to tell the team above to stop lowering for a moment, but they don't, so they improvise. Wayt and the volunteer translator take the weight of the litter and hold it in place while Lupenski sees to the patient. He clears his airway, repositions him and tightens the straps holding him in place, then gives Wayt the thumbs up. The procedure takes no more than five minutes. Wayt is having trouble feeling his fingers. It feels as if the temperature is dropping. They move the patient down another fifty feet or so and then the litter stops. They give the line a tug. They realize that somehow they're at the end of their rope, but they still have a long ways to go. There was supposed to be enough rope to reach the bottom. How many sections had there been in the rescue cache? Two? Three? They can't remember. Were they six hundred feet long, or three? They can see a group below them, a long way off. All they can do is wait, totally exposed, while the storm rages all around them.

Above, Brehm rests while Kula and Lenz pay out line. They keep lowering until they're out of rope. Brehm looks over the edge, even though there's nothing to see. The storm is sapping their strength. Skip Kula tells Chapin and the others to start putting up tents, and to be sure to stake everything down in the wind. Then he calls the park ranger at Fourteen Camp on the radio.

"Have you got 'em?" Kula asks.

"Negative," the ranger replies. "We had 'em for a while but then we lost 'em. It's blowing pretty good."

"Say again?"

"Negative," the ranger below says again. "They were maybe a third of the way down the couloir when we lost 'em."

"You're sure about that?"

"Estimated."

"We're out of rope," Kula says.

"You're still short," the ranger says.

"They have to be farther down than that."

"Well, we don't see 'em," the ranger says. "We've got a party going up to meet 'em—maybe they see 'em."

Kula crosses to Brehm.

"We need more rope!" Kula shouts above the wind.

They tie on three sections of their own personal rope, another 450 feet, but they are still short. Brehm goes from tent to tent to scrounge line. The alternative is to wait another twenty-four hours for somebody to bring rope up from below, and they don't have that much time, not with two of their guys and the Korean clinging to the headwall, exposed to the elements. The problem is that loaning your rope to somebody on a mountaintop is not unlike giving your water to somebody in the desert. It may be the most crucial part of your equipment. Nobody will give you all the rope they have, but people usually bring along spares. Brehm manages to borrow one length from the Frenchman, and another from the Koreans.

"Can you see them?" Kula shouts into the walkie-talkie. The wind is howling. His radio is fading.

"Repeat," the ranger asks.

"Can you see them now?"

"Negative."

Brehm is standing at the belaying station when he looks up and sees what he thinks is a large bird flying overhead. A bird or else some kind of low-flying aircraft. There is a kind of Eurasian crow called the chough that nests on Mount Everest at about 27,000 feet. The Everest crows feed on the garbage left behind by climbers, as well as on carrion—on whatever dies up there, which can include the bodies of unlucky climbers. The chough's favorite part of an unlucky climber is the eyes. Neither birds nor airplanes are likely to be found flying above Mount McKinley, so Brehm is puzzled until he realizes, slowly, forcing himself to accept the idea, that it isn't a bird or an airplane, but rather it's the tent they've been attempting to erect for the last hour, blown clean off the mountain. Jack Chapin, the Navy SEAL, used only a single picket to stake down the tent he was working on, and now it's gone. They have two other tents with them, low-profile models made from heavy nylon for just such environments, but it's taken all their best efforts to put up the first one, and now it's gone. Brehm experiences a sinking feeling, a momentary sense of hopelessness, a feeling that even though he knows what further steps to take, it doesn't matter. It's too late. It hurts to breathe. It hurts to swallow. It hurts to blink. He feels nauseated and weak, and senses that he's getting weaker.

Is this how I'm going to die? Brehm briefly thinks. He just as quickly pushes the idea away, but at the very least he feels certain they are about to change over from rescuers to rescuees. To a PJ, there is no worse feeling than that.

Kula calls a meeting. They've sent all their rope down the mountain. They are exhausted after rising at 5:30 in the morning and laboring non-stop since then. They haven't eaten. It's approaching 11 P.M. Somebody has to go down the rope and find out what's wrong, and perhaps establish a second belaying station from a lower elevation. Another poll is taken. Brehm's fingertips are frostbitten from taking his mittens off to tie the knots. Daigle's still not good, and Chapin and Abrams are inexperienced. It's decided that Garth Lenz will go down to see what the problem is.

"We gotta get warm," Skip says. Until Garth Lenz comes back, there's nothing they can do. All six men turn their full attention to getting out of the cold. Perhaps two hours later, they are inside their shelters, heating water over small propane stoves and mixing it with powdered cocoa. The hot fluids raise their core temperatures, and the food they eat refuels them, Ramen noodles, candy bars, rice with Tabasco sauce in it, butter, and dehydrated carbohydrates. Brehm isn't hungry. In today's fitness-conscious culture, most people think of a calorie as something that makes us fat, but a calorie is a unit of heat, not fat, measuring the amount of energy it takes to raise one cc or milliliter of water one degree centigrade at sea level. In extreme cold, you can think of each calorie you eat as per-haps another couple minutes of life. The best source of calories is fat, which is why scientists working at the poles sometimes gnaw on sticks of pure butter as if they're eating a Slim Jim, and why when a polar bear kills a bearded seal he'll eat the fat and leave the muscle tissue. Part of moun-tain sickness, ironically, includes the loss of appetite, part of the cascade of biological events that makes surviving in extreme cold so difficult. Brehm eats as much as he can force down, and it doesn't taste good, and it doesn't make him feel better, but it's fuel, and he needs fuel.

Before getting into his sleeping bag, Brehm takes his first Diamox tablet. His skull pounds. He tries to think back to the moment when he thought, *Is this how I'm going to die?* Had he felt afraid? Sad? Disappointed? He can't remember anymore. The moment has passed. The wind has blown the memory away, and that's just as well.

Down below, Mike Wayt looks up and sees a tent blowing away in the wind, and his first thought is that somebody must be in it. The wind is blowing hard enough to do that, but the tent drifts out and floats down too slowly for there to be somebody in it. He's not thinking clearly, and he knows it. He also knows they haven't moved in over an hour, and they can't stay where they are. He's exhausted. So is Lupenski. They talk over their situation. The translator looks on. He probably isn't understanding much of what's being said. They decide that Lupenski will climb down to meet the group coming up from below and borrow some rope from them. Wayt and the translator will stay with the litter.

Lupenski moves off to the right, maneuvering around the *bergschrund*. There may well be crevasses covered over with snow that he risks falling into. No one can guess anymore what time it is or how long they've been there. The wind gusts to 80 knots. Wayt watches Lupenski go. He looks up the mountain, where Garth Lenz is descending the rope into a field of *sastrugi* ice. Lenz sees a snag in the line where the rope is coiled up in the rough ice. He has no idea what the situation is down below, but he can see what the problem is here. He frees the line with his ice ax.

Below, the litter goes into sudden rapid free fall. Wayt doesn't know what's happening. The Korean translator is standing below the litter and manages to grab it. Wayt tries to hang on and stop it from falling. He digs his crampons into the ice, but it's no good. They skid down a hundred feet, gaining speed. The translator digs in, and Wayt digs in even harder, because he knows if it goes any faster, they'll never stop it, and if it goes, he goes. Wayt wrestles the litter to a stop and holds it there. The translator trades places with him as Wayt drives his ax into the ice at the bottom of the litter, swinging with all his might. The line above him "esses" down on top of him. What happened? Where is it all coming from?

He calls out for help. He doesn't remember screaming, but perhaps he did. Lupenski returns to the litter and drives his ice ax into the mountain to help secure the package. They pound pickets in and fasten the litter to the pickets with carabiners. Wayt gasps for air, exhausted, still gripping the litter with all his might. Lupenski tells him he can let go.

They reassess their new position. They're off course now, with a large crevasse directly below them. They are getting frostbitten, feeling nauseated, confused, and bone-tired, wobbly legged. They need to rest. The storm hasn't let up. The patient has to be getting worse. Time is running out on him. They pause to regain their strength, but it's waning. Gravity wants to pull the Cascade litter into the crevasse. Wayt and Lupenski use their ice axes as anchors to establish a new belaying station and begin to move the litter sideways, swinging it pendulum-fashion. Lenz reaches them two hours later, about the same time that Roger Robinson, the park ranger, climbs up from below. Then the rest of the group from Fourteen Camp, mostly guides and experienced climbers, reaches them and Mike Wayt and Steve Lupenski finally get a chance to sit. They are utterly exhausted, hands trembling, almost punch drunk and zombified. When

Wayt tries to tell Roger Robinson how tired he is, he overhears one of the others say, in what seems to be disdain, "Yeah, well, we're all tired."

Wayt doesn't have the strength to get up and punch him out, so he can only stare at the guy. He's given everything he has, and this guy wants more?

"We got 'em," Fourteen Camp radios to Skip Kula, about seven the next morning. Nearly twelve hours have passed since the rescue began.

"Say again?" Kula radios back.

"They're good—they made it in," the ranger says, just as Kula's radio goes dead, but that's all Kula needs to know. The weather has cleared. Jack Brehm looks down. He figures the storm must have raged for six or seven hours. At eight, an HH-60 Pavehawk helicopter from the 210th Air National Guard base arrives to ferry Kim Hong Bin to the hospital in Anchorage. From Seventeen Camp, Skip Kula, Jack Chapin, Jack Brehm, Brian Abrams, and Steve Daigle watch in awe as the helicopter lands and takes off below them from 14,000 feet. As far as they know, this is the highest evacuation an HH-60 has ever made. The air is so thin that it seems to take forever for the helicopter to lift off, rotors spinning at top speed for quite some time before the Pavehawk's skids break free from the mountain, giving the appearance that gravity is somehow extra strong today, which is pretty much how everybody at 17,000 feet feels.

Brehm and the others return the borrowed rope, coil up the emergency lines and put them back in the rescue cache, then return to their tents, warming themselves with hot cocoa and noshing down more candy and Ramen noodles and rice with Tabasco sauce on it. Where are Girl Scouts selling cookies when you really need them? They figure they'll see Steve and Mike back in Talkeetna, the closest town to Denali, unless of course they opted to ride the helicopter all the way back to Anchorage. After what they've been through, no one would blame them. May 24 is spent recovering. Brehm fails to even make a diary entry for that day.

Those who'd stayed at 17,000 feet now need to reach the summit. It's called Summit Fever, and it could be the number one cause of death on mountaintops, even though it's not a real disease, not in the medical sense anyway. You've come all this way, probably spent all the money you have and borrowed more to get to the mountain, spent hours upon hours training, pissed off or worried to death half the people who love you, but who you know are nevertheless rooting for you and would share your disappointment if you were to fail. Climbers face up to their physical limitations and fall short all the time, but they also push themselves further than they've ever pushed themselves before because of Summit Fever.

The round trip from 17,000 feet camp to the summit is relatively easy, but you still have to cross snowfields and rugged terrain and a landscape broad enough that you can easily get lost, which is why no one is permitted to summit unless accompanied by someone who's been there before and knows the way. Some parties leave a trail of green bamboo tomato stakes or wands jammed into the snow to mark the way back, but it can still snow hard enough to cover your trail. You travel light and leave behind anything you think you won't need. The sky is clear on May 25, the temperature a balmy zero degrees, winds still blowing between 40 and 60 knots. The remaining rescuers take the Autobahn to Denali Pass, cross the Football Field and make it to the peak at 5:30 P.M., feeling satisfied but not exhilarated. They're glad to summit, but it's a better feeling to know that Steve and Mike and the Korean are down. Besides, once you're on top of a mountain, there's really not much you can do except have your picture taken, catch your breath, drink some water, and start down. It's getting there that's important, not being there. After months of preparation and nervous anticipation, and thirteen days of climbing, they spend a mere ten minutes at the top. Brehm feels the way he sometimes feels at the end of a marathon, an almost religious sense of wonder, apart from any physical weariness or mental exhaustion, at what God has allowed him to accomplish. Briefly, he thinks of Carl Waage, back home in a hospital bed, breaking in a new set of lungs, and offers up a prayer for Carl's speedy recovery. If the theories are correct, prayers offered from 17,000 feet ought to reach their destination quicker than prayers from sea level.

They head down at 5:40 and make it back to their tents at Seventeen Camp by 8 P.M. To their amazement, Mike Wayt and Steve Lupenski are waiting for them.

"What the hell are you doing here?" is all Brehm can say to his old friend Steve.

"What do you think we're doing here?" Steve Lupenski says. "We came here to summit."

Brehm can only admire their determination, not to mention their stamina. Anybody else would have called it a day after hanging on to the side of a mountain for eleven hours.

"What do you mean 'we'?" Chapin says. "My feet look like chopped sirloin."

"We'll go alone then," Wayt says, determined. He doesn't feel one hundred percent, and neither does Steve, but given the shape they were in when they started, they figure 80 percent of a PJ is equal to a hundred percent of anybody else. Skip Kula shakes his head. The rule is, nobody goes to the summit unless accompanied by somebody who's been there before. Brehm knows how disappointed Wayt and Lupenski will be if they don't summit, and he knows that after what they've done, they deserve some kind of reward. It also occurs to him that it would be kind of cool to be able to say he summited Denali twice in two days.

"I'll go with them," Brehm says. "I know the way."

"You sure?"

"I'm sure."

They all spend the night together at 17,000 feet, and at 11:30 the next morning Brehm, Lupenski, and Wayt depart. The weather is clear, and when the sun rises in the sky it gets so warm, perhaps in the mid to high twenties, that Jack and Steve take off their Gore-Tex anoraks and, from the waist up, wear only their underwear. It soon becomes evident that something is wrong with Mike. He isn't saying anything, but he's moving way too slowly, out front, because whoever is moving the slowest goes first. It's even odder because for the whole trip, he's been the one leading the charge. By midafternoon his steps are barely a shuffle, moving him eight inches ahead with each stride, if you could still call them strides. He's resting every five steps, and he appears to be feeling the cold, dressed in full weather gear, though Jack and Steve are overheated. As Mike moves on ahead, Brehm, who is second, stops and waits for Lupenski to catch up to him. It's 2:00 P.M. and they've reached the 19,000-foot mark.

"What do you think?" he says quietly. Lupenski knows what he's referring to.

"What do *you* think?"

"You know him better than I do," Brehm says, "but I don't think he can do it."

"I think maybe you're right," Lupenski says. "He looks like he might be cramping."

"We could hang out for a while and see if he gets better, but we might not make the summit if we do." Brehm calculates that at the rate they're moving, the peak is perhaps another five hours ahead.

"We should turn back."

"You want me to tell him?" Brehm offers. "I'll do it if you want me to."

"I'll tell him," Lupenski says, volunteering for a task nobody relishes. "He's my friend." Brehm watches as Lupenski walks ahead and has a word with Mike. Wayt only listens and nods, and then, without saying a word, he turns around and heads down the mountain, trudging right past Brehm without looking at him. When Lupenski catches up, Jack asks him what he said.

"I told him *I* couldn't make it," Lupenski says.

It's brilliant thinking, particularly when you consider how hard it is to be brilliant at this altitude—better to take the blame himself than make his friend feel as though he was to blame for not making it to the summit. Climbing is something you do as a team, and no one wants to think he let his team down. It's also true that pararescuemen may be among the most competitive sons-of-bitches on the planet, challenging one another on everything from climbing a mountain to eating hamburgers. Mike Wayt doesn't want to go back, but it's the right decision.

As they descend, Mike Wayt doesn't get any better. This is odd. He keeps sitting down in the snow, then getting up, never saying anything about it when he does, and when they ask him how he is, he only grunts. Something seems to be wrong with his stomach, but when they ask him if he's cramping, he shakes his head. They trudge on, and then, at about 4:00 P.M., at about the point where the Autobahn begins, they hit a white-out, a weather system with the upper limit so sharply defined that it seems like they're walking into an opaque lake, or a flowing ocean of milk. Now the cloud cover is at your nose. Two steps forward, you're in over your head and you can't see a thing. Two steps back, the sky is blue again. Roped together, they take their bearings as best they can and head down into the white-out. They locate three tomato stakes somebody left and follow the line, but the fourth stake is missing, and the fifth, and then they don't know where they are. Brehm checks his watch. They wander for two and a half hours, not covering much ground due to Wayt's slowness. The terrain more or less funnels you in the right direction, but if you go too far off line, you can easily fall a thousand feet. Sometimes visibility is perhaps sixty or seventy feet, but most of the time it's less than ten. The whiteness gets to you, too, a disorienting lack of definition to everything, without any frame of reference to tell you not just where you are but who you are. It's also troubling to know that they could walk right past their target, miss it, and keep going. For a while, moving forward and down makes sense, but after a while, moving back, and up, or left, or right, all makes the same amount of sense. What if the tent camp they're looking for is covered with snow? By 6:30, Brehm decides it's futile. He discusses it with the others. They will dig down into the snow, huddle together, and try to wait the weather out. There's a chance the decision could prove fatal, but it seems the best option. They're beginning to dig in when Brehm sees a guy in the distance. Moving closer to him, they hear nylon tents whipping in the wind. The guy, it turns out, is taking a leak. You pee a lot in extreme cold, because your body has better things to do than keep a bladder full of urine warm.

"Hey," the Peeing Man says. "Are you the PJs who rescued the Korean? It figures only maniacs like you would be out in this shit."

Brehm and the others grunt in acknowledgment. The Peeing Man has, in a way, rescued them, but there's really no point telling him that. It turns out they were lost less than a hundred yards from their tent.

Mike Wayt has little to eat at Seventeen Camp. They wait two days for the weather to clear. The wind whips across their tent at 70 or 80 knots. Steve is beat. Mike is hurting and can't eat. Jack Brehm cooks food, and boils water, and spends long periods of time describing, in exquisite detail, all the kinds of food they're going to eat when they get down, thick juicy cheeseburgers with slabs of raw onion and fresh lettuce and tomatoes on a toasted bun, slathered with melted butter and mayonnaise and mustard and ketchup. . . . He stays crisp and motivated, and the others appreciate it, and draw strength from him. At 8:00 P.M. the evening of the second day, the wind slows, so they head down. Brehm's diary notes: *Winds stayed at 30 kts but it is still pretty shaky on the ridge going to the headwall. It took forever to descend the fixed line. Arrived camp 0030, 28 May '91. Made hot chocolate and went to bed. Four nights is too long to spend at 17,000 for anyone.*

They leave Fourteen Camp at 12:30 on the twenty-ninth but hit another white-out at 11,000 feet, stopping at 8,000 feet around 6:30 P.M. An HH-60 flies to the Kahiltna Glacier and picks them up, piloted by Steve Lupenski's brother Al, on the thirtieth at eleven in the morning and flies them to Talkeetna. On the tarmac at the Talkeetna Airport, the group assembles for a team picture. The picture is taken. Mike Wayt tries to smile. He's glad to be down from the mountain, and he hoped this would make him feel better, but it doesn't. He looks around him, at the piles of snow plowed to the edges of the runways, the signs for Hudson Av-Gas, Doug Geeting Aviation, and McKinley Flight Tours, and then it all starts to spin, and he feels as if he's been punched in the gut as he doubles over and falls to the ground. He's flown immediately to Elmendorf Hospital in Anchorage.

The final entry in Jack Brehm's diary is simply the word *BEER*. The exhilaration of coming down off a climb is both psychological and biological: psychological because you can simply feel good for having accomplished a difficult task, biological because your body is no longer under stress and you have residual levels of adrenaline and endorphins in your blood, not to mention the extra red blood cells. You also get to shower and shave for the first time in three or four weeks.

There are several bars on Talkeetna's main drag. They hole up in a place called the Fairview Inn, a historic tavern that's been there since 1923. It has white siding and a tin roof and all anybody really cares about is that the beer is cold. The team needs to do some serious decompressing, but everyone is concerned for Mike Wayt. Somebody calls the hospital and finally learns the diagnosis—he has a bleeding ulcer.

"How could he have a bleeding ulcer?" Daigle asks. They all had complete physicals before going on the climb and would have known if anybody had a bleeding ulcer. "Doesn't that take a long time to develop?"

"Has he been under a lot of stress lately?"

"He's got a new house and a new kid, but I don't think that would do it."

Someone says they heard that sometimes people who experience sheer terror for an extended period of time secrete enough stomach acids to cause bleeding ulcers in a matter of hours.

"How about the Korean?"

"He's okay. He's going to make it."

Lupenski raises his beer bottle in the air.

"To Mikey," he says.

"To Mikey," the rest join in.

At the hospital in Anchorage, Wayt is examined. The doctors find that the pyloric channel that links the small intestine to the stomach has perforated the peritoneal lining of his stomach. The layman's assessment is he busted a gut saving another man's life. When they operate, they remove a foot-long section of his small intestine. The operation is successful, but it will be two years before Wayt's insides feel right again, and five years before he can go for a run without stopping to find a bathroom every five minutes.

That night, lying in bed at the Swiss Alaska Motel, one of Talkeetna's finest, which is not saying a whole lot, Brehm holds the remote control and surfs between channels 2, 11, and 15, picking up bits of a rebroadcast of *M*A*S*H* and the sixth game of the NBA Western Conference finals between the Lakers and the Trailblazers, but the hotel's transponder works only sporadically. Brehm turns the television off and calls Peggy. He relates the whole trip for her, and they talk for over an hour. When he's finished, he says, "Tell Carl that when we're sitting on his porch drinking beers, I'm going to have a good story for him."

"John," Peggy says, "I've got bad news about Carl. He didn't make it."

"When?"

"A week ago. Eight days ago," she corrects herself. "I'm sorry."

As he falls asleep, he thinks that Carl Waage had a great life. He wonders if he appreciated it. Does anybody really appreciate it? He thinks of the view from 17,000 feet, and how the cheeseburger and Coke he ate at the Fairview Inn was the best food he's ever had in his life, and he thinks of Mike Wayt's courage.

12

THE NIGHT THE WIND BLEW

I have no interest in climbing Mount Everest, though I think I could probably do it. But to spend all that time and effort, just to stand at a very high place and hold a flag and have your picture taken? Knowing the risks involved, it sounds pretty stupid to me. Climbing Everest, you know you're rolling the dice on your health, with something like a 60 percent chance of coming back personally injured. In pararescue, you enjoy what you do, diving and jumping and what have you, but you always know you're doing it for a higher purpose than your own personal enjoyment. Sometimes when the daily routine gets to you, because you've had a lot of long boring days in a row doing nothing, sitting around the section waiting for the phone to ring, maybe then you forget what you're doing it for, but not when you're training. You're doing it for other people. Even when you think about dying, I think every PJ eventually asks himself not "Am I going to die in the line of duty?" but "How do I want to die?" And I think every PJ feels like if he's got to die, and he does, he wants to die trying to help somebody.

B Y THE END OF OCTOBER 1991, THE FROSTBITE, WHICH HAD darkened Jack Brehm's fingertips after he returned from Mount McKinley, was all but gone. It hurt to dip them in hot or cold water, so doing the dishes or holding a beer could be painful. In regard to the latter, his high tolerance for pain proved useful. It was a gorgeous autumn, the leaves resplendently afire on the hillsides and in the backyards of eastern Long Island. Jack had never missed a Halloween night trick-or-treating with the kids. The morning before Halloween, October 30, Peggy was trying to pin everybody down at breakfast as to what costumes they wanted her to make for them, but so far the only one who knew was Jeffrey, who wanted to be a witch, which meant, Peggy gathered, a black cape of some sort. Matt and Laura-Jean were still undecided. The twins were in sixth grade, and old enough now, they argued, to be allowed to skip canvassing the neighborhood for treats with the rest of the family. Tomorrow night, Elizabeth was going to a sleepover Halloween party at her best friend Emily's house in Sound Beach, one town west of Rocky Point, and was excited about helping Emily plan a scavenger hunt in the neighborhood. Emily wanted to rent a Stephen King movie. Elizabeth didn't like scary movies, didn't like being scared in general, but knew she'd probably be outvoted by the other kids at the party.

Jack got to the base at 7:30 A.M. on the thirtieth. The National Weather Service had issued a coastal flood warning the night before, predicting tides two to three feet above normal, and Nantucket had reported sustained winds of over 45 knots. At 9:05, the Coast Guard's first District Operations Center in Boston had requested assistance from the 106th in searching for a surf caster who'd disappeared off Point Judith, Rhode Island, swept from the rocks after apparently ignoring the coastal flood warnings. A C-130 was launched to look for him. The Coast Guard's Operations Center in Boston also asked, approximately one hour after the call about the fisherman, if the 106th could respond to an EPIRB, or Emergency Position Indicating Radio Beacon, coming from something in the water at 38°32'N and 69°13'W, about 180 miles south of Nantucket. By noon, there was still no word on what the SOS beacon meant. A weather system of some sort appeared to be forming far offshore, but it was moving south and west instead of north and east, the way a hurricane ordinarily moves. Because of it, at 1:00 P.M., an HH-60 crew was put on alert. The PJ section was calm, and outside the skies were blue and the air was warm. Everything seemed to be under control, so around two, Brehm decided to go for a run to the beach and back, a distance of about six miles. It was warm enough that he wore only a T-shirt. The ocean looked rough, with five- to six-foot swells, but nothing outrageous. No one at the 106th knew yet that at 38°32'N and 69°13'W, a 30-foot sailboat, the *Bazaro*, occupied by a lone forty-five-year-old Japanese yachtsman named Mikado Tomizawa, sailing from New York to Bermuda, was foundering in 35-foot seas, taking on water, while the weather around him worsened. No one knew yet that this was the beginning of what would become the "Storm of the Century," written about in Sebastian Junger's *The Perfect Storm*.

As Brehm jogged, a Coast Guard C-130 reached the *Bazaro*. When they did, Tomizawa radioed to them that he was going down. At 2:50 P.M., the 106th was asked to proceed to 37°52'N and 68°44'W, the *Bazaro* having drifted fifty miles since that morning's SARSAT fix, the location determined by the search and rescue satellite that picked up the emergency signal. By 3 P.M., the helicopter pilot for the mission, veteran (and former PJ) CAPT Dave Ruvola, thirty-four, was meeting in the briefing room in the Ops building with his copilot, CAPT Gram Buschor, LTCOL Bob Stack, the C-130 pilot, and the C-130's navigator, all going over aeronautical charts and weather reports. The Coast Guard C-130 on the scene reported a visibility of one and a half miles, winds from the northwest at 22 knots, and 25- to 35-foot seas. Ruvola and Buschor agreed that the HH-60 would need to make four midair refuelings, two going out and two coming back. There were two PJs on the schedule to be on alert that day, Jack's friend John Spillane, thirty-four, and a thirty-two-year-old tech sergeant named Arden "Rick" Smith. Smith was one of the last PJs McManus hired, a truly solid guy and one of Jack's favorites. Jack had flown a mission with him back in October of 1989, when, on the evening of the seventeenth, an earthquake registering 7.0 on the Richter scale rolled the city of San Francisco. PJs from Moffett AFB, outside of Palo Alto, including Jack's old classmate Joe Higgins, were on the scene immediately, searching the collapsed wreckage of buildings and highway bridges for survivors, despite fears of aftershocks. Jack and Rick flew to California the next day in a C-130 to assist in the rescue effort, at the request of RCC at Scott, only to be told ten minutes prior to landing that the request had been canceled. They weren't sure what the confusion was all about, but apparently it had something to do with the State of California wanting to prove it could handle its own emergencies using only state personnel. Whatever the reason, the C-130 from the 106th needed to have some mechanical work done before it could return to base, so Brehm and Rick Smith made the best of it and drove to Lake Tahoe to play blackjack. When they finally flew home, they were met at the base by a local television news crew doing a story on the dramatic return of the heroic earthquake rescue team. Jack saw the news crew's truck parked on the tarmac as they landed. He and Rick talked it over and decided the simplest thing to do would be to refuse all interviews. The local media saw their reticence as an expression of selfless heroism.

Spillane and Smith were in the Life Support section, gathering up the gear they were going to need, when Jack came in from his run. Their gear included cold-water orange Mustang immersion suits, quarter-inch wet suits, LPUs, and survival vests carrying signal mirrors, PRC-90 radios, MK-13 flares, pen gun flares, strobe lights, and survival knives.

"What's up?" Brehm asked.

"Got a mission," Spillane said, filling Jack in and explaining that a Japanese sailor, sailing solo around the world, apparently wanted off his boat. Rick Smith let Spillane do all the talking, Smith being a quiet man who tended to choose his words carefully. Brehm was happy for both of them, because you live for the missions, and even a bit disappointed that he'd been out running and couldn't take the mission himself. It's the NCOIC's job to decide who takes the missions as they come up, according to who's available and who's mission-ready, current with all his qualifications. Spillane and Smith were two of the best he had to send, and it sounded like a gravy mission. It was also going to be their first save using the new HH-60 aircraft, after switching over from the old HH-3s.

"I'll drive you to the AC," Brehm said. It's only about four hundred yards from the Operational Dispatch Center to the helicopter pods, but they needed to make haste, both because the *Bazaro* was foundering and because they wanted to be on site before the sun went down. The blades of the HH-60 Jolly 10 (with the number 110 painted on the side) were already turning when they got there. A C-130 with the number AFR 988 on the tail was taxiing to the runway. The other three C-130s assigned to the wing were down for maintenance. Dave Ruvola was the pilot. Gram Buschor was the copilot. The flight engineer was a Guardsman from New Jersey named Jim Mioli.

"You boys have a good one," Brehm said, shaking hands with his PJs before they left. "I'll see you when you get back."

The two aircraft launched around 3:30, and for the next three hours, the pilot of Air Force Rescue 988 radioed back progress reports, which were noted in the daily log. At 4:25, the tanker passed 700 pounds of fuel to the HH-60, Ruvola making contact with the drogue on the first attempt. Sunset that day came at 4:47 P.M., EST. At 5:00, Jolly 10 took on 900 more pounds to top off its tanks, expecting to be on the scene in another twenty minutes. During the second air refueling, it took Ruvola several tries to hit the drogue, due to increased turbulence. After the refueling, AFR 988 flew on ahead to help relocate the sailboat. The Coast Guard C-130 lost visual contact with it, in seas that had risen to between forty and fifty feet. When the 106th's tanker spotted the sailboat, they dropped MK-6 smoke markers, which Ruvola was able to vector in on, reaching the boat around 6:00. Ruvola and his crew spent the next twenty-five minutes trying to figure out a way to pull Tomizawa off his boat, but the weather was simply too fierce. There was a possibility that they might have to abort. It was a difficult decision, in part because the 106th had yet to abort a mission due to weather, after arriving on site, and in the larger part because the decision posed a potential death sentence for Tomizawa. Hovering directly over the *Bazaro*, Ruvola glanced at his forward airspeed indicator, which told him he was flying in winds gusting from forty to eighty knots, or nearly one hundred miles per hour. The varying wind speeds required him to constantly adjust his power and angle of attack. On two occasions, Spillane, looking out the port-side gunner's window, had to shout to Ruvola to pull up on the collective and put more distance between the helicopter and waves cresting nearly to the Jolly 10's landing gear. Jim Mioli, the flight engineer, looked below and saw waves rising and falling higher and faster than he'd be able to compensate for, even with his hoist operating at high speed, presenting the danger of having slack in the cable with men on the penetrator. Anyone getting a finger or limb caught in a loop in the slack would probably lose the finger or limb. The light was nearly gone. When Mioli told Ruvola he'd be unable to hoist, Ruvola aborted the mission. The *Bazaro* appeared to be riding fairly well in the monstrous seas; Tomizawa was perhaps not in as much danger as he thought, so the C-130 crew dropped him an MA-1 kit, containing a pair of lift rafts and survival supplies, and radioed to Westhampton, at 7:10 P.M., that they'd topped off the Jolly's tanks with their third air refueling and were returning to base. At 7:30, LTC Stack radioed the base for a weather update and was told he could expect an 8,000-foot ceiling with fifteen miles of visibility and low-level wind shear. At virtually the same time, McGuire AFB, just south of Trenton, New Jersey, was receiving weather satellite data indicating that a rain band was forming off the southern shore of Long Island, a finger of the spiraling storm fifty miles wide, eighty miles long, and ten thousand feet thick, rain so dense as to afford zero visibility.

The daily log notes that as they returned to base Spillane and Smith were both granted an extension of CDT, or crew duty time, since it looked as if the mission was going to keep them out longer than a normal crew duty day. The mission status was Ops normal, RTB. With both aircraft returning to base, Brehm's day was done. It was after eight. Before he went home, he drove the PJ truck to Whitney's Deli, about a mile from the gate, across the street from the Matchbox, and bought a six-pack of Budweiser, Rick Smith's beer of choice. Brehm left the truck parked at the helicopter pod, with the six-pack sitting on the seat, and walked back to his car.

When Jack got home, about 9:00, Peggy had just put the twins to bed. Matt, Bean, and Jeffrey had gone down long before. Peggy was making Jeffrey's costume, sewing him a black cape, and told Jack there were leftovers from dinner that he could reheat in the microwave if he was hungry. He was about to do so when the phone rang. It was Mickey's wife, Laura, who was beside herself.

"I just called the base," Laura said, "and they hung up on me. I was asking them when they thought John was coming home and they just hung up on me."

"Who were you talking to?" Jack asked.

"I don't know."

"Laura," Jack said, "just hang on a second and I'll call the base and find out what's going on and then I'll call you back, okay?"

"I mean I know it's probably nothing."

"I'm sure everything's fine. Let me just call them and check it out. I'll call you right back. Sit tight."

Brehm called the base and explained that somebody just hung up on Laura Spillane, and that she was upset about it. When he learned the reason why, his expression changed.

"What?" Peggy said. "What is it?"

"The guy had a Mayday coming in when Laura called," Jack said.

"Why a Mayday?"

"They're ditching the helicopter," Jack said.

* * * * * * * *

In a pararescue unit, a crisis affecting one PJ affects all the other PJs, and their wives and families. When their husbands are gone on a mission, the wives depend on each other in much the same way that their husbands depend on each other. They help each other with car pools and child care. They get together socially and share their worries. They see each other at functions at the base, and at barbecues and pool parties in each other's backyards, and they often wait together at airports, or in hospitals, at awards ceremonies or memorial services. Friendships between wives sometimes outlast their marriages. Being there for each other in times of crisis is something nobody ever has to question—it's a given.

Peggy immediately calls Barbara Dougherty to say they have to get over to Laura Spillane's house. There's trouble on a mission, she says, a helicopter going down, somewhere far out at sea. No, she doesn't know why.

Yes, Mickey is on the helicopter. So is Rick Smith. Somebody should call his wife, Marianne. But somebody from the base should call her first, somebody with more information. Barbara says she needs somebody to baby-sit her kids. Jimmy is three and a half, Diana is two, and Bobby is eleven months. Michele is their regular baby-sitter, so Peggy says she'll wake her daughters up. Both girls are groggy at first.

"Michele, you're going over to Aunt Barbara's to baby-sit. Elizabeth, I need you to stay here and watch the others. I'm going to call and get somebody to come sit with you, but until I do, you're in charge."

The girls think of the other PJs at the base as uncles, and their wives as aunts, particularly the Doughertys and the Spillanes.

"Can you call Carla?" Elizabeth says. Carla Waage is her favorite sitter, their next-door neighbor.

"I'll get either her or Grandma—you want to call Carla? Go ahead and call her."

"How late are you going to be?" Michele asks, putting a raincoat on over her pajamas. Neither she nor Elizabeth have ever seen their mother this frightened before. That scares them, more than anything else. Peggy knows this, and tries to stay level and calm. "Is Dad okay?"

"Your father is fine—he just left for the base. There's been an accident out at sea, and he had to go back. I have to go to Aunt Laura's."

Rain is beating against the windows. Elizabeth looks out at the trees in the front yard, whipping back and forth in the wind like a cheerleader's pom-poms. *Something is happening at sea? What? A plane crash? A sinking ship? Someone is in trouble. Will Dad have to fly out in weather like this? This is bad. This is really bad.*

Jack is in Jimmy Dougherty's truck, the two men racing back to the base. As Jimmy drives, Jack calls Laura Spillane on Jimmy's cell phone. The windshield wipers are beating at full speed, but even then sometimes it's hard to see the road. Before he dials, Brehm tries to think of what to say. This is going to be rough on her. She's five months pregnant, too. They've been friends for years, and she needs to hear the straight truth.

"Laura, it's Jack," he says. "Listen—I'm sorry I couldn't call you before now—I'm in the car with Jimmy and we're headed back to the base. The guy said hanging up on you wasn't intentional and he's sorry, but that's what I'm calling about, because there's been an accident, okay?" He wishes he'd put it differently. He wishes he had more information. "It's not an accident, actually, but something is wrong with the AC and they're going to ditch." He hears Laura gasp. "It's not a crash, Laura—it's a controlled ditch. They're doing it on purpose. It's not like they're out of control."

"Why?" she asks. He wishes he knew the answer to that.

"Probably mechanical failure," he tells her. "We don't know. This is what we practice in the dunk tank down at Virginia Beach."

"Where are they?" she asks.

"I can't answer that. I mean, I would if I could, but I don't know the answer. I don't think they're very far out. They were within one refueling of the base, somewhere south. I'll be able to learn more when I get to the base. I imagine they're getting another bird ready to go as we speak, so Jimmy and I can fly out and pick them up. They've all got survival suits and they've trained for this. Has Peg called?"

"Not yet."

"Well, she will. She's picking up Barbara and then they'll be over. You guys wait by the phone, and I'll call you as soon as I learn anything. And if I have to fly I'll let you know, and then I'll have somebody else call you. So sit tight and hang on. Okay? He's going to be all right."

They both know Jack has to say the words "He's going to be all right," and they both know Jack is not in any position to make any guarantees.

At sea, Dave Ruvola is finding it impossible to hit the drogue with his probe to effect refueling. He's been trying since 8:00. On an ordinary night, in calm air, a circular parachute around the drogue stabilizes it, and a probe light throws a shadow that allows the pilot to center the shadow on the drogue and fly forward into it. Tonight the drogue flails wildly about in the turbulence. Ruvola is afraid the probe could hit one of his rotors. His aircraft is being buffeted around so severely he's afraid he's going to hit the tail of the C-130. Much of the time, he can't even see the drogue in the blinding rain. Much of the time, he can't even see the airplane. Ruvola is wearing NVGs, night vision goggles, a device that electronically amplifies available light. The light enters through a lens and strikes a highly charged photo cathode, which then transfers the charge across a vacuum to a phosphor screen, something like a television screen, where the image is focused, and then the eyepiece magnifies the image. The image is green because the human eye can differentiate more shades of green than other phosphor colors. Night vision goggles are so effective that if you were to put them on in a pitch-black room in your basement, a room so dark you can't see your hand five inches in front of your face, you could not only see your hand, but you could read your palm. On an ordinary night in calm air a helicopter pilot will request that the tanker turn off all its lights during midair refueling, because with night vision goggles on the lights overload the goggles. Tonight, Ruvola asks Stack to turn all his lights on, and he still can't see them, flying less than a hundred feet behind the tanker. There's that much rain. Ruvola and the tanker change altitude several times, looking for better air, but the rain band is almost two miles thick. Ruvola doesn't dare fly any lower than three hundred feet. At 9:10, flying at four thousand feet, and after thirty or forty unsuccessful attempts to refuel, the pilot of Jolly 10 decides he can either make two or three more attempts to hit the drogue, or he can avoid running out of gas and falling out of the sky like a rock by putting his helicopter, as gently as possible, into an ocean that is anything but gentle. There are no parachutes on the helicopter, and bailing out would not be the best option anyway, since it would scatter everyone to the winds. The best option is to let the crew jump out ten feet above the waves. At 9:15, Ruvola tells the tanker to tell the base he's beginning his ditch sequence. His current position is 39°37′W and 71°38′N, about sixty miles southeast of Westhampton, and over twice that from where they left the *Bazaro*. The C-130, itself low on gas, will stay on the scene for as long as it can.

Peggy Brehm and Barbara Dougherty find Laura Spillane in her bathrobe, her distended belly protruding beneath the belt. After hugs, the questions fly. Have you heard anything? Who's called? Who have you called? Who was on the helicopter? Has anyone called Marianne Smith? Carmen Ruvola? Ann Buschor—does anybody know her well? Her husband, the copilot, is new to the unit, so the PJ wives don't know him or his wife as well as they know the others. Somebody who knows her should call. Jim Mioli is single—is there anybody they should contact? Laura is reluctant to tie up the phone, because she doesn't want to miss Jack's call, but she quickly dials Mickey's brothers, and gets her mom on the phone after that. They call the other PJ wives, and everybody exchanges phone numbers. In the kitchen, Peggy makes coffee. They feel better in the kitchen, where the lights are bright. Laura has been preparing the walls to be wallpapered. The smell of plaster dust is in the air. Mickey and Laura have only been in the house for a few months. The living room has a cathedral ceiling, and the floors are bare and there isn't much furniture yet, so when the rain pounds on the roof, it feels as if they're inside a drum. When the wind blows, it feels as if it blows right through the house. The kitchen is a better place to be. A bedroom may be soft and dark, but a kitchen is the most comforting room in any house.

At the base, Brehm is in Ops, the Operational Dispatch Center, and he's on the phone. There are telephones, computers, men operating radios, the SOF's (Supervisor of Flying's) desk, and on the far wall a large magnetic white-board, scored with a grid of black lines where the names of the men assigned to aircraft are posted on magnetic tags. In one group are Ruvola, Buschor, Mioli, Smith, and Spillane, and in another the names of the C-130 crew. The overhead fluorescent lights seem bright but cold. The carpeting in the outer hallway is wet all the way to the front door, as members of the 106th who've heard about the accident report in, shaking their raincoats, everybody trying to gather information and get brought up to speed. Jack is doing the same thing, talking to the Coast Guard's Operations Center in Boston. He's made a list of all the people he has to keep posted. Jim Mioli has a sister in New Jersey, according to his file. Jack dials Laura Spillane's number, but she's too upset to answer her phone. Peggy answers instead.

"Well, the good news is, Gram got off a Mayday call to a Coast Guard cutter, which is apparently only fifteen miles away. Wait a minute." She hears Jack call out to someone else in the room with him, "Fifteen miles or fifteen minutes? Miles." He talks to Peggy again. "Fifteen miles. That's only an estimate, but they think it's about fifteen miles away, and it got the SOS, so they've changed course. That's good."

"What else?" Peggy says. She's not going to say "What's the bad news?" with Laura within earshot.

"It looks like they're going in. Ten minutes ago, they were down to forty pounds, which is like running on fumes. They've already flamed out one engine. You may not need to tell Laura that."

"I know," Peggy says. "What else? What's it like?"

"We don't know. You can probably assume that whatever it's doing here, it's doing the same thing there. Probably worse. Have you talked to the girls?"

"Carla is with Elizabeth. I'm calling my mom as soon as we hang up to go sit with Carla. I'm a little worried about Michele."

"She's tough—she'll be okay."

"There's a Coast Guard cutter, fifteen miles away," Peggy says to Barbara and Laura. "They got the distress call and they're on their way."

Barbara and Laura thank God, and they all wonder how long it will take a Coast Guard cutter to sail fifteen miles. *They can go fifteen miles an hour, can't they? It's not so bad. The boys can last for an hour in the water— they're all incredible swimmers—they can all swim for longer than that.*

Plus they have survival suits and rafts—they'll be okay. Please, God, let them be okay. . . .

Michele is on the couch at the Doughertys' house, in the dark, staring out the window at the wind ripping through the trees. When Peggy calls her, Michele says only that she's okay, and that she's very tired, but she can't sleep. Peggy gives Michele the number at the Spillanes' house. At home, Elizabeth is trying to let the television take her mind off things. She wants to cry. Carla is doing homework at the kitchen table. Elizabeth surfs past a show on A&E called *Living Dangerously,* something about volcanoes, but she isn't in the mood for disasters. TBS is showing a werewolf movie called *The Howling,* but she's not in the mood for that, either. ESPN features the U.S. Women's Body Building Championships, which is only slightly less frightening than werewolves or volcanoes. MTV has Rock 'n' Jock baseball. Larry King is interviewing Brooke Shields. Elizabeth turns the television off. She sits on the couch. She's wrapped herself in a blanket her father brought home from Korea. She feels the storm raging outside and gets angry, thinking her father might have to fly out into it to save somebody. She just wants him to come home. Why is it more important to go save other people than to stay home?

At sea, Dave Ruvola radios his final position at 9:30. He's at 39°51′N and 72°00′W. He tells his crew to bail out. Only Gram Buschor thinks to keep his night vision goggles on for the low and slow, as he looks out, trying to gauge the waves below them. Spillane, Smith, and Mioli go off goggles to perform their pre-ditching duties, throwing the doors open, readying rafts, grabbing canteens and ML-4 kits, called "butt boats." Ruvola's radar altimeter fluctuates between ten and eighty feet. Falling into the crest of a wave, ten feet below, will mean falling the same distance they ordinarily jump from when they low and slow to a rescue site, a reasonably soft landing. Falling into a trough, between waves, dropping eighty feet, will be like hitting a cement parking lot at fifty miles an hour. Fast-roping into the sea isn't an option in an aircraft that might fall at any moment. Mioli shoves a raft out the starboard side door, watches it drop clear out of sight and decides not to jump in after it. Smith and Spillane are at the port-side door, watching the waves below, listening to the helicopter's turbines wind down. Spillane unclips his gunner's belt. Rick Smith is squatting at the door. Spillane puts his arm on his shoulder. Then Smith jumps. Spillane jumps in after him. He's falling. Falling and falling. He's timed it wrong. He's falling way too far.

Peggy gets her mom on the phone and asks her to go over to the house and stay with Elizabeth. Whenever the phone rings, Peggy answers it. Friends who've heard the news call to ask if they can do anything, or bring anything over, food, coffee, anything, but Laura doesn't want anybody else in the house. Peggy worries about Marianne Smith, who has a three-week-old baby to take care of, but Marianne said her brothers and her father are coming to stay with her.

Jack and Jimmy Dougherty rush to ready a second helicopter. They drive the PJ truck to an HH-60 sitting on the tarmac outside its pod and load it full of rescue gear, wet suits, Mustang immersion suits, rafts, medical kits, but the weather is getting worse. The pilots are on the base, somewhere, and should be at the helicopter, preparing for flight, but they're nowhere to be seen. As he drives back to Ops, Jack looks over his shoulder and says to Jimmy Dougherty, "We're not going anywhere—look." The wind is rocking the helicopter back and forth. If the wind gets any stronger, it's going to blow the machine over on its side before it ever leaves the ground. Base commander LTCOL David Hill gives the order that nobody is going to fly until the weather breaks. A ground crew rolls the HH-60 back into its pod. All they can do is wait.

Brehm gets the Coast Guard back on the phone. They tell him that they've launched an HU-25 Falcon jet, which can be on the scene in minutes. The Falcon will look for strobe lights. Each man is wearing a strobe light attached to his survival vest at the shoulder, which he has to activate to make work. Once activated, a white light will blink every one and a half seconds for about twelve hours. Seeing a strobe means someone is alive, or at least that he was alive long enough to activate his strobe. Without self-illumination, a man in the water will be nearly impossible to find. The men in the water also have PRC-90 radios that have a line-of-sight broadcast range as well as receive capability and emit a beacon signal. Brehm knows that AFR 988 stayed on the scene after the ditching but was unable to raise anybody on their radios, before they were forced to RTB with a blown engine of their own. They did pick up a single signal beacon. The Coast Guard launched an HH-65, a short-range recovery helicopter, smaller than an HH-60, from Floyd Bennett Field in Brooklyn, but it was nearly driven into the sea by the winds and had to abort. Jack is told the Coast Guard also launched an HH-3. Unlike the Air Force's HH-3 helicopters, the Coast Guard's HH-3s can't refuel in midair, but they have larger gas tanks than HH-60s and can fly twice as long. Jack calls Peggy and tells her to pass on the good news, that a Falcon and an HH-3 are on the way. He doesn't tell her that nobody's radio is working. He tells her he's going to set the beeper on his watch to go off every thirty minutes to remind him to call.

At Laura's house, Peggy finds some fruit and some cheese and crackers in the refrigerator and sets it out, but nobody is hungry. She's worried about Laura who, five months into her pregnancy, should be taking it easy. They talk about what they know so far.

"The Coast Guard cutter must be getting close. Did Jack say what the name of it was?"

"The *Tamaroa*."

"How big a ship is it?"

"I don't know. It's an ocean-going tug."

"How big are they?"

"You know, Dave Ruvola is a former PJ. I mean if three out of five of them are PJs, they can help each other."

"I can't stand this. I want him to call every five minutes."

"You know what I think?"

"What?"

"I think we're going to be up for a while, and if we are, we might as well get something done."

"You're right. It's better than just sitting around."

"I'd rather do something than nothing."

"Like what? I'm not knitting anything. I hate knitting."

"Why don't we wallpaper?"

"Wallpapering is good."

"We have everything we need. Don't we?"

"I was going to do it tomorrow."

"We wallpaper then."

At Brunswick Naval Air Station in Brunswick, Maine, a Navy P-3 is being made flight-ready. It's equipped with infrared equipment that can detect heat-emitting objects. Ordinarily the equipment would be used to hunt foreign submarines, but a man in a raft presents a pretty good signal. A man alone in the water presents only a head and will be nearly impossible to detect. At sea, the storm worsens. Onshore, television meteorologists wonder if it's premature to predict a "Storm of the Century." Their instruments show a cataclysmic event unfolding in three parts, made up by a high-pressure system over Canada, a hurricane to the south, and an enormous

Great Lakes low sandwiched in between. The Coast Guardsmen are calling it the No-Name Nor'easter.

Jack calls Peggy at 11:00. She tells Jack they're about to start wallpapering the kitchen. She tells him it's hard to wait thirty minutes for news—thirty minutes seems like three hours.

At 11:50, Jack gets the best news so far—the Falcon jet picked up a radio signal on 243.0 megahertz, the international emergency beacon frequency, 14.3 nautical miles downdrift from where the helicopter ditched. The Falcon's dropmaster, wearing NVGs, has also spotted four strobes in the water, three in a group and one a half-mile away, all by itself.

"That's everybody," Peggy says, losing count.

"There's one still missing," Jack says.

"How close is the cutter?"

"I'm not sure, but the Coast Guard HH-3 is only twenty minutes away. To tell you the truth, it's pretty aggravating."

"What is?"

"We want to go and we can't. We don't even have a tanker that's flyable. One's in depot and one's in periodic and the other one's being fixed for something else. The one that just came in blew a gear box."

"Can't you go without a tanker? How far offshore are they?"

"Sixty miles," Jack says. He explains that it may seem close, but without tankers to refuel them, they'd only have fifteen or twenty minutes of loiter time once on scene, and even if they knew exactly where to go, even in good weather there's no guarantee that they'd be able to get a guy up in the helicopter in fifteen or twenty minutes. "Colonel Hill says they're not going to send another HH-60 out in the same conditions we lost the last one in. Actually they're not the same conditions—the weather's getting worse. Apparently."

"I'm sorry," is all Peggy can say. She can hear the anxiety in Jack's voice.

"Everybody's pretty frustrated," Jack says. "We're all just sitting on our hands, waiting for the Coast Guard to call us." Peggy knows Jack's frustration, knows what it's like to feel helpless, waiting for the phone to ring, just as she knows the respect the PJs and the Coast Guard have for each other. The irony of it is that half the time the PJs make a rescue, some local news stations get it wrong and give the credit to the Coast Guard. It's one reason nobody's ever heard of the PJs. "I gotta go, but I'll call again. Call me if you need to, but I'm on the phone almost constantly. I finally got a number for Mioli's sister Cathy in New Jersey—the number we had was wrong."

"I called Lorraine and told her to drive Elizabeth over to Barbara's to stay with Michele. I don't want Michele there all by herself all night."

When Brehm reaches Jim Mioli's sister, she's grateful for the news and says she'll inform the rest of the family. Her concern is for her brother but also for her brother's dog.

"His dog?"

"He takes her everywhere. She's probably in his van. Somebody should walk her. Her name is Maggie."

Jack finds somebody to get the dog. By midnight, the Ops building is crowded with airmen ready to help, pilots and copilots, navigators and mechanics. It feels as if the whole base is present, everybody trying to pull together. Men and women drink coffee, smoke cigarettes, hit the soda machines and the candy machines for sustenance. Everybody wants to pitch in, but Brehm has to send guys home, because the Air Force requires that a flight crew has to rest for twelve hours before a mission, including eight hours of uninterrupted sleep and four hours of uninterrupted non-duty time. Jack recalls that Mark Judy's team was flying two missions in one day. If the whole team spends the whole night in the Ops building, there'll be nobody fit to fly tomorrow, and they may need guys to fly tomorrow, if the weather eases up and lets them.

"Michele," Elizabeth asks her sister. "Do you think Uncle Mickey is in the ocean?"

"Maybe he's at the base."

"Who's in the ocean? Is it PJs?"

"I think so."

"I want to call Dad."

"Don't," Michele says. "They'll call us when they know something."

"I want to call him anyway."

"Elizabeth, no—we can't."

"I want to call Mom."

"She said she'll call. Just wait."

"I don't want to be here. I want to just go home."

"We can't go home."

"I'm scared."

"Don't be."

There are no streetlights. Occasionally a car goes past. Elizabeth can't help but cry, imagining her father's friends in the water, and she can't help but worry that her dad is going to go after them, which makes her cry even more. She hates this, the storm, the darkness, the Doughertys' black dog Patty, which always scared her. Out the window, there's no lightning, no thunder, just a relentless wind-driven rain. Elizabeth finally calls her grandmother, who helps calm her down.

Jack gets good news at ten after midnight and calls Peggy to tell her the Coast Guard's HH-3 is hovering above three men. No, he doesn't know which three men, but he'll call back when he knows.

The Coast Guard doesn't have PJs, but they do have rescue swimmers who can swim with the best of the Navy SEALs or Air Force para-rescuemen. The Coast Guard, to state the obvious, trains primarily for water rescues, and its methods differ accordingly. For one, where PJs carry victims up on a penetrator, a Coast Guard helicopter will lower a basket, essentially a five-sided metal cage, into which the victim can swim, either under his own power or assisted by a rescue swimmer. Expectations at the 106th are high, but by 1:00 A.M., Jack Brehm has received the bad news that the HH-3 can't make the rescue. The wind is blowing the basket straight back toward the HH-3's tail. With the pilot working the cyclic and the copilot operating the collective they still can't put the basket in the water. The HH-3 pilot reports that in a hover above the men, his forward speed indicator told him he was flying at 80 knots or 100 mph. What he can do is give the *Tamaroa* accurate locations for the men. The *Tamaroa* is 205 feet long, but waves are cresting above the ship and breaking over its decks. Brehm tries to imagine how high the seas must be. He knows how dangerous it can be, picking people up out of heavy seas. Having a ship on the scene is good, but it's no guarantee of anything. He's worried about hypothermia, which will eventually affect even someone in a survival suit. By now his friends have been in the water for what seems like a very long time. He keeps his worries to himself, and calls Peggy to tell her the Coast Guard cutter is almost there. She's frustrated, and says she thought it was only fifteen miles away. He says it was. She asks what's taking it so long. He says that from the sound of it, they can only make two or three knots, but he's sure they're doing the best they can and adds that you have to also consider that the guys in the water have probably drifted from their original location. Peggy says she's sorry, she knows everybody is doing the best they can.

"I'm worried about Laura—she needs to rest. Someone five months pregnant shouldn't be going through something like this. We finished the kitchen. We're going to bed, but you still have to call us any time you know anything, all right?"

"As soon as I know anything."

"I doubt you'll wake us up. We're bringing the phone next to the bed, so promise me you'll call."

"I will," Jack says.

Peggy, Barbara, and Laura all get into the same queen-size bed. They can't sleep, but they think it might do some good to lie still with their eyes closed. They turn the lights off and hold hands, with Laura in the middle. They listen to the rain and the wind, now hard, now soft, now loud, now quiet. Perhaps it's a natural biological function, a way the body compensates for extreme stress, or acts to relieve it, but somehow, the mood starts to shift from serious to silly. It begins with a heavy sigh, and another, and then a snicker. Eventually hysterical laughter.

"What?"

"Nothing."

"What?"

"Nothing. It's not funny."

"Tell me!"

"I was just thinking what we must look like."

It feels good to laugh. They think about slumber parties they had as adolescents, and how far they've come in their lives since then. Ten minutes later, laughter has dissolved to silent prayer.

Around 1:30, the Coast Guard's HH-3 lands at Westhampton Beach to refuel, and the crew comes into the Ops building to warm up, dry off, use the bathroom, and debrief. They are peppered with questions. They try to describe what it's like out there, how fierce the winds are, how the sea is just a whorl of foam and spray, mountainous waves rolling into each other in infinite combinations. They say it's incredible, unbelievable, that they've never seen anything like it. It was too rough to drop a rescue swimmer. They saw strobe lights, that's all—they can't say who was down below. Eventually, the phone rings at Laura Spillane's house, and Peggy answers. It's another PJ's wife.

"I just wanted to say how sorry I am," she says.

"Why?"

"Well, my father-in-law is at the base," she says, "and he says he was talking to some guys who were saying the conditions are so bad they don't see how anybody could survive."

"Well, it's just really too soon to know," Peggy says. "We don't really know anything yet."

"Well, I know, but my father-in-law says—"

"I'm sorry to cut you off but there's somebody on call waiting—I'll let you know when we know anything."

There isn't another call coming in on call waiting. Peggy just said that. She tells Barbara about the call, but not Laura. When the phone rings again, it's Elizabeth.

"Did I wake you guys up?" Elizabeth says.

"No, hon'," Peggy says. "We're still up. Are you still up? Have you gone back to sleep?"

"We can't."

"Well, you don't have to, if you can't, so don't worry about it, but if you can you should try to sleep."

"When are you coming over?"

"I don't know, hon'—probably in the morning. I'll come and get you as soon as we hear something, but we don't know when that's going to be. You guys are being very brave. How's Michele?"

"She's okay," Elizabeth says. "You haven't heard anything?"

"They flew a helicopter to the scene and now there's a Coast Guard ship that's there, so they should be rescuing people any minute now. Why don't you see if there's something on Nick at Night?"

"Who flew a helicopter?"

"The Coast Guard."

"Is Uncle Mickey in the ocean?"

"Honey, just try not to worry about everything. Your dad and Uncle Jimmy are doing everything they can to get them back—everything is going to be okay. All right?"

"Okay."

"I'm very proud of you. I love you both very much."

"Okay."

At 2:15, the phone rings again. It's Jack.

"They've got one," he says.

"Oh my God," Peggy says, repeating the news for the others, "They've got one! Who? Do they know who?"

"We don't know who . . ."

"John, if you know something, and you're not telling anybody, you have to promise you'll tell me."

"Peggy, honestly, we don't know who it is. I asked the guy at RCC and he said he didn't know. As soon as I hear anything I'll let you know. What I'm telling people now is that they've got the assets at the splash point and they're making recoveries. Right now, that's all we can say."

"But that's good."

"That's very good."

"How many?"

"One."

"No—how many in the water."

"Four. I mean, three, now. There's one still missing, but he's going to be in approximately the same area."

At sea, the *Tamaroa* is risking crewmen every time they put anybody on the deck. The first man they rescue is the copilot, Gram Buschor. They lower a cargo net over the side for him to grab. They haul him aboard and take him inside. His core temperature is 94 degrees, so they immediately begin to warm him by giving him hot fluids and wrapping him in blankets. When Jack learns it's Buschor, his first thought is, if they can get Gram, they can get anybody, primarily because, of the five men on Jolly 10, Buschor is in the worst shape. He doesn't train like a PJ. He's a bit overweight and he smokes. They used to joke that if he ever needed rescue, he wouldn't need flares—they would just look for his cigarette lighter. Everyone else on board was a much better swimmer than Gram Buschor. Brehm's hopes rise. After picking up Buschor, the *Tamaroa* heads for where the HH-3 said the others were. They see strobes in the water. They light flares, aim spotlights, and throw lines overboard with chemlights tied to the ends. They want to come in by drifting down on the men in the water, which means the *Tam'* will have to turn broadside to the waves to make the pickup, a maneuver that in seas that high is terribly dangerous to the ship. On the third try, one of the men in the water manages to grab the net, and they haul him onboard. As soon as he's on deck, they can tell he's in terrible pain. They bring him into a cabin, cut his wet suit off him, give him an IV to rehydrate him and a catheter to measure his urine output. His blood pressure is 140 over 90, and his pulse is 100. Instead of being hypothermic, he's running a slight fever. He's hurting everywhere, and his eyes are glazed. They give him a seasickness patch and Tylenol 3.

The phone rings at Laura Spillane's house.

"John," Peggy says. "I hope this is good news."

"It is," he says. "They've got Mick."

"They've got Mick," Peggy says to the others. She bursts into tears. "Oh my God, they've got Mick, thank God, they've got him. Here—let me put Laura on."

Brehm repeats what he knows. He tells Laura that he's also been told that Mickey is injured. He doesn't really know how badly, but if Mickey was able to swim, and to assist in his own rescue, then maybe he's not hurt so bad. He's receiving medical attention. Jack reminds her that her husband was in great shape before any of this happened, getting ready to run a marathon. He's alive. That's all good news.

By 3:00 A.M., four men have been recovered from the water, and Brehm knows their names. He wants to tell the wives of the men who've been recovered, Carmen Ruvola, Ann Buschor, Laura Spillane, and he wants to tell Jim Mioli's sister, but he dreads telling Marianne Smith that Rick is still out there. Yet he doesn't want her to hear it from someone else, and he knows how the telephone network works. He calls her. The only concrete positive news he has for her is that Mickey remembers seeing Rick leave the helicopter in full survival gear. He says they all have high confidence they'll find Rick. By now, the entire PJ community worldwide seems to know there's been an accident, and that some of their own are in trouble, because units from all over are calling in, offering to send aircraft or men to help in the search. All Brehm can tell them is that the Coast Guard is coordinating the search—anyone with assets to offer should call the First District Operations Center in Boston. The mood at the section is mixed. Knowing they've picked up Dave Ruvola, Jim Mioli, Gram Buschor, and Mickey Spillane has lifted everybody's spirits, but not getting Rick is unacceptable, aggravating at best and infuriating at worst to the PJs who know they have the training and the tools to help but can't use them. Everybody knows that Rick Smith was the strongest swimmer among them, one of the strongest swimmers the PJs have ever produced. It's hard to wait. It should only be a matter of minutes now. The phone should ring, any second. They feel certain.

Four o'clock arrives, and Brehm and the others are nervous again. By 5:00, a collective low-level depression has sunk in, in part simply because people are tired, and spirits can sag when the body gives out and the caffeine doesn't work anymore. Brehm calls Peggy at 5:30, needing support himself before he calls Marianne Smith.

"Everybody thought Rick would be the first guy they got, not the last," Brehm says. "He's the best of all of them."

"What are you going to tell Marianne?"

"Just what we know. It's going to be light soon, and when it is, there's going to be a lot of airplanes going out. We're getting a lot of calls from other units."

Peggy asks the question she's afraid to ask.

"Will you be going?"

"We still can't fly," Jack says. "It's Hill's decision. The math says that Rick's probably blowing away from us, meaning we'd have less loiter time now than we had before. For the moment, it's fixed wings only."

"Have they fixed the tankers?"

"They're working on 'em. How are you doing?"

"Okay," Peggy says. She's relieved, on one level, and saddened on another. "I was going to let your parents sleep a little while longer, but then I wanted to call them before they hear anything on the news and start to wonder. Do they know anything more about Mickey?"

"All we were told is broken bones," Jack says. "Ribs. I'm sure they'll med-evac him as soon as it's feasible. It's still pretty rough out there, I gather. Jim Mioli was hypothermic because he wasn't wearing an immersion suit for some reason."

"It's just unbelievable," Peggy says, looking out the kitchen window to see if the sky has begun to lighten any. "We're all going to go over to Marianne's. My mom is going to get the kids off to school."

"How about the twins?"

"We're still figuring that out. Somebody'll get 'em. Barbara wants to be home when her kids wake up."

Jack calls Marianne Smith after hanging up with Peggy, tells her Rick is not yet recovered and tries to reassure her. Her father has arrived from Delaware, and her brothers are there. He tells her about all the airplanes rushing to the North Atlantic to join the search, C-130s and Talons from Florida, P-3s, Coast Guard Falcons, probably fifteen planes today and more tomorrow if they're needed—every search and rescue asset on the East Coast, basically. He tells her they know that Rick had all his gear when he left the helicopter, a survival vest and a wet suit, and that he could probably survive in a raft for days. Peggy, Barbara Dougherty, and Laura Spillane are on their way over to Marianne's to be with her.

When he calls Marianne back at 7:30 A.M., he wishes he had something to report, but he doesn't. He gives her as much positive information as he can. The Coast Guard is collecting data from marker buoys, including a radio marker buoy the *Tamaroa* dropped into the water where she'd picked the four men out of the Atlantic. The buoy indicates what the Coast Guard calls the datum, a term that describes the central point in a search, calculated from the last point of contact and factoring in how far somebody would drift according to the winds and currents at the site. Finer calculations determine how far from the splash point a man swimming in the water might have drifted in the ten hours since the ditching, against how far a man in a life raft with a higher wind profile might have drifted. He tells Marianne they have a really good idea where to look. The 106th's C-130, AFR 988, has repaired the gear box flux in its faulty engine and is again operational, but their other planes are still grounded with mechanical problems. Jack tells her that in addition to the *Tamaroa*, a high endurance Coast Guard cutter, the 327-foot *Spencer*, is on the scene. The weather at 39°27'N and 72°04'W is still tough, winds gusting to fifty miles an hour, rain and only an 800-foot ceiling to fly in, which will limit the territory any one search plane can cover by narrowing the tracks they have to fly. Jack can hear a television in the background and can only imagine what the morning news is telling Marianne. Overnight, six houses in Westhampton Beach were swept into the sea. Four other homes were heavily damaged. Sailboats off Connecticut, Nantucket, Long Island, and even Daytona Beach, Florida, were lost. Boats were blown ashore in Rhode Island, Connecticut, Virginia, Cape Cod, Martha's Vineyard. Waves are still pounding North Carolina's Outer Banks. Hatteras Island has lost power. The Pilgrim nuclear power plant in Plymouth, Massachusetts, has been shut down as a precaution. Oceanfront homes in Brooklyn, just east of Coney Island, are being battered by the sea, where homeowners are stacking sandbags to protect their property. TV weathermen can't believe the size of this thing, calling the storm an "extra-tropical hurricane," having some of the properties of a hurricane, including a counterclockwise swirling motion, but moving west and south, opposite of the way hurricanes move, and they add that it looks like it's going to stick around a lot longer than a typical hurricane.

Marianne Smith puts Peggy on the phone.

"You must be tired," Peggy says.

"I'm all right," Jack says. "I'm just glad they got Rick."

"What did you say?"

"I said I'm glad they got Rick."

Peggy's heart races.

"John, tell me exactly what it is you're saying," Peggy says.

"Did I say Rick?" Jack says, realizing his Freudian slip. "Oh geez. I meant Mick. Mickey. God. I must be more tired than I thought I was."

"That wasn't good," Peggy says, calming herself, glad she didn't blurt his words out for the others to hear. "Think if it'd been Marianne you were talking to and not me."

"I'm not going to be here much longer," Jack tells his wife. "I'll see you at home."

Neighbors stop by Marianne's to check in on her. They've seen the news on TV. They bring coffee cakes and baked goods. Marianne's oldest girl is seven, and she wants to wear her Halloween costume to school. After getting the kids off and putting the baby down for a nap, Marianne Smith retreats to the kitchen, where she seems extremely somber. Peggy asks her how she's doing.

"He's not coming back," Marianne says, sounding very calm and together. "I just know he's not coming back." Peggy knows what it's like to have that feeling. Twice, when Jack was hurt on the job, both times with broken arms, she'd had premonitions, and knew even before he called home that he'd been injured. Other times, she'd called the base and said, "John—don't fly today—I have a bad feeling." But sometimes he'd flown despite her misgivings and everything had been okay.

"Don't give up," Peggy says to Marianne. "You just can't give up."

* * * * * * * *

Over the next week, the details of the accident were pieced together. After ordering his crew to bail out, Dave Ruvola put the helicopter into the water as softly as possible, kicked out his door, something he'd forgotten to do while the aircraft was still in the air, inflated his life vest, and popped to the surface. He saw Jim Mioli's strobe a short time later and swam to him. Mioli was hurt, so Ruvola tied himself to his flight engineer with a piece of parachute cord and held on to him. The water temperature was in the mid-fifties. In the rush to ditch, Mioli had failed to don his survival suit, and Ruvola knew hypothermia would be a problem in waters that cold. Buschor was relatively unhurt, and had the only working radio among the five of them. Mickey Spillane was in trouble as soon as he hit the water, hard, at perhaps fifty or sixty miles per hour, fracturing his left leg, the radius and ulna of his left arm, the ulna and middle finger of his right arm and hand, cracking four ribs, bruising his pancreas, and rupturing a kidney. He was dazed, semiconscious. At one point, he found the nine-man raft that Jim Mioli pushed out his door, but the water was too rough for Spillane to hold on to it. He eventually grabbed a rubberized sack full of blankets and used that for supplemental flotation. When he saw Ruvola and Mioli's strobes bobbing in the distance, his first thought was that he'd only be a burden if he swam to them, and he felt something like the way he'd felt running marathons, an I'm-in-pain-leave-me-the-hell-alone attitude, until he remembered that his PJ training at Lackland taught him team members should stick together. It took him two hours to swim over to his pilot and flight engineer.

Jack Brehm was back at the base by two the following afternoon, Thursday. During the day, Spillane had been moved from the *Tamaroa* to the *Spencer*. At three o'clock, the 106th asked permission to fly out to the *Spencer* and take Mickey off, but the captain denied them permission, saying the seas were still far too rough to have any helicopters hovering over his decks. Around the same time, a familiar and welcome figure walked into the dispatch center. Mike McManus had flown down from Alaska to take part in a conference in Washington, D.C., and drove up to Long Island as soon as he heard there was trouble. It wasn't the kind of weather you want to be driving in, but that didn't stop McManus. Jack gave his mentor a hug when he saw him. Mike asked what the situation was. Jack filled him in.

"It's rough," Jack concluded. "The pisser is that we still haven't launched the helos. They got the tanker flying again, but Hill says we still have to wait." He added that the primary search area had drifted so far to the south that any helicopter on scene would have to refuel every half hour to avoid going below bingo fuel. As a rule, helicopters only search close to shore. In the mid-Atlantic, you search with fixed-wing aircraft, and once you find what you're looking for, you send helicopters to the exact location of the rescue. Using helicopters to search the mid-Atlantic would be ludicrous.

"I know," Mike said. "It's not just Hill—I heard the generals talking about it in D.C."

"The boys want to fly," Jack said.

"Of course they want to fly," Mike said, "but Hill's got more than just PJs to worry about. You know, you guys could swim in this shit, but the pilots don't train like you. The flight engineers don't train like you. You gonna put those guys in the water?"

"It's nice to have somebody around here who understands," Jack said.

At 5:30 that day, as the light was beginning to fade, a Coast Guard C-130 reported seeing a large patch of green marker dye in the water, with what appeared to be a man in the middle of it, or at least a dark shape that looked like a man. The C-130 dropped another marker buoy, as well as a raft, a flare kit, and radios. The Coast Guard launched an HH-3 to fly to the site. Jack called Marianne to tell her they thought they'd found somebody. An hour later, he had to call her back and apologize, and tell her it was a false alarm. The dye had been dropped by another search pilot to mark something he thought he'd seen. The dark shape was probably just a piece of flotsam. (An article in the New York *Daily News* would erroneously report the next day, November 1, that searchers had spotted a lone individual in choppy seas east of Atlantic City.) There was another false alarm at 9:30 that night, when a Coast Guard helicopter pilot radioed that he'd spotted Smith near the marker buoy the *Tamaroa* had dropped. Jack told Marianne, because she said she wanted to know whenever there was any new information, even if it was a false alarm, but then the Coast Guard pilot corrected himself and said he'd only seen a raft. The weather was still atrocious, bad enough that Elizabeth Brehm and her friend Emily had to cancel the scavenger hunt they'd planned. They bobbed for apples instead, and played games, and ate candy. Some kids wore costumes. Everybody watched the Stephen King movie *It*. Elizabeth thought the movie was okay, but how could it be frightening, after what she'd been through the night before?

Her Uncle Mickey was med-evac'ed from the *Spencer* at eight Friday morning and taken to a hospital in Atlantic City, New Jersey. As soon as they heard, Peggy drove Laura to Atlantic City, leaving at ten in the morning, a five-hour drive. Thirty minutes from the hospital, the two women heard a loud noise when the master brake cylinder blew on Peggy's Plymouth Voyager, so they limped the last thirty miles, driving on the shoulder of the New Jersey Turnpike, listening to the rumble strip beneath the wheels. At the hospital, it was a joyous reunion, tempered by the reality that Mickey was in bad shape, white as a ghost, immobile, with a blank stare on his face. He was, as Peggy Brehm remembers, "in never-never land—he could barely whisper." He was in too much pain to be hugged. Laura held his hand but didn't squeeze it. Peggy drove home that night.

On Saturday, the *Tamaroa* sailed into Shinnecock Inlet for the Coast Guard Station at Hampton Bays. Jim Mioli, Gram Buschor, and Dave Ruvola were met by their loved ones on the docks, then driven to the base for physicals. Mioli and Buschor appeared overjoyed to be home. Ruvola looked distraught, as if, Brehm thought, he might be blaming himself. That afternoon, Brehm, Colonel Hill, and the base chaplain, a guardsman named John Hecht, drove to Marianne's house on the South Shore near the end of the William Floyd Parkway, in the town of Shirley. Her father, stepmother, and two of her brothers were there, as were her children,

Erica, who was seven, Kristin, five, and Caroline, only three weeks old. Marianne looked exhausted, limp. Jack could see the resignation in her face, but he told her they weren't giving up. If anybody could last this long, Rick could, and finally, the weather was getting better. According to the weather patterns, Rick would have blown south, where the water was warmer. The calmer the seas, the easier it was going to be to spot someone. Jack told her to hold on if she could, because nobody was giving up yet. They both knew, however, that realistically, the chances of finding Rick Smith were slim and getting slimmer.

The search lasted a full week, involving hundreds of aircraft and thousands of men, to date one of the largest search and rescue operations in the history of the Coast Guard. There were more false alarms. One plane would see something, drop a raft, just in case it was Rick, and a couple hours later, another plane would call in, saying they'd spotted a raft. The PJs flew out and knifed the empty rafts, so they wouldn't have to investigate them twice. Aircraft from the 106th flew every day, often in a formation of two HH-60s with a tanker between them to serve as a mobile gas station, but the helicopters had to refuel frequently, and every time they did the attention paid to refueling procedures compromised the search. The search area grew larger and larger, as the datum shifted farther and farther away. Areas that had been searched in rough seas were searched again in calm seas. On November 7, the Coast Guard abandoned its search. On the same day, a helicopter from the 106th, Jolly 14, returned from Atlantic City, bringing Mickey Spillane home.

On November 8, nine days after the accident, a Sergeant Mounger from RCC at Scott AFB called to say that the Air Force's search, officially mission 2-2341A, was closed. That evening, Jack Brehm was called into Colonel Hill's office. There'd been a number of debriefings with Dave Ruvola and the other members of the crew of Jolly 10. Speculation as to what happened to Rick Smith was only that—speculation—but the best guess was that he'd probably hit the water as hard or harder than Mickey Spillane had hit it, lost consciousness, and drowned. Another theory suggested he and Spillane may have collided on impact with the sea. A third theory posited that under the stress of preparing to ditch, he may have forgotten to release his gunner's belt and had gone under with the helicopter. Jack wasn't sure what Colonel Hill wanted and was surprised to see a civilian sitting opposite the colonel's desk. The colonel introduced the man and asked him to repeat, for Sergeant Brehm, what he'd just told the wing commander. The man was about thirty, with long scraggly hair, dirty, parted in the middle. He was wearing tennis shoes, jeans, a brown shirt and a jacket over it, and he had a folder in his hands.

"I was telling your colonel," the man said, extending the folder, "that I have psychic abilities, and that I was hoping you'd let me help you. I should tell you that when I do this kind of work, I always anticipate skepticism, but I do have numerous newspaper clippings and documents here, if you'd care to read them, about the times I've worked with various police departments and with the FBI. At any rate, as I was telling Colonel Hill, I think your friend Rick Smith is still alive, because I believe I've seen him."

Brehm took the clippings The Psychic offered and glanced at them without reading them.

"You've seen him?" Brehm said. A skeptic all his life, Brehm didn't believe in psychics. Yet he found himself reserving judgment, reluctant to be the one who says no, this is impossible. He wanted to believe rescue was still possible. Everybody did. This gave him a chance to do that. The Psychic's manner was humble and matter-of-fact, and he sounded reasonable and sincere in his desire to help.

"Yes," The Psychic said. "I've had the vision several times. I see him in the water. There's something shiny on his face, and he's wearing a black suit. And he keeps grabbing for his right leg. I don't know why, but there's something on his right leg. I can give you the coordinates if you'd like."

"Would you mind waiting out in the hall for a second?" Colonel Hill asked The Psychic. When he was gone, Hill asked Brehm what he thought. Hill said he'd called some of the references The Psychic had provided, police departments that said that while the guy hadn't exactly led them directly to what they were looking for, he'd steered them in the right direction, asked good questions, and had indeed proved helpful. Brehm shook his head, more in bewilderment than in doubt.

"I don't know what to think," Brehm said. Brehm knew that there were things in this universe that he couldn't explain. "I guess the shiny thing on his face could be Rick's mask. And he's wearing a black wet suit."

"What about the right leg?" Hill asked. Brehm shrugged.

"I have no idea. I suppose he could be reaching for his knife, or else he's hurt. I don't know what to say. What do you think, Colonel?"

"I don't know, either," Colonel Hill said. "I really don't. Except that I don't see what we have to lose. We've tried everything else. These other people said he'd helped. One voice says 'Why?' and the other says, 'Why not?' The guy says he can give us coordinates."

"Well then . . ."

The next morning at 6:43 A.M., the C-130 AFR 988 took off. AFR 974 and AFR 114 were by now repaired and on standby. The Psychic had explained himself, his purpose, and his vision, to the entire squadron at a preflight briefing. No one expressed any doubts or misgivings about using him. They wanted it to work. No one wanted to cross the line and say, "Forget it, it's over, Rick's gone." The Psychic even requested that he be allowed to fly on the C-130, feeling he'd be able to get a better sense of things if he were actually on the scene. Permission was denied. Instead they let The Psychic speak with the pilot on the radio.

"We're seeing something in the water off to starboard," the pilot radioed back at one point.

"It's going to be a square piece of wood, about two foot by two foot," The Psychic said. Everyone in the Ops room waited.

"It looks like a shipping pallet or something," the pilot radioed in after closer examination. "Just a piece of wood, maybe two foot square."

No one in Ops knew what to say. Some felt chills as The Psychic correctly predicted the sighting. Those who wanted to believe in him saw it as a positive sign. Those who didn't tried to figure out how he could have known. The proof would come when AFR 988 reached the coordinates the psychic had given them. When it did, the anticipation was intense.

"Do you see anything?" The Psychic asked.

"Negative," the pilot said. "Scanners report negative."

"You're certain?"

"As certain as I can be," the pilot said. "Seas maybe ten feet, good visibility. We got nothing."

"Okay," The Psychic said, "that's all right—now, turn east twenty degrees. You should see something white in the water."

Brehm's skepticism returned. If the guy was truly psychic, why wouldn't he just take them straight to Rick? Why send them somewhere, then make them change course? He didn't expect it to make perfect sense, but he did expect it to make *some* sense. For the next ten hours, The Psychic gave the pilot his feelings and impressions, until, at 4:30 in the afternoon, the C-130 was ordered to return to base. Searching the open ocean is an exhausting thing to do. The people manning the scanning windows need a twenty-minute break every hour because focusing and concentrating that hard wears you out. They'd been out for ten hours. By the time they landed, everybody had the feeling they'd been used and misled, if not jerked around outright. Flights had been scheduled for the next two days, but by 8:15 that evening, all flights were canceled, pending reevaluation. The Psychic was politely informed that he'd be called if and when there was any further need for his services.

Marianne called Jack the following afternoon.

"Would you mind coming over?" Marianne asked. "He's here."

"Who is?"

"Well, this guy who says he's a psychic . . ."

Jack was at Marianne Smith's house in a matter of minutes. The Psychic was sitting in her living room, wearing what looked like the same clothes he'd worn the day before. Jack wondered how he'd gotten Marianne's address. He wondered if the guy had slept in his car. He wondered if he lived in his car.

"What's up?" Jack asked, trying to hide his rising ire.

"You're thinking of stopping the search, aren't you?" The Psychic said. *God,* Brehm thought, *you really are a psychic.* "You can't give up hope, Jack." *Don't call me Jack.* "He's still alive. I'm as certain of that as I am of anything. I just can't be of any help unless I can get out there. I'm frustrated, because I'm really having a hard time working from these distances. I just think you'd be crazy to give up now when we're so close."

"Hang on a second," Brehm said. "I want to talk with Marianne."

Jack followed Marianne Smith into the kitchen. Out the kitchen window, he noticed how stark and bare everything was. Before the storm, there'd been leaves on all the trees, but now they'd all blown off, black tree limbs against a cold autumn sky.

"What do you think?" Marianne asked. "He wants to rent a boat and go out there."

"He's going to rent a boat?" Jack asked.

"Well, no," Marianne said. "He wants me to rent the boat."

"Marianne," Jack said, "I hate to put it this way, but I think this is a crock of shit. I think by now we both know Rick is gone, and I think this guy is just some sick jerk who gets a kick out of preying on the hopes of people in tough situations. How else can you explain it? He knows it's going to be hard for you to admit Rick is gone, so he's just . . . I don't know what he's doing. I just think it's a bunch of crap."

"So do I," Marianne said. "I agree. I just needed to hear somebody else say it. Would you mind asking him to leave?"

Brehm confronted The Psychic in the living room.

"Marianne's not interested," he told the man. "I don't know how you found out where she lives, and I don't care—don't bother her again. We don't want your help. Got it? Don't see her, and don't call her. Do we understand each other? So grab your stuff and I'll walk you to your car."

13

KRYPTONITE

The book that came out about the '91 Nor'easter was called The Perfect Storm, *and most of the guys who read it were pretty impressed with how the author got it right. At the time though, we probably wouldn't have agreed that the storm was "perfect" in any way.*

I don't want to defend myself without giving anybody with a different opinion a chance to have a say in the matter. I can live without addressing it. I regret losing Rick, but I don't regret any decisions I made, because I know they were sound. I was thinking as clearly as anybody could. It was time to be practical. Beyond that, there was nothing I could do. If I'd had my druthers, I would have been on the helicopter myself. When they left for the mission, I was jealous. It was going to be a historic mission, the first rescue for the unit using the new HH-60s. The storm caught the whole East Coast unprepared—why should the 106th be any different? After the storm, it was like a mortar round had hit the unit. Guys were devastated, and I understood that, but to be questioned and told your motives were somehow less than clear or righteous, when you know you were trying to do the best by everyone, is horrible. In a way, it was the most traumatic thing that ever happened to me. Everything fell apart.

Humans need answers and reasons for everything. We need to know why horrible traumatic things happen. I think of the U.S. prisoners of war in North Vietnam, guys held for years in hopeless heartbreaking conditions, knowing there was no rational justification for what they were going through. It's your faith, in God or in country or in your family, that gets you through something like that.

IN THE END, WE ASK, WHY WAS THERE A STORM? WE CAN LOOK AT all the meteorological data we want, but in an ontological sense, there's no answer to that question. If we believe in God, we can say, "God sent the storm," but *why* did God send the storm? Why would God choose October 30, 1991, as the night Rick Smith had to die? There's no answer to that, either. But grief invariably poses the question, "Why?" It's human nature to insist that the deaths of the people we love have meaning, because otherwise it would seem that we live in a meaningless universe, where actions and consequences disconnect, and justice goes unserved, and fairness doesn't matter, and things don't make sense anymore. Love seems meaningless, because when all is said and done, love can't really save anybody. Yet because of love, we can't stop asking questions that have no answers, over and over again, until we get angry that we're not getting any answers. We get angry with God, or with Nature, angry with the ocean and the sky. We feel guilty for surviving, angry at ourselves, and enraged at feeling so helpless. We can lash out in defiance, like Captain Ahab with his lightning rods, screaming at God. We can scream at God, or at the ocean, or at the sky, but that usually doesn't satisfy, because unless we get a sign, it's hard to tell when anyone is listening. Then it's human nature to look for someone or something else to blame. Ahab blamed the whale. Some of the PJs at the 106th blamed Jack Brehm.

It makes no sense, but it can, perhaps, be partially deconstructed. It could be argued that the seeds of discord were planted prior to the accident. Even before McManus put Jack's name up to succeed him as NCOIC it was clear in the section that Jack and Mike had a good relationship, one others might envy. Jack admired Mike's courage and toughness, and Mike admired Jack's dedication and spirit. Was McManus ever guilty of favoritism? Probably, if you call it favoritism to give the best assignments to guys he knew could get the job done willingly and cheerfully, guys like Jack, and not to guys Mike had his doubts about, guys prone to acting more out of self-interest than for the good of the team. A handful of PJs who held seniority over Jack questioned Mike's decision to recommend Jack for NCOIC. McManus made the recommendation anyway. Before he left for Alaska, Mike McManus was satisfied that he'd left the unit in the best possible hands.

Yet the feeling in the PJ section among a certain faction was that Jack could have and should have done more to get the PJs in the air the night Jolly 10 ditched. Beginning the very first night, some thought Jack should have gone into Colonel Hill's office and turned his desk upside down if he had to, and pounded his fists and demanded that they be allowed to fly to go rescue their friend. Never mind that the 106th didn't have a flyable refueler, with all four of their C-130 tankers down for repairs. Never mind that that meant any HH-60 arriving on the scene flying without refueling capability would only be able to loiter for fifteen or twenty minutes before it would have to RTB, and even if they knew exactly where to look, in seas that rough there was no guarantee they'd be able to hoist down and pick anybody up in fifteen minutes. Never mind that a Coast Guard HH-3 had already reached the splash point within a few hours of the ditching, but failed to make a pickup due to the weather, and the weather had gotten worse since then. Never mind that when McManus showed up at the base to help out during the search, he backed Jack up one hundred percent, and said that suspension of flying was the right decision, and there was nothing he nor anybody else could have done to reverse it, even if it was the wrong decision. Never mind that it wasn't Jack's call in the first place— it was wing commander Hill's call, and it was the Pentagon's call, too.

Hill had a number of sound reasons to make his decision, but he also had a broader perspective than the PJs had. He was concerned with the entire helicopter crew, not just the PJs, and with the aircrafts. He lived near the base and knew, by listening for them, when his helicopters were late coming home. At 9:00 P.M. the night of the storm he'd been dining in a local restaurant with members of a visiting logistics team when he realized he hadn't heard Jolly 10 flying over and knew it was tardy, at which point he called the base from a pay phone and first learned of the imminent ditching. The logistics team was visiting because the 106th had received a shipment of auxiliary internal fuel tanks for their HH-60s, tanks that would have extended their flying time by about two hours, but the auxiliary tanks couldn't be installed because the shipment was missing the hoses needed to connect the tanks to the HH-60's fuel system. Somewhere along the way, somebody had failed to kit-proof the shipment. It was as if, during the storm, everything that could go wrong did. There was nothing the 106th could do about it but wait for the fuel-line assemblies to arrive.

Hill's perspective was different in another way. He knew that his PJs were upset at not being able to fly the night of the accident, and more so the next day, and he heard them grumble when they learned maintenance wasn't going to be able to install the internal fuel tanks. Hill could see that his PJs, men who could be fairly tightly wound under normal circumstances, were too emotionally invested, to the extent that it might have been a bad idea to fly, even if they'd had tankers available—a Bat 21 mentality was becoming evident. Civilians might recall *Bat 21* as the title of a movie starring Gene Hackman, a fairly inaccurate Hollywood rendition, if you ask most PJs, of an April 1972 rescue in Vietnam of an EB-66 pilot named LTCOL Iceal "Gene" Hambleton who'd been shot down behind enemy lines in the middle of the DMZ, the heart of "bad guy" country, while trying to jam SAM sites during the NVA's Easter Offensive. Bat 21 was the identifying call number of his airplane. By 1972 the North Vietnamese had realized that U.S. forces generally refrained from bombing places where our personnel had been shot down, for fear of hitting our own people. The North Vietnamese used Hambleton's downing as an opportunity to move several armored tank divisions into the area where he was evading, perhaps as many as 10,000 troops in broad daylight. They also knew that somebody was going to come and get him, so rather than capture him they surrounded him and waited, using him as bait to set up a "flak trap." The United States lost several airplanes and a helicopter trying to get Hambleton out, with two HH-53s so shot up they barely made it back to Da Nang, the Air Force thinking all the while, "He's our guy, he's one of us, and he's in trouble, and we gotta go save him." Hambleton was recovered eleven days after being shot down. Lost were two PJs, TECH SGT Allen Avery and SGT William Pearson.

Hill knew being emotionally invested isn't always a good thing. Hoo-yah and gung ho can go too far. There are times when it's foolish to persist, no matter how badly you want to launch—times when courage is counterindicated.

It was a difficult concept for the PJs of the 106th to accept. Some men who might not have stood up to Mike McManus got in Jack Brehm's face. McManus never used Novocain when he went to the dentist. At the end of a night of drinking at the Matchbox, McManus routinely ate his beer glass. Despite his diminutive stature, Mike was somebody you didn't want to take on. "Leadership," Sun Tzu writes in the classical Chinese text *The Art of War*, "is a matter of intelligence, trustworthiness, humaneness, courage, and sternness." Jack had intelligence, trustworthiness, humaneness, and courage, but he didn't have an evil bone in his body. There are occasions when a leader needs to crack a few heads, or eat a few beer glasses, to make a point. Emotions after the accident were out of control. The men suffered from overwhelming feelings of grief and frustration and sadness and an infuriating helplessness. Some tried to self-medicate with alcohol, a poor choice that only made things worse, because alcohol flattens REM (rapid eye movement) sleep, which is the brain's way of processing trauma and healing itself. At the section, cheap shots and low blows abounded. Fingers were pointed. Men whispered behind each other's backs, and meetings were held behind closed doors. One day Jack discovered that somebody had stolen his jacket. Another day, as he prepared to fly to Kuwait on a TDY, he discovered that somebody had hidden a bottle of hooch in his kit bag. Kuwait is an Islamic country where alcohol is strictly forbidden. Smuggling booze into country could have gotten Jack into enormous trouble, had anyone found the bottle. He was lucky to find it and dispose of it, but it became evident that somebody was trying to drive him from the unit.

Jack had men on his side, guys like Jimmy Dougherty and Mickey Spillane, but the argument was dividing the unit. He had Peggy, too, who talked to him and held him and told him he'd done the right thing. She went over the details of the search for Rick with Jack, when he needed to review the decisions made during those difficult hours, but she told him not to second-guess himself, too. She'd never seen him so distraught, a man who'd probably been in about three or four bad moods since the day she met him. Ordinarily, Jack tried, as much as possible, not to bring the office home with him, but now Peggy encouraged him to talk about it, because she could see that what was tearing up the team was tearing him up too.

Colonel Hill knew what was going on, knew someone had stuck a bottle of hooch in Jack's bag, but he couldn't take disciplinary action against anybody without evidence or testimony, and he couldn't get that, because he couldn't crack the "code of silence" that shielded the section, not unlike the way police departments or fire departments sometimes develop a protective code of silence. Hill had also lost a certain amount of face at the awards ceremony that followed the storm. The purpose of the ceremony was to commend people for their efforts and hopefully to initiate a healing process. Air Medals were given to the pilots who flew the search planes, and to the crew members who flew with them. One Air Medal was even given to a parachute packer who'd manned a scanning window on a C-130 for an afternoon. Hill had recommended to Washington that the crew of Jolly 10 receive the Air Force's Airman's Medal for valor in the line of duty. The Airman's Medal is a higher award than the Air Medal. As of the eve of the ceremony, Ruvola, Mioli, Buschor, and Spillane expected the Airman's

Medal. They'd been told that's what they were going to get, and they clearly had a right to feel they deserved it, though they might never have come right out and said so. Hill was informed, the night before the ceremony, that the Pentagon's awards committee had declined the Airman's Medal, ruling that it wasn't an award that could be given out in a noncombat situation. Hill flipped. He picked up the telephone and appealed to the generals above him, arguing that Jolly 10 had ditched in the line of duty—it wasn't as if some irresponsible young fighter jock had trashed an F-15 on a test range out of recklessness or negligence. Several of Hill's superiors agreed with him, but not enough to sway the members of the awards committee. It was too late to call off the awards ceremony, so Hill did the next best thing he could do. Ruvola got an Aerial Achievement Medal. The rest of the crew received Air Force Commendation Medals. Both are lower awards than the Air Medals the scanners were getting.

It did little to assuage the discord in the unit.

Then Dave Ruvola flew to Washington, D.C., in late November to give a special briefing on the accident, and at the hearing he was told he was a hero, and that the Air Force was proud of the way he'd handled himself and saved as many of his crew as he could. Yet when Ruvola mentioned to the man who'd called him a hero, a general, how unfair the meager Aerial Achievement Medal seemed, the general replied coldly, "Well, the bottom line is, you lost the aircraft."

It seemed to Colonel Hill and to Jack Brehm, as well as to many others in the unit, that some sort of mass insanity was afoot, something inexplicable and weird, wrong-headed and bizarre, but nevertheless something that had a life of its own, like an illness that needed to run its course, or a fever that needed to burn itself out. Colonel Hill knew that in the military, once a leader loses the confidence of his men, he loses the ability to lead, and it doesn't matter whether the reasons for that loss of confidence are valid or invalid.

In hindsight, one action that might have been taken, a tool the Air Force had resorted to on other occasions, albeit usually in post-combat situations, would have been to hold a CISD, or Critical Incident Stress Debriefing. CISD was a tool the Air Force, in 1991, was just beginning to be aware of, but one commonly used today. The idea was pioneered by Dr. Jeffrey T. Mitchell, founder of the International Critical Incident Stress Debriefing Foundation, a nonprofit United Nations affiliated organization in Ellicott City, Maryland. Mitchell, currently a clinical associate professor

of emergency health services at the University of Maryland, is also a former fireman and paramedic who, in the mid-seventies, began looking at
the way emergency workers and rescue teams handle the stress of their
jobs. Mitchell looked at the aftermath of a variety of calamities and disasters, from the 1942 fire at the Coconut Grove, a Boston nightclub, to the
1985 Mexico City earthquake and a 1986 midair collision in the skies over
Cerritos, California, a gruesome accident involving a private plane and a
commercial airliner that left what was thought to be over ten thousand
body parts on the ground. He looked at what happens after a crisis to
policemen, firemen, medical personnel, anybody who might have come in
contact with a traumatic event. Many of them reported one or more symptoms of stress: physical symptoms such as fatigue, dizziness, chest pains,
and headaches; cognitive symptoms such as nightmares, uncertainty,
hypervigilance, suspiciousness, and the blaming of others; and emotional
symptoms such as fear, guilt, panic, denial, irritability, and intense anger
to the point of losing emotional control. He found behavioral symptoms
such as withdrawal, antisocial acts, inability to rest, and increased alcohol
consumption, and he found spiritual symptoms, too, men and women who
fought with their God or questioned their basic beliefs, withdrew from
their places of worship, and felt empty and lost, without a sense of meaning or purpose. Mitchell observed untreated stress leading to divorce,
alcoholism, and suicide attempts. The effect on rescue units was frequently devastating, often marked by an increase in sick days taken, a
higher rate of disability claims, and a greater number of qualified people
leaving their career fields prematurely and retiring from sheer burnout. In
a nutshell, Mitchell found that too often the last thing people who dedi-
cate their lives to saving others remember to do is save themselves. They
tell themselves, "It's just part of my job—I'm trained to handle this," when
no one can really be trained to handle that much grief and loss and pain,
or to pick up the body parts of a fellow human being.

The goal of a Critical Incident Stress Debriefing is to stop the progress
of post-traumatic psychological deterioration and stabilize the cognitive
and affective processes. First, you reduce the stimulation levels and get
everybody to calm down physically by removing them from the source of
the crisis—you give them a sense of psychological distance from it. You
might break the rescue team up into small groups, those who were directly
involved in one group, those more tangentially involved in another, or you
might divide them up according to rank, enlisted men in one circle, offi-

cers in another. Then you talk about what's going on. You acknowledge that there's a crisis. You don't critique the mission or go over what went wrong and you don't write up reports on anybody—you talk about the emotions you're all feeling, somebody starting simply with "I can't sleep," or "I'm not hungry," or "I'm having flashbacks." You talk about the symptoms, that it's perfectly normal and common to be angry or to look for someone to blame, which is a quick way to release tension and at the same time avoid dealing with it. You talk in general about what stress is, a biological mechanism designed to alert us to imminent danger and protect us from it by preparing us either to fight or flee, but that unlike almost every other species on the planet, humans have a tendency to hang on to the defense mechanism long after the danger has passed.

During the crisis, the men of the 106th spent nine days either waiting in vain for good news, as a storm raged outside, or searching the vast, open ocean, flying long hours, trying to see, trying to concentrate and stay focused. They went without sleep, ate lousy food, drank too much coffee on duty and too much booze off duty, and struggled to contain the things they were feeling, the doubts and the fears, without a clue as to what they were really dealing with. They were dealing with a lot. In fact, after years of field experience, Dr. Mitchell developed a list of things that can stress emergency workers, ranked in order of seriousness, and the worst thing that can happen is to lose a member of your team in the line of duty. It's a clock-cleaner, a proven destroyer of units, time after time, an emotional mortar round, as bad as losing a family member. A rescue team is indeed like a family. PJs spend almost as much time with one another as they do with their families. The bond is made more profound by the fact that frequently their very lives depend on one another. According to Mitchell, the only way losing a team member in the line of duty could be made worse would be if you thought his death was your fault.

And that's exactly how the PJs of the 106th felt.

Someone could have told them, "The worst thing that can happen to a human being just happened to you, and just because you became a pararescueman doesn't mean you gave up being human." The great irony of post-traumatic stress is that, like a Chinese finger puzzle, the harder you fight to escape, the more firmly you're trapped, so you have to do something extremely counterintuitive and quit struggling. PJs would have a harder time doing that than most people. Their strengths would work against them. Self-doubt is, to a PJ, what kryptonite is to Superman, and it's easy to confuse self-examination with self-doubt. The Wizard of Wig at the bottom of the pool at Lackland is real, the embodiment of everything a PJ fears. PJs are taught, from the opening day of Indoc, to deny their emotions. How do you move beyond your comfort level? You deny that you're uncomfortable. How do you keep going when everybody else is exhausted and spent? You deny that you're exhausted and spent. How do you proceed in the face of enormous risk? You deny that you're scared. How do you deal with tremendous physical trauma, patients with gaping head wounds or severed limbs? You pretend it doesn't affect you. How do you deal with the loss of a patient? You tell yourself the guy's number was up, that you don't care. How do you cope with losing a friend? You deny that it happened for no reason, and that there was nothing anybody could have done. You try to figure it out, because we need answers, so badly that we'll supply them even when there are no answers. Denial might work temporarily, but it never works over the long haul. Emotions eventually come out. Sometimes they explode suddenly in ugly painful displays, and sometimes it's more like a slow leak, a debilitating malfunction over a period of years, but either way, inevitably, they come out. The PJs at the 106th got angry at Jack Brehm because they were angry at God, and at the ocean, and the sky, and because they couldn't imagine getting angry at the one person they really were angry at.

Rick Smith.

Anger is a normal part of the grieving process, yet the hardest thing for a bereaved individual to admit is that he's angry at the deceased, pissed off at being left behind and abandoned. We get mad at the people who leave us without asking our permission. Who said they could break off the friendship? We get mad that we can't tell them we're mad. When Tolstoy wrote, "Hell is the inability to love," he didn't mean hell is not knowing what love is, because then we wouldn't know what we're missing. Hell is knowing exactly what love is, and feeling it precisely and fully, with all our hearts, but being unable to express it or give it away. When loved ones die, we can't love them anymore. We can cherish our memories of them, but that's not the same thing. That doesn't do the trick. That doesn't dispose of all the love that keeps building up inside, with nowhere to go until it becomes toxic and dangerous. Rick Smith didn't do anything wrong, he didn't want to die, it wasn't his fault, he was a great guy—how could anybody justify being mad at him? What sense would that make?

But it didn't make sense. It was simply an accident, a random event, in a universe that's sometimes ordered and often random. The universe might not be forgiving, but we can be.

On December 3, 1991, Jack Brehm stepped down as NCOIC. It was for the good of the unit. He'd talked it over with Colonel Hill, who suggested that Jack move aside and let somebody else try to bring stability to the 106th. Jack had the support of a loving family to fall back on, one of the best coping mechanisms there is. Afterward he called Mike, who told him, "Hey man—if you haven't been fired at least three times in this job, you're not trying. All you can do is stay true to yourself."

Jack knew he'd stayed true to himself. There was a sense of peace in that.

After stepping down as NCOIC, Jack moved down the hall in the Ops building and served the unit in Standardization and Evaluation, tasked with making sure everyone in the section was current with his skill levels, training, and qualifications. He worked for a while in the clinic. He enrolled in leadership school for senior NCOs at Gunther AFB in Montgomery, Alabama. At the 106th, an interim non-PJ NCOIC was assigned, CMSGT Ed King, who came from headquarters in Newburgh, New York, to help unruffle feathers and restore a sense of purpose to the team. King helped everybody move on while the application process to find a permanent NCOIC restarted. Eventually, a PJ from outside the unit was brought in, and stability returned. It was exactly the idea of staying true to himself that kept Jack from ever seriously entertaining the idea of quitting. He and Peggy talked about the other things he could do, but when all was said and done, he was trained to save lives. He was good at it. People were alive because of him—how many guys can say that? The idea of throwing away fifteen years of experience was unthinkable. Talking things through with Peggy saved him, as surely as he'd ever saved anybody else. After the bombing of the Murrah Federal Building in Oklahoma City, the divorce rate among the emergency workers involved in the rescue work following the bombing rose by 300 percent; after "the perfect storm" and throughout its aftermath, Jack and Peggy grew closer.

And as disappointed as Jack was at losing the NCOIC position, there was a brighter side. He'd always known that his family was more important than his job, and the transition gave him more time to spend with his family—how could that be a bad thing? He played ball with his kids, and catch, and taught his children how to ride bikes and skateboards. He came to their schools and gave first-aid demonstrations and talked about what it was like to parachute or scuba-dive. He took them to the beach to fly kites or run down the sand dunes. He took them to movies, parades, and fairs. He cheered from the side lines at hockey games and soccer games and basketball games. He took them to dance recitals and baton-twirling competitions, visibly bursting with pride from the front row, tears welling up in his eyes and a huge smile on his face, to where his kids were almost embarrassed that he was there all the time. Attending to his children never seemed to get in the way of giving time to his wife. He and Peggy still held hands everywhere they went, like teenagers, still talked endlessly, and still apologized when they were wrong, knowing the importance of forgiving each other for the mistakes they made.

As keen as he'd been to assume a leadership role, he realized in the end that that wasn't what was important. The team was important. You do what's right for you, and stay true to yourself, as Mike had said, but above that you do what's right for the team. The team needed experienced PJs. Jack still needed the team. In a way, life was simpler under the new NCOIC, CMSGT Alan Manuel, because it allowed Jack to return his primary focus to the mission. All PJs live for the mission, jones for the mission, dream the mission, and Jack was no different. He knew that sooner or later, other leadership opportunities would come along.

* * * * * * * *

Early October. Midafternoon. The Coast Guard's Rescue Control Center in Elizabeth City, North Carolina, notifies the 106th that the captain of a Malaysian freighter, the *Bunga Saga Tiga*, is having heart trouble. It's a jump mission. The ship is sailing from Penang for Calais, France, and is currently 900 miles east of New York in the middle of the Atlantic. Jack Brehm and PJs Sean Brady and Steve Arrigotti fly out in a C-130 and reach the ship around 5:00 P.M. The weather is good for the first 890 miles, but as they circle the ship, a cloud deck at 2,000 feet forces them to jump S-17 round chutes off a static line from 1,000 feet. As he falls, Brehm notes that the sky, the water, the ship, everything is gray, save for the golden sun on the ship's smokestack.

A launch picks them up a couple hundred yards off the *Bunga Saga Tiga*'s port beam, in rolling fifteen-foot seas, conditions not terribly harsh or difficult, but the crew on the launch seems edgy, unhappy to be on the open ocean in such a small boat. They're led by the first mate, a thin, short, jittery Malay man in his mid-twenties who speaks broken English, his rank indicated by the epaulets on his shirt, his youth by the wispy mustache on his upper lip. Getting the launch back up to the ship proves a nightmare, a procedure that involves attaching twin chains from a winch on the freighter to hooks at either end of the launch, but the launch's crew manages to hook up to only one of the chains, such that whenever a wave drops out from under the launch, the boat and the men in it dangle at a nearly vertical angle. Brady and Arrigotti opt to climb a rope ladder to the deck of the freighter. Brehm stays with the gear in the launch, and tells them to see to the captain. He'll catch up to them when he can.

When he finally gets onboard, Brehm learns from Brady that the captain is dead.

"For how long?"

"I'm not sure," Brady says. "Not long. I guess RCC called to terminate, but we were already under canopy."

"Swell," Brehm says, noticing a sign on a plaque over the dining hall that reads, *PRAISE BE TO ALLAH*. It's an Islamic ship with an Islamic crew. That means they could be stuck for three or four days on a ship with no beer.

"Guess who called RCC?" Arrigotti says.

"Who?"

"The captain's wife."

"She's onboard?"

"Apparently. We haven't seen her."

Brehm finds the first mate and pulls him aside.

"I'm afraid I've got some bad news," Brehm says. "Your captain has died. I'm sorry for your loss." The first mate doesn't seem particularly grieved. "Do you have a cooler on the ship?"

"A what?"

"A cooler. COOL-ER. Refrigerator. Freezer. Icebox."

"Yes, yes," the mate says, glancing nervously over Brehm's shoulder. "Refrigerator."

"A big one?"

"Big."

"You need to get some men and move the captain's body to the refrigerator," Brehm says. The mate nods. "Have you talked to the captain's wife?"

"No one talk to wife," the mate says.

"What do you mean?"

"No talk. Not allowed. Captain's order."

"Well somebody's got to talk to her," Brehm says, feeling like he's talking to himself. "Please direct me to the captain's quarters."

When he gets there, he sees a woman sitting behind the captain's desk, talking on the phone. She's beautiful, in her mid-thirties, twenty years younger than the captain, with sleek black hair and remarkable dark eyes. Brehm can't tell if she's been crying. Her name is Raji Sekhar. She refers to her deceased husband only as Shaka. After telling her he's sorry for her loss, Brehm asks her a few medical questions, how long her husband suffered, what kinds of pains he reported, what his symptoms were. She answers the questions calmly, but she seems to be in shock.

He wants to say something consoling, but then her telephone rings, and she has to answer it.

At dinner, Brehm asks the cook, using the first mate to translate, whether or not the captain's wife has eaten anything. When he's told she hasn't, Brehm puts together a plate of food, chicken, and teriyaki vegetables, and brings it to her, telling her she should eat. She smiles.

"Please, come in," she says. "Unless you are busy. . . ."

"Busy?" Brehm smiles. "I've got all the time in the world," Brehm says, wondering how and when he'll be able to leave the ship. He can imagine she might need someone to talk to, even if she weren't on a ship where the crew was forbidden to speak with her. There are two black leather couches in the captain's quarters, a Persian rug on the floor (the only rug he's seen on the entire ship), a safe, a bookshelf, a large desk, a pair of nautically themed paintings on the walls (which seems a bit redundant), and a brass lamp. There's a lone picture frame on the desk. A door, sitting ajar, leads to what Brehm presumes is the bedroom, where they found the captain's body. Brehm takes one of the couches. Raji takes the other. Brehm speaks first.

"The first mate said nobody's allowed to talk to you."

"First mate," she says with scorn. She nibbles at a chicken leg. "First buffoon would be more like it."

"You're not too fond of the guy, I guess," Brehm says.

"He's an idiot," she says. "He's the cause of this, you know."

"Of what?"

"Of Shaka's heart attacks," she says.

"How so?"

"Oh," she says, rolling her eyes. "How so indeed. How so is that he was in charge of loading the ship, making sure everything is balanced and what have you, but Shaka was the type of man who attended to everything, you know—he couldn't trust other people, so he had to do it all himself. And especially that man, but this time, he didn't have time to check the First Buffoon's calculations before we sailed. Shaka said he would check the First Buffoon's figures later. When he did, he found out we were overloaded by ten tons. Ten tons! Shaka was furious."

"I don't know much about ships," Jack says. "That's a big problem?"

"Aha! It is indeed a big problem," Raji says, "if you are sailing through the Panama Canal. I've sailed with Shaka since we were first married—do you know what they do in the Panama Canal? They measure your water line, you see, and if you are overweight, you can't go through, because you'll run aground. They won't let you. They make you unload your excess cargo onto a barge, which you have to tow behind you, and then on the other side, you can reload, but they don't just give you the barge—you have to rent one. On top of the delay it causes, it can cost the company half a million dollars. Shaka was beside himself. He was livid. He'd be responsible. He's very respectful to his company—he never makes mistakes like that." She catches herself using the present tense. "We were very lucky—ultimately the weather was too rough to allow the canal authority to mark the water line, so they just waved us through and we didn't run aground, but it didn't make Shaka feel any better. Shaka was a fanatic for details. If it wasn't for the first mate, Shaka wouldn't have had a heart attack. He was too worried about what his First Buffoon was up to. No one respects the mate, you know. The whole crew are idiots. Do you know that the First Buffoon had to pull a knife to get one of the crew members to go out on the launch to pick you up?"

"Really?"

"It's true. It is. I tried to call the Coast Guard after Shaka died to tell them it was too late. I'm sorry you had to come all this way."

"It's not a problem," Brehm says, wishing he could take it back—it was not a problem for him, but the whole situation was clearly hard for her.

"Would you like a glass of wine?" she offers.

"You have wine?" Brehm says. "I didn't think you were allowed to have alcohol on an Islamic ship."

"You're not," Raji says, "But Shaka and I had our secrets. He had a weakness for cigars. I would buy wine whenever we were in port." She crosses to the ship's safe and opens it. "Would you like red wine or white wine?"

Jack tries to remember what he learned in survival school. He had chicken for dinner, and you're not supposed to drink red wine with chicken. He's good to go.

"White."

"Would you like a cigar?" she adds. "I have plenty of them and I am certainly not going to smoke them."

"No thanks," Brehm says. It's no time to be passing around cigars, and particularly not the dead captain's cigars.

She opens the bottle of Chablis and pours him a glass.

"That man is such a fool. I don't know how he got to be first mate. He's too young. He should be home, reading schoolbooks. Where are you from, Sergeant Brehm?" He likes the way she rolls the *R* when she pronounces his name.

"You can call me Jack if you want," Brehm says. "I'm from New York."

"You like New York?"

"Very much."

"Why do you like it?"

"Well, for one thing," he says, "when you're from New York, everywhere you go, people are friendlier." She smiles, but her English isn't good enough to catch the humor.

"I have never been to New York City."

"I'm from eastern Long Island, actually," Brehm says.

"And do you have a family, Jack?"

"I have a wife and five kids," Brehm says.

"Boys or girls?"

"Both. Two boys, three girls. The oldest girls are fifteen."

"My daughter is sixteen," Raji says. "When she was little, I could take her with us, but when she got bigger, I stayed home with her. Now she's fully grown."

"In America, we don't consider sixteen fully grown."

"I was married when I was sixteen," Raji says with a laugh.

"Really?" Brehm says. "Wow. I can't imagine my girls getting married, a year from now. Did you think that was too young?"

"Too young?" she smiles. "I thought that was too old. My friends had all married at fourteen. I thought I'd been passed by. I came home for dinner one night and there was a captain sitting at the table, and I knew right away that he was a captain, and what he was there for. My mother told me, 'Raji, we have a guest for dinner tonight,' and I knew right away."

"How'd you feel about that?"

"I felt very lucky. I didn't know much about the business of ships, but I knew it would be better than marrying a shopkeeper."

She says she loved her husband, despite the fact that the marriage was arranged. She and Jack talk. She asks him about his job. He asks her about her hometown. The way she seems to be handling things reminds him of

Peggy. Eventually, she asks him if he minds if she makes a phone call. She has to call her sister. Brehm sips his wine, drains his glass, and then refreshes it. Raji is speaking in English with her sister, and he tunes it out, until he realizes she is looking at him and answering questions. "Yes," she says, to a question her sister asks. He wonders what it might be. Raji glances at him. Brehm wonders why she keeps giggling. "Yes. Yes, very much." She glances at him again. "Oh, I don't know, maybe thirty or thirty-five—my age. Yes," she says, "he's handsome. He's very handsome. Uh huh. Uh huh. Yes. No, not now . . ."

"My sister is a very bad girl," Raji says, holding her hand over the mouthpiece. "If you were single, I would introduce you."

When Jack Brehm finally leaves, he tells the captain's widow she really needs to eat, even if she doesn't feel like it. He tells her he'll bring her lunch tomorrow.

The next morning, before checking in on Raji he needs to call the base to find out what transportation arrangements have been made to bring him, Brady, and Arrigotti back to the base. He heads for the bridge, hoping to use the ship's satellite telephone. When he gets there, he's greeted by the First Buffoon, who says, "Good morning, Captain." Brehm thinks to correct him, and say, "I'm a sergeant, not a captain," but he lets it go. What's the point?

"Can I use your phone?" Brehm asks.

"Certainly."

"Where should I tell them we're going?"

"Excuse me please?"

"Where are we going?"

"Wherever you want to go, Captain."

Then it dawns on Brehm—the first mate wants the PJ to be captain of the *Bunga Saga Tiga*. From the first mate's point of view, the more responsibility he can pass off, the better. Brehm's first thought is, *You've got to be kidding*. His second thought is, *That might not be a bad way to get home*.

"Let me get back to you on that," Brehm tells the mate. "First I need to use the phone." He wants to add, "And that's an order." He calls the Rescue Command Center in Elizabeth City. He gives his story to the duty officer at RCC, who can't believe it, either.

"They said what?"

"They said they'll take us anywhere we want to go."

"No shit?"

"No shit."

"Do they realize they're probably going to be fined by their company for every day they fall behind schedule?" the duty officer asks.

"Probably not," Brehm says. "The guy's not too sharp."

"Well," the duty officer says, "I don't know what to tell you. If it's okay with them, it's okay with us. I guess your closest port of call is Halifax. When you get there, call the harbormaster and they'll send out a pilot to bring you in."

"Anything else I should know?" Brehm asks.

"Yeah—don't hit anything."

Brehm tells the first officer he wants to go to Halifax. Ten minutes later, he can feel the ship changing course. It's good to be the captain.

The next day RCC calls back and says they've found a ship willing to change course to pick them up in mid-ocean, a smaller freighter that can rendezvous with them at 0200 hours. That way, the *Bunga Saga Tiga* won't have to fall behind schedule. Brehm, Brady, and Arrigotti talk it over. The crew had a hard enough time sending out the launch in broad daylight in relatively calm seas. The weather has worsened, and this time, they'll have to do it at two in the morning. Brehm doesn't want to have to pull a knife on anybody. Maybe if they were transferring to a luxury liner . . . but another freighter? Brady and Arrigotti are against the rendezvous. Captain Brehm makes the executive decision to maintain a heading for Halifax.

He calls the coroner in Halifax to tell him they'll be bringing in a body. The coroner asks him if he's sure the guy is dead. Brehm laughs at the question. "Well, if he wasn't when we put him in the freezer yesterday," Brehm says, "he is now." He makes arrangements with the shipping company to have someone from the company meet the widow at the dock. She'll need a hotel room, airline tickets back to Penang, and somebody has to escort the body home and see to the details to make sure it arrives safely—the widow shouldn't have to do that. Brehm brings Raji dinner that night and explains to her the gist of what he's arranged. He tells her they'll be in Halifax at eight the following evening. The coroner will meet them. There'll be policemen as well, to investigate any possible wrongdoing. She isn't worried. She thanks him. She's more subdued and solemn today, as the reality of it all starts to sink in. There are things you can postpone, at sea, that you can't postpone once you're back on land—it's why so many men go to sea. She thanks him for being so considerate. She breaks out a bottle of Merlot, and they talk for hours, about everything.

"It's really funny, isn't it?" she says at last. "In a way."

"What is?"

"That two total strangers from two entirely different countries and cultures can meet each other in the middle of the ocean and become friends. And then we'll probably never see each other again. Without you, I would have been sitting here in this room, with no one to talk to."

"Surrounded by idiots," Brehm says.

"Yes," she agrees.

The next day in Halifax, the ship is met by the coroner, as well as by two representatives from the Royal Canadian Mounted Police, who are required to investigate the circumstances of the captain's death. Raji has things to attend to, so Brehm says good-bye to her at the dock. A handshake, and then a hug. Brehm recalls the old saying about ships passing in the night. He tells her he and his buddies are joining a couple of Canadian PJs for a night on the town before a flight home in the morning. Raji could probably use a night on the town, but he knows an invitation would probably be inappropriate.

"So take care of yourself, Raji," Brehm says.

"Thank you again for everything," she says. "Wait a minute." She takes a pen and a piece of paper and writes down her address for him. "If you are ever in Penang, you must call me."

"Absolutely," he says, "and if you're ever in Long Island, look me up."

"New York," she says. "Where everybody is friendlier."

"Yeah," Brehm says. "Something like that."

14

DO YOU LIKE VAMPIRE MOVIES?

The ocean has a way of really humbling anybody who thinks he's strong enough to beat it. Sometimes it's something you think is going to be really simple that turns into something you can't control. One time we had what seemed like a fairly straightforward task, a training mission where four of us were supposed to deploy off the PJ boat about four hundred meters from the beach, maybe half a mile down from the Shinnecock Inlet on the southern shore of Long Island, about ten miles east of the base. The idea was to drop to the bottom and follow our compasses to a specific point on the shore. It'd be something like standing in a field or park, picking something across the park four hundred yards away, taking a compass bearing, and then trying to walk to it just looking at the compass and never lifting your head up to see where you're going. The visibility in the water off Long Island can be so poor that when you're on the bottom, you can't see more than three or four feet in any direction. What also happens, though, underwater, is that you can accurately follow a heading, but while you're doing that a current you didn't expect can take you down the shore without you knowing it. Something like walking across that field with a wind pushing you off your line.

It seemed like we were swimming longer than we should have been, and I was running out of air, so I decided to surface. When I did, I found myself right in the middle of the inlet, and the tide was ripping. I couldn't swim out of it. I was wearing twin 72-cubic-foot tanks, which made swimming a bit difficult, and then the waves caught me. I'd played in the surf as a kid a thousand times, so in a way I couldn't believe what was happening to me, because these waves were trying to kill me. The inlet runs between two jetties, made from gigantic granite boulders the size of refrigerators, covered with barnacles and mus-

sels and such—not exactly something you want to get bashed against. The first wave that caught me sent me in backward, so I took the blow on my tanks, but it sort of knocked the wind out of me. I managed to drop my weight belt, but I kept the tanks on for protection because I didn't want to break my back. On the second wave, I hit sideways and tried to break the impact with my arm, and it felt like I broke it, and maybe some ribs as well. I was trying to swim out between waves, but it was impossible, so I figured I'd just try to get myself in a good crash position instead. The third wave threw me up harder than the first two. I tried to grab on to something but I couldn't. That was when I knew that if I didn't figure something out, it was possible I was going to get knocked out and maybe drown. No way could I take a beating like that much longer. I didn't figure anything out, but the fourth wave lifted me up high enough that my tanks wedged between some rocks and I managed to climb out. My dive partner, Mike McManus, had virtually the same thing happen to him. I sat there, feeling equal parts lucky and stupid. I looked down the beach and saw that two of the other guys made the beach. I thought, man, you can't take the ocean for granted. Just when you think you're in control of it, it's going to show you different.

IT'S THE KIND OF MISSION YOU THOUGHT ABOUT, BACK WHEN YOU were going through hell at Lackland and the instructors yelled in your face, "Do you really want to be a PJ? Do you refuse to train? Do you *really* want to be a PJ?" You thought of the reasons why you wanted to be a PJ, and about saving lives, that was the main thing, the really important thing, but sometimes you also fantasized about training missions in Florida, where you'd spend your days scuba diving in the warm Florida waters and your nights drinking beer at open-air beachside bars and nightclubs, all on the Air Force's dime. And those weren't even the off days.

It's Friday, February 23, 1996, another six months to go before Jack Brehm's fortieth birthday, but it's never too soon to start treating yourself right. Particularly when you thought you weren't going to make it to thirty. PJs from the 106th have flown down to cover a space shuttle launch, but Jack needs to get in a few deep dives and a compass swim to knock out his dive requirements for the year. The others take the C-130 back to Westhampton. Jack drives down from Patrick AFB in Cocoa Beach, Florida, just south of Cape Canaveral, to Key Largo to meet up with Mike McManus and some PJs from Alaska. He hasn't seen Mike since Rick Smith's funeral. He also doesn't mind getting away from a winter that has dumped record amounts of snow in the Northeast. It's a year that a lot of northerners have headed for Florida, just to stay sane.

Today Brehm and McManus have three dives planned. They're going south of Pennecamp Coral Reef State Park, diving into a couple of wrecks not far from Mosquito Bank Light #35. The first dive, at 1:30 P.M., takes them down 115 feet to a wreck called the *Bibb.* They spend eighteen minutes at the bottom, exploring the wreck, then ascend, stopping to pause for five minutes at fifteen feet. You have to schedule safety stops into your ascent, and you have to exhale as you rise, because the air in your lungs expands as the water pressure around you decreases. On the surface, your lungs hold about four liters of air, but at sixty-six feet below the surface, those four liters compress to the size of a fist, and you need twelve liters instead of four to keep your lungs inflated. The pressure of the water squeezing your body doubles at thirty-three feet, increasing by a factor of one atmosphere. The scuba tank's regulator is designed to measure the pressure and allow enough air into your lungs to compensate for it. A hundred feet down, at a pressure four times that of the air pressure on the surface, you might have seventeen liters of air in your lungs, but if you rise as little as eight feet without exhaling, the air in your lungs can expand to where a lung might tear or pop a leak. A person in a car accident can suffer from a collapsed lung if he holds his breath when he sees the accident coming, hits the steering wheel or the dashboard, and puts too much pressure on his chest. Think of a lung as a balloon, inflating and deflating inside a jar. The jar represents the chest cavity, an airtight chamber. If the balloon leaks, the air escapes into the chest cavity. The lung then deflates and can't reinflate because there is now air in the chest cavity, and that air has nowhere to go.

The second dive at 2:30 P.M. takes them thirty feet down, to another wreck. They spend thirty minutes on the bottom, then ascend, pausing for four minutes at fifteen feet. The third dive, at 3:30, is identical, diving to thirty feet, with thirty minutes of bottom time and one four-minute safety stop at fifteen feet on the ascent. That night, Jack and Mike hit a few of the local hot spots. Brehm calls Peggy from his motel, the Marina Del Mar, about ten, and they talk about the kids' progress reports, Elizabeth's cheer-leading accomplishments (she's the one they throw up in the air, the cheer-leading equivalent of a HALO jump), the weather.

"Are you having a good time?" Peggy asks.

"I'm having a great time," Jack tells her. "Tomorrow we're diving into the wreck of an old freighter. They say it's one of the more famous wrecks around here. The water is just beautiful. I think it was eighty-five today. What's it there?"

"I don't want to talk about it," Peggy says. "It's cold."

"Well, it's not cold here."

"I said I don't want to talk about it."

"Is it snowing?"

"I don't want to talk about it."

"After we finished diving today we just lay on the beach. . . ."

"I'm hanging up now," Peggy says. "Be careful tomorrow."

"You know me," he says.

"Yes, I know you," she says. She knows that the thing most likely to get him in trouble is his enthusiasm. "Be careful anyway."

The next day, Saturday, February 24, breaks clear and bright, blue skies and bright sun, perfect diving conditions. Brehm, McManus, and PJ Steve Daigle, who climbed Mount McKinley with Jack, meet at the dive center in the morning. They load their gear onto a wooden 28-foot dive boat, open and flat in the back, allowing divers to step off into the sea. They leave port at around 9:00. They reach the dive site, suit up, and enter the water around 11:00. Brehm is wearing an eighth-inch wet suit (the water is cold a hundred feet down, even in Key Largo) and a single 80-cubic foot scuba tank, which will give him about an hour of air at thirty feet, or twenty or thirty minutes' worth of air one hundred feet down. The wreck they're diving to today, a ship called the *Dwane*, is 120 feet down. They will spend eighteen minutes on the bottom, then ascend, pausing for five minutes at fifteen feet. One hundred twenty feet is fairly deep for a recreational dive, about the limit for a sports scuba certification, but Brehm dove to 115 feet the day before on the *Bibb* and didn't have any problems. His personal deepest dive is 130 feet, done while in scuba school in Key West. One hundred twenty feet is about the height of an eight-story building. As you descend, you can feel the pressure change in a number of ways, as the weight of the water presses on the air-filled cavities of your body. You feel a pain in your ears, until you have to hold your nose and blow your eardrums back out, or sometimes work your jaw until your ears pop and feel normal again. Your mask gets squeezed to your face, so you have to blow air into it through your nose to equalize the pressure. A neoprene wet suit that is a quarter-inch thick on the surface will be crushed at 110 feet to the thickness of a T-shirt, as the light gets murky and the temperature drops.

It takes Brehm and McManus about five minutes to reach the wreck. For Jack, descending is the fun part. When he first enters the water and turns around to look down, a kind of euphoric feeling comes over him because he's weightless and gently falling toward something very beautiful. There's another kind of euphoric feeling, one Brehm is aware of and monitoring himself for. It's called nitrogen narcosis, and it can mean different things to different people. Some people feel light-headed, or light-hearted, buzzed. Some feel intoxicated and giddy, not unlike the way the nitrous oxide the dentist gives makes you feel. The rule of thumb says that every fifty feet you descend is equal to drinking one martini. Some divers feel a sense of tunnel vision, and some people hallucinate. The story goes that Jacques Cousteau, who helped invent scuba diving, felt so happy when he first experienced nitrogen narcosis that he tried to offer his mouthpiece to fish and had to be stopped by his dive partners from doing so, or he might have drowned. Other people feel tense, or even paranoid. Thought processes under the influence of nitrogen narcosis can become as murky as the water; a diver might lose the ability to do long division or other relatively easy math problems, which can lead to diving accidents, especially when conditions below change, forcing the diver to recalculate his dive underwater, say if a swift current or reduced visibility makes the tasks he needs to accomplish take longer or require greater exertion, increasing his air consumption. Sometimes a diver can get a bit loopy, until it seems as if when one thing goes wrong, four things go wrong: he drops his light, and then he drops his compass, retrieving the light, and then he snags his fin on something, and suddenly, he's in trouble. Nitrogen narcosis happens when the nitrogen in the compressed air a diver breathes gets forced or absorbed into the blood and tissues of the body as the pressure increases. What we call "air" is only 21 percent oxygen, 76 percent nitrogen, and 3 percent other gases, and a diver breathes enormous amounts of air when he dives deep.

Nitrogen narcosis is what can happen as a diver descends. The bends can happen when he ascends. A diver gets bent if he comes up without pausing to allow the nitrogen in his blood or tissues to be expelled through his lungs. As the pressure decreases as the diver ascends, the nitrogen in his tissues expands and forms bubbles, something like the way the carbon dioxide in a soda bottle will fizz or foam when you take the cap off the bottle. A diver who ascends without pausing at all, in a panic situation, can get the full-blown systemic bends, which can be fatal, even if he's rushed to a hyperbaric chamber. A hyperbaric chamber treats decompression illnesses by recompressing the victim, which stops the nitrogen from expanding uncontrollably and forces it back into the blood. Once it's in solution in the blood, the lungs can remove it. Even a diver who ascends with caution and planned decompression stops can sometimes take a bends hit in a specific area, where a number of tiny nitrogen bubbles have coalesced to form a larger expanding bubble, sometimes in a joint, in a muscle, or sometimes within the nerve tissue itself, which can be excruciatingly painful. Sometimes there's permanent damage. Researchers today think there are also dive events called micro-bends, which have a subtler effect. Some Navy divers who've dived to extreme depths have been found subsequently to have a neurological condition that seems to permanently rob them of their sense of humor. After a deep dive, some divers find that it can take hours to regain fine motor control over their muscles, and that they can't play the guitar, or write legibly, or they have trouble driving. Perhaps the biggest danger is that you usually don't feel anything happening until you're back on land and you think you're safe. The deepest recorded dive with scuba gear, breathing regular air, is 525 feet. The deepest dive of all time using scuba gear is 925 feet, accomplished in 1996 by two men, Jim Bowden and Sheck Exley, in the Gulf of Mexico, using thirty tanks and fourteen different gas mixtures of oxygen, nitrogen and helium, but even at a depth where the pressure was strong enough to crush a quarter-inch thick cast aluminum battery case, Bowden didn't feel any extraordinary pain. Exley died making the dive.

Today, as he approaches the wreck, Brehm feels good. Confident. Like he's got the best job in the world, but then, he's also felt that sense of satisfaction on dry land. He has a slight case of nitrogen narcosis, but it's nothing he hasn't experienced before. If anything he feels perhaps a bit cocky. Usually he experiences nitrogen narcosis as the equivalent of drinking two beers, nothing dramatic, but definitely pleasant. He tries to caution himself against feeling too cocky. Feeling too good about yourself is as dangerous as feeling scared, both forms of impaired thinking, but it's hard to stop yourself from feeling good about something. He follows McManus as they explore the wreck. The wreck has been picked clean by other divers over the years, no souvenirs to take home to Matt or Jeff, but it is nevertheless interesting. According to reports, there is supposed to be a large grouper living somewhere on the wreck, and Jack wants to find it. At one point, he comes to a wall, about eight feet high, and has to swim up and over it. As he does, he feels a slight ping just above his heart, slightly to the left. It's a small pain. He's felt such pains before, though never in this exact place. Sometimes they go away.

He dives again at noon, a mere forty-foot dive for forty minutes bottom time, into a wreck perhaps three miles away from the first. The second dive goes fine, but when it's over, around two, Brehm realizes he still has the pain over his heart, a very slight ache, but a specifically located ache all the same. He thinks, it's probably nothing.

At nine the next morning, he tries to go for a six-mile run from his motel, heading south on Route 1, but after only a quarter-mile, he feels a sharp stabbing pain in his heart that makes him stop in his tracks, grab his chest and cry out. He bends over. He wonders if he's having a heart attack. He takes his pulse. After a moment, the pain lessens, but he decides to give up on the idea of running. Walking back to the hotel, he is in constant pain, with sharp attacks coming every few seconds. He sees Mike McManus in a coffee shop and joins him.

"What's up, Jack?" McManus says. "You don't look so good."

"I'm not so good," Brehm says, telling McManus his symptoms. He's hesitant to tell McManus just how bad it is. He fears he has a serious problem.

"When did you first notice it?" McManus asks.

"Yesterday, during the first dive."

"It sounds like maybe you took a hit," McManus says. "It's probably not anything serious, but if you are bent, you should go back to the motel and see if you can find a local dive chamber."

Sometimes the symptoms of a dive injury can be so vague that divers don't seek attention for days or weeks. Symptoms can resemble those of a virus: headaches, nausea, fatigue, vomiting, intestinal disturbances, parathesia, muscle or joint pain. On the phone, Brehm hopes to find a local doctor who specializes in diagnosing dive-related injuries, but when he calls the nearest dive chamber in Key Largo, he gets an answering machine, informing him that it's closed because it's Sunday. That sounds a bit odd, for what is ostensibly an emergency medical facility. He leaves his number. No one calls back. He drives with the team back to Patrick at noon. Everyone is laughing and talking about the weekend, so he keeps his complaints to himself. When they stop for gas north of Miami, Mike McManus asks him, out of earshot from the others, how he's feeling. "Like shit," Brehm replies. At 4:30, he calls the emergency room at Patrick, and at 5:30, he sees the flight surgeon, Dr. Ted Foondos, who examines him and asks him a series of questions. Does he feel any joint pains? Any need to cough? Did he feel like he pulled anything, loading or unloading equipment, either onto the C-130 he flew in on or on the boat before or after the dive? Dr. Foondos listens to Jack's chest through a stethoscope. Brehm's heart sounds fine. His breathing sounds normal. Foondos calls Brooks AFB in San Antonio, the Air Force's main medical facility for studying and treating fliers, and consults with a Dr. Mike Ainscough. The conversation lasts about ten minutes.

"We don't think you're bent," Dr. Foondos says at last. "My guy at Brooks agrees. If you were, there ought to be other symptoms. It seems more likely that you pulled a muscle."

"Really?" Brehm says. "You know, Doc, I'm in pretty good shape. . . ."

"I'm going to write you a prescription," Foondos says. "You take these and call me in the morning. Tell me if anything changes."

The prescription is for Motrin.

At 9:00 the next morning, Monday, Jack is back in the doctor's office. The pain has moved. What was once located on his left side, above his heart, seems to have shifted to below his zyphoid process, the bottom of his breastbone, near the diaphragm. How could a muscle pull relocate? Foondos doesn't know, but suggests that if the pain persists, Jack should call his flight surgeon when he gets back to Long Island. Brehm doesn't press the point, but nothing he knows about medicine has ever explained to him how a muscle pull might relocate. By 4:00, Brehm is on a commercial airliner, headed home.

His flight surgeon in Long Island is a Dr. Pasternak, a guardsman and, in civilian life, a cardiologist. When Jack calls him the next day, Tuesday, he's told that the doctor won't be back to the base clinic again until 2:00 Friday. The problem is that now the pain not only persists but it's shifted again, moving from his diaphragm to mid-sternum. Basically it feels as if he's swallowed a large ice cube. This is getting weird, he thinks. At Peggy's suggestion, he locates a dive chamber on Long Island and speaks to a nurse who specializes in dive injuries. He describes the progression of the pain. The nurse is busy, but listens and expresses her opinion when he's done.

"What'd she say?" Peggy asks him when he gets off the phone.

"She says it doesn't seem dive-related," Jack says.

"That's ridiculous," Peggy says. "You're okay, you dive, you're not okay anymore—that's dive-related. Call Dr. Pasternak back."

"I'm seeing him on Friday."

"Well, call him back and get him on the phone. Leave a message and make him return your call. If this is a problem, you're not going to wait until Friday to take care of it."

You sometimes get the sense that if Peggy Brehm had been on the *Titanic*, there would have been plenty of lifeboats to go around, they would have all sailed away fully occupied, and the ship probably wouldn't have struck the iceberg in the first place.

Pasternak returns Jack's call at 7:15 that evening. Jack tells him he originally had a sharp stabbing pain over his heart, which became a dull ache in his diaphragm, which turned into a feeling like he'd swallowed a large ice cube. Pasternak listens and asks some of the same questions Dr. Foondos did. He asks about the dive in question and if anything unusual took place during it. The dive was planned perfectly, and Brehm and McManus and the others dove the plan. No one else on the dive experienced any difficulties, and they followed the same procedures Jack did. Pasternak's over-the-phone assessment matches that of the woman from the dive chamber at St. Agnes. It simply doesn't seem, at least from the way Jack describes it, to be a dive-related injury. They'll know more on Friday when they can meet at the clinic. Until then, he says, Jack should take it easy and skip his daily workouts.

In the interim, the feeling changes yet again. By Friday, it feels as though there's a weight inside his chest, tied to a string around his heart. He thinks he can feel something flapping around loose. Sometimes he almost thinks he can *hear* something flapping around loose, though that's probably unlikely. One night he lets Peggy put her ear to his chest, but she hears nothing but his heart beating. She borrows his stethoscope, but can't tell anything. The last time she put on a stethoscope, they were listening to the separate heartbeats of the twins, Michele and Elizabeth, when they were still in her womb. It reassures her to hear his heart beating. Her concern is for him. His concern is for himself, too, but also for his family, and how he might provide for them in the future, because there are rules regarding what types of injuries might disqualify a man from being a PJ. Getting knocked unconscious, for example, automatically disqualifies you from serving in pararescue, because it's known that one spell of unconsciousness can lead to future blackouts or seizures, and PJs work under circumstances and in situations where they can't afford to black out. Needless to say, between getting sucker-punched in a bar fight or simply going one Kamikaze or Jell-O shot over the line and passing out, PJs do, in some way or other, become unconscious from time to time, so it helps to have a flight surgeon on your side. It also helps to work in hospitals where you can gain access to your own medical records, and it helps to know how to work a bottle of Wite-Out or the delete button on a computer keyboard. Serious injuries, however, can't be hidden, and shouldn't be, and good PJs know that. Lying in bed the night before his examination, Jack hopes it is just a muscle pull, because if it's something else he might have to start looking for a new line of work, and that thought is as uncomfortable as the pain in his chest. The more he thinks about it, the more certain he is that this is a career-ending injury. He tries not to think about it.

Jack meets Dr. Pasternak at the clinic at 4:00 on Friday, March 1. He describes the pain as a loose feeling and says that sometimes he thinks he can even hear it, so Pasternak puts a stethoscope to his chest and listens. Everything sounds normal. He repeats that it doesn't seem to be a dive-related injury, but he knows that Jack is not satisfied with this diagnosis. Brehm knows he probably should be satisfied, because three separate people who ought to know, Dr. Foondos, the dive clinic nurse, and now Dr. Pasternak, have all said the same thing.

"Look," Pasternak says, "why don't you call the physiological center down at Brooks and talk to them? Maybe they can reassure you."

Brehm calls from Pasternak's desk, only to be told that all flight surgeons at Brooks are gone for the weekend. Pasternak recommends that Jack be patient. They can go further with this if the conditions persist, or worsen, but if it's a severe muscle pull it will simply take time to heal. Brehm asks if he should resume his physical training. Pasternak says he can, as long as he keeps it light and stops if he feels any discomfort. Relaxing and not worrying about it sound like good ideas—after all, everybody else is telling him it's minor. Maybe worrying too much about it is the real problem.

Deep down, Jack still thinks he knows better.

On Saturday, Brehm tries to obey doctor's orders and does nothing. The pain and the loose feeling are still there. On Sunday night, he has a hockey game with his team, "The Lost Cause," so he tries to play, but he becomes quickly winded. He thinks it's been so long since he's put in a decent workout that he's gotten rapidly out of shape. On Monday, he manages to run four miles on a treadmill at the small gym in the Ops building at the base, but he can barely maintain a nine-minute mile pace, and he feels very weak.

He feels somewhat better when he wakes up on Tuesday morning. He reports to work. At 7:00 A.M., he tries to go for a six-mile run. He gets a mile and a half before he is fatigued and out of breath. This is not a pulled muscle. He doesn't know what this is, but this is not a pulled muscle. He turns back to the base. A mile from the gate, he decides to go all out and run as fast as he can. He uses the stopwatch function on his watch to time himself.

By the time he reaches the gate, he feels as if he's going to collapse, gasping for air. His time is eight minutes and thirty-three seconds. Now he knows something is wrong. He feels a hundred years old. He's afraid. This is a career-ending injury. The twins are applying to colleges. How will he pay for that? What can he tell them? How will they handle the disappointment?

At the base he showers, dons a flight suit, and finds an empty office with a door he can close behind him. At a quarter to two in the afternoon, he calls Brooks AFB and asks to speak with a flight surgeon from the physiological center. He speaks with a Dr. Butler, who tells him to start at the beginning. It takes Brehm nearly an hour to recite the chronology of the last two weeks. Butler listens patiently and asks a few questions, mainly to make sure he has the dive depths and the times correct. Jack tells him he just tried to run an all-out mile and did it in eight and a half minutes.

"That sounds pretty good to me," Butler says. "I'd love to run an eight-and-a-half-minute mile. How fast would you normally run it?"

"I'm a PJ and a triathlete," Brehm tells him. "I usually run that in less than six."

Jack finishes his synopsis. Finally Dr. Butler reaches an opinion.

"I'm guessing you have medistinal air, probably a pneumothorax," he says. Brehm knows from his paramedic training what that means. He may have a collapsed lung. "I'm going to call Pasternak right now and arrange for you to get some chest X-rays. What's the closest hospital to you?"

Brehm gives Dr. Butler Dr. Pasternak's number, as well as the number to Central Suffolk Hospital. Butler tells him to report to Central Suffolk immediately. Jack clears it with his supervisors and leaves for the hospital.

The X-rays are taken at 4:00. The X-ray technician is a pretty young brunette woman, maybe twenty-five years old. She asks Jack to wait until she develops the film, to make sure the film comes out clear. It does. Ten minutes later, she tells him they're fine.

"They're fine?" Jack says. "What do they show?"

"I'm only the technician," she says. "I can't read the X-rays. I just meant they're fine as in, the pictures came out okay, and I won't need to reshoot them."

"Well when will the doctor be able to read them?"

She shrugs. "The radiologist just left for the day. He'll be back in the morning."

It sounds a bit fishy, since Dr. Butler told him to get to the hospital immediately, but Brehm figures if he could wait nine days, he can wait another twelve hours.

On his way home, he stops off at Barbara Dougherty's house to see how she and the kids are doing. Jimmy is in Turkey on a TDY. She asks Jack if he remembers the Ukrainian sailor her husband recently rescued. Jack says he certainly does. Alexander Taranov. The sailor was from a Ukrainian cargo ship that had rolled over in a storm and was sinking in the mid-Atlantic. Looking down from the airplane, the crew counted thirty-four Ukrainian sailors in the water, holding on to anything that floated, bobbing about in twenty- to thirty-foot seas. The C-130 dropped all the life rafts they had onboard, a total of six, along with survival kits and radios. They managed to make radio contact with the Ukrainians, and told them they'd be back at first light with helicopters and to sit tight. When the HH-60s arrived the next morning at the break of day, they circled the area for thirty minutes, unable to discover a single raft, with no trace of the ship. Finally Dougherty spotted a lone survivor clinging to some flotsam. Dougherty low and slowed in and hoisted Taranov out. The rest of the sailors' shipmates, Dougherty learned, had been killed by sharks during the night or drowned.

"What about him?" Jack asks.

"He's defecting," Barbara Dougherty says. "He's in Manhattan with his lawyer, and he wants to know if I want to come into the city to meet them for drinks. I was wondering if you'd go with me."

Jack says he doesn't feel so good, but he'll go if it will cheer her up. When Laura Spillane calls, checking in, they decide that Laura will go and Jack won't have to, since he's not feeling up to it.

Jack doesn't know that just after he left Central Suffolk Hospital ("Central Suffering," some called it), the twenty-five-year-old X-ray technician had shown Jack's X-rays to a doctor who just happened to be passing by. The doctor said, "I hope this guy is in surgery."

"He's not," she told the doctor. "He just went home."

"When?"

"Two minutes ago"

"Well run out to the parking lot and see if you can catch him," the doctor told her. "This guy should be in surgery. Now."

Jack drives home from Barbara Dougherty's house but passes Peggy coming from the opposite direction. Peggy frantically waves him down and pulls off the road. Jack gets out of the car and sees that his wife has been crying hysterically.

"What's the matter?" he asks.

"You," she says. "A doctor from Texas just called the house and told me he sent you to the hospital with a collapsed lung. Then I called the hospital and they tell me you left—where have you been? Why didn't you call me?"

"They can't read the X-rays until tomorrow," he explains. "There's nothing to tell you until then. I was at Barbara's. I almost went into the city with her. That Ukrainian guy is defecting and he and his lawyer—"

"Nothing to tell me?" Peggy says. "I'm thinking you're in a hospital with a collapsed lung, and you say you have nothing to *tell me*?"

"I didn't know you knew anything," he said. "If I thought you were worried, I would have called."

"How can I know anything if you don't call me?"

"But if you don't know anything, then why would I assume you were worried about—" Jack begins, but quickly abandons this line of reasoning because he knows he's wrong. "I'm sorry. I should have called you."

At home, Peggy asks him again how he feels. She says he doesn't look very well.

"I'm fine . . . I just . . . think maybe I should . . . lie down for . . . a while."

"Listen to you," she says. "You can't even finish a sentence without taking a breath every three words."

The phone rings. It's Dr. Pasternak. He tells Jack his left lung is 80 percent collapsed and that he needs to get to the nearest hospital as soon as possible. Jack tells him that would be Mather Hospital in Port Jefferson, and that he's on his way.

Meanwhile, Peggy has checked the answering machine. There are three messages, one from Jack's NCOIC, Chief Manuel; one from Dr. Butler;

and one from Central Suffolk Hospital. All three messages say the same thing. Get to a hospital, now.

Immediately.

Do not wait.

Peggy drives. Jack doesn't want her to worry, so he tries to tell her that he sees collapsed lungs all the time, and that the procedure to remedy the situation is fairly simple. In the field, lacking anesthesia, he would perform a thoracentesis, inserting a large-bore fourteen-gauge needle, about the diameter of a toothpick, to purge the air in the chest cavity. In a hospital, under anesthesia, a chest tube would be used. The balloon-inside-a-jar analogy isn't quite accurate, because in fact both lungs occupy the same chest cavity, with the heart between them. As one lung collapses, venting air through the tear into the chest cavity, the chest wall around the healthy lung slowly fills with air, restricting the healthy lung's expansion. The pressure in the chest cavity increases with each exhalation, until the damaged lung collapses entirely. Then the pressure begins to push the heart into the healthy lung. If it pushes it too far, it stresses the vena cava, the vein that returns blood to the heart. An artery like the aorta is fairly sturdy, but the vena cava is comparatively flimsy and can easily become twisted or kinked. When this happens, it's called a tension pneumothorax. If the vena cava is constricted completely, no blood can return to the heart, and the patient dies.

Jack tells her only that he sees collapsed lungs all the time.

He reaches the Mather emergency room at ten minutes to seven. He's taken into triage at ten minutes after seven, and at seven-thirty, new X-rays are taken. Peggy is with him, holding his hand, asking him how he feels. He feels fine, really, relieved to be in a hospital and finally getting treatment, but Peggy isn't satisfied that the man she loves is out of danger. It's also true that for all the times in his life that Jack has been in danger, she has never been there with him. She has never been able to do anything about it.

"You're sure you're okay?" she says.

"I'm good," he says. "Really."

She pats his hand. He squeezes hers. She tries to think of what else she can do.

At 8:00, an ER doctor comes by to examine Jack. He asks Peggy to wait on the other side of the curtain. He listens to Jack's chest, and tells him that the new X-rays have revealed that his left lung is 100 percent collapsed and is restricting his right lung by 10 percent. The ER doctor asks the nurse when the thoracic surgeon will arrive. He's told that the thoracic surgeon is due in about twenty minutes.

"This guy doesn't have twenty minutes," the ER doctor says.

Peggy hears this. She throws aside the curtain.

"Look—I don't know what you have to do, but I want you to do it right now," she says.

"Please wait behind the curtain," she's told.

"I'm not waiting behind the curtain," she says. Jack reaches for her hand.

"Peg, it's all right," he says, struggling to breathe. "I don't feel that bad, plus the guy is right here with the needle and he knows what to do with it if he has to. It's not that big a deal."

"Who's going to do this thing?" Peggy asks, turning to the ER doctor. "Are you?"

"We're hoping the thoracic surgeon will arrive shortly," he says.

"What's his name? I want to speak with him."

"It's Dr. Van Bemmelen," the doctor says. "I believe he's on his way to the hospital at the moment."

"He's on his way? You don't know where he is?"

"Peggy," Jack says, "it's going to be all right. Come here."

He puts his arm around her. She kisses his cheek. He whispers to her, "I really think we should just wait until the doctor gets here. I'll be okay until then."

Van Bemmelen arrives at 8:30. He looks at the X-rays, and asks the ER doctor when they were taken. Told that the pictures are half an hour old, Van Bemmelen frowns. He informs Jack that there's no time to wait for an operating room. Unfortunately, that means that there's no time to wait for anesthesia, either. He wants to insert a chest tube immediately.

"Do it," Jack says.

"There's going to be some pain," Van Bemmelen says.

"Do it," Brehm says.

Van Bemmelen picks up a sterilized scalpel from a tray. The idea is to make an incision below Jack's left clavicle and insert the chest tube, a clear plastic tube about the diameter of your index finger. The technical term for it is a thorascotomy.

"Should I be here?" Peggy asks.

"Well," Van Bemmelen asks her, "do you like vampire movies?" She says she doesn't. "Then you might want to step out for a second."

Jack knows she's within earshot, so he doesn't cry out when the surgeon stabs him with the scalpel. He says only, "Oh God . . ." Peggy hears him. It hurts, but it's a good pain, Jack has to admit. When Peggy returns, he's smiling. The chest tube has allowed his left lung to reinflate. Within three breaths, he feels as though it's full again. The tube will stay in for as long as it takes for the tear in his lung to heal.

"Oh my God," she says when she sees the bloody tube sticking out of his chest. "How do you feel?"

"A hundred percent better," he tells her.

"I've got to call the kids," she says.

While she's on the phone, Jack wonders if trying to run a mile in under six minutes was what finally blew the lung open. He probably had a slow leak before that. He feels like a thick-headed idiot. He'd tell Peggy as much, but she already knows.

He doesn't kick himself for showing poor judgment—he's always pushed it, always been a bit reckless, in the belief that luck comes to those who press their luck, and so far he's been right. What nags him is a different idea. Muscle tissue is something you can change through exercise. You can build muscle tissue, and make yourself stronger, but there's nothing you can do to strengthen the tissues in your lungs. The lungs simply grow older, and as the tissue ages, it weakens. You can't help it, and you can't reverse it. The body ages. You lose bone strength, and muscle strength, and brain cells, and who knows what else. You can't help it. You can't reverse it. You can't give in to it, either.

Would his lung have collapsed twenty years ago? Why now? Does it mean anything? Is it a sign, of aging—of mortality? Or of something smaller than mortality—a sign that it's simply time to start thinking about a different line of work?

*   *   *   *   *   *   *

At home, while he recuperated and waited to return to flight status, Jack signed up for a paramedic class, hedging his bets. If the doctors ruled that he couldn't return to flight status, he might look for work as a medic. He did odd jobs around the house, and he shoveled snow. Lots of snow, snow that filled the backyard and covered the deck. There were eighteen major snowstorms that year. One day, after the snow had piled up at the end of the deck to where it nearly reached the roof, Jack and Jeffrey built an igloo, the kind of snow shelter Jack had learned to build during winter training exercises, complete with a protected entryway and benches inside to sleep on. Jeffrey wanted to spend the night in the igloo, and Jack agreed. Jeffrey went in at 8:00 that night, and Jack joined him long enough to stick a handful of green chemlights in the snow for illumination. He told Jeffrey that he wanted to watch television until ten, and that he'd join him after that. When Peggy learned that Jeffrey was in the igloo all by himself, she decided to keep him company, even though she wasn't really an outdoors enthusiast, and not the kind of person who would ordinarily spend any more time than she had to in a snow shelter. Jack gave her his sleeping bag. She brought a book with her and said she was going to read.

Most people who stay in snow shelters are surprised at how comfortable they are. When Jack went in to get Peggy at ten, she was sound asleep, and so was Jeffrey, so he left them there, safe and warm in their down bags. He turned off the lights. In the backyard, the igloo glowed a dull phosphorescent green in the late winter night.

15

THE HAND OF GOD IN THE
HEART OF PITTSBURGH

Mike and I were on a TDY in Thailand in 1988 where we were ordered to teach a Thai captain how to free fall. I believe he's a general or something by now, but at the time, he was still a V.I.P. who wanted to learn how to free fall, and we were chosen to help him. We knew him as Captain Sui Gin. He was in his mid-twenties, maybe five foot six, with a perpetual smile on his face. First of all, in the Pipeline, there's a procedure you have to go through before you can free fall. You go to jump school at Fort Benning and learn how to land and how to jump off a static line. You go to the wind tunnel at Fort Bragg, North Carolina, which is essentially a big hole in the ground with a fan at the bottom with a net over it, and the fan blows air up at 125 miles per hour, and you jump in and learn how to float and how to turn, and how to stabilize yourself, in a safe, controlled environment. You don't just read a few books and then step out the back of an airplane. The guy did wear jump school wings, so we assumed he'd jumped before, but whether he'd ever done free fall remained to be seen. Second, Mike and I didn't have our AFF qualifications, which you need to instruct accelerated free fall, but there was no one else available. Better us than nobody. Third, the guy didn't speak a word of English, which made instructing him slightly more difficult. I pantomimed, and I used hand signals, and I drew the guy pictures—I had no idea how much of it he picked up on. He just sort of smiled and nodded at everything I said. We did this every night for a week. When it came time to jump, to be safe, Mike and I grabbed on to him, one on each arm, and we went out the door with him, but the guy didn't exit square to the wind and immediately he started tumbling, flip-flopping every-

where. Mike wanted no part of it and flew out. It was sort of "Here you go, Jack—let's see how you handle this." I tried to do what I could to get the guy stable, but it was no use, and I was running out of time, so eventually I pulled his main chute and hoped he remembered some of the things I taught him. Away he went, on a square chute he didn't really know how to steer, or brake, riding with the wind. The drop zone was fairly large, a field alongside a country road, but beyond that there were trees and farms and mountains in the distance. If he hit a tree . . . even if he landed in an open field, he could still hit it at thirty miles an hour if he landed with the wind. Mike and I made the DZ without any complications. We had no idea where CAPT Sui Gin went. When we finally caught up with him, he was walking down the road, about four miles away, carrying his parachute under his arm, and he was totally psyched. He wanted to go again. Considering we'd lucked out not killing him the first time, we declined.

But I've always said that Mike and I have led charmed lives. We've both walked away, time and again, from parachute malfunctions and other screw-ups. Sometimes you feel lucky. Other times you feel like there's more than luck involved. Sometimes you feel like maybe somebody's watching over you.

J ACK BREHM AND MIKE MCMANUS SHARED A CHARMED EXISTENCE, almost from the start. They'd missed the crash in Plattsburgh, a flight they both could have been on. They survived the pounding on the rocks of Shinnecock Inlet, anecdotally one of the most dangerous inlets in the United States. They were able to bail out of a Thai helicopter after it lost an engine at 10,000 feet. They'd survived hangovers that would have put ordinary men in hospital, and bar fights that would have put ordinary men in jail. McManus had saved Jack's life, simply by teaching him to hang tough. It was McManus who got Jack into running marathons and Iron Man competitions, advising him that the way to get ahead in a race was to imagine that the guy in front of you was a mass-murdering rapist psychopath who wasn't going to stop until he got to your house. There were always going to be other mass-murdering rapist psychopaths to pass, but the point was to focus on the one in front of you, and take them one at a time. Brehm

returned the favor by saving McManus's life one night on a visit to
Anchorage. The two men were debriefing the day's activities over beers at
an Alaskan institution called the Alaskan Bush Company, a strip joint on
East International Airport Road just off Old Seward Highway, decorated in
Old West Yukon frontier motifs, lacking only swinging doors and someone
named Miss Kitty at the door, with a staircase against the back wall that led
to the dressing rooms. They were drinking their second beers when Mike
described to Jack a weird thing that had been happening to his heart lately,
palpitations that came and went and didn't seem to be related to exertion
or stress, accompanied by a strange light-headedness. McManus was getting a lap dance at the time, and had a pair of hooters in his face like you
read about in books, but Brehm excluded the lap dance from his diagnosis,
took a beverage napkin and wrote down the words *Wolff-Parkinson-White
Syndrome* with a felt-tipped pen. WPW is essentially a short-circuiting of
the heart's electrical system, in which an extra electrical pathway develops
between the atria and the ventricles, causing extra contractions that speed
the heart rate, easily reparable with surgery but potentially fatal.

"Five bucks says I'm right," Brehm proclaimed. "We just read about it
last week in my paramedics class."

An examination by a cardiologist shortly after that was inconclusive,
until Mike asked the doctor to look for WPW and proved Brehm's diagnosis correct. McManus carried the beverage napkin in his wallet ever
since. McManus was, however, lucky before he ever met Jack, according
to a story Brehm frequently tells, when he tries to explain to people why
Mike McManus is the toughest guy he knows.

McManus was stationed in Tachikawa AFB in Japan. It was 1968. The
section got a call that a fishing boat had had an explosion, five hundred
miles off the coast of Japan in the North Pacific. The ship was dead in the
water, adrift in a storm. It wasn't known whether there were any survivors
on the ship, only that an emergency SOS beacon had been activated.
McManus launched in a C-130 at 2100 hours, along with another PJ
named Ted Martin. They homed in on the beacon but didn't find the ship
until midnight, partly because there were no lights on the boat and partly
because the weather was so rough, maybe forty-foot seas and fifty-knot
winds. The weather was bad enough that the pilot wanted to abort the rescue, but Mike had flown with him on five other jump missions, and
together they had a pretty good track record, and besides, McManus
argued, there could be people trapped in the overturned hull of the ship.

The radio operator couldn't raise the ship. Mike concluded that there was nothing left but to go down there and see what happened.

Ordinarily when a jumper leaves an airplane, it suddenly gets very quiet. It was the only time, in Mike's memory, that it ever got louder outside the plane. He heard the ocean literally roaring below him, loud as a freight train, and it scared the crap out of him. He thought, "Oh boy, this is going to be fun."

They deployed from a thousand feet, about two and a half miles upwind from the ship, using round parachutes that couldn't be steered or turned, though McManus did have some control over his rate of descent. Ted Martin immediately had a malfunction, pulled his reserve chute, and sailed off into the night. McManus watched him disappear. He saw the ship below, in a mass of foam, directly on his wind line, and knew he had two choices, either to fly over it and swim back or drop in short and swim to it. He didn't want to hit it, so he decided to drop in short. His landing was rough. He hit the top of a wave with his fins, popped his capewells to release his chute, and immediately did a flip into the sea, smacking the water so hard it ripped the regulator out of his mouth. As a teenager he'd worked as a clown diver, entertaining vacationers in Florida resort pools, so he knew a bit about aquabatics. He'd swam in the open ocean in his early days as a PJ, recovering film cartridges dropped to earth from spy satellites, risking his life for cassettes with signs on the side that said, "If found, please return to . . ." with an address and an offer of a $25 reward for anybody who came across one washed up on a beach, though they were, of course, worth far more than that.

Nothing he'd ever done prepared him for this.

The previous estimate of forty-foot seas proved a tad conservative. The seas were overwhelming, preposterous, ridiculous, hellacious. The Japanese fishing boat drifted away from him in the wind. He swam toward it for a while, but it was no use. It was drifting too fast. He tried to raise the C-130 on his radio, but the radios they gave PJs back then didn't work very well when they got wet, which was most of the time, so he got rid of it because he didn't need the extra weight. He got rid of his scuba tanks for the same reason, dumping them before they beat him to death. He had an inflatable one-man butt boat with him, but the water was too rough to stay in it. The winds were too strong and kept flipping him over. He got back in the water and hung on to the raft. Much of the difficulty came from the fact that there was no pattern or predictability to the waves, the way you can watch waves crashing rhythmically on a beach. Waves lifted him high in the air and dropped him on his face. Waves crashed over his head. He'd take a gulp of air, go under, surface, and wait for the next wave to hit, though they were coming at random, and he never knew when the next one would pound on him. Saltwater blew in his face and down his throat. He threw up frequently. Sometimes he'd ride four or five waves in a row, but then the next one would toss him. He had no sense of time passing, living moment to moment, knowing only that he was growing tired and cold. When he fired a flare the C-130, which was still circling overhead, tried to drop him a twelve-foot in diameter twenty-man raft. Twenty-man rafts weigh about seventy pounds. McManus watched it flip end over end and blow away, skipping like a stone across the surface of the water.

He fired more flares, but there was nothing anybody could do. He knew it would be crazy to send another man in after him. There was no sign of Ted Martin, no other flares in the sky to indicate what might have happened to him. McManus was on his own. For six hours, he fought the ocean. He felt if he could just make it to the morning, he'd be all right. They'd come get him. For six hours, he rode up and down thirty- and forty- and fifty-foot swells, hanging on to his raft while the wind and the waves conspired to rip it from his hands. A wave would crash over him, he'd wait for it to clear, catch a breath, and wait for it to happen again. For six hours.

McManus wasn't a churchgoer and he didn't pray, or at least he wasn't into the "Please help me" approach to deities, but he did talk to the Big Guy from time to time, and felt they had an understanding, that when it was time they'd get it on. McManus believed that God had a sense of humor, and that he was definitely the Big Guy's entertainment that night.

Around 6:00 A.M., as the sky was beginning to lighten, he saw a ship, a Japanese fishing boat, coming toward him, though it was too far away to have seen him yet. The weather was still nasty, twenty-five foot breakers and thirty-knot winds. He had one flare left. He waited, then popped it when the fishing boat was about two hundred yards off. He was in luck. The boat turned toward him.

Ordinarily a boat coming to the rescue of someone in the water will either send out a smaller boat or, more likely, lower a cargo net over the side for him to grab. McManus wasn't sure what they were going to do, and he wasn't sure how much strength he had left to grab any cargo nets.

Enough, he hoped. As the fishing boat approached, he looked for men tending the deck, but in the roller-coaster seas, it was hard to keep a fix on it. He didn't see anybody. When he dropped low, the boat would disappear altogether. Then he'd rise up and see it. Then the entire boat would disappear again behind a wave.

Then suddenly it was upon him, just as a colossal wave lifted him up. The fishing boat plunged into a trough, approaching from his right. The wave crested, then came crashing down on the deck of the ship, carrying Mike with it. He hit hard but managed to hang on to the railing, as the water cleared the decks.

He caught his breath, polling all the parts of his body for broken bones or worse. He was okay.

"Damn," he thought, "I don't know how they did that, but these guys are good."

He gathered himself together for a moment, then took his fins off, threw his butt boat overboard, and walked around to the side of the pilot house, hanging on to the railing lest another wave wash him overboard, in which case they'd have to start over, and he didn't see how they'd be able to catch him twice. The door to the pilot house was closed to the heavy seas, so he pounded on it. There was no answer. He pounded on it again, and then the door opened. There were three Japanese fishermen inside, each of them with eyes wide as saucers.

They hadn't seen him.

They hadn't seen his flare.

They'd only turned in his direction to run with the weather and keep from capsizing. They were in shock, wondering how a small American man in a wet suit had managed to climb onboard their boat in the middle of a typhoon.

The storm raged for three more days. If the fishing boat hadn't picked him up, McManus most likely would have died. Without flares to signal his position, he'd have little hope of rescue. Spotting a lone man floating in the ocean would have been difficult, even in calm seas. A C-130 crew the next day said they couldn't even spot the twenty-man raft they'd dropped him. Ted Martin got picked up by a luxury liner that was riding out the storm and spent the next three days drinking Scotch in the lounge. McManus was transferred to a Japanese Coast Guard cutter, where he helped treat victims of the storm. When they found the boat that had originally emitted the emergency beacon, there were no survivors onboard.

Before he retired, McManus became a member of the Air Force STARS, an expert parachuting team the Air Force uses as a recruiting tool, putting on demonstrations at air shows and football or baseball games. After he left the STARS, McManus got Jack to apply for the vacant position, one which Jack eventually filled by attending a try-out involving jumping and hitting the target ten times in a row, sticking the landing each time. McManus did a jump into a Texas Rangers game at Arlington Stadium in the spring of 1998, executing a perfect hook slide into third base on his landing and getting the thrill of a lifetime. It was a thrill that he wanted his protégé to experience.

Other than as a recruiting tool, stadium jumps have little practical value. If an American pilot were ever to get shot down and eject into the middle of a stadium, there would probably already be somebody there to attend to his medical needs and recover him. At the same time, stadium jumps are among the most difficult PJs or any demonstration jumpers ever attempt. To get a sense of it, put a Cheerio on the floor, maybe ten or twelve feet in front of you, and then imagine trying to fly down into it. The winds involved in a stadium jump are extremely difficult to predict because they change constantly, blowing way across the top of the bowl, swirling in different directions inside the bowl, then shifting again at ground level, where there may be winds blowing in from open loading doors or gaps in the stadium walls. Most stadiums are located in urban areas, surrounded by parking lots, lit barbecue grills from tailgate picnics, lampposts, people, flagpoles, buildings, traffic, and most dangerous of all, those annoying, nearly invisible high-voltage power lines. You train to be as accurate as possible, but nobody in the military trains or draws up plans for jumping into cities or urban areas. Urban insertions are done with helicopters and hoists or fast ropes. In any jump, you have a drop zone (for military training purposes, drop zones must be clear of obstacles for one hundred yards in any direction from the center of the target), but if conditions in the drop zone change or become dangerous, you need to designate an alternate drop zone. If the target zones in stadium jumps are iffy, the alternate drop zones can be even iffier. You don't, however, have a choice—you have to pick somewhere to land. It's one of the more unbreakable laws of parachuting—you must land on the ground the same number of times as you jump out of airplanes.

Brehm's classmate, John Smith, did a stadium jump in Niceville, Florida, near Fort Walton Beach, that went more than a little awry.

Conditions were favorable, a warm autumn night, moderate winds. Smith and a team of PJs from Eglin had executed a practice jump earlier in the day without a hitch. The real jump was scheduled for roughly eight o'clock at night. The plan was to land on the 50-yard line during pregame activities at Niceville High School's homecoming football game. It seemed fairly low risk, flying into a high school stadium, not one of the massive college or professional bowl stadiums full of swirling winds that can give jumpers fits. Smitty was flying a different type of chute from the kind he ordinarily flies, a "sharpshooter" canopy in a vector container, one with a quick-access pilot chute stowed in a pocket on the leg strap of the harness, which he simply needed to grab hold of and throw out into the wind, instead of pulling a rip cord. He exited the plane, saw the aircraft and the stars in the sky, and thought that because it was a night jump it would be wise to locate the hand-deploy early. When he reached for the pilot chute, he couldn't find it. He looked for it, but in the darkness he couldn't tell where it might be. He'd loosened his leg straps during the long wait, crouched in a cramped airplane, and forgot to cinch them down again before he jumped, which may have been a factor. There wasn't time to figure it out. When the emergency beeper went off in his ear, warning him that he'd reached his minimum pull altitude, he immediately went to his reserve canopy. He had a good reserve opening, but by then he was too low to make the target. He started looking for an alternate place to land. The main thing he wanted to avoid were power lines. He saw a brightly lit intersection on a main road that looked pretty good to him and turned toward it, only to see a traffic light change from red to green a few blocks ahead. He saw the oncoming traffic and decided not to challenge any cars or trucks for the right of way. He turned again and headed for a small grove of oak trees. PJs train to land in trees, and in emergencies often prefer to land in trees, which present a fairly consistent set of variables. PJs have special jumpsuits designed for tree landings, akin to the jumpsuits worn by smoke jumpers in Montana and Idaho who fly in to fight forest fires, with low crotches that are reinforced with heavy nylon straps that run beneath the feet and up the inside of the legs. You can kick a man wearing such a suit in the groin and it won't hurt him. Smith wasn't wearing such a suit, which briefly gave him pause, but all things considered, hanging up in a tree was still his safest bet. By now he was too low to maneuver into the wind, so he flew in a deep brakes position, arms straight at his sides, toggles all the way down, to bleed off as much forward speed as possible and enter the tree on a steep vertical descent. At the last moment, however, he saw the last thing he wanted to see—power lines, running through the tree's foliage. He let go of the toggles. The canopy surged dramatically over his head and whipped him up over the power lines, but he hit the tree so hard he broke off a large branch. As Smith fell on the branch, the branch fell on the power lines, causing them to arc, blue sparks flying up into the night. It smelled something like the overheated transformer from an electric train set. The arcing power lines blew out a nearby transformer, which blew out a series of transformers down the line, which blacked out a large part of the city. By the time Smith hit the wires, they were already dead, which was good, because if they weren't, he would have been. He landed on the ground, on his feet, with nothing but a small scratch on his arm.

Brehm got his stadium jump in September of 1998. He had to think hard about it, because he knew the dangers, but Mike had told him what a thrill it was, and Jack couldn't help but fantasize about making a splashy landing in front of sixty thousand people, and many more than that if they showed the game on national television. The whole idea of the Air Force STARS team (Special Tactics And Rescue Specialists) was to get publicity for the Air Force. The plan was to jump onto the field prior to the coin flip and deliver the game ball to the referee at a Pittsburgh Steelers game in Three Rivers Stadium, Pittsburgh. Peggy saw it as an unnecessary risk that Jack didn't have to take, but when she saw the gleam in his eye, she knew there was no stopping him. "The biggest little kid in the world," Randy Mohr had always called him, and he was right. Jack fantasized spiking the ball in the end zone, and he liked the idea of his kids seeing him on television. For a belated eighteenth birthday present, he'd taken his daughter Michele on a jump at a local skydiving club in August, a place where beginning jumpers hooked up in tandem to an instructor. Jack had gone out the jump door of the stripped-down Cessna after her (a plane built in 1956, he noted, the year he was born), and he'd seen the smile on her face when she screamed and gave him a double thumbs-up sign—he was happy for her, because he knew how she felt, but he was also happy for himself, because he knew that for the first time someone in his family finally understood how he felt when he jumped out of airplanes. Fathers hear their teenage children say "You just don't understand me" all the time. Fathers usually have to hold their tongues at such moments, when what they really want to say is, "Well, it would be nice if you understood me, too." Jumping into a stadium, on television, with his children watching, appealed to him. He told Peggy he might even be able to get her tickets to the game.

"I'm a lot less interested in getting tickets to the game than I am in getting you home safe," she said.

"So it's okay for me to go into a war zone but it's not okay to jump into Pittsburgh," he teased.

"It's not okay for you to do, either," she said. "Why don't you get a job in a deli? There's no dishonor in slicing meat, you know."

"This we do, that others may eat salami," he said. "I don't know, Peg—it just doesn't sound the same to me."

*   *   *   *   *   *   *   *

A week later, on September 26, Jack Brehm is in the air over Three Rivers Stadium. Six thousand feet below, where the Allegheny, Monongahela, and Ohio rivers meet, Three Rivers Stadium looks smaller than a donut. It's the day before the game, Saturday afternoon, and time for a practice jump. There are four jumpers. Brehm is the third. All will exit the plane at 6,000 feet. The first man will free fall to 4,000 feet and pull, the second to 4,500 feet, Brehm will pull at 5,000 feet, and the last man will pull five hundred feet above him.

It feels wrong from the start. He's used to jumping from much higher altitudes, anywhere from 10,000 to 26,000 feet. He's also used to jumping over water, grass, deserts, even jungles. Below, he sees where I-279 crosses the Allegheny River on the Dusquesne Bridge, and where U.S. 19 crosses the Ohio River on the West End Bridge, and where U.S. 30 crosses the Monongahela River on the Fort Pitt Bridge. The roads are full of cars, which he'd hate to hit. He sees a Navy ship below, the USS *Requin,* now a tourist attraction, docked where the three rivers meet, just south of the stadium. He sees the rooftops of Allegheny Community College on Ridge Road, the Andy Warhol Museum on Sandusky, and the Carnegie Library in Allegheny Square. He sees the tracks of the Conrail railroad running past the stadium, and the skyscrapers of downtown Pittsburgh. He sees the Art Institute, Heinz Hall, Fort Pitt, the Gateway Center, Point State Park, and he sees the pointed steeples of all the nearby churches, St. Mary of Mercy, St. Peter's, Emmanuel Episcopal, and Friendship Baptist. They look like so many pungee sticks, set in the ground to spear him.

He wonders if he's getting too old for this. He and Peggy have talked about his retirement plans and what he might do when he's no longer a pararescueman. He's heard that guys start to psyche themselves out the closer to retirement they get. They start noticing how far out to sea they're going to fly on a mission, and how many air refuelings will be involved, and they start asking what the weather is going to be like when they get there, where before they just went and accepted the dangers, without really worrying about or anticipating them.

Thirty seconds from the drop, he gets the final wind report over his headset. A large scoreboard at the east end of the field marks the twelve o'clock position. A STARS team spotter on the rim of the stadium says winds there are coming from the two o'clock position at eleven knots. A spotter on the ground says winds are five knots from the ten o'clock position.

Brehm exits the plane about a half a mile from the stadium. If something goes wrong, the alternate drop zone will be one of the rivers, whichever river seems closest. He falls to 5,000 feet and pulls, experiencing the familiar and ever-reassuring shock of an opened chute, which yanks him suddenly from a horizontal to a vertical position, feet to earth. His adrenaline begins to pump, then pumps harder when he realizes something is wrong. He looks up and sees that the cells of his chute, a special red-white-and-blue demonstration chute, smaller and faster than the chutes he ordinarily uses, able to turn on a dime and penetrate higher head winds, is only 70 percent inflated. The end cells on the left side of the chute haven't inflated. This isn't an uncommon malfunction, and pumping the brakes usually corrects it.

He pumps the brakes.

It doesn't work.

He's at 4,300 feet.

He realizes he's in a severe left-hand spiral. The city spins beneath him, whirling counterclockwise. It's dizzying. To equalize the curvature of his canopy and fly straight, Brehm has to pull 85 percent right brake and zero left brake. He looks up again, and sees that he has a malfunction called a tension knot, which is not correctable by the jumper, and must be cut away.

He's at 4,000 feet.

You can't deploy a reserve chute until you've rid yourself of a malfunctioning chute—otherwise the reserve will get tangled in the bad chute. The procedure, therefore, is to grab the reserve chute's rip cord with your left hand and grab something called a cutaway handle with your right. The reserve chute rip cord handle is a square aluminum ring, about the size of a cigarette pack. The cutaway handle is shaped differently from a rip cord's

D-ring, so that the two never get confused. The cutaway handle is a small beanbag, about the size of a dill pickle, red fabric filled with sand, attached to the right harness strap with a set of mated Velcro strips. Pulling the cutaway handle flips a series of three interlocking rings, which releases the main. It's attached solely with Velcro, but when Jack tries to pull it with one hand, it won't break loose. It should, but it won't. He goes after it with both hands, which means he has to release the brakes, which again sends him into a severe downward left spiral, but ridding himself of the malfunction is more important. He can't free the cutaway handle from the harness. He absolutely can't pull his reserve until he releases his main.

He grabs the brakes to fly straight again.

He's at 3,700 feet.

He can't land with his malfunctioning chute—he'll die if he tries.

He releases the brakes, spiraling left again. The city rotates beneath him, getting closer and closer. He grabs the cutaway handle with both hands, but just before he does, he offers up a brief sort of prayer, not a formal heavenly address, just the words, "Don't let me die doing something stupid." This time, he pulls as hard as he can on the cutaway handle with both hands. Instantly he feels separation, and transitions back into free fall, face to earth. Now the city rushes at him, antennae and steeples and telephone poles and lampposts, and it all wants to skewer him.

He's at 3,200 feet.

He pulls his reserve and fires it off. He's jerked back to vertical, feet to earth, a small white square chute now open over his head, but he's not out of trouble. He glances to his right, and sees his fancy main chute, so pretty in the colors of the flag, with the words *Aim High Air Force* stitched into it, drifting down toward downtown Pittsburgh. What if it hits somebody? It's not his problem anymore.

He's at 2,700 feet.

He looks for an alternate landing site, but nothing appeals to him, particularly not the cold gray waters of the river below him. When he spots his jump partners, he realizes, to his amazement, that he hasn't lost that much altitude and has maintained his position in the stack. All his maneuverings in the cutaway process must have happened in just a few seconds, though it seemed to take much longer. He decides to try for the stadium.

"We have a cutaway," the voice in his helmet radio says. "Repeat, we have a cutaway and a good reserve deployment."

He thinks, "Thanks for paying attention."

He's at 950 feet.

He follows the number two jumper over the lip of the stadium, crossing the wall at the three o'clock position. He immediately turns left toward the six. It's crazy. He's falling *inside* something. The stadium lights and tiers and seats fly past in a blur. The winds are swirling. It feels as if there are cables everywhere, threatening to cut his suspension lines. He spots the windsock on the 50-yard line, which shows ground winds coming from eleven o'clock at five knots. Turning to land means he has to get close to the far end zone's cable. He hopes he can see it to avoid it. He can't see it—there's too much in the background. He hopes he misses it.

He misses it.

He turns to his final approach at two hundred feet and experiences severe turbulence. It rocks his canopy. He has to release his brakes to stabilize his canopy, but this sends him shooting past the 30-, the 40-, the 50-yard line. As the turbulence subsides, he brakes hard, then makes a final crab to the left to land directly into the wind, at which time he sees a stack of plywood sheets directly in his path at the 20-yard line, just off the field. He manages to land on top of the stack of plywood (instead of hitting the side of it), runs off, jumps, slips on the blue plastic tarpaulin used to cover the field during rains, and slides into the 10-yard line.

Shit damn.

Stadium jumps.

Cheeses.

He's glad to be alive. He feels a tingling in his extremities, the aftereffects of having the crap scared out of him. He is glad Peggy wasn't there to see this. He's glad 100,000 people weren't there to see this. He's glad it wasn't on national television. He is mainly full of disbelief, amazed that he'd come so close to frapping on something so ridiculous, so trivial, a *practice* jump, for a *demonstration,* in *Pittsburgh!* After all the things he's done in his life, to almost die that way . . .

He hears a voice behind him. It's the voice of Wayne Norad, the team chief.

"Sergeant Brehm," Wayne says. "Can you tell me what you did with my five-thousand-dollar United States Air Force STARS parachute?"

"Sorry, Chief," Brehm says. Unbelievable. Does the man not realize what almost happened, or does he know and is simply making light of it? "Not a clue—I had my eyes on the stadium the whole time. I suspect it's somewhere in the heart of Pittsburgh."

Brehm walks to where the other jumpers have gathered. He examines his harness. It's then that he realizes something. He observes the cutaway handle. It looks funny—there are loose threads hanging from it. His first thought is that somebody sewed the knap and hook components of the Velcro together. The knap component is commonly attached to the bean-bag, and the hook component is sewn to the harness.

Closer examination reveals that there is no hook component attached to the harness. That is to say, there used to be, but in his panic, or rather, in his desperate effort to pull the cutaway handle, Brehm ripped the stitching from the harness and removed *both* halves of the Velcro. It would take incredible strength to do that.

It would certainly take two hands—or three, he thinks, if you include the hand of God.

That night, Brehm calls McManus to tell him what happened.

"See?" Mike says. "I told you they were fun."

The next day's jump is canceled, due to high winds.

16

ANYONE ELSE BUT ME

Dear Dad,

How are you doing? When are you coming home? Dad do not forget to get me some thing o by the way soon as you left Mom started crying. I love you.

Love,
Jeff

ON SUNDAY, APRIL 11, 1999, THE NEWSPAPERS REPORT THAT NATO is committing eighty-two more planes to Operation Allied Force, sending over twenty-four F-16s, four A-10 Thunderbolts, six EA-6B Prowlers, thirty-nine KC-130 tankers, two more KC-10 tankers, and seven C-130 transports, bringing the total number of airplanes flying in the Baltics close to seven hundred. A report of explosions at the airport in Montenegro suggests the war might be expanding. The next day, NATO requests an additional three hundred planes. New NATO ally Hungary, where Russian tanks rolled in 1956, stops a convoy of seventy-three Russian trucks headed for Yugoslavia, but the Soviets still seem intent on getting involved. For the first time, Pentagon spokesman Kenneth Bacon suggests that an expanding campaign could require calling up reservists and Guardsmen. By Tuesday, a defense department spokesman is saying reservists could be called up any time, adding that the president has the power to activate up to 200,000 men for as long as 270 days. Logic suggests that if the war expands, and more PJs are needed, that it would be easier for the Air Force to keep in place the men who are already there, rather than fly over troops less prepared.

On Saturday, April 10, Peggy has a luncheon at the base for the Family Support Group. She's been so busy driving her brother-in-law Jim to and from Sloan-Kettering that she's missed the last couple of meetings, and the idea is, after all, that people show up and help each other. She picks up Barbara Dougherty and leaves a note for Matt, telling him what yard work needs to be done. The whole yard needs to be raked out, and particularly the flower beds, where she intends to lay stone instead of mulch this year—it is almost standard that each time Jack goes away, she does something radical to the house, partly to surprise him and give him something to look forward to coming home to, and partly, she supposes, out of some subconscious need to rule the roost by redecorating it. At the support group meeting, they talk about the scholarship fund, but she has a hard time paying attention. On top of everything else, in a week she'll be attending a fund-raiser for Jim that Michele has arranged at the Ramada Inn in Riverhead, a party to help defray his medical costs. Elizabeth will be coming home for it, and says she's bringing her boyfriend Drew—a really nice boy, but isn't the house small enough already? Michele says she and her Aunt Carol will do all the cooking, but there are still a million details to attend to.

When Peggy gets home, around two, she sees that the yard work hasn't been touched.

"Where's Matt?" she asks Michele. "Didn't he see my note?"

"He said he was going to his friend Vinnie's," Michele says, digging into a late lunch she's prepared for herself, white rice and ketchup.

"Vinnie's?" Peggy says. *The nerve of him, to totally ignore my note.* She picks up the phone and dials Vinnie's mother, who says she doesn't know where the boys are.

"Unbelievable," Peggy says.

She gets in her car and goes looking for her oldest son. She drives past Vinnie's house, past the school, past several of Matt's friends' houses. *How dare he? The nerve of that boy! He totally ignored me. He's definitely not afraid of me anymore. How could he? He knows at a time like this we have to pull together. That's what he does—that's exactly what he does—he's just seeing how far he can push, because John isn't here. If John were here, he wouldn't dare. The nerve.* She drives past Vinnie's house again, wondering where they went. To the beach? The park? *Maybe this is just normal? It's normal for a fifteen-year-old boy to rebel—maybe this is nothing to worry about? One thing is clear though—if I don't get control back, the other kids are going to start following Matt's lead. How dare he defy me? I don't need his defiance—this is not the time nor the place for it.*

Then she spots him at the 7-Eleven on Route 25A, where he isn't allowed to go because the traffic is too heavy. She pulls over to the curb. She considers that, at fifteen, it may be time to let him go to the 7-Eleven alone. Vinnie is with him, their bikes leaning against the store window. Then she sees Matt give Vinnie something. Matt looks guilty, suspicious, as if he were making some kind of drug deal. Drugs? She knows him well enough to know that's not it, but it's something. Then Matt spots her, but apparently he thinks she doesn't see him, because he runs away.

Now he's running away from me? He's running *from me? This boy is in big trouble.*

She pulls into the parking lot next to the Rocky Point Diner, down from the convenience store, and waits. She's not in the mood to chase after him, and she has a pretty good idea that if she waits long enough, he's going to come back to get his bike. When he does, she pulls into the 7-Eleven lot and orders him to get in the car.

Now!

He throws his bike in the back.

"Do you have any idea the kind of trouble you're in? Do you have *any* idea? Like it's not bad enough that you ignored my note—what were you up to?"

"When?"

"Now? Just now—at the 7-Eleven."

"Nothing."

"What were you giving Vinnie? I saw you give him something."

"Nothing."

"Don't tell me nothing, I saw you give him something. I want to know what it was?"

"Mom . . ."

"What did you give him?"

"I gave him firecrackers," he finally admits.

"Firecrackers?" she says. "And where did you get firecrackers?" She knows roughly where he got them—everywhere they stopped in North Carolina on the drive home from Myrtle Beach they were selling firecrackers, bottle rockets, Roman candles, and worse.

"I bought 'em at one of the gas stations we stopped at on our way home," Matt says. He'd begged her for fireworks, until she relented and bought him some, a brick of basic Black Cat firecrackers, which she'd wrapped and stored away, telling Matt he wasn't allowed to open them until his father came home.

"You went behind my back, when I was filling up the car with gas, and bought fireworks?" she asks him. He nods. Part of her wants to laugh, because she knows there's probably some sort of genetic attraction to fireworks in the family, some consanguineous appeal, though Matt definitely doesn't get it from her side. She hates fireworks. Back when she was pregnant with Matt, Jack got in trouble at the base when a group of PJs started shooting off their pen guns, which are Vietnam-era flares designed to shoot up seven hundred feet and penetrate the jungle canopy to signal rescue helicopters. They were shooting them in the general direction of the C-130 fleet when the base commander caught them. Another time Jack hurt his eye, playing with fireworks at a Fourth of July beach party. But it wasn't funny then, and it isn't funny now.

"You've made a lot of really bad decisions today, Matthew," Peggy says. "Really bad. And for your information, you now have two hours of yard work and one hour of indoor work ahead of you. Do you understand me?"

"Yes, Mom."

"Do I have to say it again? Have I made myself clear?"

"You've made yourself clear."

The next day, Peggy goes to her sister Carol's house after mass for breakfast and calls home to make sure Matt is doing his yard work. He grumbles, insolent. When she comes home, she finds he's gone back to bed. His cheekiness amazes her. She makes him get up. When she goes to the laundromat to do laundry, her cell phone rings. It's Jeffrey, asking her to settle another argument he's having with his brother. She tries to listen to both of them, but she doesn't even care what it's about, and they're both wrong, and they're both grounded until Jack comes home.

Jeffrey, she can tell, is losing it. He has a two-week limit when Jack is gone, and now his two weeks are up. When school starts again after Easter break, Jeffrey complains that his ribs hurt, enough that he doesn't want to go to school. She makes a deal with him—she'll give him a couple of Tylenol and send him to school, but if he still hurts, he can come home. After he leaves, she calls the school nurse to warn her that he's hit his limit, and that if he comes in, all he'll need is sympathy, maybe an icepack, fifteen minutes of quiet time, and a hug. "If he's really teary," Peggy says, "call me and I'll come get him. He's also not going to be able to concentrate on his schoolwork."

When the nurse calls and says she thinks Jeffrey has a real problem with his ribs, Peggy takes him to the doctor, who says Jeffrey has a strained muscle and bruised cartilage on his rib cage. Peggy doesn't like bringing her children to doctor's visits alone, and again thinks, *I never asked to be the single mother of five.* Jeffrey is actually glad, because his injury means he has two weeks free of yard work, but that night, when Peggy goes to her sister's for Chinese food and some deeply needed "adult time," Jeffrey calls three times, needing to be told what position to sleep in, needing to be told when to take his medicine—needing to know that his mother will come in and kiss him good night when she gets home.

Michele is stressing, too, but seems to be coping. The work she's doing for her Uncle Jim's fund-raiser on Saturday is phenomenal. While working at the Olive Garden, going to school full-time, and finishing up her EMT training, Michele has also been running around to local shops and restaurants getting them to donate prizes and free dinners for two and for four, which she'll be able to raffle off at the fund-raiser. Elizabeth is helping as much as she can from Boston, but she's mainly worried about her mother, worried that she keeps so much to herself. Elizabeth thinks that if her father could only hear the weariness in Peggy's voice and see how worn down and tired she is, maybe this would be his last trip.

Thursday is the worst day of all. Peggy wonders why she's having such a hard time keeping it together, why she can't seem to get a grip. She doesn't want to be alone anymore. It's as simple as that. No other explanation is necessary. Bean left at 4:30 A.M. for a school field trip to Washington, D.C., and that further fragments the family. That afternoon, Jim gets a report on a new CAT scan, which seems to show a four-centimeter tumor on the right plura, the blood vessel near his heart, as well as a blood clot that the doctors are worried about. She knows Jim doesn't need more bad news, two days before his big party. *How much more emotional stress can I handle?* She wants Jack to call, even though the next call isn't scheduled until tomorrow. She feels an overwhelming sadness. She can't allow it to grow, but it seems to get bigger and bigger all the time.

The next day, he doesn't call. Elizabeth is home from school to help with the fund-raiser. Nobody at the dinner table dares to bring up the fact that Jack hasn't called. They try to talk about the good news—further analysis and a second opinion on Jim's CAT scan has revealed that what they thought was a new tumor is nothing more than scar tissue from where the old tumor was removed, and the blood clot is just some surgical Gore-Tex used to patch up the vena cava. They talk about tomorrow's party. They make small talk, and they try to keep talking, because in the silences between the words they can all hear the phone not ringing.

Jack doesn't phone because on Thursday, Groundhog Day finally comes to an end. The team gets a call at 1200 hours to deploy to the Forward Operating Location, somewhere on the border of Turkey and Iraq. They load the aircraft, draw their weapons and taxi out onto the ramp, only to be told that their clearance to fly doesn't come into effect until 1430 hours. Finally, at 1500 hours, they're in the air. After they land and unload the helicopter, there's only time to eat dinner and hit the sack. Brehm can't believe it's taken this long to arrive. There are no telephones at the FOL, which makes him sorry that he won't be able to call home, but there's nothing he can do about it. He's glad to finally get a chance to "play," however, and tries to focus on the task at hand.

The next morning, at 0730, he reports to work. They reload the helicopters, prepare their radios, test their sat-coms, update their intelligence reports, and go over their gear. They don't know how many flights over Iraq they can expect today, but they expect to be told soon. An hour later, the word comes.

"The box will not open today," they're told by headquarters. "Stand down."

"The box will not open today." That's it? That's all? Everyone is pissed off. They're ready. There's nothing they can do to be more ready. They're willing, eager, trained, and if they don't go, they're going to feel as if they've wasted their time.

At noon, they're told to pack up their personal gear because they're going to be replaced. For all the delays in getting them there, it takes the Air Force a mere thirty minutes to land a C-130 to take them back to Incirlik to outprocess.

Brehm can't believe it.

On the flight, he ends up talking to a younger PJ, who asks him if he ever thinks that maybe he's getting too old for this sort of thing.

"What do you mean by that?" Brehm asks the kid.

"I don't mean that you can't do the job—I just mean, you know, that you have, what, five kids?"

"Five," Jack says.

"It just seems like that's a lot to lose."

"Well, of course I don't want to lose it," Brehm says. "I've got a great life—what are you going to do? *Not* have a great life, because there's a chance you're going to lose it?"

"I suppose not," the younger PJ says.

"The way I figure it, I'm forty-two years old, and I've done more stuff than most people do in a hundred years. I mean, that they would do if they lived a hundred years."

"I know what you mean."

"I've been more places."

"Hoo-yah to that."

"What's the point to being alive if you don't believe in something strongly enough to risk your life for it?" The younger PJ doesn't say anything. "I mean, who's to say the day I decide to retire I won't get hit by a car? There's a sign outside the main gate of the base where I work that says, 'YOU ARE ABOUT TO ENTER ONE OF THE MOST DANGEROUS AREAS IN THE WORLD. A PUBLIC HIGHWAY. FASTEN YOUR SEAT BELT AND DRIVE DEFENSIVELY.' I see that sign every day. Who's to say I won't die in a car accident two miles from my house? If that's the case, then I'd rather die rescuing somebody. When and where I die isn't exactly under my control."

He didn't mean to go off on the guy, but standing around for three weeks doing nothing, only to be replaced, has gotten him thinking about what he's doing here. It's weird. He's elated to be going home, and deeply disappointed at the same time. He finds himself thinking of a quote he learned back in high school, his freshman English class, Mr. Snow, the teacher's name was. It was something by Shakespeare, and he can't remember it precisely, but it went something like, "Cowards die many times before their deaths; the valiant never taste of death but once. Of all the wonders that I yet have heard, it seems to me most strange that men should fear; seeing that death, a necessary end, will come when it will come."

He has, in fact, remembered it precisely. If he could remember the context, he'd be aware of the irony. The lines come from Shakespeare's *Julius Caesar*, Act 2, scene 2. The speaker is Caesar, addressing his wife, Calphurnia, on a stormy night full of lightning and thunder, while conspirators are afoot, out to do him harm, and the omens are all bad ("A lioness hath whelped in the street") and she wants him to stay home and play it safe.

"What can be avoided whose end is purpos'd by the mighty Gods?" Caesar wants to know. "Caesar should be a beast without a heart, if he should stay at home today for fear."

Jack arrives at Incirlik and finally manages to call Peg. She happens to be home alone when he calls.

The fund-raiser at the Ramada Inn in Riverhead is a smashing success. They raise over $13,000 to put toward Jim's medical expenses, and everybody is thrilled to see Jim dancing with his wife and to learn that his latest test results are negative. All of Peggy's enormous extended family has shown up, as well as friends from the base, and friends of Jim's from the car dealership where he works. Peggy looks terrific, in a gray-blue dress that flatters her. Michele shines. Elizabeth, in a black velvet skirt slit up the side nearly to the hip, her long curly blond hair cascading down her shoulders, has glammed up and looks like a forties' movie starlet. The food is delicious, large flat pans full of pastas, lasagna, ziti, and salads. They raffle off tickets to Jets games, dinners at local restaurants, free haircuts and manicures and massages, baskets full of Girl Scout cookies and bottles of champagne. The place is decorated with crepe paper and Christmas lights. Matt and Laura-Jean hang out with their friends. Jeffrey has his eye on a pair of walkie-talkies being raffled. Jack and Peggy's next-door neighbor Dennis is a DJ and spins the tunes. The best dancers on the floor are all under six years of age, including one little boy in sunglasses who has disco fever so bad he needs a pediatrician. When friends ask Peggy if she's heard from Jack, she silently shakes her head and bites her lip. When they ask her how she's doing, she says, "Hanging in there, but just barely." Everyone is sensitive that, on an evening when everybody else seems to be coupled up, Peggy is alone.

It's possible that somebody, paying close attention, might notice something slightly different about Peggy, something a bit sly or deceptive in the way she answers questions or glances about the room. Most eyes are on Jim and Lorraine, slow dancing cheek to cheek in the middle of the dance floor.

Elizabeth, her boyfriend Drew, Greg, Bean, and Matty all work in the garden the next day, placing rocks and trying to make things look nice for when Jack comes home. Lorraine and Carol come over for dinner. Carol's kids come, too. After dinner, Michele and Elizabeth and their boyfriends go over to Carol's to watch a movie. They get home around eleven to find Matt watching television.

"Where's Mom?"

"She went to a movie with Aunt Sally," Matt says.

"What movie?"

"I dunno."

"Wow," Elizabeth says. "Good for her."

But it's not like her mother to go to a late movie. When Peggy's not home by 1:00 A.M., Elizabeth starts to worry. It doesn't help to know how upset her mother has been lately, how on edge. She wakes up Michele. They whisper in the hallway.

"Mom's not home."

"What time is it?"

"It's after one."

"Did she say what time she was coming home?"

"To who? Matty was home when she left."

"She's probably at Aunt Sally's."

"Should we call?"

"Not if it's going to wake her up."

"She's probably okay."

"Oh God, of course she is. She probably just zonked out on the couch or something."

"Probably."

But Peggy isn't at her sister-in-law's house, zonked out. She's in a motel room, with her husband. Jack left Turkey at 2:30 in the morning, Saturday, and flew to Italy, from there to Germany, and from there to Baltimore, where he took a tortuous seven-hour bus ride back to the base, where Peggy met him around ten o'clock. She didn't tell anybody at the fundraiser that Jack was on his way, because she didn't want everybody to get their hopes up when the situation was still subject to change. Mostly, she didn't tell anybody because she wanted him all to herself. She had a right to that. Nobody who really knew what she'd been through could possibly argue with that. When she met him at the airfield, she ran to him and threw her arms around him and felt whole again. It didn't take long for Jack to fill her in on what he'd been up to. It took a lot longer for her to tell him all the things that had been going on at home, but that's the way it usually went when Jack went away—he could spend a month in some foreign country, some exotic distant place, but when he came home, what had been happening in the family in his absence was always more important to him. They talked and talked. Then they didn't want to use words anymore.

Peggy and Jack arrive home Monday morning, April 19, around eleven. Michele and Elizabeth sigh with relief when they see their mom and dad together again. Jack gets Matt and Jeffrey and Bean out of school, and everybody goes to lunch at the diner. Some of the kids are dying to tell Jack everything that happened in his absence. Others are just happy that he's here, home, tangible, and present. Over cheeseburgers and onion rings, everyone's internal emotional guidance system recalibrates. The King is back on his throne, next to the Queen, and there's no longer a power vacuum for everyone to deal with. For the kids, it's as simple as having two sets of eyes watching over them instead of one. They feel safer with two. For Jack, this is the moment he thinks of when he's far away, the image of being surrounded by his family, the thing he carries with him. After a trip it isn't until this moment that he knows he's truly returned to base.

17

' 7 8 - 0 3

I've always had this idea that when we die and meet our maker, God will ask us one question. He'll say, "So—how was it?" If you answer, "Wow, what a ride," he'll welcome you with open arms, but if you complain about all the unfair events that might have caused you an unjust amount of pain, you'll get sent back because you missed the main drift. Life is good. There are bad things in the world. There are situations where you might find yourself out of control or in dire straights, but even then, there is good. It may be hard to find, but it's there.

IN THE MORNING, WHEN JACK BREHM GOES RUNNING, WHETHER HE'S training for a marathon or an Iron Man or just running to stay in shape, he pauses briefly to stretch in the living room of his house. He knows he should pay more attention to stretching, but he just doesn't. Each year, he's a bit sorer and a bit stiffer in the morning, and it's been a while since he ran his personal best marathon time of 2:51, but he can still race with the young guys, and he still enjoys running.

He knocks the sand from his running shoes into the wastebasket. He sees the fireplace he put in, and the ceiling fan, and the grass wallpaper that Peggy put up one weekend in his absence. His entertainment center features a Pioneer turntable, a JVC tuner, a 28-inch Goldstar TV, a Symphonic five-disk CD changer, and a Broksonic VCR, but Brehm doesn't turn any of it on. He hears only the humming of the refrigerator. He glances out the bay window at the weather, and at the vine-strangled oak trees in his front yard. He checks the anniversary clock on the mantel sitting in its bell jar. The clock is surrounded by photographs of his kids, including pictures of Elizabeth and Laura-Jean in their cheerleading uniforms, the blue and white colors of Rocky Point High. Elizabeth's uniform has the word *Eagles* stitched across the chest in gold. It matches her curly blond hair. In a photo album, Jack keeps a picture of Elizabeth flying high in the air, tossed straight up by her fellow cheerleaders. She is smiling as she does the splits, arms straight out from her side as she touches her toes. She never stretched much, either, but when you're that young, you don't have to.

He takes it easy at first, loping down Locust Drive to Eos, where he turns right, then left on King, and right on Odin to Route 25A. He runs east on 25A for a few blocks and turns left on Woodville Road, which brings him back to Long Island Sound. The narrow streets of Rocky Point are lined with old cottages and newly constructed, expansive landscaped homes. He runs past a cottage a PJ purchased years ago. The previous occupants had been Italians, who'd paved their yard with concrete, as was the fashion at the time. The new owner couldn't afford a demolition crew on a National Guardsman's salary, but he could afford a few cases of beer, to give to a bunch of sledgehammer-wielding PJs who tore into the cement only to find that whoever had put it in had reinforced it with any sort of metal junk he could get his hands on, bedsprings and teaspoons, extension cords and chicken wire. It took forever to get it up and out of there. Just as they finished, an old Italian neighbor strolled by to admire their hand-iwork, and said, "I'm so glad we have young people in the neighborhood again—maybe now we can get some fresh concrete in here."

Brehm likes to run on the beach, on the sand where it's hard-packed above the tide line, marble-sized pebbles the colors of toffee and putty and brick. He runs up and down sand dune cliffs that would make an ordinary runner's thighs burst into flames, but before hitting the beach, he always stops at a cliff above the ocean, where there's a stone bench for people to sit on and gaze out at the sound. It's seventeen miles across to Connecticut. Brehm and Jimmy Dougherty kayaked it once. He puts his feet up on the bench to elevate them and begins his push-ups. He does a hundred push-ups every morning to stay in shape, and then he does one more, for Randy Mohr, and one more, for Mark Judy.

After the space shuttle *Challenger* blew up, a massive effort was made to recover any piece of the spacecraft that might provide a clue as to why the accident happened. The effort included launching an unmanned sub-marine to search the ocean floor. The submarine found pieces of the *Challenger*, but it also observed a wreckage of a helicopter that could have been the helicopter Mark Judy had gone down in, sitting on the bottom in two thousand feet of water, about fifty miles off Cape Canaveral. A recov-ery vessel called the *Frank Cable* managed to fasten a line to the fuselage, but the line broke. It was determined that it wouldn't be cost effective to bring the wreckage to the surface, so it was declared a gravesite and left undisturbed.

Jack Brehm runs because he's the last man in his class still serving as a PJ. The others have all moved on to other things.

Randy Mohr thinks about "The Jude" from time to time. After "seeing the light," he moved back to Olean, New York, and took a job at Olean Wholesale, the same place where his dad drove a truck, delivering food to the SureFine chain of supermarkets. Randy had worked there before he enlisted in the Air Force. After leaving pararescue, Mohr spent time on his grandparents' 125-acre horse farm, swimming in the pond and hunting deer on the back acres, and then he married a girl named Diane Gardner, a half Cherokee Indian from nearby Allegheny and someone Randy had played with when they were little kids. She gave birth to a boy, Christian, in July of 1983, and two years later had a girl, Amber-Jude, named after Mark Judy. They bought a huge house in the town of Portville, a "mansion," Mohr says. The town was full of broken homes and dysfunctional families. In junior high school, Christian Mohr got in trouble with some of the other kids at school, including the son of a local cop, who poured ink on Christian's New England Patriots jacket and pressured him into shoplifting a pack of cigarettes, then denied it after Christian got caught. They stole Christian's bicycle, made threats, sprayed graffiti on the garage. To protect his boy, Randy Mohr moved his wife and kids out of their "mansion" to a mobile home on the family horse farm, on a lot behind the big house where his brother lives. Christian hasn't been in trouble since. They have Clydesdales, Arabians, and quarter horses on the farm, even a cow or a bull now and then, all bred for show and sale. They have five-pound bass in the pond and ten-point bucks in the woods. To Randy Mohr, moving his family out of town was a no-brainer, even if it meant going from a mansion to a trailer, because that's what you're supposed to do—live your life "that others may live." He never got an actual save as a PJ, but he still lives the motto—the golden light didn't change that part of it.

He and Jack get together once a year, driving the 370 miles between their houses to drink coffee (Mohr has been on the wagon for eight years) and retell old stories, about the time they were four-wheel driving in the Baja and Jack leapt out of a bush to tackle Mohr, snarling and growling to the point Mohr was convinced he'd been attacked by a bear. They talk about the time Mohr, Jack, the Jude, and Matelski nearly got handed their sombreros in a bar in Juarez, across the border from El Paso, by fifteen or twenty cantinistas after Jack got upset when he paid for a beer with a twenty-dollar bill and the girl wouldn't give him his change. The girl pretended he'd given her a five, then cried *lobo* and screamed bloody murder when Jack said she was cheating him. The bar's patrons rose to defend her, so the PJs went ballistic, breaking pool cues and bottles and throwing bar stools, knowing that the best defense is a good offense. They were allowed to leave after Mohr lifted a stool and threatened to break the mirror behind the bar and destroy half the bar's liquor stock. Jack got his change back, too.

"Jack gets kind of goofy when he drinks," Mohr says. "One time we were in a bar in Long Island, and there was this girl with gigantic ta-tas who was dancing all by herself, really putting on an exhibition, and she was wearing this knit black tube dress, you know, where the only thing holding it up was her boobs, so Jack was drinking his beer and looking at her, and apparently she took offense because she came over and said, 'Why don't you try looking me in the eyes?' Jack was really hammered, so he just kept looking at her boobs and said, 'Oh—you have eyes? And where would those be?' "

Joe Higgins stayed a PJ for eight and a half years. He recalls, with particular fondness, a jump mission six hundred miles west of San Francisco, where a sailor on the research vessel the USS *Dutton* was in need of medical assistance. The call came at three in the morning. They launched at first light. The water was choppy, so heavily whitecapped that they couldn't see the smoke marker they'd dropped to give them wind direction. The *Dutton* dispatched a long boat, which picked them up after they'd been in the water for ten or fifteen minutes. The *Dutton* extended davits over the side to winch the long boat to the deck. It was as they waited to be hoisted out of the water that Higgins noticed a sailor high up on the superstructure of the ship, aiming a high-powered rifle at him and watching him through the rifle's scope.

"What's with the sharpshooter?" Higgins asked the bo'sun.

"Sharks," the bo'sun said.

"Here?"

"Yeah," the bo'sun said. "They're everywhere. This water is full of 'em."

"You might have told us that before we jumped into it," Higgins said.

"We might have," the bo'sun agreed, "but then you might not have come."

While serving with the 129th at Moffett, Joe Higgins got lucky. A lieutenant colonel named Charlie Cross saw something he liked in the young PJ and told him he had a flight slot open. The problem was that to become an officer in the Air Force, you have to have graduated from a four-year college, and Higgins was only two and a half years into his degree. You also have to be twenty-six-and-a-half years old or younger to start the program. Cross said he could waive the college requirement if Higgins promised to finish his degree once he was commissioned, but he couldn't waive the age limit. Higgins started Officer Training School immediately, and from there he went on to flight school. He's currently a lieutenant colonel in the California Air National Guard, where he first flew HH-3E and later HH-60G helicopters, pulling seamen out of the Pacific Ocean and climbers off Northern California's mountainsides. He trained Slovenian pilots in rescue techniques in a program called Partnership for Peace, in which Americans helped retrain military personnel in countries that were once part of, or under the influence of, the former Soviet Union. Higgins recalls a time when Jack Brehm, in Hawaii on a training mission, was waiting in full uniform at a bus stop in downtown Honolulu with a flight engineer who didn't know him very well. A woman at the bus stop asked him what it was he did in the military.

"Well," Brehm said with a mock mysteriousness, "I could tell you, but then I'd have to kill you."

"Don't let him give you that bullshit," the FE said. "His name is Jack Brehm and he's a PJ from Long Island and he's here on a training mission."

"Jack suddenly got this wild look on his face," Higgins recalls, "and then he screamed this blood-curdling scream and said to the woman, 'Now I must kill you!' and leapt at her and proceeded to pretend to strangle her. Jack and the woman had a good laugh out of it, but the flight engineer didn't know what to make of it. He almost had a heart attack. He told me later, 'Your buddy Brehm is kind of wacked,' and I said, 'Yeah, that's about the size of it.'"

Dave Higgins stayed a PJ for twenty years. He stood alert at Edwards AFB in California when the space shuttles landed there, prepared to muscle astronauts out of the cockpit were something to go wrong upon landing. He nearly got washed off the deck of a submarine in the Pacific by a rogue wave while rescuing an overweight seaman with a hernia, "sort of a whiner who I think they just wanted to get off the boat, so on the way back, we practiced our IV sticks on him—you don't get much of a chance to practice that on an actual moving vibrating helicopter—we sort of made a pincushion out of the guy." Another time, D.T. flew to a U.N. observation post on an island in the Yellow Sea off North Korea and treated a father and infant son who'd been burned in a house fire, the HH-60G helicopter accompanied by F-16 fighter planes, given their proximity to the demilitarized zone. Higgins flew with a test team in Hawaii, where PJs from Hickham AFB were charged with recovering whatever hardware had fallen to earth from space and splashed down in the Pacific. He was an instructor at Kirtland for five years. He worked at Hurlburt Field, Florida, in Special Tactics for AFSOC, but didn't care much for the politics of the operations he helped plan there, complicated missions where PJs had to let Command and Control guys help them talk on the radio, while a small company of soldiers rode along to provide security—it seemed as if they were constantly planning for sending twenty guys to do a two-man job. His last administrative job was setting up a pararescue team at Pope AFB in North Carolina. He went to Cuba for the "Great Haitian Vacation," the invasion of Haiti that didn't happen, and pulled a ninety-day rotation in Bosnia in 1995. He retired in July of 1997, but not before seeing his wife, Jill, an Air Force sergeant he'd met when he outranked her, perform so well and win so many awards as a non-commissioned officer that she was recommended for OTS, moving from the ranks of the enlisted to the officers corps, or as Higgins puts it, "She did the impossible." She's a captain now, which means that when she gets transferred somewhere, Higgins has to follow her, but that's all right with him. His sons, Brian and David, are proud of their mother. D.T. is currently trying to finish his undergraduate degree in economics at Campbell University in Buies Creek between Fayetteville and Raleigh, attending classes with kids half his age.

"Going to school at forty sucks," he admits. "I have to read everything at least twice. For every new piece of information you take in, you have to dump something that's already there."

Slip O'Farrell recalls a training exercise in scuba school where he and Brehm were supposed to do high-speed castoffs from the fantail of a patrol boat and then swim 1,000 meters to shore. Brehm lost a fin, hitting the water at about twenty knots. It took the duo forever to reach the beach, where, for losing his fin, an instructor sentenced both Brehm and O'Farrell to two hundred flutter kicks while lying on their twin 72-cubic-foot scuba tanks. "This was the high point of the Pipeline, for me," O'Farrell recalls.

O'Farrell lived in extremes, ever since his instructor at Survival Instructors School showed him how to bite the head off a snake. "I knew then I had found my home." It was living to extremes that finally turned on him. He SIE'd from the PJs in April of 1982, while stationed with the 41st ARRS at McClellan AFB in Sacramento, California. He didn't tell any of the other PJs on his team why he did it. He was reassigned to the base life-support section, two blocks down the street, but for the most part, he avoided his former friends, didn't want to talk about it when he ran into any of them, because he felt guilty for quitting. His gradual fall from grace began when he busted his ass, literally. In Florida, before he was transferred to Okinawa, he and a team of PJs had practiced low-and-slowing from a helicopter, tumbling into the sea at ten knots from a mere ten feet above the water, performing flips and belly flops and cannonballs. It was play, joyful and oblivious. O'Farrell was jumpmastering a low and slow exercise in Okinawa, in a similar playful mood, when he accidentally led two other PJs out of an HH-53 from thirty feet at thirty knots, only to learn he wasn't as tough as he thought he was. He broke his coccyx. Another PJ broke a few ribs.

O'Farrell's fortunes continued to turn. While he waited to heal, he got married "for all the wrong reasons" to a woman he describes as a "beautiful, intelligent, articulate alcoholic" who was being discharged from the Air Force "for all the appropriate reasons." He married her anyway, didn't see a problem. After all, he told himself, he rescued people for a living—why couldn't he save her? He didn't know anything about enabling, or codependency. The marriage was, in a word, tumultuous. In another word, boozy. Extreme. He started turning down temporary duty tours because he was afraid of leaving his wife alone, afraid of what she might do if he wasn't there. For a PJ, the mission was supposed to come first, but it didn't anymore. Worse, he began to fear for his own mortality, in part because of his injury, but to a larger extent because his shattered, shredded marriage made everything seem fragile or doomed. He was spooked. He didn't believe in karma, but he knew his karma was bad. His friends tried to warn him, saying, "Slip, man, you're fucking up," but he only thanked them and walked away. One night, he was supposed to fly aboard a C-130 on a full moonlit night over the California desert, a mission in which the pilots were to use night vision goggles but not terrain-following radar. Without radar, it simply seemed too dangerous. Guys died in training exercises all the time. If an actual rescue were involved, that would have been different, but to die in a training exercise . . .

He quit.

O'Farrell separated from his wife three times before finally divorcing her, fleeing the Air Force, a VA mortgage, a codependent wife—fleeing the whole enchilada. For a while he worked for a private rescue systems company in Colusa, California, where the medical director was Jeffrey MacDonald, known to readers of Joe McGinniss's book *Fatal Vision* as the ex-military doctor who was convicted of killing his wife and family. O'Farrell went from there to delivering oxygen bottles and fixing wheelchairs. "In fourteen months, I went from Sky God to piss-foam," he recalls. After his divorce, he started going to Al-Anon, while attending paramedic school. He worked as a paramedic in Sacramento from 1985 to 1991. He was working in Chico as a paramedic student in 1989 when he met his current wife, Teresa, over an emergency room double overdose, two teenage girls who'd taken barbiturates (they lived). Slip and his family fled the People's Republic of California for the freer expanses of Spokane, Washington, in 1991, where he currently works as an ER nurse, still saving lives and "living by the motto." His daughter is learning to run, swim, jump, dive, climb, and fly. "She can't outshoot me yet," O'Farrell says, "but her ambition is to be a scuba-diving nurse." He tried to sell his parachutes, but they were too old. He uses his scuba gear a few times a year and dreams about pararescue nearly every single night. His deepest regret is that he'll never get to fly his perfect mission, "a last-light low level C-130 jump onto a beeper signal in a blizzard, only to find the survivor hypovolemic and hypothermic, with a grizzly bear sniffing him."

He would probably be the first man ever to bite the head off a grizzly bear.

Mike Wilkey disappeared, last believed to be living in the Salt Lake City area. No one seems to know where he served or where he is now. Chuck Matelski nearly disappeared. After serving for a year and a half at Fairchild, Matelski transferred to Hickham AFB in Hawaii, where he ran the medical supply section. He stayed at Hickham until 1981, then got out. Looking back, he sometimes thinks he should have stayed in, but acknowledges, "Back then, I was stubborn and hard-headed and basically young and stupid. I wanted out to go to school, thinking I was going to be a marine biologist and get a job back in Hawaii. I went to school, but my study habits were poor and my personality wasn't conducive to academics. Part of the problem maybe was that in the Pipeline they build you up to think you're invincible. When I was running with the PJs, we partied up a storm, taking advantage of every bar and girl we could get our hands on. I knew I couldn't do that for twenty years."

After school didn't pan out, Matelski worked as a security guard at a research plant in Santa Barbara, then at a shop that manufactured custom countertops. He took odd jobs in L.A., the Malibu area, doing anything to make money. He stopped drinking in 1992, after waking up from a three-day binge only to hear a voice in his head say, clear as a bell, "That's it." He's currently part owner of a construction company that contracts painting for new construction. He's married to a woman named Anna and has a twenty-one-year-old stepson named Christopher.

Smitty did well for himself. After graduation from the PJ school, John Smith was assigned to the 55th ARRS at Eglin, where he upgraded to jumpmaster and team leader within two years. From Eglin, he was assigned to the 39th at Patrick, where he was part of the Space Shuttle Astronaut Rescue Team. He wrote the rescue procedures for the 099 (*Columbia*) and 101 (*Challenger*) vehicles. From Patrick, Smith transferred to Woodbridge, England, and the 67th ARRS. While there, he participated in the recovery of human remains from an Air India 747 that went down in the Irish Sea. He escorted President Carter to Egypt and President Reagan to Iceland, when Reagan met with Gorbachev. On the same mission, Smitty met Reagan and shook his hand on the tarmac at the airport. Smith led the rescue effort during the U.S. bombing of Libya. He returned to Eglin in 1986, where he stayed a year before moving on to the headquarters of the 23d Air Force at Hurlburt Field, Florida, to work for the Special Tactics Group. There, Smith was in charge of advanced skills training for the entire Air Force Special Operations Command. He participated in Just Cause, Desert Shield, Desert Storm, and Desert Thunder. He was also on the rescue attempt in Bosnia as the primary planner of the mission to extract two French NATO pilots shot down during Operation Deny Flight.

John "Smitty" Smith retired October 30, 1998, after a total of 26 years, 4 months, and 18 days of service. His military decorations include the Bronze star with "V" for valor, the Meritorious Service Medal with four Oak Leaf Clusters, the Air Medal with two Oak Leaf Clusters, the Aerial Achievement Medal with Oak Leaf Cluster, a Joint Service Commendation Medal, an Air Force Commendation Medal with three Oak Leaf Clusters, an Air Force Achievement Medal with Oak Leaf Cluster, and numerous foreign decorations. He was awarded the Sikorsky Winged "S" seventeen times for skill and courage during a life-saving mission using a Sikorsky helicopter. Over the course of his career he was credited with saving the lives of ninety-eight people, twenty-three in combat. One of his favorite missions came on the July 4th weekend of 1983, one of his first assignments out of Woodbridge, a marathon seven-hour flight over the North Atlantic involving three midair refuelings each way in an HH-53 to recover a sailor who'd taken ill aboard an old Boomer-class nuclear submarine. Smith knew the dangers and he knew the story of an unfortunate PJ from the rescue group in Iceland who'd been hoisted down to the deck of a submarine, where the deck tenders had tethered him to the deck for safety because the seas were rough, but the tether they used was too long, such that when a wave washed the PJ off the deck, the forward motion of the sub trapped him underwater. Cutting him loose would have sent him through the screw of the ship. He drowned. Before launching to the Boomer, Smith recalled a sign he'd seen in Jonestown, posted over Jim Jones's throne: "Those who do not remember the past are doomed to repeat it."

The sub's captain refused to surface until the HH-53 was on station. Smith and a fellow PJ named Craig Teeters were hoisted down to the deck without difficulty. They politely but firmly declined when the deck tenders offered them tethers. Down below, the sailor was having cardiac problems, chest pains, skin pallor, fast respiration and rapid pulse, with a blood pressure reading that should have blown the guy's head off. Smith and Teeters were still treating the patient when the captain sent the ship's executive officer to inform them they had fifteen minutes to get the guy off the boat. A Soviet satellite pass was due, and the captain couldn't allow the sub to stay on the surface when that happened. The patient could neither walk to the hatch nor climb up the ladder, so Smith and Teeters fashioned a rope harness for him and lifted him out of the sub. Teeters and the patient went up the hoist first. Smith stayed behind. When the executive officer gave the order to "clear the deck" and asked Smith what his intentions were, he said he'd stay on deck to wait to be hoisted off. The executive officer closed the hatch behind him. Minutes passed. Standing on the deck of the giant ship, he felt quite small and quite alone. It seemed to be taking forever to get the patient off the penetrator. Smith heard the sub's ballast tanks blow just as the HH-53 finally came for him. He felt the submarine sinking into the ocean below him as he grabbed the penetrator. The water came up over the sides of the hull, met in the middle and splashed the bottoms of his feet.

Bill Skolnik began to have problems as soon as he left Lackland. At Jump School in Fort Benning, Georgia, Skolnik, himself an ex-Marine, wanted to show the other Marines training there that PJs were as tough as any Marine. Some branches of the military traditionally consider the Air Force "soft," and others had never heard of the PJs, so to rectify the situation, every time a Marine got dropped for disciplinary pushups, Skolnik dropped with him. To show team unity, every time Skolnik dropped, his fellow PJs dropped too. The Marines didn't want to be shown up, so every time a PJ got dropped, the Marines dropped. Pretty soon the Navy SEALs saw that everybody was doing more pushups than they were, so they started dropping. Then the Green Berets and the Army Rangers got in on it too, even though the PJs were eating the SEALs and the Green Berets for lunch. The interservice competition culminated when the various branches entered a local raft race in which teams paddled about twenty miles down the Chattahoochee river, a race traditionally won every year by the Army Rangers, but this year, the PJs, led by Skolnik, beat them by more than a few boat lengths. The PJs beat the entire field by a distance of two and a half miles. The headlines in the next day's papers read, "AIR FORCE BEATS ARMY," and afterward a Marine captain admitted to Skolnik, "As far as I'm concerned, you PJs are one of the finest groups of military men I've ever had the pleasure to meet."

It would be some time before anybody considered the Air Force "soft" again; nevertheless, Skolnik's enthusiasm and exuberance brought him directly into a personality conflict with John Smith, the team leader, who considered Skolnik's hoo-yahing to be inappropriate and excessive. The personality conflict started small and escalated. Skolnik pushed Smith's buttons, and Smith pushed Skolnik's, and eventually, Smith had enough and recommended to the commander that Skolnik be dropped from the program for disrupting team unity. The commander agreed. Skolnik appealed to McManus, who made some phone calls.

"I always liked Bill's spirit," McManus says. "After all, if it's your son or daughter out there in the middle of the ocean, who do you want going after them—somebody with spirit or somebody without it?"

McManus used his powers of persuasion to get his candidate reinstated, and invited a third party pararescue NCOIC from Scott AFB to interview Skolnik, who agreed that Bill had exactly the kind of attitude pararescue was looking for. Eventually Skolnik was brought back into the Pipeline, but now he was in the class behind Jack. At Scuba School in Key West, Skolnik was with two fellow PJs one night, one of them a young Latino man from Colombia, South America, and they were trying to enter a bar when one of the bouncers told them they didn't admit Cubans. The bouncer probably didn't welcome Skolnik's fist in his face either, but that's what he got. Later, at Kirtland, Skolnik and a PJ named Bill Griffin were involved in an altercation in a twenty-four-hour chow hall on the base where guys coming in from missions at all hours could grab something to eat. Skolnik asked the sergeant behind the counter if he could whip them up some omelets. It was approaching midnight, and the cook was more interested in handing people pre-made sandwiches than relighting the grill.

"You fucking PJs just think you're gods, don't you?" the cook said.

"Yeah, as a matter of fact, we are gods," Skolnik replied.

The cook speculated as to the romantic propensities of Bill Griffin's mother. Skolnik suggested the cook's sister really loved to entertain. In the fight, some witnesses said the cook came over the counter wielding a knife, and most sensible people would agree that it's probably unwise to provoke a cook in his own kitchen, when he knows where all the knives are. Again an investigation ensued, where it was determined that Skolnik hadn't thrown the first punch. His record was, however, beginning to show a troubling pattern of first punches being thrown at him.

Bill Skolnik eventually became a PJ and was assigned to the 106th a few months after Jack Brehm, but he never had a cherry mission. He'd gone on a training mission out of Fort Polk, Louisiana, where he and Bill Hughes practiced escape and evasion techniques in the Louisiana woods, moving twenty-five miles from insertion to pickup point while being searched for by a squad of Special Forces troops. He'd done a good job, and felt good about himself afterward. He asked McManus to put him up for a training mission to climb Mt. McKinley, and was scheduled to go when Mike told him, at a party in the enlisted man's club on the base, that he was going to have to bump him because another PJ with seniority needed the mission more.

Skolnik didn't take the news that he'd been bumped well. He stood by the door, drinking a beer, getting angrier and angrier. Stewing. Then he was bumped again, literally, when a chief master sergeant from maintenance named Dave DeJohn arrived at the party, didn't see Skolnik, and hit him with the door. Skolnik hit DeJohn back, but not with the door. He hit him with a right cross that landed them both on the floor, with everyone there watching him, including the base commander. He knew immediately that it was wrong, a stupid thing to do, but it was too late. He was asked the next day to leave the team.

Today Bill Skolnik is the head wine maker at Leelanau Wineries in Traverse City, Michigan, where he makes pinot noirs, chardonnays, and rieslings. For several years he was the head wine maker at the Osprey's Dominion vineyard, on the north fork of eastern Long Island, and almost every week a C-130 or an HH-60 from the 106th flew over his vineyard, and when they did, his emotions were mixed. In part he felt regret, sorry that one night in an NCO club he'd let Mike McManus down, McManus a man Skolnik loved like a father. For the main part though, whenever the men from the 106th flew overhead, Skolnik simply felt proud to have been one of them, and proud of the work they did, and proud to have been part of it—once a PJ, always a PJ. Hoo-yah.

When Mike McManus retired, Skolnik sent him a case of wine.

Mike McManus, in retirement, is a lion in winter. Mostly he's riding his 1997 Harley-Davidson, a soft-tailed Heritage Springer with a red custom finish and a twin 1400cc engine, with black leather saddlebags and a windshield, crossing the great dry basins of Nevada or slicing up the landscape of Texas's Hill Country. His wife, Debby, might be next to him, riding her Harley Fat Boy. Occasionally he considers his options.

"I don't want to do anything medical," he says. "I suppose I could get a job, but they'd probably want me to come to work on time, and produce something while I'm there, and stay all day. I was never really into fishing. I could take up hunting, but hell, I get moose walking up my driveway. I suppose I could wait for one to walk into my garage and then strangle him."

He lives in a mountainside house above the clouds, at least when the fog rolls in low on the Prince William Sound, south of Anchorage. They have Western art on the walls, Christmas cacti and spider plants in hanging baskets, two fat cats and a German shepherd that barks from the deck at whatever moves below. When the sky is clear he can see the Turnagain Arm, an inlet of Prince William Sound where, when the tide goes out, tourists get stuck in the mud flats on a fairly regular basis. When the tide goes out, the mud dries hard enough to walk on, except in those places where it's not, and then somebody's foot goes through, and then the whole leg goes in, and the person can't get out. Occasionally boats get stranded in the mud, too, but usually it's a hiker who ought to have known better. When the tide roars back in, the sea in the Turnagain Arm rises high above the head of anybody unfortunate enough to be stuck in the mud. It was a PJ from the 210th rescue squadron out of Kulis AFB in Anchorage named

Brent Widenhouse who invented a device to free people from the mud, a three-foot long probe, hooked up to a compressed air tank, which the rescuers insert to pump air into the mud around a victim's foot or leg, making extraction possible by breaking the vacuum.

Mike's last rescue mission came in June of 1997. He and Widenhouse were in a C-130 preparing for a training jump when the pilot reported he'd intercepted a Mayday distress call from a nearby private plane having some kind of engine trouble, hoping to make it to a nearby airfield. There were three people on board, the pilot, another man, and his wife. The C-130 diverted to look for the private plane. They found it, newly crashed in a clearing in a wooded area adjacent to the airfield. McManus and Widenhouse jumped down to the crash site, arriving on scene within minutes of the accident. The airplane was upside down. Widenhouse examined the passenger and reported that he was dead. McManus examined the pilot, who was hanging upside down in a puddle of blood, his head cracked open.

"This guy's bled out," McManus said, looking in the back of the plane. "I thought there were three. Didn't they say three?"

"Shhh—hang on a second," Widenhouse said.

Over the sound of the wind in the trees, they both heard a faint moaning.

"Check that guy again," Widenhouse said.

"Trust me—it's not him."

They widened their search to the area around the plane, until they found a woman in her forties lying in a ditch, thrown about thirty yards from the crash. She was badly hurt, with head and chest injuries, and she was barely breathing. Widenhouse opened her air passage, while Mike radioed for a helicopter. He also asked the C-130 to drop an extra medical kit and a stretcher. The helicopter med-evac'ed her to a hospital in Anchorage. As McManus helped load the stretcher into the helicopter, he winced.

"You okay?" Widenhouse asked him.

"Yeah yeah," he said, declining to add that he'd felt a bit of a twinge then and earlier, especially when his chute opened. The yank a jumper feels when his chute opens to transition him from a free fall to a feet-to-earth position can be severe, but it usually doesn't hurt. Mike felt a twinge, more than a twinge, actually, when his chute opened because he'd broken three ribs in a car accident the day before, information he kept to himself because he had a TDY in Washington, D.C., coming up, a conference on

Search and Rescue that he wanted to attend, and he didn't want to be taken off flight status by some overefficient flight surgeon.

McManus has always had a high threshold for pain, and he's needed it. The most difficult thing he ever had to endure was his divorce. The pain of dealing with his wife's alcoholism was incessant. The intractable futility of it all was hard to accept, because he saw himself as a problem solver. When he moved to Alaska, his kids stayed behind, and that was hard, too, but then life had always been hard. His father hated his job in the steel mill, and came home and drank after work every evening. Among his siblings, Mike's younger brother Ed lives in Florida and doesn't drink at all, but his younger sister Michele died of alcoholism, and his baby brother Marty died of a heroin overdose. Mike's daughter Kelly moved to Anchorage and followed in her father's footsteps by joining the National Guard, where she seems quite happy. He stops by the PJ section at Kulis every once in a while, too, just to check in, or hang around in the day room with the guys. Other times, he rides his Harley. The sound of a 1400cc engine can drown out all kinds of pain.

Jack Brehm runs on the beach. Offshore, Brehm sees a white dinghy, with three men in it, fishing. Back in 1982, PJs from Westhampton on a TDY in Panama went out to rescue a crew of Portuguese fishermen who'd lost their boat in a storm. Their ship had gone down so suddenly that they never managed to send an SOS and weren't looked for until they were overdue in port. Seven men spent five days in a four-man dinghy, without food or water. A team from the 106th jumped when they spotted the dinghy. The men on the boat were delirious, hallucinating, and thought at first that the men falling from the sky were angels descending from heaven to take them away. A month and a half after the rescue, the unit got a letter from the Portuguese captain. His English wasn't the best, but they could make out the gist of what he wanted. They expected he was writing to thank them for saving his crew, but instead, the captain said he wanted money. For a new boat.

"You saved me," he wrote, "now what am I supposed to do?"

Most PJs would reply that once they save somebody's life, their job is pretty much done, and it's really up to the survivor to think of what to do next. Running on the beach, Brehm thinks of the Portuguese captain's letter, because as far as he knows, it's the only time he or anybody else from the 106th has ever heard from somebody they saved. If you ask a hundred PJs, or a thousand, you might not find one who ever received a thank you from a survivor. They don't do it for the glory, and they don't do it for the credit, or the thanks, and they certainly don't do it for the money. They do it, "That others may live," even though they never really know exactly what that means, or how those lives continue.

For Kim Hong Bin, his rescue allowed him to resume his climbing career. In 1992, Kim Hong Bin summited Mount Nangaparbat. In 1997 he summited Mount Elbrus (5,642m) in Europe and Mount Kilimanjaro (5,895m) in Africa. In 1998 he summited Mount Aconcagua (6,962m) in South America and Mount McKinley. He is planing to climb Mount Everest in the spring of 2000 if he can find a sponsor, completing his conquest of mountain peaks on all five continents. Kim's accomplishments are all the more remarkable because after being brought off Mount McKinley in 1991, he lost his hands, and now climbs using prosthetics. When he first came to in the hospital, his hands were bandaged, but he felt as if he had ten full fingers. He had a dream one night that his body was being consumed by cannibals. After a month in hospital, his doctor told him his fingers had turned black and couldn't be saved. He couldn't believe it when he heard it, and he couldn't believe it after the operation. At first he wondered why anybody saved him. Today he is thankful from the bottom of his heart that the PJs saved his life, even though the quality of his life has changed. In 1993, he married his nurse. From 1994 to 1996, he worked at a golf course, but ultimately he was dismissed due to his handicap.

Kim feels that he got in trouble because of poor nutrition. Rather than pack Korean food for the climb, he tried to switch to a Western diet, for example substituting bread for rice, but found the food unappetizing and he missed his spicy Korean condiments. He'd been with a group from the Seoul Chung Hae Mountain Climbing Club, but when they faltered at 13,500 feet, he went on alone. The last thing he remembers before passing out on his way to the summit was being attended to by members of the Sau Mok Po University Climbing Club.

"I think I'm a more careful climber now, and I gather more information and material before I climb. I'm more thorough. I'm thankful the PJs saved me, even though the conditions of my life have clearly changed. It's difficult to find a job in my country with my disability," he says. "Sometimes I wish I'd stayed in Alaska."

As he runs, Jack wonders about a girl in Greece somewhere, unless she's moved to Paris, or maybe New York. He prefers to think she's still in Greece. She's probably twenty-four or twenty-five years old by now. He tries to imagine her life. She has dark hair, unless she's dyed it blond. Maybe she's married by now, with children, maybe a daughter named after her sister, who died when she was two. He wonders if the girl remembers that night, on a boat in the middle of the stormy ocean, when she flew in a helicopter with her mother. He wonders if her mother and father are still around, and if they were there at the wedding. He tries to picture a Greek wedding, but all he knows of Greek weddings are what he's seen in the movies. He pictures a circle of men, holding hands, fingers interlocked above their heads as they step sideways to the music. He can almost see the girl, first in her white wedding dress, laughing with a glass of wine in her hand, then pushing a stroller along some sun-bleached beachfront promenade. He likes to think things worked out for her, though maybe they didn't. Her memories of the night, twenty-one years ago, when she rode in a helicopter are no doubt dim and faded. Maybe all she remembers is that her lungs hurt, and that it was very loud. He's just happy that she has any memories at all. She's probably never heard of the PJs, or of the U.S. Air Force's pararescue program, but that's all right with Jack. As a rule, the people who find themselves flying through the air in the arms of a PJ, being hoisted into a helicopter, usually have more on their minds than making a mental note to remember the names of the guys who are helping them.

There is an exception to the rule. While it's true that civilians almost never say thank you, military survivors do, because they appreciate what's at stake, and know the risks PJs take. As Jack runs, he thinks of one such survivor who recently visited the section. The mission the man flew on remains classified, and will probably remain classified for years—for as long as there's trouble in the Balkans. His F-117 Stealth fighter was shot out of the sky outside of Belgrade on March 27, 1999. He was on a speaking tour, visiting the various pararescue bases around the country, and he stopped by the 106th for a few hours because he had something to say. He spoke of the six hours he spent on the ground, hiding, hearing dogs barking in the distance, wondering if they were military guard dogs looking for him. He spoke of the American flag he'd tucked inside his uniform, and how he knew it stood for the guys who were coming to get him, and for all the people he knew were praying for him, and that gave him the strength he needed to endure. He was a clean-cut kid, a real all-American boy. Jack wondered, upon seeing him, how the Air Force keeps finding pilots like that.

"So I just wanted you guys to know," the pilot concluded, "that some-times if you're ever sitting around here, frustrated or something because you're not sure what the value of your mission is, I just want you to think about me, and I want you to know that you didn't save just me. You saved my whole flying squadron, all the guys I have on my team, just like you have guys on your team. I was down in the heart of bad-guy territory, and six hours later I was standing in front of my unit. This is the sort of thing that's going to have an impact on them for years to come. And you didn't just save me—you saved my mother. You saved my wife. You may think you saved one guy, but when you do that, you have an effect on a whole lot of people. And all those people are as grateful to you as I am."

Jack runs and realizes that's exactly the point of it all. Every seaman or sailor or mountain climber or heart attack victim he's ever treated or med-evac'ed to a hospital is someone's son or daughter, and possibly somebody else's husband or wife, and if so, likely somebody's father, or uncle, or friend. To save one person is to save the entire web of relationships that depend on that one person, which means that, for Jack, to save one per-son is to save everything he believes in, the love of a good wife, the ado-ration of a child, the circle of family and friends that keeps you going and catches you when you fall. To save one person is, by proxy, to save himself. The pilot's speech was more than inspiring, more than motivational. How bad would it be to reenlist, sign on for another six years?

Maybe he'd better talk it over with Peggy first.

Maybe he'd better think about what he's going to say before he talks it over with Peggy.

Jack runs. It's a fine sunny day. He feels glad to be alive. He thinks about the friends he's known and lost, and he's glad to have known them. He thinks about the places he's been and he's glad to have been there. He thinks about the country he serves and is happy to serve it. He thinks about all the love he has in his life and he's thrilled to have it, and hopes only that he can reciprocate. He thinks about his job, and he thinks it's the perfect job, because it allows him to be selfish and selfless at the same time. It lets him do the things he loves, sky dive, scuba dive, but it's not just for him that he does it.

Jack Brehm runs on the beach. He breathes the salt air. He passes a young couple, a boy and a girl, both about twenty, and they remind him of himself and Peggy when they first met. He sees a massive sand cliff rising to his left, a steep slope of heavy wet sand. Someday he will be too old to do this, and then maybe he'll take up golf, but for now, his body still allows him the privilege, so he turns and runs up the cliff, zigzagging, switching back, digging in, sending sand cascading down the slope, and his thighs burn and his lungs aches, but he won't stop. It doesn't feel good to do this, but feels good to have done it. He does it to stay in shape. He does it for the same reason he does everything else.

That others may live.

GLOSSARY

AC   Slang abbreviation for "aircraft."

ACC   Air Combat Command, headquartered at Langley AFB in Virginia, one of seven commands in the Air Force, along with the Education and Training, Materiel, Reserve, Space, Special Operations, and Mobility Commands.

AFB   Air Force Base.

AFF   Accelerated Free Fall.

AFSOC   Air Force Special Operations Command, headquartered at Hurlburt Field, Florida.

ANGB   Air National Guard Base.

AR   Air refueling.

ARRS   Aerospace Rescue and Recovery Service, the command pararescue fell under in the seventies and eighties. Pararescue now is organized under either ACC or AFSOC.

ARS   Air Rescue Service.

BC   Buoyancy Compensator, a vest worn by divers that can be inflated with a CO_2 cartridge to increase buoyancy, or deflated to decrease buoyancy.

BDU   Battle Dress Uniform.

BENDS   An illness that can affect divers if they ascend too quickly, occurring when nitrogen in the bloodstream forms bubbles and expands as the surrounding pressure decreases.

BERGSCHRUND   An area of crevasses and cracks where a glacier flowing down a mountain has broken off.

CAPEWELL   A clasp that separates a parachute from the harness, used by parachutists to avoid being dragged by ground winds.

CARP   Controlled Aerial Release Point, a parachute tactic usually performed at altitudes at or below 800 feet, a way of putting men on the ground in the shortest amount of time.

CDC   Career Development Course.

CDT   Crew Duty Time.

CEREBRAL EDEMA   A hemorrhaging of the tissues surrounding the brain.

CHEMLIGHT   A device that supplies illumination via a chemical reaction. Some are shaped like large fountain pens, while others take the form of small disks.

CHOUGH   A Eurasian crow, found at high elevations.

CISD   Critical Incident Stress Debriefing, a counseling tool usually used to help emergency relief personnel cope with job-related stress.

COLLECTIVE   The lever-like control a helicopter pilot uses to change his up/down direction by changing the pitch of the rotor blades.

CORNICE   In mountain climbing, an overhang of snow or ice at the top of a ridge or crest.

COULOIR   A mountain ravine or gorge.

CP   Copilot, as found in a flight log abbreviation.

CRICOTHYROTOMY   A surgical procedure where an air passage is cut into a patient's throat.

CYCLIC   The stick-like control a helicopter pilot uses to change his forward or backward direction.

DECADRON   A synthetic adrenocortical steroid used to reduce swelling in the case of high altitude cerebral edema.

DIAMOX   A carbonic anhydrase inhibitor that promotes diuresis and controls fluid secretions.

DNIF   The status designation of an airman who is qualified only for Duty Not to Include Flying. The work status an airman is placed in after becoming injured, resulting in his not being able to fly, lasts from one day to two years.

DROGUE   The basket on the end of the hose that is extended by a midair refueling tanker, the female receptacle into which the receiving aircraft's probe is inserted to on-load fuel.

DUCK BUTT   Slang for a mission in which rescue personnel are assigned to escort another aircraft.

DZ   Drop Zone, the designated area where a parachutist attempts to land.

ECW   An Extreme Cold Weather clothing system.

ELT   Emergency Locating Transmitter, a marker beacon signal given off by a ship or aircraft in trouble.

EPIRB   Emergency Position Indicating Radio Beacon, a marker beacon activated by individuals in trouble.

EVAL   Evaluations or tests.

FE   Flight Engineer, as referred to in a flight log abbreviation.

FLARING   The act of stalling one's parachute by entering deep brakes just before touching ground.

FLIR   Forward Looking Infrared Radar, a system used to detect enemy movements by picking up heat signatures from ground troops or from the motors of enemy vehicles.

FOL   Forward Operating Location.

FRAP   Slang for hitting the ground if your parachute fails to open.

GPS   Global Positioning System.

HACE   High Altitude Cerebral Edema.

HAHO   High Altitude High Opening, a parachute tactic where the jumper opens his chute at high altitudes and glides to the target, covering distances of thirty miles or more, depending on the prevailing winds. Supplemental oxygen is required.

HALO   High Altitude Low Opening, a kind of parachute tactic where men jump from 25,000–35,000 feet, using supplemental oxygen, and open their chutes at around 3,000 feet, used in covert SARs.

HAS   Hardened Aircraft Shelter.

HEED BOTTLES   Helicopter Emergency Egress Device, a small oxygen bottle supplying about three to five minutes of oxygen, used by helicopter crew members in case of an accidental submersion.

HOVER REFERENCE   A stable reference point which a helicopter pilot needs to fix on, in order to maintain his hover position.

HYPERBARIC   High barometric pressure.

HYPERGOLIC   Refers to volatile gases that mix in open air and can spontaneously explode.

HYPOBARIC   Low barometric pressure.

HYPOTHERMIC   Low body temperature.

HYPOVOLEMIC   Low blood volume.

HYPOXIA   Low oxygen levels.

JDAM   Joint Direct Attack Munitions or "smart bombs."

JOLLY   Short for "Jolly Green Giant," a nickname for Air Force rescue helicopters.

JSTARS   Joint Surveillance Target Attack Radar System.

JUMPMASTER   The crewman in charge of telling jumpers when to leave the aircraft.

KINGBIRD   A radio designation given to C-130s flying top cover for helicopters.

KLICK   Kilometer.

LPU   Life Preserver Units, inflatable air pouches worn under the armpits and attached to a vest-like harness.

LZ   Landing Zone, the place where a parachutist lands. Also the place designated for a helicopter to land.

MED-EVAC'ED   Abbreviation for "medically evacuated," pronounced "med-i-vacked."

MT-IX RAM-AIR CHUTE   A square, steerable, double-layered 375-square-foot chute with an open nose that inflates the chute like an airplane's wing to provide lift.

NCO   Non-Commissioned Officer.

NCOIC   Non-Commissioned Officer In Charge.

NITROGEN NARCOSIS   A drunken feeling experienced by divers as they descend, when nitrogen is forced into the bloodstream as the surrounding pressure increases.

NVA   North Vietnamese Army.

NVG   Night Vision Goggles, a device that electronically amplifies available light.

OD   Olive Drab.

OL-J   Operation Location J—the site, at Lackland AFB in San Antonio, Texas, where the pararescue indoctrination school is located. Also called Indoc or Superman School.

OTS   Officer Training School.

P   Pilot, as referred to in a flight log abbreviation.

PCS   Permanent Change of Station.

PEN GUN   A small flare launcher, about the size of a fountain pen, that can send a signal flare 600 feet up in the air.

PENETRATOR A forest penetrator, designed to penetrate the canopy in the jungles of Vietnam, a milk can–shaped device that can be lowered via a hoist from a helicopter, used to extract survivors.

PHOSPHEGENE An industrial pesticide, similar to the phosgene gases used in WWI.

PJ Pararescue Jumper, a flight log abbreviation.

PNEUMOTHORAX Collapsed lung. A *tension pneumothorax* happens when the pressure inside the chest cavity of a collapsed lung increases to the point that it dislodges the heart and affects the other lung.

PRC Personal Radio Communicator.

PT Physical Training.

PULMONARY EDEMA A hemorrhaging of the lung tissues.

RANK In the Air Force, from bottom to top: Airman Basic, Airman, Airman First Class, Senior Airman, Staff Sergeant, Technical Sergeant, Master Sergeant, Senior Master Sergeant, Chief Master Sergeant, and among the officers, Second Lieutenant, First Lieutenant, Captain, Major, Lieutenant Colonel, Colonel, Brigadier General (one star), Major General (two stars), Lieutenant General (three stars) and General (four stars).

RCC Rescue Control Center. The RCC at Scott AFB, outside of St. Louis, is sometimes referred to as AFRCC, or Air Force Rescue Control Center.

RECON Short for "reconnaissance."

RTB Return To Base, a flight log abbreviation.

RQS Rescue squadron.

SAM Surface to Air Missile.

SAR Search and Rescue. SARs can be covert (men performing HALO or HAHO jumps or flying in low, preferably at night, in helicopters to rescue downed pilots) or they can be overt SARs in which the rescue is made in daylight under protective covering fire.

SARSAT Search and Rescue Satellite, a satellite operated jointly by the United States, Canada, and Russia that picks up EPIRBs and ELTs.

SAR TECH Search And Rescue Technician, the Canadian equivalent of the PJ.

SASTRUGI Ice that the wind has formed into various waves, sawtooths and stalactites.

SAT-COM A radio with a communications satellite uplink.

SCHIST A crystalline rock with a laminar structure that splits easily into layers—for example, slate.

SERE TRAINING A training program used by the Air Force to teach Survival, Evasion, Resistance, and Escape techniques.

SIE Self-Initiated Elimination.

SOF Supervisor Of Flying.

STARS The Air Force's demonstration parachute team, called Special Tactics And Rescue Specialists.

STOKES LITTER A metal basket, used to move an injured or immobilized victim.

TDY   Temporary Duty, a tour of duty, often abroad, lasting anywhere from a day to six months.

THORACENTESIS   A surgical procedure that purges the air in the chest cavity of a collapsed lung by inserting a large-bore needle into the chest.

THORASCOTOMY   A surgical procedure that purges the air in the chest cavity of a collapsed lung by inserting a chest tube into the chest.

TL   Team Leader.

TOGGLE   The red nylon loop at the end of the lines that a parachutist pulls on to control and change the shape of his chute, thereby steering it.

TRIPLE A   Anti-Aircraft Armaments.

VENA CAVA   The vein that returns blood to the heart.

WPW   Wolff-Parkinson-White syndrome, a short-circuiting of the heart's electrical system, in which an extra electrical pathway develops between the atria and the ventricles, causing extra contractions that speed the heart rate.

ABOUT THE AUTHORS

Jack Brehm has been a pararescue jumper for twenty years. He lives with his wife, Peggy, and their five children in Rocky Point, New York.

Pete Nelson is a prolific author and magazine writer. His articles have appeared in *Harper's, Esquire, Men's Health, Outside, Rolling Stone, Playboy,* and other publications. He lives in Northampton, Massachusetts. His Web site is: www.pete-nelson.com